CIMA
STUDY TEXT

Intermediate Paper 8

Management Accounting: Performance Management

BPP's NEW STUDY TEXTS FOR CIMA's NEW SYLLABUS

- Targeted to the **syllabus** and **learning outcomes**

- **Quizzes** and **questions** to check your understanding

- Incorporates CIMA's new Official Terminology

- Clear layout and style designed to save you time

- Plenty of **exam-style questions**

- **Chapter Roundups** and summaries to help revision

- **Mind Maps** to integrate the key points

New in this July 2001 edition

- A bank of **multiple choice questions** at the back

BPP's **MCQ cards** also support this paper

BPP Publishing
July 2001

First edition 2000
Second edition July 2001

ISBN 0 7517 3164 1 (previous edition 0 7517 3138 2)

British Library Cataloguing-in-Publication Data
A catalogue record for this book
is available from the British Library

Published by

BPP Publishing Ltd
Aldine House, Aldine Place
London W12 8AW

www.bpp.com

Printed in Great Britain by Ashford Colour Press

We are grateful to the Chartered Institute of Management Accountants for permission to reproduce past examination questions and questions from the pilot paper. The suggested solutions to the illustrative questions have been prepared by BPP Publishing Limited.

Contents

		Page

THE BPP STUDY TEXT — (v)

HELP YOURSELF STUDY FOR YOUR CIMA EXAMS — (vii)
The right approach - suggested study sequence - developing your personal Study plan

SYLLABUS AND LEARNING OUTCOMES — (xii)

THE EXAM PAPER — (xvii)

WHAT THE EXAMINER MEANS — (xix)

TACKLING MULTIPLE CHOICE QUESTIONS — (xix)

PART A: STANDARD COSTING
1	Standard costing	3
2	Variance analysis	25
3	Further variance analysis	49
4	Interpretation of management control information	69

PART B: BUDGETING
5	Budgets	89
6	Preparing forecasts for budgetary plans	126
7	Budgetary control and performance measurement	153
8	Cost and profit centres. Transfer pricing	178

PART C: ALLOCATION AND MANAGEMENT OF RESOURCES
9	The modern business environment	193
10	Activity based costing	218
11	Cost reduction	229
12	Multiple product CVP analysis	245
13	Limiting factor analysis	263
14	Linear programming: the graphical method	279
15	Linear programming: the simplex method	304

APPENDIX: MATHEMATICAL TABLES — 325

EXAM QUESTION BANK — 331

EXAM ANSWER BANK — 345

MULTIPLE CHOICE QUESTIONS — 379

ANSWERS TO MULTIPLE CHOICE QUESTIONS — 385

INDEX — 393

REVIEW FORM & FREE PRIZE DRAW

ORDER FORM

BPP PUBLISHING

MULTIPLE CHOICE QUESTION CARDS

Multiple choice questions form a large part of the exam. To give you further practice in this style of question, we have produced a bank of 150 **multiple choice question cards**, covering the syllabus. This bank contains exam style questions in a format to help you revise on the move.

COMPUTER-BASED LEARNING PRODUCTS FROM BPP

If you want to reinforce your studies by interactive learning, try BPP's **i-Learn** products, covering major syllabus areas in an interactive format. For self-testing, try **i-Pass** which offers a large number of objective test questions, particularly useful where multiple choice questions form part of the exam.

See the order form at the back of this text for details of these innovative learning tools.

THE BPP STUDY TEXT

Aims of this Study Text

To provide you with the knowledge and understanding, skills and application techniques that you need if you are to be successful in your exams

This Study Text has been written around the **Management Accounting: Performance Management** syllabus.

- It is **comprehensive**. It covers the syllabus content. No more, no less.

- It is written at the **right level**. Each chapter is written with CIMA's precise learning outcomes in mind.

- It is targeted to the **exam**. We have taken account of the pilot paper, questions put to the examiners at the recent CIMA conference and the assessment methodology.

To allow you to study in the way that best suits your learning style and the time you have available, by following your personal Study Plan (see page (x))

You may be studying at home on your own until the date of the exam, or you may be attending a full-time course. You may like to (and have time to) read every word, or you may prefer to (or only have time to) skim-read and devote the remainder of your time to question practice. Wherever you fall in the spectrum, you will find the BPP Study Text meets your needs in designing and following your personal Study Plan.

To tie in with the other components of the BPP Effective Study Package to ensure you have the best possible chance of passing the exam (see page (vi))

BPP
PUBLISHING

Recommended period of use	Elements of the BPP Effective Study Package
Three to twelve months before the exam	**Study Text** Use the Study Text to acquire knowledge, understanding, skills and the ability to use application techniques. You might also use BPP's **i-Learn** product to reinforce your learning.
Throughout	**MCQ cards and i-Pass** Revise your knowledge and ability to use application techniques, as well as practising this key exam question format, with 150 multiple choice questions. **i-Pass,** our computer-based testing package, provides objective test questions in a variety of formats and is ideal for self-assessment.
One to six months before the exam	**Practice & Revision Kit** Try the numerous examination-format questions, for which there are realistic suggested solutions prepared by BPP's own authors. Then attempt the two mock exams.
From three months before the exam until the last minute	**Passcards** Work through these short, memorable notes which are focused on what is most likely to come up in the exam you will be sitting.
One to six months before the exam	**Success Tapes** These audio tapes cover the vital elements of your syllabus in less than 90 minutes per subject. Each tape also contains exam hints to help you fine tune your strategy.
Three to twelve months before the exam	**Breakthrough Videos** Use a Breakthrough Video to supplement your Study Text. They give you clear tuition on key exam subjects and allow you the luxury of being able to pause or repeat sections until you have fully grasped the topic.

HELP YOURSELF STUDY FOR YOUR CIMA EXAMS

Exams for professional bodies such as CIMA are very different from those you have taken at college or university. You will be under **greater time pressure before** the exam - as you may be combining your study with work. There are many different ways of learning and so the BPP Study Text offers you a number of different tools to help you through. Here are some hints and tips: they are not plucked out of the air, but **based on research and experience**. (You don't need to know that long-term memory is in the same part of the brain as emotions and feelings - but it's a fact anyway.)

The right approach

1 The right attitude

Believe in yourself	Yes, there is a lot to learn. Yes, it is a challenge. But thousands have succeeded before and you can too.
Remember why you're doing it	Studying might seem a grind at times, but you are doing it for a reason: to advance your career.

2 The right focus

Read through the Syllabus and learning outcomes	These tell you what you are expected to know and are supplemented by Exam Focus Points in the text.
Study the Exam Paper section	Past papers are a reasonable guide of what you should expect in the exam.

3 The right method

The big picture	You need to grasp the detail - but keeping in mind how everything fits into the big picture will help you understand better. • The **Introduction** of each chapter puts the material in context. • The **Syllabus content, learning outcomes** and **Exam focus points** show you what you need to **grasp.** • **Mind Maps** show the links and key issues in key topics.
In your own words	To absorb the information (and to practise your written communication skills), it helps to **put it into your own words.** • **Take notes.** • Answer the **questions** in each chapter. As well as helping you absorb the information, you will practise the assessment formats used in the exam and your written communication skills, which become increasingly important as you progress through your CIMA exams. • Draw **mind maps.** We have some examples. • Try 'teaching' a subject to a colleague or friend.

Give yourself cues to jog your memory	The BPP Study Text uses **bold** to **highlight key points** and **icons** to identify key features, such as **Exam focus points** and **Key terms.** • Try **colour coding** with a highlighter pen. • Write **key points** on cards.

4   **The right review**

Review, review, review	It is a **fact** that regularly reviewing a topic in summary form can **fix it in your memory.** Because **review** is so important, the BPP Study Text helps you to do so in many ways. • **Chapter roundups** summarise the key points in each chapter. Use them to recap each study session. • The **Quick quiz** is another review technique to ensure that you have grasped the essentials. • Go through the **Examples** in each chapter a second or third time.

Suggested study sequence

Tackle the chapters in the order you find them in the Study Text. Taking into account your individual learning style, you could follow this sequence.

Key study steps	Activity
Step 1 **Topic list**	Each numbered topic is a numbered section in the chapter.
Step 2 **Introduction**	This gives you the **big picture** in terms of the **context** of the chapter, the **content** you will cover, and the **learning outcomes** the chapter assesses - in other words, it sets your **objectives for study.**
Step 3 **Knowledge brought forward boxes**	In these we highlight information and techniques that it is assumed you have 'brought forward' with you from your earlier studies. If there are topics which have changed recently due to legislation for example, these topics are explained in more detail.
Step 4 **Explanations**	Proceed methodically through the chapter, reading each section thoroughly and making sure you understand.
Step 5 **Key terms and Exam focus points**	• **Key terms** can often earn you *easy marks* if you state them clearly and correctly in an appropriate exam answer (and they are highlighted in the index at the back of the text). • **Exam focus points** give you a good idea of how we think the examiner intends to examine certain topics.
Step 6 **Note taking**	Take brief notes if you wish, avoiding the temptation to copy out too much.
Step 7 **Examples**	Follow each through to its solution very carefully.

Key study steps	Activity
Step 8 **Case examples**	Study each one, and try to add flesh to them from your own experience – they are designed to show how the topics you are studying come alive (and often come unstuck) in the real world.
Step 9 **Questions**	Make a very good attempt at each one.
Step 10 **Answers**	Check yours against ours, and make sure you understand any discrepancies.
Step 11 **Chapter roundup**	Work through it very carefully, to make sure you have grasped the major points it is highlighting.
Step 12 **Quick quiz**	When you are happy that you have covered the chapter, use the **Quick quiz** to check how much you have remembered of the topics covered and to practise questions in a variety of formats.
Step 13 **Question(s) in the Exam Question bank**	Either at this point, or later when you are thinking about revising, make a full attempt at the **Question(s)** suggested at the very end of the chapter. You can find these at the end of the Study Text, along with the **Answers** so you can see how you did. We highlight those that are introductory, and those which are of the standard you would expect to find in an exam. If you have purchased the **MCQ cards**, use these too.
Step 14 **Multiple choice questions**	Use the bank of MCQs at the back of this Study Text to practise this important assessment format and to determine how much of the Study Text you have absorbed. If you have bought the MCQ cards, use these too.

BPP PUBLISHING

Developing your personal Study Plan

Preparing a Study Plan (and sticking closely to it) is one of the key elements in learning success.

Step 1. How do you learn?

First you need to be aware of your style of learning. There are four typical learning styles. Consider yourself in the light of the following descriptions and work out which you fit most closely. You can then plan to follow the key study steps in the sequence suggested.

Learning styles	Characteristics	Sequence of key study steps in the BPP Study Text
Theorist	Seeks to understand principles before applying them in practice	1, 2, 3, 4, 7, 8, 5, 9/10, 11, 12, 13 (6 continuous)
Reflector	Seeks to observe phenomena, thinks about them and then chooses to act	
Activist	Prefers to deal with practical, active problems; does not have much patience with theory	1, 2, 9/10 (read through), 7, 8, 5, 11, 3, 4, 9/10 (full attempt), 12, 13 (6 continuous)
Pragmatist	Prefers to study only if a direct link to practical problems can be seen; not interested in theory for its own sake	9/10 (read through), 2, 5, 7, 8, 11, 1, 3, 4, 9/10 (full attempt), 12, 13 (6 continuous)

Step 2. How much time do you have?

Work out the time you have available per week, given the following.

- The standard you have set yourself
- The time you need to set aside later for work on the Practice & Revision Kit and Passcards
- The other exam(s) you are sitting
- Very importantly, practical matters such as work, travel, exercise, sleep and social life

Note your time available in box A.

A [Hours ____]

Step 3. Allocate your time

- Take the time you have available per week for this Study Text shown in box A, multiply it by the number of weeks available and insert the result in box B.

B [____]

- Divide the figure in Box B by the number of chapters in this text and insert the result in box C.

C [____]

Step 4. Implement

Set about studying each chapter in the time shown in box C, following the key study steps in the order suggested by your particular learning style.

This is your personal **Study Plan**.

Short of time: Skim study technique?

You may find you simply do not have the time available to follow all the key study steps for each chapter, however you adapt them for your particular learning style. If this is the case, follow the **skim study** technique below (the icons in the Study Text will help you to do this).

- Study the chapters in the order you find them in the Study Text.

- For each chapter, follow the key study steps 1-3, and then skim-read through step 4. Jump to step 11, and then go back to step 5. Follow through steps 7 and 8, and prepare outline answers to questions (steps 9/10). Try the Quick quiz (step 12), following up any items you can't answer, then do a plan for the Question (step 13), comparing it against our answers. You should probably still follow step 6 (note-taking), although you may decide simply to rely on the BPP Passcards for this.

Moving on...

However you study, when you are ready to embark on the practice and revision phase of the BPP Effective Study Package, you should still refer back to this Study Text, both as a source of **reference** (you should find the index particularly helpful for this) and as a **refresher** (the Chapter roundups and Quick quizzes help you here).

And remember to keep careful hold of this Study Text – you will find it invaluable in your work.

BPP PUBLISHING

SYLLABUS AND LEARNING OUTCOMES

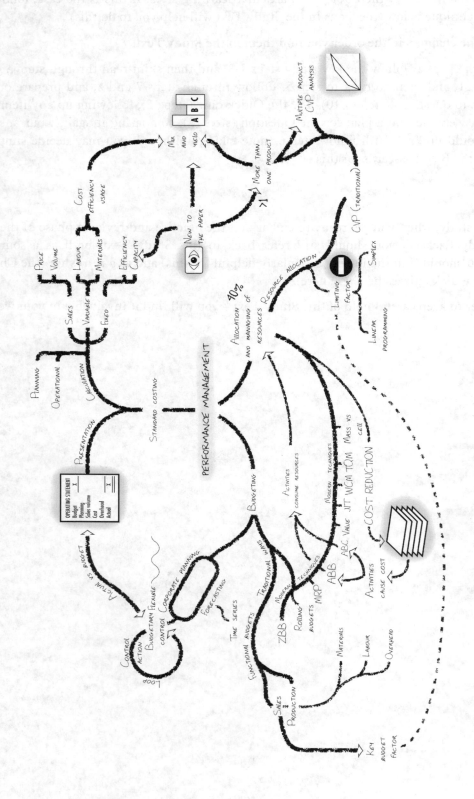

Syllabus overview

Performance management builds on the introduction to standard costing and budgeting provided by Management Accounting Fundamentals, and covers the allocation and management of resources.

While this paper will develop students' ability to apply a range of management accounting techniques, quantitative methods and resource management strategies to the modern business environment, students will also have to demonstrate understanding of these tools and the issues that surround their use.

Students must also appreciate the contribution made by information technology to management accounting.

Aims

This syllabus aims to test the student's ability to:

- Apply and evaluate standard costing
- Prepare and evaluate plans, budgets and forecasts
- Apply and evaluate techniques for allocating and managing resources

for a wide range of sectors, including manufacturing, retail and services.

Assessment

There will be a written paper of 3 hours. Section A will use objective testing for 20% of the marks. Section B will be a compulsory question for 30% of the marks. Section C will offer a choice of one question from two for 25% of the marks, and Section D will offer a choice of one question from two for 25% of the marks.

Learning outcomes and syllabus content

8(i) Standard costing - 20%

Learning outcomes

On completion of their studies students should be able to:

- Explain why costing systems and standard costs must be reviewed on a regular basis
- Explain why it is necessary to take account of the learning curve effect to produce meaningful standards
- Calculate the standard cost for a product which exhibits the learning effect
- Calculate and interpret material, labour, variable overhead, fixed overhead and sales variances
- Prepare and discuss a report which reconciles budget and actual profit using absorption and/or marginal costing principles
- Calculate and explain planning and operational variances
- Prepare reports using a range of internal and external benchmarks and interpret the results
- Discuss the behavioural implications of standard costing

Syllabus content

		Covered in chapter
•	Criticisms of standard costing	1
•	Learning curve (Note: derivation of the learning index and the learning rate is not required)	1
•	Material mix and yield variances	3
•	Labour mix and yield variances	3
•	Fixed overhead capacity and efficiency variances	2
•	Sales price and volume variances (Note: the volume variance will be calculated on a units basis using sales revenue, contribution or gross profit.)	2
•	Interpretation of variances: interrelationship, significance	4
•	Planning and operational variances	3
•	Benchmarking	4
•	Behavioural implications	1

8(ii) Budgeting - 40%

Learning outcomes

On completion of their studies students should be able to:

- Explain why organisations prepare plans

- Calculate future sales and costs using forecasting techniques and evaluate the results

- Explain and interpret the effect of amendments to budget/plan assumptions

- Explain why it is necessary to identify controllable and uncontrollable costs

- Evaluate performance using fixed and flexible budget reports

- Discuss alternative approaches to budgeting

- Evaluate the balanced scorecard

- Discuss the behavioural implications of planning and budgeting

- Compare and contrast cost and profit centres

- Explain the principles of transfer pricing

- Compare and contrast transfer pricing systems

Syllabus content

		Covered in chapter
•	Planning	5
•	Time series and regression	6
•	'What-if' analysis	6
•	Controllable and uncontrollable costs	8
•	Fixed and flexible budgeting	7
•	Incremental budgeting	5
•	Rolling budgets	5
•	Zero-based budgeting	5
•	Activity based budgeting	5,10
•	Balanced scorecard	7
•	Behavioural implications	7
•	Cost and profit centres	8
•	Principles of transfer pricing	8
•	Transfer pricing systems: cost/standard cost, cost/standard cost plus, market price, market price less savings	8

8(iii) Allocation and management of resources - 40%

Learning outcomes

On completion of their studies students should be able to:

- Describe the modern business environment
- Compare and contrast alternative production and management strategies
- Compare and contrast value analysis and functional analysis
- Explain activity-based costing
- Explain total quality management
- Prepare and discuss cost of quality reports
- Calculate and interpret the break even point, profit target, margin of safety and profit/volume ratio for multiple products
- Prepare break even charts and profit/volume charts for multiple products
- Discuss multiple product CVP analysis
- Calculate and interpret the profit-maximising sales mix for a company with a single resource constraint and limited freedom of action
- Solve a two-plus constraint/limitation problem for two-plus products using the Simplex method and interpret the results
- Discuss the linear programming model

Syllabus and learning outcomes

Syllabus content

		Covered in chapter
•	Modern business environment	9
•	Resource planning systems: MRPI, MRPII AND ERP	9
•	Just-in-time	9
•	Activity-based costing	10
•	Cost reduction programmes	11
•	Value and functional cost analysis	11
•	Total quality management	9
•	Multi-product CVP analysis including break even, profit target, margin of safety, contribution/sales ratio, break even charts, contribution, profit/volume graphs	12
•	Single limiting factor analysis where a company has restricted freedom of action	13
•	Linear programming	14,15

THE EXAM PAPER

Format of the paper

		Number of marks
Section A:	objective test questions	20
Section B:	one compulsory question	30
Section C:	one question from two	25
Section D:	one question from two	25
		100

Time allowed: 3 hours

Examiner's note

The examiner has confirmed that topics previously covered in the old syllabus Paper 10 *Management Accounting Applications* (such as the behavioural aspects of budgeting, mix and yield variances and planning and operational variances) or completely new topics (such as linear programming) will **first** appear in optional questions, then as a small part of a compulsory question, before becoming the basis for an entire compulsory question.

Analysis of papers

May 2001

Section A
1.1 Variances
1.2 Forecasting
1.3 Breakeven analysis
1.4 Flexible budgets
1.5 Behavioural aspects of budgeting
1.6 Limiting factor analysis
1.7 Breakeven analysis
1.8 Variances
1.9 Variances

Section B
2 Limiting factor analysis; learning curves; profit statements

Section C
3 Activity based costing; pricing; modern business environment
4 Cost reduction; value analysis; ZBB; relevance of standard costing

Section D
5 Planning and operational variances; mix and yield variances
6 Activity based costing

The exam paper

Pilot paper

Section A

1.1 Seasonal variations
1.2 Cash budget
1.3 Incremental budgeting system
1.4 Flexible budget cost allowance
1.5 Learning curve
1.6 Balanced scorecard
1.7 ABC
1.8 Quality costs

Section B

2 Planning and operational variances. Operating statement. Transfer prices

Section C

3 Budgeting. Behavioural issues. Spreadsheets
4 JIT

Section D

5 Linear programming
6 Maximising the benefit from available resources

BPP
PUBLISHING

WHAT THE EXAMINER MEANS

The table below has been prepared by CIMA to help you interpret exam questions.

Learning objective	Verbs used	Definition
1 Knowledge What you are expected to know	• List • State • Define	• Make a list of • Express, fully or clearly, the details of/facts of • Give the exact meaning of
2 Comprehension What you are expected to understand	• Describe • Distinguish • Explain • Identify • Illustrate	• Communicate the key features of • Highlight the differences between • Make clear or intelligible/state the meaning of • Recognise, establish or select after consideration • Use an example to describe or explain something
3 Application Can you apply your knowledge?	• Apply • Calculate/compute • Demonstrate • Prepare • Reconcile • Solve • Tabulate	• To put to practical use • To ascertain or reckon mathematically • To prove the certainty or to exhibit by practical means • To make or get ready for use • To make or prove consistent/compatible • Find an answer to • Arrange in a table
4 Analysis Can you analyse the detail of what you have learned?	• Analyse • Categorise • Compare and contrast • Construct • Discuss • Interpret • Produce	• Examine in detail the structure of • Place into a defined class or division • Show the similarities and/or differences between • To build up or complete • To examine in detail by argument • To translate into intelligible or familiar terms • To create or bring into existence
5 Evaluation Can you use your learning to evaluate, make decisions or recommendations?	• Advise • Evaluate • Recommend	• To counsel, inform or notify • To appraise or assess the value of • To advise on a course of action

BPP
PUBLISHING

TACKLING MULTIPLE CHOICE QUESTIONS

Of the total marks available for this paper, objective test questions comprise:

A   10%
B   20%
C   30%
D   40%
E   50%

The correct answer is B.

The multiple choice questions (MCQs) in your exam contain four possible answers. You have to **choose the option that best answers the question**. The three incorrect options are called distracters. There is a skill in answering MCQs quickly and correctly. By practising MCQs you can develop this skill, giving you a better chance of passing the exam.

You may wish to follow the approach outlined below, or you may prefer to adapt it.

Step 1.   **Skim read** all the MCQs and **identify** what appear to be the easier questions.

Step 2.   Attempt each question – **starting with the easier questions** identified in Step 1. Read the question thoroughly. You may prefer to work out the answer before looking at the options, or you may prefer to look at the options at the beginning. Adopt the method that works best for you.

Step 3.   Read the four options and see if one matches your own answer. **Be careful with numerical questions**, as the distracters are designed to match answers that incorporate common errors. Check that your calculation is correct. Have you followed the requirement exactly? Have you included every stage of the calculation?

Step 4.   You may **find that none of the options matches your answer**.

- Re-read the question to ensure that you understand it and are answering the requirement
- Eliminate any obviously wrong answers
- Consider which of the remaining answers is the most likely to be correct and select the option

Step 5.   If you are still **unsure** make a note **and continue to the next question**.

Step 6.   **Revisit unanswered** questions. When you come back to a question after a break you often find you are able to answer it correctly straight away. If you are still unsure have a guess. You are not penalised for incorrect answers, so **never leave a question unanswered!**

Exam focus. After extensive practice and revision of MCQs, you may find that you recognise a question when you sit the exam. Be aware that the detail and/or requirement may be different. If the question seems familiar read the requirement and options carefully – do not assume that it is identical.

Part A
Standard costing

Chapter 1

STANDARD COSTING

Topic list		Syllabus reference	Ability required
1	The uses of standard costing	(i)	Comprehension
2	Setting standards	(i)	Application/ comprehension
3	The learning curve effect	(i)	Application/ comprehension
4	The behavioural implications of standard costing	(i)	Application/ comprehension
5	Updating standards	(i)	Comprehension
6	Criticisms of standard costing	(i)	Evaluation
7	Budgets and standards compared	(i)	Evaluation

Introduction

Just as there are **standards** for most things in our daily lives (cleanliness in hamburger restaurants, educational achievement of nine-year olds, number of underground trains running on time) there are standards for the unit costs of products and of services rendered in a commercial organisation. Moreover, just as the standards in our daily lives are not always met, the standards for the costs of products and services rendered are not always met. We will not, however, be considering the cleanliness of hamburger restaurants in this chapter but we will be looking at **standard costs** and **standard costing.**

Standard costing was covered at Foundation, where you learned about the principles of standard costing and how to calculate a number of cost and sales variances. We obviously look at the topic in more depth for your Paper 8 studies.

In this chapter we will be reviewing the main principles of standard costing, as well as looking in detail at the way in which standard costs are set.

Learning outcomes covered in this chapter

- **Explain** why costing systems and standard costs must be reviewed on a regular basis
- **Explain** why it is necessary to take account of the learning curve effect to produce meaningful standards
- **Calculate** the standard cost for a product which exhibits the learning effect
- **Discuss** the behavioural implications of standard costing

Syllabus content covered in this chapter

- Criticisms of standard costing
- Learning curve
- Behavioural implications

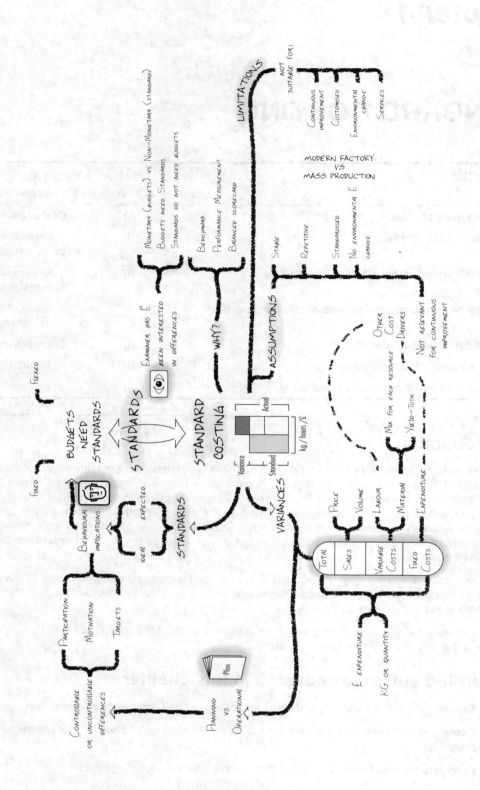

1 THE USES OF STANDARD COSTING

What is a standard cost?

> **KEY TERM**
>
> A **standard cost** is a carefully predetermined estimated unit cost.

1.1 Standard costs are usually drawn up for a unit of production or a unit of service rendered but it is also possible to have a standard cost per routine task completed, or a standard cost per £1 of sale. A standard cost per unit of production may include administration, selling and distribution costs, but in many organisations, the assessment of standards is confined to production costs only.

What is standard costing?

> **KEY TERM**
>
> The CIMA *Official Terminology* definition of **standard costing** is 'A control technique which compares standard costs and revenues with actual results to obtain variances which are used to stimulate improved performance'.

1.2 Standard costing is the **preparation of standard costs** to be used in the following circumstances.

(a) To assist in **setting budgets** and **evaluating managerial performance**.

(b) To act as a **control device** by establishing standards, highlighting (via **variance analysis**) activities that do not conform to plan and thus alerting management to those areas that may be out of control and in need of corrective action.

(c) To enable the principle of '**management by exception**' to be practised. A standard cost, when established, is an average expected unit cost. Because it is only an average, actual results will vary to some extent above and below the average. Variances should only be reported where the difference between actual and standard is significant.

(d) To **provide a prediction of future costs** to be used in decision-making situations.

(e) To **value stocks and cost production** for cost accounting purposes. It is an alternative method of valuation to methods like FIFO, LIFO or replacement costing.

(f) To **motivate staff and management** by the provision of challenging targets.

(g) To **provide guidance on improvement of efficiency**.

1.3 Although the use of standard costs to simplify the keeping of cost accounting records should not be overlooked, we will be **concentrating** on the **control and variance analysis** aspect of standard costing.

When standard costing is used

1.4 Standard costing can be used in a variety of costing situations.

- Batch and mass production
- Process manufacture

- Jobbing manufacture (where there is standardisation of parts)
- Service industries (if a realistic cost unit can be established)

However, the **greatest benefit** from its use can be gained if there is a **degree of repetition** in the production process. It is therefore most suited to **mass production** and **repetitive assembly** work. However, a standard cost can be calculated **per task if there is a similarity of tasks**. In this way standard costing can be used by some **service organisations**.

2 SETTING STANDARDS

2.1 A standard cost implies that a standard or target exists for every single element that contributes to the product: the types, usage and prices of materials and parts, the grades, rates of pay and times for the labour involved, the production methods, tools and so on. The standard cost for each part of the product is recorded on a **standard cost card**, an example of which is given below.

```
                        STANDARD COST CARD
                   Product: the Splodget, No 12345

                          Cost           Requirement
                                                        £        £
Direct materials
    A                  £2.00 per kg       6 kgs       12.00
    B                  £3.00 per kg       2 kgs        6.00
    C                  £4.00 per litre    1 litre      4.00
Others                                                 2.00
                                                                24.00
Direct labour
    Grade I            £4.00 per hour     3 hrs       12.00
    Grade II           £5.40 per hour     5 hrs       27.00
                                                                39.00
Variable production overheads  £1.00 per hour  8 hrs            8.00
Fixed production overheads     £3.00 per hour  8 hrs           24.00
Standard full cost of production                               95.00
```

2.2 Standard costs may be used in **both marginal and absorption costing systems**. The card illustrated has been prepared under an absorption costing system, with selling and administration costs excluded from the standard.

2.3 The **responsibility for setting** standard costs should be shared between **managers able to provide the necessary information** about levels of expected efficiency, prices and overhead costs. Standard costs are **usually revised once a year** (to allow for the new overheads budget, inflation in prices, and any changes in expected efficiency of materials usage or of labour). However they may be **revised more frequently if conditions are changing rapidly**.

Setting standards for materials costs

2.4 **Direct material prices** will be estimated by the purchasing department from their existing knowledge.

- Purchase contracts already agreed
- Pricing discussions with regular suppliers
- Quotations and estimates from potential suppliers
- The forecast movement of prices in the market
- The availability of bulk purchase discounts
- Material quality required

2.5   **Price inflation** can cause difficulties in setting realistic standard prices. Suppose that a material costs £10 per kilogram at the moment, and during the course of the next 12 months, it is expected to go up in price by 20% to £12 per kilogram. **What standard price should be selected?**

- The **current price** of £10 per kilogram
- The **expected price** for the year, say, £11 per kilogram

2.6   Either price in Paragraph 2.5 would be possible, but neither would be entirely satisfactory.

(a)   If the **current price** were used in the standard, the reported price variance would become adverse as soon as prices go up, which might be very early in the year. If prices go up gradually rather than in one big jump, it would be difficult to select an appropriate time for revising the standard.

(b)   If an **estimated mid-year price** were used, price variances should be favourable in the first half of the year and adverse in the second half, again assuming that prices go up gradually. Management could only really check that in any month, the price variance did not become excessively adverse (or favourable) and that the price variance switched from being favourable to adverse around month six or seven and not sooner.

2.7   Standard costing for materials is therefore more **difficult in times of inflation but it is still worthwhile**.

(a)   Usage and efficiency variances will still be meaningful.

(b)   Inflation is measurable: there is no reason why its effects cannot be removed from the variances reported.

(c)   Standard costs can be revised, so long as this is not done too frequently.

Setting standards for labour rates

2.8   **Direct labour rates per hour** will be set by discussion with the personnel department and by reference to the payroll and to any agreements on pay rises and/or bonuses with trade union representatives of the employees. A separate average hourly rate or weekly wage will be set for each different labour grade/type of employee (even though individual rates of pay may vary according to age and experience).

Setting standards for material usage and labour efficiency

2.9   To estimate the materials required to make each product (material usage) and also the labour hours required (labour efficiency), **technical specifications** must be prepared for each product by production experts (either in the production department or the work study department).

2.10   Material usage and labour efficiency standards are known as **performance standards**.

Types of performance standard

2.11   The setting of standards raises the problem of how demanding the standard should be. Should the standard represent a perfect performance or an easily attainable performance? The type of performance standard used can have behavioural implications. There are four types of standard.

BPP PUBLISHING

Type of standard	Description
Ideal	These are based on **perfect operating conditions**: no wastage, no spoilage, no inefficiencies, no idle time, no breakdowns. Variances from ideal standards are useful for pinpointing areas where a close examination may result in large savings, but they are likely to have an unfavourable motivational impact because reported variances will always be adverse. Employees will often feel that the goals are unattainable and not work so hard.
Attainable	These are based on the hope that a standard amount of work will be carried out efficiently, machines properly operated or materials properly used. **Some allowance is made for wastage and inefficiencies.** If well-set they provide a useful psychological incentive by giving employees a realistic, but challenging target of efficiency. The consent and co-operation of employees involved in improving the standard are required.
Current	These are based on **current working conditions** (current wastage, current inefficiencies). The disadvantage of current standards is that they do not attempt to improve on current levels of efficiency.
Basic	These are **kept unaltered over a long period of time**, and may be out of date. They are used to show changes in efficiency or performance over a long period of time. Basic standards are perhaps the least useful and least common type of standard in use.

2.12 Ideal standards, attainable standards and current standards each have their supporters and it is by **no means clear which of them is preferable**.

Question 1

Which of the following statements is not true?

A   Variances from ideal standards are useful for pinpointing areas where a close examination might result in large cost savings.

B   Basic standards may provide an incentive to greater efficiency even though the standard cannot be achieved.

C   Ideal standards cannot be achieved and so there will always be adverse variances. If the standards are used for budgeting, an allowance will have to be included for these 'inefficiencies'.

D   Current standards or attainable standards are a better basis for budgeting, because they represent the level of productivity which management will wish to plan for.

Answer

The correct answer is B.

Statement B is describing ideal standards, not basic standards.

The learning curve effect

2.13 Another factor which may affect the standard time allowed to perform a standard task is the possible existence of a learning curve effect. We look at the learning curve effect in the next section.

Setting standards for overheads

2.14 The **standard overhead absorption rate** is the same as the **predetermined overhead absorption rate** as calculated for an absorption costing system.

2.15 The **standard absorption rate** will **depend** on the **planned production volume** for a period. Production volume will **depend on two factors**.

(a) **Production capacity** (or 'volume capacity') measured perhaps in standard hours of output.

(b) **Efficiency of working**, by labour or machines, allowing for rest time and contingency allowances. This will depend on the type of performance standard to be used (ideal, current, attainable and so on).

2.16 Suppose that a department has a workforce of ten employees, each of whom works a 36 hour week to make standard units, and each unit has a standard production time of two hours. The expected efficiency of the workforce is 125%.

(a) **Budgeted capacity**, in direct labour hours, would be $10 \times 36 = 360$ production hours per week.

(b) **Budgeted efficiency** is 125% so that the workforce should take only 1 hour of actual production time to produce 1.25 standard hours of output.

(c) This means in our example that **budgeted output** is 360 production hours $\times$ 125% = 450 standard hours of output per week. At two standard hours per unit, this represents production activity or volume of 225 units of output per week.

2.17 Output, capacity and efficiency are inter-related items, and you should check your understanding of them by attempting the following problem.

Question 2

ABC Ltd carries out routine office work in a sales order processing department, and all tasks in the department have been given standard times. There are 40 clerks in the department who work on average 140 hours per month each. The efficiency ratio of the department is 110%.

Required

Calculate the budgeted output in the department.

Answer

Capacity	=	$40 \times 140 = 5,600$ hours per month
Efficiency	=	110%
Budgeted output	=	$5,600 \times 110\% = 6,160$ standard hours of work per month

---

Capacity levels

2.18 Capacity levels are needed to establish a standard absorption rate for production overhead, when standard absorption costing is used. Any one of three capacity levels might be used for budgeting.

KEY TERMS

- **Full capacity** is 'output (expressed in standard hours) that could be achieved if sales orders, supplies and workforce were available for all installed workplaces'.

- **Practical capacity** is 'full capacity less an allowance for known unavoidable volume losses'.

- **Budgeted capacity** is 'standard hours planned for the period, taking into account budgeted sales, supplies, workforce availability and efficiency expected'.

(CIMA *Official Terminology*)

(a) **Full capacity** is the **theoretical** capacity, assuming continuous production without any stoppages due to factors such as machine downtime, supply shortages or labour shortages. Full capacity would be associated with **ideal standards**.

(b) **Practical capacity** acknowledges that **some stoppages are unavoidable**, such as maintenance time for machines, and resetting time between jobs, some machine breakdowns and so on. Practical capacity is below full capacity, and would be associated with **attainable standards**.

(c) **Budgeted capacity** is the capacity (labour hours, machine hours) **needed to produce the budgeted output**, and would be associated with **current standards**, which relate to current conditions but may not be representative of normal practical capacity over a longer period of time.

2.19 **Idle capacity** would be defined as the **practical capacity** in a period **less the budgeted capacity** measured in standard hours of output. It represents unused capacity that ought to be available, but which is not needed because the budgeted volume is lower than the practicable volume that could be achieved.

Capacity ratios

2.20 Capacity ratios can be calculated. They provide similar information to fixed overhead variances (which we cover in the next chapter).

Question 3

Given the following information, calculate an idle capacity ratio, a production volume ratio and an efficiency ratio and explain their meanings.

Full capacity	10,000 standard hours	Standard hours produced	6,500
Practical capacity	8,000 standard hours	Actual hours worked	7,000
Budgeted capacity	7,500 standard hours		

Answer

$$\text{Idle capacity ratio} = \frac{\text{Practical capacity} - \text{budgeted capacity}}{\text{Practical capacity}} \times 100\%$$

$$= \frac{8,000 - 7,500}{8,000} \times 100\% = 6.25\%.$$

This means that 6.25% of practical capacity will be unused because budgeted volume is lower than the volume that could be achieved.

$$\text{Production volume ratio} = \frac{\text{Standard hours produced}}{\text{Budgeted capacity}} \times 100\%$$

$$= \frac{6,500}{7,500} \times 100\% = 86^2/_3\%$$

This means actual output was only $86^2/_3\%$ of budgeted output.

$$\text{Efficiency ratio} = \frac{\text{Standard hours produced}}{\text{Actual hours worked}} \times 100\% = \frac{6,500}{7,000} \times 100\% = 92.86\%$$

This means that the labour force were working at 92.86% efficiency.

Setting standards for selling price and margin

2.21 As well as standard costs, standard selling prices and standard margins can be set. The standard selling price will depend on a number of factors including the following.

- Anticipated market demand
- Competing products and competitors' actions
- Manufacturing costs
- Inflation estimates

2.22 The standard sales margin is the difference between the standard cost and the standard selling price.

3 THE LEARNING CURVE EFFECT   5/01

3.1 Whenever an individual starts a job which is **fairly repetitive** in nature, and provided that his **speed of working is not dictated to him by the speed of machinery** (as it would be on a production line), he is likely to become **more confident and knowledgeable** about the work as he gains experience, to become **more efficient**, and to do the work **more quickly**. The **resulting reduction in time** taken is called the **learning curve effect**.

3.2 If such a learning effect exists, it must be **taken into account** when **standards** are set. Otherwise, the standards will not be useful for control purposes because they will not represent a **realistic target** for the time allowed, and favourable variances would arise.

3.3 **Eventually**, however, when the individual has acquired enough experience, there will be nothing more for him to learn, and so the **learning process will stop**. After this point there should be no allowance for time savings due to the learning effect.

When might the learning curve affect standard costs?

3.4 Labour time should be expected to get shorter, with experience, in the production of items which exhibit any or all of the following features.

- Made largely **by labour effort** (rather than by a **highly mechanised** process)
- Brand **new** or relatively **short-lived** (learning process does not continue indefinitely)
- **Complex** and made in **small quantities** for **special orders**

The learning curve theory

> ### KEY TERM
>
> The **learning curve** is 'The mathematical expression of the phenomenon that when complex and labour-intensive procedures are repeated, unit labour times tend to decrease at a constant rate. The learning curve models mathematically this reduction in unit production time.'   (CIMA *Official Terminology*)

3.5   More specifically, the learning curve theory states that the **cumulative average time per unit** produced is assumed to **decrease by a constant percentage every time total output of the product doubles**.

3.6   For instance, where an **80% learning effect** occurs, the **cumulative average time required per unit of output is reduced to 80% of the previous cumulative average time when output is doubled**.

> ### ATTENTION!
>
> - By **cumulative average time**, we mean the **average time per unit for all units produced so far**, back to and including the first unit made.
>
> - The **doubling of output** is an **important feature** of the learning curve measurement. With a 70% learning curve, the cumulative average time per unit of output will fall to 70% of what it was before, every time output is doubled.

3.7   Don't worry if this sounds quite **hard to grasp** in words, because it is (until you've learned it!). It is best explained by a numerical example.

3.8   EXAMPLE: AN 80% LEARNING CURVE

If the first unit of output requires 100 hours and an 80% learning curve applies, the production times would be as follows.

Cumulative number of units produced		Cumulative average time per unit		Total time required		Incremental time taken		
		Hours		Hours	Total hours	Hours per unit		
1		100.0	(× 1)	100.0				
2*	(80%)	80.0	(× 2)	160.0	60.0	÷ 1		60.0
4*	(80%)	64.0	(× 4)	256.0	96.0	÷ 2		48.0
8*	(80%)	51.2	(× 8)	409.6	153.6	÷ 4		38.4

* Output is being doubled each time.

Notice that the incremental time per unit is reducing at a much faster rate than the average time per unit.

Graph of the learning curve

3.9   This learning effect can be shown on a **graph** as a learning curve, either for **unit times** (graph (a)) or for **cumulative total times or costs** (graph (b)).

(a) (b)

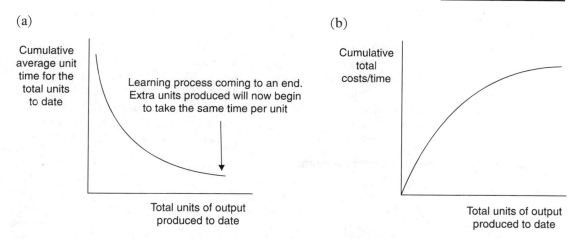

Cumulative average unit time for the total units to date

Learning process coming to an end. Extra units produced will now begin to take the same time per unit

Total units of output produced to date

Cumulative total costs/time

Total units of output produced to date

3.10 The curve on graph (a) becomes horizontal once a sufficient number of units have been produced. At this point the learning effect is lost and production time should become a constant standard, to which a standard efficiency rate may be applied.

3.11 EXAMPLE: THE LEARNING CURVE EFFECT

Captain Kitts Ltd has designed a new type of sailing boat, for which the cost and sales price of the first boat to be produced has been estimated as follows.

	£
Materials	5,000
Labour (800 hrs × £5 per hr)	4,000
Overhead (150% of labour cost)	6,000
	15,000
Profit mark-up (20%)	3,000
Sales price	18,000

It is planned to sell all the yachts at full cost plus 20%. An 80% learning curve is expected to apply to the production work. Only one customer has expressed interest in buying the yacht so far, but he thinks £18,000 is too high a price to pay. He might want to buy two, or even four of the yachts during the next six months.

He has asked the following questions.

(a) If he paid £18,000 for the first yacht, what price would he have to pay later for a second yacht?

(b) Could Captain Kitts Ltd quote the same unit price for two yachts, if the customer ordered two at the same time?

(c) If the customer bought two yachts now at one price, what would be the price per unit for a third and fourth yacht, if he ordered them both together later on?

(d) Could Captain Kitts Ltd quote a single unit price for

(i) Four yachts
(ii) Eight yachts

if they were all ordered now?

Assuming there are no other prospective customers for the yacht, how would the questions be answered?

3.12 SOLUTION

Number of yachts		Cumulative average time per yacht		Total time for all yachts to date		Incremental time for additional yachts
		Hours		Hours		Hours
1		800.0		800.0		
2	(× 80%)	640.0	(× 2)	1,280.0	(1,280 – 800)	480.0
4	(× 80%)	512.0	(× 4)	2,048.0	(2,048 – 1,280)	768.0
8	(× 80%)	409.6	(× 8)	3,276.8	(3,276.8 – 2,048)	1,228.8

(a) **Separate price for a second yacht**

	£
Materials	5,000
Labour (480 hrs × £5)	2,400
Overhead (150% of labour cost)	3,600
Total cost	11,000
Profit (20%)	2,200
Sales price	13,200

(b) **A single price for the first two yachts**

	£
Materials cost for two yachts	10,000
Labour (1,280 hrs × £5)	6,400
Overhead (150% of labour cost)	9,600
Total cost for two yachts	26,000
Profit (20%)	5,200
Total sales price for two yachts	31,200
Price per yacht (÷ 2)	15,600

(c) **A price for the third and fourth yachts**

	£
Materials cost for two yachts	10,000
Labour (768 hours × £5)	3,840
Overhead (150% of labour cost)	5,760
Total cost	19,600
Profit	3,920
Total sales price for two yachts	23,520
Price per yacht (÷ 2)	11,760

(d) **A price for the first four yachts together and for the first eight yachts together**

		First four yachts		First eight yachts
		£		£
Materials		20,000		40,000
Labour	(2,048 hrs)	10,240	(3,276.8 hrs)	16,384
Overhead	(150% of labour cost)	15,360	(150% of labour cost)	24,576
Total cost		45,600		80,960
Profit (20%)		9,120		16,192
Total sales price		54,720		97,152
Price per yacht	(÷ 4)	13,680	(÷ 8)	12,144

Question 4

A 90 per cent learning curve applies to the manufacture of product X. If the time taken for the first unit is three hours, what will be the average time per unit for units 5 to 8?

A 1.944 hours   B 2.187 hours   C 7.776 hours   D 17.496 hours

Answer

The correct answer is A.

You should have been able to eliminate options C and D because they are longer times than the three hours taken for the first unit. In fact they are the total time for units 5 to 8 and for units 1 to 8 respectively.

Option B is incorrect because it is the average time for units 1 to 8.

Cumulative number of units produced		Cumulative average time per unit	Total time
		Hours	Hours
1		3	
2	(90%)	2.7	
4	(90%)	2.43	9.720
8	(90%)	2.187	17.496
Time taken for units 5 to 8			7.776
Average time per unit (÷ 4)			1.944 hours

A formula for the learning curve

FORMULA PROVIDED IN THE EXAM

The formula for the learning curve shown in Paragraph 3.9(a) is $Y_X = aX^b$

where Y = cumulative average time per unit to produce X units
X = number of units made so far

a = time to produce the first unit
b = the learning coefficient or learning index (log of the learning curve improvement rate divided by log2)

3.13 You will be provided with the formula and the learning index in the exam if it is needed, as was the case in the May 2001 exam.

3.14 You might also be expected to use the formula to calculate expected labour times for inclusion in a standard cost.

3.15 EXAMPLE: USING THE FORMULA

Suppose, for example, that the following learning curve formula applies to production of item ABC.

$$Y = aX^{-0.322}$$

To date, (the end of June year 8) 230 units of ABC have been produced. Budgeted production for July year 8 is 55 units.

The time taken to produce the very first unit of ABC, in January year 8, was 120 hours.

Required

Calculate the standard total labour time for July year 8 and the average standard labour time per unit in year 8.

3.16 SOLUTION

To solve this problem, we need to calculate three things.

(a)   The cumulative total labour time needed so far to produce 230 units of ABC

(b) The cumulative total labour time needed to produce 285 units of ABC, that is adding on the extra 55 units for July

(c) The extra time needed to produce 55 units of ABC in July, as the difference between (b) and (a)

Calculation (a)

$Y = aX^{-0.322}$ and we know that for 230 cumulative units, a = 120 hours (time for first unit), X = 230 (cumulative units) and so $Y = 120 \times 230^{-0.322} = 20.83$.

So when X = 230 units, the cumulative average time per unit is 20.83 hours.

Calculation (b)

Now we do the same sort of calculation for X = 285.

If X = 285, $Y = 120 \times 285^{-0.322} = 19.44$

So when X = 285 units, the cumulative average time per unit is 19.44 hours.

Calculation (c)

Cumulative units	*Average time per unit*	*Total time*
	Hours	Hours
230	20.83	4,791
285	19.44	5,540
Incremental time for 55 units		749

Average time per unit, between 230 and 285 units = 749/55 = 13.6 hours per unit approx

3.17 Instead of the formula you can use the graphical methodology (Paragraph 3.9) to determine cumulative average time per unit but you will need considerable drawing skill to obtain an accurate result.

Incremental time model

3.18 The model described so far is the cumulative average time model and is the one most commonly encountered. An alternative is the incremental (**or marginal or direct**) model. This model uses the same formula as the cumulative average time model but Y represents the time required to produce the final unit.

Exam focus point

When learning curve theory is incorporated in an examination question, you can assume that the cumulative average time model is applicable unless explicit instructions are given to the contrary.

What costs are affected by the learning curve?

3.19 (a) **Direct labour time and costs** are obviously **affected** by the learning curve effect and output capacity increases as the workforce gains experience.

(b) **Variable overhead costs** will also be **affected** by the learning effect, but only to the extent that variable overheads vary with direct labour hours worked.

(c) **Materials costs** are usually **unaffected** by learning among the workforce, although it is conceivable that materials handling might improve, and so wastage costs be reduced.

(d) **Fixed overhead expenditure** should be **unaffected** by the learning curve (although in an organisation that uses absorption costing, if fewer hours are worked in producing a unit of output, and the factory operates at full capacity, the **fixed overheads recovered or absorbed per unit** in the cost of the output **will decline** as more and more units are made).

The relevance of learning curve effects in management accounting

3.20 Learning curve theory can be **used** in the following situations.

(a) To **calculate the marginal (incremental) cost of making extra units** of a product.

(b) To **quote selling prices for a contract**, where prices are calculated at cost plus a percentage mark-up for profit. An awareness of the learning curve can make all the difference between winning contracts and losing them, or between making profits and selling at a loss-making price.

(c) To **prepare realistic production budgets** and more **efficient production schedules**.

(d) To **prepare realistic standard costs** for cost control purposes.

3.21 The further considerations that should be borne in mind are as follows.

(a) **Sales projections, advertising expenditure and delivery date commitments**. Identifying a learning curve effect should allow an organisation to plan its advertising and delivery schedules to coincide with expected production schedules. Production capacity obviously affects sales capacity and sales projections.

(b) **Budgeting with standard costs**. Companies that use standard costing for much of their production output cannot apply standard times to output where a learning effect is taking place. This problem can be overcome in practice by **establishing standard times for output once the learning effect has worn off** or become insignificant and **introducing a 'launch cost' budget** for the product for the duration of the learning period. Alternatively, a **standard average time per unit** can be estimated for a budgeted volume of output, which makes allowance for the expected learning rate.

(c) **Cash budgets**. Since the learning effect reduces unit variable costs as more units are produced, it should be allowed for in cash flow projections.

(d) **Work scheduling and overtime decisions**. To take full advantage of the learning effect, **idle production time should be avoided** and work scheduling/overtime decisions should take account of the expected learning effect.

(e) **Pay**. Where the workforce is paid a productivity bonus, the time needed to learn a new production process should be allowed for in calculating the bonus for a period.

(f) **Recruiting new labour**. When a company plans to take on new labour to help with increasing production, the learning curve assumption will have to be reviewed.

(g) **Market share**. The significance of the learning curve is that by increasing its share of the market, a company can benefit from shop-floor, managerial and technological 'learning' to achieve economies of scale.

Cost experience curves

3.22 A 'learning curve' is a term usually applied to the time taken by skilled labour element in shop floor production.

KEY TERM

A **cost experience curve** is a term applied to the 'corporate embodiment' of the shop floor, managerial and technological learning effects within an organisation and it expresses the way in which the average cost per unit of production changes over time due to technological and organisational changes as well as changes to factory size, product design, materials used and so on, not just 'learning' by skilled workers.

The experience curve is best exploited by growth and achieving a sizeable market share, so that an organisation can benefit from mass production techniques.

Limitations of learning curve theory

3.23 The limited use of learning curve theory is due to several factors.

(a) The learning curve phenomenon is **not always present**.

(b) It **assumes stable conditions at work** which will enable learning to take place. This is not always practicable (for example because of labour turnover).

(c) It must also **assume a certain degree of motivation** amongst employees.

(d) **Breaks** between repeating production of an item must not be too long, or **workers will 'forget'** and the learning process would have to begin all over again.

(e) It might be difficult to **obtain enough accurate data** to decide what the learning curve is.

(f) **Workers might not agree** to a gradual reduction in production times per unit.

(g) **Production techniques might change,** or product design alterations might be made, so that it **takes a long time for a 'standard' production method to emerge**, to which a learning effect will apply.

In **variance analysis**, a **choice between average or incremental hours** as being the most relevant measure of time taken to produce a certain number of units has to be made. Incremental hours probably gives the most meaningful results but the merits of the two approaches depend on circumstances.

4 THE BEHAVIOURAL IMPLICATIONS OF STANDARD COSTING

4.1 Setting standards and using them as a yardstick for cost control is not simply an exercise in dealing with numbers. It also involves dealing with people, and a standard costing system will only be **effective if it is designed with full understanding of its potential behavioural effects**. We have already seen how the type of performance standard used can have behavioural implications. For example the adverse variances which tend to be reported when ideal standards are used can be demotivating for the individuals who are working to achieve the standard.

4.2 **Other behavioural implications to be considered in the design and operation of a standard costing system**

(a) **Communication is of the utmost importance**. Because of the technical nature of much of the standard setting process, production employees and their supervisors may need to be involved. This will help to win their support for the resulting standards and they are more likely to be willing to work to achieve them. Moreover, the employees' practical knowledge will contribute towards a more accurate and useful standard for cost planning and control.

(b) **The variance reporting system should not be used punitively**. There must be no undue pressure or excessive blame attached to the non-achievement of standards. Managers who are treated in this way may resent the use of the standard costing system and thus reduce its effectiveness.

(c) **Care must be taken to distinguish between controllable and non-controllable costs in variance reporting**. It can be demotivating for managers who feel that they are being held responsible for costs and variances over which they cannot exercise control.

(d) **Variance control reports must be produced promptly and accurately**. Inaccuracy will lead to managers losing faith in the value of the information and they may not bother to act upon it. Late information may cause frustration if managers feel that they could have acted earlier if they had known that problems existed.

Question 5

(a) Describe the possible problems which could arise when setting standards.
(b) List possible advantages of standard costing.

Answer

(a) (i) Deciding how to incorporate inflation into planned unit costs.

    (ii) Agreeing a short-term labour efficiency standard (current, attainable or ideal).

    (iii) Deciding on the quality of materials to be used (a better quality of material will cost more, but perhaps reduce material wastage).

    (iv) Deciding on the appropriate mix of component materials, where some change in the mix is possible (for example in the manufacture of foods and drink).

    (v) Estimating materials prices where seasonal price variations or bulk purchase discounts may be significant.

    (vi) Finding sufficient time to construct accurate standards. Standard setting can be a time-consuming process.

    (vii) Incurring the cost of setting up and maintaining a system for establishing standards.

    (viii) Dealing with possible behavioural problems. Managers responsible for the achievement of standards might resist the use of a standard costing control system for fear of being blamed for any adverse variances.

(b) (i) Carefully planned standards are an aid to more accurate budgeting.

    (ii) Standard costs provide a yardstick against which actual costs can be measured.

    (iii) The setting of standards involves determining the best materials and methods which may lead to economies.

    (iv) A target of efficiency is set for employees to reach and cost consciousness is stimulated.

    (v) Variances can be calculated which enable the principle of 'management by exception' to be operated. Only the variances which exceed acceptable tolerance limits need to be investigated by management with a view to control action.

    (vi) Standard costs and variance analysis can provide a way of motivating managers to achieve better performance. However, care must be taken to distinguish between controllable and non-controllable costs in variance reporting.

5 UPDATING STANDARDS

5.1 When an organisation introduces a system of standard costing, it is quite possible that the standards initially set will not be the most accurate reflection of what occurs 'on average'.

Initial standards may need **substantial revision** in the early period of a standard costing system's life before they are really useful measures for control purposes.

5.2 The evolution of standards does not stop after a couple of accounting periods, however. Standards must be **continuously reviewed** to ensure that they do **mirror** what is **currently happening** and that they are the **most accurate 'average'**.

5.3 **Out-of-date standards** will produce **variances** that are **illogical bases** for planning, control, decision making or performance evaluation. Current operational performance cannot be compared to out-of-date standards.

> 'Labour and material usage standards normally are set by the industrial engineering department. Material price normally is considered the responsibility of purchasing. Similarly, the labour rates are set by the personnel department. As the production processes change (improve), past standards become less than realistic, and should be revised. It is the responsibility of departments that originally created the standard to inform the accounting department about the need for revising the standards.
>
> But, unfortunately, some managers prefer to keep the old standards because the new improved production process makes their performance look better with old standards.'
>
> (LU Tatikonda, 'Production Managers Need a Course in Cost Accounting', *Management Accounting* (June 1987), published by Institute of Management Accountants, Montvale, N J)

Improvement of standard setting process

5.4 Standard setting procedures may be refined and extended to enable more accurate standards to be set.

(a) **Work study** methods may be established within the organisation. These enable accurate estimates of labour time to be made.

(b) The introduction of **computerised information systems** provides more reliable standards.

5.5 With CADCAM (computer-aided design/computer aided manufacture) systems the planning of manufacturing requirements can be **computerised,** with the useful spin-off that standard costs can also be constructed by computer, thus saving administrative time and expense while providing far more accurate standards.

Revision of standards

5.6 In practice standard costs are usually revised **once a year** to allow for the new overheads budget, inflation in prices and wage rates, and any changes in expected efficiency of material usage, labour or machinery.

5.7 Some argue that standards should be revised **as soon as there is any change in the basis upon which they were set.** Clearly, for example, if a standard is based on the cost of a material that is no longer available or the use of equipment which has been replaced, it is meaningless to compare actual performance using the new material and equipment with the old standard.

5.8 Coates, Rickwood and Stacey in their book *Management Accounting in Practice* put forward the following reasons for revising standards.

> '(a) Manufacturing methods are **significantly** changed due to plant layout, machinery alterations, change in product design, use of different materials, etc.
>
> (b) The relationship of normal capacity and actual activity is **significantly** out of balance.

(c) The disparity between the standard and expected performance is **so significant** that the standard as a measurement loses its value.

(d) An existing standard is discovered to be incorrectly set and a **significant** difference exists.'
(JB Coates, CP Rickwood, RJ Stacey, *Management Accounting in Practice,* CIMA)

5.9 **Frequent changes** in standards can cause **problems**.

(a) They may become **ineffective as motivators and measures of performance,** since it may be perceived that target setters are constantly 'moving the goal posts'.

(b) The **administrative effort** may be too time consuming (although the introduction of computer systems renders this objection less forceful).

Coates *et al* concede the following point.

'Revisions should be **held to a minimum**, despite the fact that standards may not be precise, in order to provide for relative comparisons between operating periods and/or versus budget.'

5.10 The most **suitable approach** would therefore appear to be a policy of revising the standards **whenever changes of a permanent and reasonably long-term nature occur,** but not in response to temporary 'blips' in price or efficiency.

6 CRITICISMS OF STANDARD COSTING 5/01

6.1 Some commentators have argued that **traditional variance analysis is unhelpful and potentially misleading** in the modern organisation, and can make managers focus their attention on the wrong issues. Here are just two examples.

(a) **Efficiency variance**. Traditional variance analysis emphasises adverse efficiency variances should be avoided, which means that managers should try to prevent idle time and to keep up production. In a total quality management environment, just in time may be used (JIT being defined in CIMA *Official Terminology* as 'A system whose objective is to produce or procure products or components as they are required by a customer or for use, rather than for stock.') In these circumstances, manufacturing to eliminate idle time could result in the manufacture of unwanted products that must be held in store and might eventually be scrapped. Efficiency variances could focus management attention on the wrong problems.

(b) **Materials price variance**. In a JIT environment the key issues in materials purchasing are supplier reliability, materials quality, and delivery in small order quantities. Purchasing managers should not be shopping around every month looking for the cheapest price. Many JIT systems depend on long-term contractual links with suppliers, which means that material price variances are not relevant for management control purposes.

6.2 **Other criticisms of using standard costing in today's environment**

(a) Variance analysis concentrates on only a **narrow range of costs**, and does not give sufficient attention to issues such as quality and customer satisfaction.

(b) Standard costing places **too much emphasis on direct labour costs**. Direct labour is only a small proportion of costs in the modern manufacturing environment and so this emphasis is not appropriate.

(c) Many of the variances in a standard costing system focus on the control of **short-term variable costs**. In most modern manufacturing environments, the majority of costs, including direct labour costs, tend to be fixed in the short run.

(d) The use of standard costing relies on the existence of **repetitive operations** and relatively **homogeneous** output. Nowadays many organisations are forced continually

BPP PUBLISHING

to respond to customers' changing requirements, with the result that output and operations are not so repetitive.

(e) Standard costing systems were **developed** when the **business environment** was more **stable** and **less prone to change**. The current business environment is more dynamic and it is not possible to assume stable conditions.

(f) Standard costing systems **assume** that **performance to standard is acceptable.** Today's business environment is more focused on continuous improvement.

(g) Most standard costing systems produce **control statements weekly or monthly.** The modern manager needs much more prompt control information in order to function efficiently in the dynamic business environment.

Exam focus point

A May 2001 exam question required an explanation of how standard costing systems based on absorption costing principles might be inappropriate in the modern manufacturing environment. Information in this section would have provided an excellent answer.

6.3 This long list of criticisms of standard costing may lead you to believe that such systems have little use in today's business environment. Standard costing systems can be **adapted to remain useful,** however.

Question 6

Can you think of some ways in which a standard costing system could be adapted so that it is useful in the modern business environment?

Answer

Here are some ideas.

(a) **Non-financial measures** can be included within management control reports. Examples include number of defects, percentage of on-time deliveries, and so on.

(b) Even when output is not standardised, it may be possible to identify a number of **standard components and activities** whose costs may be controlled effectively by the setting of standard costs and identification of variances.

(c) The use of computer power enables standards to be **updated rapidly** and more frequently, so that they remain useful for the purposes of control by comparison.

(d) The use of **ideal standards** and **more demanding performance levels** can combine the benefits of **continuous improvement** and standard costing control.

(e) **Information,** particularly of a non-financial nature, can be **produced more rapidly** with the assistance of **computers.** For example the use of on-line data capture can enable the continuous display of real time information on factors such as hours worked, number of components used and number of defects.

7 BUDGETS AND STANDARDS COMPARED

7.1 You will recall from your earlier studies that a **budget** is a **quantified monetary plan** for a **future period,** which **managers will try to achieve.** Its major function lies in **communicating plans** and **coordinating activities** within an organisation.

On the other hand, a **standard** is a **carefully predetermined quantity target** which can be **achieved in certain conditions.**

7.2   Budgets and standards are **similar** in the following ways.

(a)   They both involve looking to the future and **forecasting** what is likely to happen given a certain set of circumstances.

(b)   They are both **used for control purposes**. A budget aids control by setting financial targets or limits for a forthcoming period. Actual achievements or expenditures are then compared with the budgets and action is taken to correct any variances where necessary. A standard also achieves control by comparison of actual results against a predetermined target.

7.3   As well as being similar, **budgets and standards are interrelated**. For example, a standard unit production cost can act as the basis for a production cost budget. The unit cost is multiplied by the budgeted activity level to arrive at the budgeted expenditure on production costs.

7.4   There are, however, **important differences between budgets and standards**.

Budgets	Standards
Gives planned **total aggregate costs** for a function or cost centre	Shows the unit resource usage for a **single task**, for example the standard labour hours for a single unit of production
Can be prepared for **all functions**, even where output cannot be measured	Limited to situations where **repetitive actions** are performed and output can be measured
Expressed in **money terms**	**Need not be expressed in money terms**. For example a standard rate of output does not need a financial value put on it

7.5   In summary, budgets and standards are very similar and interrelated, but there are important differences between them.

Chapter roundup

- A **standard** is a **predetermined unit of cost** for stock valuation, budgeting and control.

- A **standard cost card** shows full details of the standard cost of each product.

- The standard for each type of cost (labour, material and so on) is made up of a **standard resource price** and a **standard resource usage**.

- **Performance standards** are used to set efficiency targets. There are four types: ideal, attainable, current and basic.

- The **learning curve effect** must be taken into account to produce meaningful standards.

- **Learning curve theory** is that the **cumulative average time per unit produced is assumed to fall by a constant percentage every time total output doubles**. Cumulative average time is the average time per unit for all units produced so far, back to and including the first unit made.

- The formula for the learning curve is $Y_x = aX^b$ where b is the learning coefficient or learning index, Y is the cumulative average time per unit to produce X units, a is the time for the first unit, X is the number of units made so far.

- An effective standard costing system should take account of **behavioural implications** in its design.

- Standards should reflect technical and other factors **expected for the period** in which the standards are to be applied.

- There are a number of **criticisms** of the use of standard costing, particularly in the modern manufacturing environment.

BPP PUBLISHING

Quick quiz

1   *Match the types of performance standard to the correct descriptions.*

Performance standards	Descriptions
(a) Ideal	(1) If well set, can provide a useful psychological incentive
(b) Attainable	(2) Do not attempt to improve on current levels of efficiency
(c) Current	(3) Least common type of standard in use
(d) Basic	(4) Likely to have an unfavourable motivational effect

2   An attainable standard is based on perfect operating conditions. True or false?

3   The time taken to produce the first unit of product B was 4.5 hours. An 80% learning effect applies. How long will it take to produce the second unit of product B?

   A   4.5 hours
   B   2.7 hours
   C   7.2 hours
   D   3.6 hours

4   Fill in the gaps.

   (i)   Budgets are prepared for .... costs; standards are for a ....

   (ii) .... can be prepared for all functions; .... are only suitable for repetitive actions where output can be measured.

   (iii) .... are expressed in money terms; .... need not be expressed in money terms.

5   *Choose the appropriate words from those highlighted.*

   Standard costing places too much emphasis on **direct material costs/direct labour costs/ overheads**. **Direct material/direct labour/overheads is/are** a **small/large** proportion of costs in the modern manufacturing environment and so this emphasis is **appropriate/inappropriate**.

Answers to quick quiz

1   (a)   4

    (b)   1

    (c)   2

    (d)   3

2   False. An ideal standard is based on perfect operating conditions.

3   B   (4.5 × 80% × 2) − 4.5 = 2.7 hours

4   (i)   aggregate total
          single task

    (ii) budgets
          standards

    (iii) budgets
          standards

5   Standard costing places too much emphasis on direct labour costs. Direct labour is only a small proportion of costs in the modern manufacturing environment and so this emphasis is inappropriate.

Now try the question below from the Exam Question Bank

Number	Level	Marks	Time
Q1	Introductory	n/a	15 mins

Chapter 2

VARIANCE ANALYSIS

Topic list	Syllabus reference	Ability required
1 Variances	(i)	Application/analysis
2 Direct material cost variances	(i)	Application/analysis
3 Direct labour cost variances	(i)	Application/analysis
4 Variable production overhead variances	(i)	Application/analysis
5 Fixed production overhead variances	(i)	Application/analysis
6 Sales variances	(i)	Application/analysis
7 Operating statements	(i)	Application/analysis
8 Variances in a standard marginal costing system	(i)	Application/analysis
9 Deriving actual data from standard cost details and variances	(i)	Application/analysis

Introduction

The **actual results** achieved by an organisation during a reporting period (week, month, quarter, year) will, more than likely, be **different** from the expected results (the expected results being the **standard costs and revenues** which we looked at in the previous chapter). Such differences may occur between individual items, such as the cost of labour and the volume of sales, and between the total expected profit/contribution and the total actual profit/contribution.

Management will have spent considerable time and trouble setting standards. Actual results have differed from the standards. The wise manager will **consider the differences** that have occurred and use the results of these considerations to assist in attempts to attain the standards. The wise manager will use variance analysis as a **method of control**.

In your studies for Paper 2 you will have covered the calculation of basic cost and sales variances. Because students often find variance analysis quite difficult (although, really, it isn't) we are going to go over the basic variances again in detail.

When we study fixed overhead variances we will go a stage further than in your Paper 2 studies and sub-divide the volume variance. Within sales variances we will also study a more detailed sub-analysis than in your Paper 2 studies.

In Chapter 3 we will build on your revision of basics in this chapter by examining more complex variances, mix and yield variances and planning and operational variances, so ensure that you have mastered the basics!

Learning outcomes covered in this chapter

- **Calculate and interpret** material, labour, variable overheads, fixed overheads and sales variances

- **Prepare and discuss** a report which reconciles budget and actual profit using absorption and/or marginal costing principles

Syllabus content covered in this chapter

- Fixed overhead capacity and efficiency variances

- Sales price and volume variances

1   **VARIANCES**   **Pilot paper**

> **KEY TERM**
>
> A **variance** is the 'Difference between planned, budgeted, or standard cost and the actual cost incurred. The same comparisons may be made for revenues'.
>
> (CIMA *Official Terminology*)

1.1   The process by which the **total difference between standard and actual** results is **analysed** is known as **variance analysis**.

> **KEY TERM**
>
> **Variance analysis** is defined in CIMA *Official Terminology* as 'The evaluation of performance by means of variances, whose timely reporting should maximise the opportunity for managerial action'.

1.2   When **actual results are better than expected results,** we have a **favourable** variance (F). If, on the other hand, **actual results are worse than expected results,** we have an **adverse** variance (A).

1.3   Variances can be divided into three main groups.

- Variable cost variances
  - Direct material
  - Direct labour
  - Variable production overhead
- Fixed production overhead variances
- Sales variances

2   **DIRECT MATERIAL COST VARIANCES**

2.1   The **direct material total variance** (the difference between what the output actually cost and what it should have cost, in terms of material) can be **divided into two sub-variances.**

(a) **The direct material price variance**

This is the **difference between the standard cost and the actual cost for the actual quantity of material used or purchased.** In other words, it is the difference between what the material did cost and what it should have cost.

(b) **The direct material usage variance**

This is the **difference between the standard quantity of materials that should have been used for the number of units actually produced, and the actual quantity of materials used, valued at the standard cost per unit of material.** In other words, it is the difference between how much material should have been used and how much material was used, valued at standard cost.

2.2   EXAMPLE: DIRECT MATERIAL VARIANCES

Product X has a standard direct material cost as follows.

10 kilograms of material Y at £10 per kilogram = £100 per unit of X.

During period 4, 1,000 units of X were manufactured, using 11,700 kilograms of material Y which cost £98,600.

Required

Calculate the following variances.

(a) The direct material total variance
(b) The direct material price variance
(c) The direct material usage variance

2.3 SOLUTION

(a) The direct material total variance

This is the difference between what 1,000 units should have cost and what they did cost.

	£
1,000 units should have cost (× £100)	100,000
but did cost	98,600
Direct material total variance	1,400 (F)

The variance is favourable because the units cost less than they should have cost.

Now we can break down the direct material total variance into its two constituent parts: the direct material price variance and the direct material usage variance.

(b) The direct material price variance

This is the difference between what 11,700 kgs should have cost and what 11,700 kgs did cost.

	£
11,700 kgs of Y should have cost (× £10)	117,000
but did cost	98,600
Material Y price variance	18,400 (F)

The variance is favourable because the material cost less than it should have.

(c) The direct material usage variance

This is the difference between how many kilograms of Y should have been used to produce 1,000 units of X and how many kilograms were used, valued at the standard cost per kilogram.

1,000 units should have used (× 10 kgs)	10,000 kgs
but did use	11,700 kgs
Usage variance in kgs	1,700 kgs (A)
× standard cost per kilogram	× £10
Usage variance in £	£17,000 (A)

The variance is adverse because more material than should have been used was used.

(d) Summary

	£
Price variance	18,400 (F)
Usage variance	17,000 (A)
Total variance	1,400 (F)

Materials variances and opening and closing stock

2.4 Suppose that a company uses raw material P in production, and that this raw material has a standard price of £3 per metre. During one month 6,000 metres are bought for £18,600, and

BPP
PUBLISHING

5,000 metres are used in production. At the end of the month, stock will have been increased by 1,000 metres. In variance analysis, the problem is to decide the **material price variance**. Should it be calculated on the basis of **materials purchased** (6,000 metres) or on the basis of **materials used** (5,000 metres)?

2.5 The answer to this problem depends on **how closing stocks** of the raw materials will be **valued**.

(a) If they are valued at **standard cost**, (1,000 units at £3 per unit) the price variance is calculated on material **purchases** in the period.

(b) If they are valued at **actual cost (FIFO)** (1,000 units at £3.10 per unit) the price variance is calculated on materials **used in production** in the period.

2.6 A **full standard costing system** is usually in operation and therefore the price variance is usually calculated on **purchases** in the period. The variance on the full 6,000 metres will be written off to the costing profit and loss account, even though only 5,000 metres are included in the cost of production.

2.7 There are two main **advantages** in extracting the material price variance at the time of **receipt**.

(a) If variances are extracted at the time of receipt they will be **brought to the attention of managers earlier** than if they are extracted as the material is used. If it is necessary to correct any variances then management action can be more timely.

(b) Since variances are extracted at the time of receipt, **all stocks will be valued at standard price**. This is administratively easier and it means that all issues from stocks can be made at standard price. If stocks are held at actual cost it is necessary to calculate a separate price variance on each batch as it is issued. Since issues are usually made in a number of small batches this can be a time-consuming task, especially with a manual system.

Question 1

What is the price variance based on the information in Paragraph 2.4?

A   £3,100 (A)
B   £600 (A)
C   £3,100 (F)
D   £600 (F)

Answer

The correct answer is B.

The price variance would be calculated as follows.

	£
6,000 metres of material P purchased should cost (× £3)	18,000
but did cost	18,600
Price variance	600 (A)

3   DIRECT LABOUR COST VARIANCES

3.1 The calculation of direct labour variances is very similar to the calculation of direct material variances.

The **direct labour total variance** (the difference between what the output should have cost and what it did cost, in terms of labour) can be **divided into two sub-variances**.

(a) **The direct labour rate variance**

This is similar to the direct material price variance. If is the **difference between the standard cost and the actual cost for the actual number of hours paid for**.

In other words, it is the difference between what the labour did cost and what it should have cost.

(b) **The direct labour efficiency variance**

This is similar to the direct material usage variance. It is the **difference between the hours that should have been worked for the number of units actually produced, and the actual number of hours worked, valued at the standard rate per hour.**

In other words, it is the difference between how many hours should have been worked and how many hours were worked, valued at the standard rate per hour.

3.2 EXAMPLE: DIRECT LABOUR VARIANCES

The standard direct labour cost of product X is as follows.

2 hours of grade Z labour at £5 per hour = £10 per unit of product X.

During period 4, 1,000 units of product X were made, and the direct labour cost of grade Z labour was £8,900 for 2,300 hours of work.

Required

Calculate the following variances.

(a) The direct labour total variance
(b) The direct labour rate variance
(c) The direct labour efficiency (productivity) variance

3.3 SOLUTION

(a) **The direct labour total variance**

This is the difference between what 1,000 units should have cost and what they did cost.

	£
1,000 units should have cost (× £10)	10,000
but did cost	8,900
Direct labour total variance	1,100 (F)

The variance is favourable because the units cost less than they should have done.

Again we can analyse this total variance into its two constituent parts.

(b) **The direct labour rate variance**

This is the difference between what 2,300 hours should have cost and what 2,300 hours did cost.

	£
2,300 hours of work should have cost (× £5 per hr)	11,500
but did cost	8,900
Direct labour rate variance	2,600 (F)

The variance is favourable because the labour cost less than it should have cost.

(c) **The direct labour efficiency variance**

1,000 units of X should have taken (× 2 hrs)	2,000 hrs
but did take	2,300 hrs
Efficiency variance in hours	300 hrs (A)
× standard rate per hour	× £5
Efficiency variance in £	£1,500 (A)

The variance is adverse because more hours were worked than should have been worked.

(d) **Summary**

	£
Rate variance	2,600 (F)
Efficiency variance	1,500 (A)
Total variance	1,100 (F)

Idle time variance

3.4 A company may operate a costing system in which any idle time is recorded. Idle time may be caused by machine breakdowns or not having work to give to employees, perhaps because of bottlenecks in production or a shortage of orders from customers. When idle time occurs, the labour force is still paid wages for time at work, but no actual work is done. Time paid for without any work being done is unproductive and therefore inefficient. In variance analysis, **idle time is an adverse efficiency variance**.

3.5 When idle time is recorded separately, it is helpful to provide control information which identifies the cost of idle time separately, and in variance analysis, there will be an idle time variance **as a separate part of the total labour efficiency variance**. The remaining **efficiency variance** will then relate only to the productivity of the labour force during the **hours spent actively working**.

3.6 EXAMPLE: LABOUR VARIANCES WITH IDLE TIME

Refer to the standard cost data in Paragraph 3.2. During period 5, 1,500 units of product X were made and the cost of grade Z labour was £17,500 for 3,080 hours. During the period, however, there as a shortage of customer orders and 100 hours were recorded as idle time.

Required

Calculate the following variances.

(a) The direct labour total variance
(b) The direct labour rate variance
(c) The idle time variance
(d) The direct labour efficiency variance

3.7 SOLUTION

(a) **The direct labour total variance**

	£
1,500 units of product X should have cost (× £10)	15,000
but did cost	17,500
Direct labour total variance	2,500 (A)

Actual cost is greater than standard cost. The variance is therefore adverse.

(b) **The direct labour rate variance**

The rate variance is a comparison of what the hours paid should have cost and what they did cost.

	£
3,080 hours of grade Z labour should have cost (× £5)	15,400
but did cost	17,500
Direct labour rate variance	2,100 (A)

Actual cost is greater than standard cost. The variance is therefore adverse.

(c) **The idle time variance**

The idle time variance is the hours of idle time, valued at the standard rate per hour.

Idle time variance $= 100$ hours $(A) \times £5 = £500$ (A)

Idle time is **always** an **adverse** variance.

(d) **The direct labour efficiency variance**

The efficiency variance considers the hours actively worked (the difference between hours paid for and idle time hours). In our example, there were $(3,080 - 100) = 2,980$ hours when the labour force was not idle. The variance is calculated by taking the amount of output produced (1,500 units of product X) and comparing the time it should have taken to make them, with the actual time spent **actively** making them (2,980 hours). Once again, the variance in hours is valued at the standard rate per labour hour.

1,500 units of product X should take (× 2 hrs)	3,000 hrs
but did take (3,080 – 100)	2,980 hrs
Direct labour efficiency variance in hours	20 hrs (F)
× standard rate per hour	× £5
Direct labour efficiency variance in £	£100 (F)

(e) **Summary**

	£
Direct labour rate variance	2,100 (A)
Idle time variance	500 (A)
Direct labour efficiency variance	100 (F)
Direct labour total variance	2,500 (A)

3.8 Remember that, if idle time is recorded, the actual hours used in the **efficiency variance** calculation are the **hours worked and not the hours paid for.**

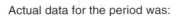

Question 2

Growler Ltd is planning to make 100,000 units per period of product AA. Each unit of AA should require 2 hours to produce, with labour being paid £11 per hour. Attainable work hours are less than clock hours, so 250,000 hours have been budgeted in the period.

Actual data for the period was:

Units produced	120,000
Direct labour cost	£3,200,000
Clock hours	280,000

Required

Calculate the following variances.

(a) Labour rate variance
(b) Labour efficiency variance
(c) Idle time variance

Answer

The information means that clock hours have to be multiplied by 200,000/250,000 (80%) in order to arrive at a realistic efficiency variance.

(a) **Labour rate variance**

	£'000	
280,000 hours should have cost (× £11)	3,080	
but did cost	3,200	
Labour rate variance	120	(A)

(b) **Labour efficiency variance**

120,000 units should have taken (× 2 hours)	240,000	hrs
but did take (280,000 × 80%)	224,000	hrs
Variance in hours	16,000	hrs (F)
× standard rate per hour	× £11	
Labour efficiency variance	£176,000	(F)

(c) **Idle time variance**

280,000 × 20%	56,000	hrs
	× £11	
	£616,000	(A)

4 VARIABLE PRODUCTION OVERHEAD VARIANCES

4.1 Suppose that the variable production overhead cost of product X is as follows.

> 2 hours at £1.50 = £3 per unit

During period 6, 400 units of product X were made. The labour force worked 820 hours, of which 60 hours were recorded as idle time. The variable overhead cost was £1,230.

Calculate the following variances.

(a) The variable overhead total variance
(b) The variable production overhead expenditure variance
(c) The variable production overhead efficiency variance

4.2 Since this example **relates to variable production costs**, the total variance is **based on actual units of production**. (If the overhead had been a **variable selling cost**, the variance would be **based on sales volumes**.)

	£
400 units of product X should cost (× £3)	1,200
but did cost	1,230
Variable production overhead total variance	30 (A)

4.3 In many variance reporting systems, the variance analysis goes no further, and expenditure and efficiency variances are not calculated. However, the adverse variance of £30 may be explained as the **sum of two factors**.

(a) The hourly rate of spending on variable production overheads was higher than it should have been, that is there is an **expenditure variance**.

(b) The labour force worked inefficiently, and took longer to make the output than it should have done. This means that spending on variable production overhead was higher than it should have been, in other words there is an **efficiency (productivity) variance**. The variable production overhead efficiency variance is exactly the same, in hours, as the direct labour efficiency variance, and occurs for the same reasons.

4.4 It is usually assumed that **variable overheads are incurred during active working hours**, but are not incurred during idle time (for example the machines are not running, therefore power is not being consumed, and no direct materials are being used). This means in our example that although the labour force was paid for 820 hours, they were actively working for only 760 of those hours and so variable production overhead spending occurred during 760 hours.

4.5 (a) **The variable production overhead expenditure variance**

This is the **difference between the amount of variable production overhead that should have been incurred in the actual hours actively worked, and the actual amount of variable production overhead incurred**.

	£
760 hours of variable production overhead should cost (× £1.50)	1,140
but did cost	1,230
Variable production overhead expenditure variance	90 (A)

(b) **The variable production overhead efficiency variance**

If you already know the direct **labour efficiency variance**, the variable production overhead efficiency variance is **exactly the same in hours**, but **priced at the variable production overhead rate per hour**. In our example, the efficiency variance would be as follows.

400 units of product X should take (× 2 hrs)	800 hrs
but did take (active hours)	760 hrs
Variable production overhead efficiency variance in hours	40 hrs (F)
× standard rate per hour	× £1.50
Variable production overhead efficiency variance in £	£60 (F)

(c) **Summary**

	£
Variable production overhead expenditure variance	90 (A)
Variable production overhead efficiency variance	60 (F)
Variable production overhead total variance	30 (A)

5 FIXED PRODUCTION OVERHEAD VARIANCES

5.1 The method of calculating variances is essentially the same for labour, materials and variable overheads. As we will see, fixed production overhead variances are very different. In an absorption costing system, they are simply **an attempt to explain the under or over absorption of fixed overheads**.

5.2 The **fixed production overhead total variance** may be broken down into **two parts** as usual.

(a) An **expenditure variance**

(b) A **volume variance. This in turn may be split into two parts.**

   - An **efficiency variance**
   - A **capacity variance**

You will have learned about the expenditure variance and volume variance in your Paper 2 studies, but the subdivision of the volume variance into its two component parts is new to your Paper 8 syllabus.

5.3 The fixed production overhead volume variance sometimes causes confusion and may need more explanation. The most important point is that the **volume variance applies to fixed production overhead costs only** and not to variable production overheads.

(a) Variable production overheads incurred change with the volume of activity. If the master budget is to work for 300 hours and variable overheads are incurred and absorbed at a rate of £6 per hour, the variable overhead budget will be £1,800. If only 200 hours are actually worked, the variable overhead absorbed will be £1,200 and the expected expenditure will also be £1,200, so that there will be no under or over absorption of overhead because of volume changes.

(b) Fixed production overheads are different because the level of expenditure does not change as the number of hours worked varies. If the master budget is to work for 300 hours and fixed overheads are budgeted to be £2,400, the fixed overhead absorption rate will be £8 per hour. If actual hours worked are only 200 hours, the fixed overhead absorbed will be £1,600, but expected expenditure will be unchanged at £2,400. There is an under absorption of £800 because of the volume variance of 100 hours shortfall multiplied by the absorption rate of £8 per hour.

ATTENTION!

You will find it easier to calculate and understand fixed production overhead variances if you keep in mind the whole time the fact that you are trying to explain the reasons for any under- or over-absorbed production overhead. Remember that the absorption rate is calculated as budgeted fixed production overhead ÷ budgeted level of activity.

5.4 Generally the level of activity used in the overhead absorption rate will be units of production or hours of activity. More often than not, if just one product is being produced, the level of activity is in terms of units produced. If, however, more than one product is produced, units of output are converted to standard hours.

5.5 You will remember from your earlier studies that if either the budgeted overhead expenditure or the budgeted activity level or both are incorrect then we will have under- or over-absorbed overhead.

(a) The fixed overhead **expenditure variance** measures the under or over absorption caused by the **actual overhead expenditure being different from budget**.

(b) There are two reasons why the **actual production or hours of activity may be different from the budgeted production or budgeted number of hours** used in calculating the absorption rate.

   (i) The **work force may have been working at a more or less efficient rate than standard** to produce a given output. This is measured by the fixed overhead **efficiency variance**.

   (ii) Regardless of the level of efficiency, the **total number of hours worked could have been less or more than was originally budgeted** (employees may have worked a lot of overtime or there may have been a strike). Other things being equal, this could lead to under- or over-absorbed fixed overhead and the effect is measured by the fixed overhead **capacity variance**.

How to calculate the variances

> **KEY TERMS**
>
> - **Fixed overhead total variance** is the difference between fixed overhead incurred and fixed overhead absorbed (the under- or over-absorbed fixed overhead).
>
> - **Fixed overhead expenditure variance** is the difference between the budgeted fixed overhead expenditure and actual fixed overhead expenditure.
>
> - **Fixed overhead volume variance** is the difference between actual and budgeted production/volume multiplied by the standard absorption rate per *unit*.
>
> - **Fixed overhead efficiency variance** is the difference between the number of hours that actual production should have taken, and the number of hours actually taken (that is, worked) multiplied by the standard absorption rate per *hour*.
>
> - **Fixed overhead capacity variance** is the difference between budgeted hours of work and the actual hours worked, multiplied by the standard absorption rate per *hour*.

5.6   You should now be ready to work through an example to demonstrate all of the fixed overhead variances.

5.7   EXAMPLE: FIXED OVERHEAD VARIANCES

Suppose that a company budgets to produce 1,000 units of product E during August. The expected time to produce a unit of E is five hours, and the budgeted fixed production overhead is £20,000. The standard fixed production overhead cost per unit of product E will therefore be 5 hours at £4 per hour (= £20 per unit). Actual fixed production overhead expenditure in August turns out to be £20,450. The labour force manages to produce 1,100 units of product E in 5,400 hours of work.

Task

Calculate the fixed production overhead total variance and its sub-variances.

5.8   SOLUTION

(a)   **Fixed production overhead total variance**

	£
Fixed overhead incurred	20,450
Fixed overhead absorbed (1,100 units × £20 per unit)	22,000
Fixed production overhead total variance (= under-/over-absorbed overhead)	1,550 (F)

The variance is favourable because more overheads were absorbed than budgeted.

(b)   **Fixed production overhead expenditure variance**

	£
Budgeted fixed overhead expenditure	20,000
Actual fixed overhead expenditure	20,450
Fixed production overhead expenditure variance	450 (A)

The variance is adverse because expenditure was greater than budgeted.

(c)   **Fixed production overhead volume variance**

The production volume achieved was greater than expected. The fixed production overhead volume variance measures the difference at the standard rate.

	£
Actual production at standard rate (1,100 × £20 per unit)	22,000
Budgeted production at standard rate (1,000 × £20 per unit)	20,000
Fixed production overhead volume variance	2,000 (F)

The variance is favourable because output was greater than expected.

This **volume variance arises for two reasons**.

(i)   The labour force may have worked efficiently, and produced output at a faster rate than expected. More overhead will be absorbed if units are produced more quickly. This efficiency variance is exactly the same in hours as the direct labour efficiency variance (and variable overhead efficiency variance), but is valued in £ at the standard absorption rate for fixed overhead.

(ii)   The labour force may have worked longer hours than budgeted, and therefore potentially produced more output, so there may be a capacity variance.

(d) **Fixed production overhead efficiency variance**

The efficiency variance is calculated in the same way as the labour efficiency variance.

1,100 units of product E should take (× 5 hrs)	5,500 hrs
but did take	5,400 hrs
Efficiency variance in hours	100 hrs (F)
× standard fixed overhead absorption rate per hour	× £4
Fixed production overhead efficiency variance in £	£400 (F)

The labour force has produced 5,500 standard hours of work in 5,400 actual hours and so output is 100 standard hours (or 20 units of product E) higher than budgeted for this reason and the variance is favourable.

(e) **Fixed production overhead capacity variance**

The capacity variance is the difference between the budgeted and actual hours of work.

Budgeted hours of work	5,000 hrs
Actual hours of work	5,400 hrs
Capacity variance in hours	400 hrs (F)
× standard fixed overhead absorption rate per hour	× £4
Fixed production overhead capacity variance in £	£1,600 (F)

Since the labour force worked 400 hours longer than budgeted, we should expect output to be 400 standard hours (or 80 units of product E) higher than budgeted and hence the variance is favourable.

Question 3

Brain Ltd produces and sells one product only, the Blob, the standard cost for one unit being as follows.

	£
Direct material A - 10 kilograms at £20 per kg	200
Direct wages - 5 hours at £6 per hour	30
Fixed production overhead	50
Total standard cost	280

The fixed overhead included in the standard cost is based on an expected monthly output of 900 units.

During April the actual results were as follows.

Production	800 units
Material A	7,800 kg used, costing £159,900
Direct wages	4,200 hours worked for £24,150
Fixed production overhead	£47,000

Required

(a)   Calculate material price and usage variances.

(b)   Calculate labour rate and efficiency variances.
(c)   Calculate fixed production overhead expenditure and volume variances.
(d)   Calculate fixed production overhead efficiency and capacity variances.

Answer

(a)   **Material price variance**

	£
7,800 kgs should have cost (× £20)	156,000
but did cost	159,900
Price variance	3,900 (A)

Material usage variance

800 units should have used (× 10 kgs)	8,000 kgs
but did use	7,800 kgs
Usage variance in kgs	200 kgs (F)
× standard cost per kilogram	× £20
Usage variance in £	£4,000 (F)

(b)   **Labour rate variance**

	£
4,200 hours should have cost (× £6)	25,200
but did cost	24,150
Rate variance	1,050 (F)

Labour efficiency variance

800 units should have taken (× 5 hrs)	4,000 hrs
but did take	4,200 hrs
Efficiency variance in hours	200 hrs (A)
× standard rate per hour	× £6
Labour efficiency variance in £	£1,200 (A)

(c)   **Fixed production overhead expenditure variance**

	£
Budgeted expenditure (£50 × 900)	45,000
Actual expenditure	47,000
Expenditure variance	2,000 (A)

Fixed production overhead volume variance

	£
Budgeted production at standard rate (900 × £50)	45,000
Actual production at standard rate (800 × £50)	40,000
Volume variance	5,000 (A)

(d)   **Fixed production overhead efficiency variance**

Fixed production overhead standard rate per hour = £50/5 = £10 per hour

From the labour efficiency variance,	
Efficiency variance in hours	200 hrs (A)
x standard fixed production overhead absorption rate per hour	× £10
Fixed production overhead efficiency variance in £	£2,000 (A)

Fixed production overhead capacity variance

Budgeted hours of work (900 units x 5 hours)	4,500 hrs
Actual hours of work	4,200 hrs
Capacity variance in hours	300 hrs (A)
x standard fixed production overhead absorption rate per hour	× £10
Fixed production overhead capacity variance in £	£3,000 (A)

Check: efficiency variance + capacity variance = volume variance
£2,000 (A)   +   £3,000 (A)   =   £5,000 (A)

BPP PUBLISHING

6 SALES VARIANCES

Selling price variance

6.1   The **selling price variance** is a measure of the effect on expected profit of a different selling price to standard selling price. It is calculated as the **difference between what the sales revenue should have been for the actual quantity sold, and what it was.**

6.2   Suppose that the standard selling price of product X is £15. Actual sales in year 3 were 2,000 units at £15.30 per unit. The selling price variance is calculated as follows.

	£
Sales revenue from 2,000 units should have been (× £15)	30,000
but was (× £15.30)	30,600
Selling price variance	600 (F)

The variance is favourable because the price was higher than expected.

Sales volume profit variance

6.3   The **sales volume profit variance** is the difference between the actual units sold and the budgeted quantity, valued at the standard profit per unit. In other words, it measures **the increase or decrease in standard profit as a result of the sales volume being higher or lower than budgeted.**

6.4   Suppose that a company budgets to sell 8,000 units of product J for £12 per unit. The standard full cost per unit is £7. Actual sales were 7,700 units, at £12.50 per unit.

The sales volume profit variance is calculated as follows.

Budgeted sales volume	8,000 units
Actual sales volume	7,700 units
Sales volume variance in units	300 units (A)
× standard profit per unit (£(12−7))	× £5
Sales volume variance	£1,500 (A)

The variance is adverse because actual sales were less than budgeted.

Question 4

Jasper Ltd has the following budget and actual figures for year 4.

	Budget	Actual
Sales units	600	620
Selling price per unit	£30	£29

Standard full cost of production = £28 per unit.

The selling price variance and the sales volume profit variances are

	Selling price variance	Sales volume profit variance
A	£620 (F)	£40 (A)
B	£600 (A)	£40 (F)
C	£620 (A)	£40 (F)
D	£620 (A)	£600 (F)

Answer

The correct answer is C.

	£
Sales revenue for 620 units should have been (× £30)	18,600
but was (× £29)	17,980
Selling price variance	620 (A)
Budgeted sales volume	600 units
Actual sales volume	620 units
Sales volume variance in units	20 units (F)
× standard profit per unit (£(30 – 28))	× £2
Sales volume profit variance	£40 (F)

The significance of sales variances

6.5   The possible **interdependence** between sales price and sales volume variances should be obvious to you. A reduction in the sales price might stimulate bigger sales demand, so that an adverse sales price variance might be counterbalanced by a favourable sales volume variance. Similarly, a price rise would give a favourable price variance, but possibly at the cost of a fall in demand and an adverse sales volume variance.

6.6   It is therefore important in analysing an unfavourable sales variance that the overall consequence should be considered, that is, has there been a counterbalancing favourable variance as a direct result of the unfavourable one?

Exam focus point

Sales variances are liable to come up both as part of a longer question or as MCQs.

7   OPERATING STATEMENTS

7.1   So far, we have considered how variances are calculated without considering how they combine to **reconcile the difference between budgeted profit and actual profit** during a period. This reconciliation is usually presented as a report to senior management at the end of each control period. The report is called an operating statement or statement of variances.

KEY TERM

The CIMA *Official Terminology* definition of an **operating statement** is 'A regular report for management of actual costs and revenues, as appropriate. Usually compares actual with budget and shows variances'.

7.2   An extensive example will now be introduced, both to revise the variance calculations already described, and also to show how to combine them into an operating statement.

7.3   EXAMPLE: VARIANCES AND OPERATING STATEMENTS

Sydney Ltd manufactures one product, and the entire product is sold as soon as it is produced. There are no opening or closing stocks and work in progress is negligible. The company operates a standard costing system and analysis of variances is made every month. The standard cost card for the product, a boomerang, is as follows.

STANDARD COST CARD - BOOMERANG		£
Direct materials	0.5 kilos at £4 per kilo	2.00
Direct wages	2 hours at £2.00 per hour	4.00
Variable overheads	2 hours at £0.30 per hour	0.60
Fixed overhead	2 hours at £3.70 per hour	7.40
Standard cost		14.00
Standard profit		6.00
Standing selling price		20.00

Selling and administration expenses are not included in the standard cost, and are deducted from profit as a period charge.

Budgeted output for the month of June year 7 was 5,100 units. Actual results for June year 7 were as follows.

Production of 4,850 units was sold for £95,600.
Materials consumed in production amounted to 2,300 kgs at a total cost of £9,800.
Labour hours paid for amounted to 8,500 hours at a cost of £16,800.
Actual operating hours amounted to 8,000 hours.
Variable overheads amounted to £2,600.
Fixed overheads amounted to £42,300.
Selling and administration expenses amounted to £18,000.

Required

Calculate all variances and prepare an operating statement for the month ended 30 June year 7.

7.4   SOLUTION

		£
(a)	2,300 kg of material should cost (× £4)	9,200
	but did cost	9,800
	Material price variance	600 (A)
(b)	4,850 boomerangs should use (× 0.5 kgs) 2,425 kg	
	but did use	2,300 kg
	Material usage variance in kgs	125 kg (F)
	× standard cost per kg	× £4
	Material usage variance in £	£ 500 (F)

		£
(c)	8,500 hours of labour should cost (× £2)	17,000
	but did cost	16,800
	Labour rate variance	200 (F)
(d)	4,850 boomerangs should take (× 2 hrs)	9,700 hrs
	but did take (active hours)	8,000 hrs
	Labour efficiency variance in hours	1,700 hrs (F)
	× standard cost per hour	× £2
	Labour efficiency variance in £	£3,400 (F)
(e)	Idle time variance 500 hours (A) × £2	£1,000 (A)

		£
(f)	8,000 hours incurring variable o/hd expenditure should cost (× £0.30)	2,400
	but did cost	2,600
	Variable overhead expenditure variance	200 (A)
(g)	Variable overhead efficiency variance in hours is the same as the labour efficiency variance:	
	1,700 hours (F) × £0.30 per hour	£ 510 (F)

		£
(h)	Budgeted fixed overhead (5,100 units × 2 hrs × £3.70)	37,740
	Actual fixed overhead	42,300
	Fixed overhead expenditure variance	4,560 (A)

		£
(i)	Actual production at standard rate (4,850 units × £7.40)	35,890
	Budgeted production at standard rate (5,100 units × £7.40)	37,740
	Fixed overhead volume variance	1,850 (A)

(j) Fixed overhead efficiency variance in hours is the same as the labour efficiency variance:

1,700 hrs (F) × £3.70 per hour £6,290 (F)

(k)	Budgeted hours of work (5,100 units x 2 hours)	10,200 hrs
	Actual hours of work	8,000 hrs
	Capacity variance in hours	2,200 hrs (A)
	× standard fixed overhead absorption rate per hour	× £3.70
	Fixed overhead capacity variance in £	£8,140 (A)

(l)	Revenue from 4,850 boomerangs should be (× £20)	97,000
	but was	95,600
	Selling price variance	1,400 (A)

(m)	Budgeted sales volume	5,100 units
	Actual sales volume	4,850 units
	Sales volume profit variance in units	250 units
	× standard profit per unit	× £6 (A)
	Sales volume profit variance in £	£1,500 (A)

7.5 There are several ways in which an operating statement may be presented. Perhaps the most common format is one which reconciles budgeted profit to actual profit. In this example, **sales and administration costs will be introduced at the end of the statement,** so that we shall **begin with 'budgeted profit before sales and administration costs'.**

7.6 **Sales variances are reported first,** and the **total of the budgeted profit and the two sales variances** results in a figure for **'actual sales minus the standard cost of sales'.** The **cost variances** are then reported, and an **actual profit** (before sales and administration costs) calculated. **Sales and administration costs** are then **deducted** to reach the **actual profit.**

SYDNEY LTD - OPERATING STATEMENT JUNE YEAR 7

		£	£
Budgeted profit before sales and administration costs			30,600
Sales variances:	price	1,400 (A)	
	volume	1,500 (A)	
			2,900 (A)
Actual sales minus the standard cost of sales			27,700

Cost variances	(F)	(A)	
	£	£	
Material price		600	
Material usage	500		
Labour rate	200		
Labour efficiency	3,400		
Labour idle time		1,000	
Variable overhead expenditure		200	
Variable overhead efficiency	510		
Fixed overhead expenditure		4,560	
Fixed overhead efficiency	6,290		
Fixed overhead capacity		8,140	
	10,900	14,500	3,600 (A)
Actual profit before sales and admin costs c/f			24,100

BPP PUBLISHING

	£	£
Actual profit before sales and administration costs b/f		24,100
Sales and administration costs		18,000
Actual profit, June year 7		6,100

Check	£	£
Sales		95,600
Materials	9,800	
Labour	16,800	
Variable overhead	2,600	
Fixed overhead	42,300	
Sales and administration	18,000	
		89,500
Actual profit		6,100

8 VARIANCES IN A STANDARD MARGINAL COSTING SYSTEM

8.1 In all of the examples we have worked through so far, a system of standard absorption costing has been in operation. If an organisation uses **standard marginal costing** instead of standard absorption costing, there will be two differences in the way the variances are calculated.

(a) In marginal costing, fixed costs are not absorbed into product costs and so there are no fixed cost variances to explain any under or over absorption of overheads. There will, therefore, be **no fixed overhead volume variance**. There will be a fixed overhead expenditure variance which is calculated in exactly the same way as for absorption costing systems.

(b) The **sales volume variance** will be valued at **standard contribution margin** (sales price per unit minus variable costs of sale per unit), **not** standard **profit** margin. It will be called the **sales volume contribution variance.**

Preparing a marginal costing operating statement

8.2 Returning once again to the example of Sydney Ltd, the variances in a system of standard marginal costing would be as follows.

(a) There is **no fixed overhead volume variance**, and therefore no variances for fixed overhead efficiency and capacity.

(b) The standard contribution per unit of boomerang is £(20 – 6.60) = £13.40 and so the **sales volume contribution variance** of 250 units (A) is valued at (× £13.40) = £3,350 (A).

8.3 The other variances are unchanged. However, this operating statement differs from an absorption costing operating statement in the following ways.

(a) It **begins with the budgeted contribution** (£30,600 + budgeted fixed production costs £37,740 = £68,340).

(b) The subtotal before the analysis of cost variances is **actual sales** (£95,600) **less the standard variable cost of sales** (£4,850 × £6.60) = £63,590.

(c) **Actual contribution** is highlighted in the statement.

(d) Budgeted fixed production overhead is adjusted by the fixed overhead expenditure variance to show the **actual fixed production overhead expenditure**.

8.4 Therefore a **marginal costing** operating statement might look like this.

SYDNEY LTD - OPERATING STATEMENT JUNE YEAR 7

		£	£	£
Budgeted contribution				68,340
Sales variances:	volume		3,350 (A)	
	price		1,400 (A)	
				4,750 (A)
Actual sales minus the standard variable cost of sales				63,590

	(F)	(A)	
	£	£	
Variable cost variances			
Material price		600	
Material usage	500		
Labour rate	200		
Labour efficiency	3,400		
Labour idle time		1,000	
Variable overhead expenditure		200	
Variable overhead efficiency	510		
	4,610	1,800	
			2,810 (F)
Actual contribution			66,400
Budgeted fixed production overhead		37,740	
Expenditure variance		4,560 (A)	
Actual fixed production overhead			42,300
Actual profit before sales and administration costs			24,100
Sales and administration costs			18,000
Actual profit			6,100

8.5 Notice that the actual profit is the same as the profit calculated by standard absorption costing because there were no changes in stock levels. Absorption costing and marginal costing do not always produce an identical profit figure.

Question 5

MilBri Limited, a manufacturing firm, operates a standard marginal costing system. It makes a single product, LI, using a single raw material AN.

Standard costs relating to LI have been calculated as follows.

Standard cost schedule - LI	*Per unit*
	£
Direct material, AN, 100 kg at £5 per kg	500
Direct labour, 10 hours at £8 per hour	80
Variable production overhead, 10 hours at £2 per hour	20
	600

The standard selling price of a LI is £900 and MilBri produce 1,020 units a month.

During December, 1,000 units of LI were produced. Relevant details of this production are as follows.

Direct material AN

90,000 kgs costing £720,000 were bought and used.

Direct labour

8,200 hours were worked during the month and total wages were £63,000.

Variable production overhead

The actual cost for the month was £25,000.

Stocks of the direct material AN are valued at the standard price of £5 per kg.

Each LI was sold for £975.

Required

Calculate the following for the month of December.

(a)   Variable production cost variance
(b)   Direct labour cost variance, analysed into rate and efficiency variances
(c)   Direct material cost variance, analysed into price and usage variances
(d)   Variable production overhead variance, analysed into expenditure and efficiency variances
(e)   Selling price variance
(f)   Sales volume contribution variance

Answer

(a)   This is simply a **'total' variance**.

	£
1,000 units should have cost (× £600)	600,000
but did cost (see working)	808,000
Variable production cost variance	208,000 (A)

(b)   **Direct labour cost variances**

	£
8,200 hours should cost (× £8)	65,600
but did cost	63,000
Direct labour rate variance	2,600 (F)

1,000 units should take (× 10 hours)	10,000 hrs
but did take	8,200 hrs
Direct labour efficiency variance in hrs	1,800 hrs (F)
× standard rate per hour	× £8
Direct labour efficiency variance in £	£14,400 (F)

Summary

	£
Rate	2,600 (F)
Efficiency	14,400 (F)
Total	17,000 (F)

(c)   **Direct material cost variances**

	£
90,000 kg should cost (× £5)	450,000
but did cost	720,000
Direct material price variance	270,000 (A)

1,000 units should use (× 100 kg)	100,000 kg
but did use	90,000 kg
Direct material usage variance in kgs	10,000 kg (F)
× standard cost per kg	× £5
Direct material usage variance in £	£50,000 (F)

Summary

	£
Price	270,000 (A)
Usage	50,000 (F)
Total	220,000 (A)

(d)   **Variable production overhead variances**

	£
8,200 hours incurring o/hd should cost (× £2)	16,400
but did cost	25,000
Variable production overhead expenditure variance	8,600 (A)

Efficiency variance in hrs (from (b))	1,800 hrs (F)
× standard rate per hour	× £2
Variable production overhead efficiency variance	£3,600 (F)

Summary

	£
Expenditure	8,600 (A)
Efficiency	3,600 (F)
Total	5,000 (A)

(e) **Selling price variance**

	£
Revenue from 1,000 units should have been (× £900)	900,000
but was (× £975)	975,000
Selling price variance	75,000 (F)

(f) **Sales volume contribution variance**

Budgeted sales	1,020 units
Actual sales	1,000 units
Sales volume variance in units	20 units (A)
× standard contribution margin (£(900 – 600))	× £300
Sales volume contribution variance in £	£6,000 (A)

Workings

	£
Direct material	720,000
Total wages	63,000
Variable production overhead	25,000
	808,000

9 DERIVING ACTUAL DATA FROM STANDARD COST DETAILS AND VARIANCES

Exam focus point

Examination questions usually provide you with data about actual results and you have to calculate variances. One way in which the examiner can test your understanding of the topic, however, is to provide information about variances from which you have to 'work backwards' to determine the actual results. This section should equip you to deal with such questions which can appear in the multiple choice section, or as longer questions in the remainder of the paper.

9.1 EXAMPLE: WORKING BACKWARDS

The standard cost card for the trough, one of the products made by Pig Ltd, is as follows.

	£
Direct material 16 kgs × £6 per kg	96
Direct labour 6 hours × £12 per hour	72
Fixed production overhead 6 hours × £14 per hour	84
	252

Pig Ltd reported the following variances in control period 13 in relation to the trough.

Direct material price: £18,840 favourable

Direct material usage: £480 adverse

Direct labour rate: £10,598 adverse

Direct labour efficiency: £8,478 favourable

Fixed production overhead expenditure: £14,192 adverse

Fixed production overhead volume: £11,592 favourable

Actual fixed production overhead cost £200,000 and direct wages, £171,320. Pig Ltd paid £5.50 for each kg of direct material. There was no opening or closing stocks of the material.

Required

Calculate the following.

(a) Budgeted output
(b) Actual output
(c) Actual hours worked
(d) Average actual wage rate per hour
(e) Actual number of kilograms purchased and used

9.2 SOLUTION

(a) Let budgeted output = q

Fixed production overhead expenditure variance = budgeted overhead – actual overhead = £(84q – 200,000) = £14,192 (A)

$$\therefore 84q - 200,000 = -14,192$$
$$84q = -14,192 + 200,000$$
$$q = 185,808 \div 84$$
$$\therefore q = 2,212 \text{ units}$$

(b)

	£
Total direct wages cost	171,320
Adjust for variances:	
labour rate	(10,598)
labour efficiency	8,478
Standard direct wages cost	169,200

$$\therefore \text{ Actual output} = \text{Total standard cost} \div \text{unit standard cost}$$
$$= £169,200 \div £72$$
$$= 2,350 \text{ units}$$

(c)

	£
Total direct wages cost	171,320.0
Less rate variance	(10,598.0)
Standard rate for actual hours	160,722.0
÷ standard rate per hour	÷ £12.0
Actual hours worked	13,393.5 h

(d) Average actual wage rate per hour = actual wages/actual hours = £171,320/13,393.5 = £12.79 per hour.

(e) Number of kgs purchased and used = x

	£
x kgs should have cost (× £6)	6.0x
but did cost (× £5.50)	5.5x
Direct material price variance	0.5x

$$\therefore £0.5x = £18,840$$
$$\therefore x = 37,680 \text{ kgs}$$

Question 6

The standard material content of one unit of product A is 10kgs of material X which should cost £10 per kilogram. In June, 5,750 units of product A were produced and there was an adverse material usage variance of £1,500.

The quantity of material X used in June was

A   56,000 kg
B   57,350 kg
C   57,650 kg
D   59,000 kg

Answer

The correct answer is C.

Let the quantity of material X used = Y

5750 units should have used (× 10kgs)	57,500 kgs
but did use	Y kgs
Usage variance in kgs	(Y − 57,500) kgs
× standard price per kg	× £10
Usage variance in £	£1,500 (A)

∴   10(Y − 57,500)   = 1,500
      Y − 57,500   = 150
∴   Y   = 57,650 kgs

Chapter roundup

- Much of this chapter should have been revision for you, but do make sure that you have worked through all of the examples and exercises because they test points that earn relatively easy marks in examinations.

- **Price, rate and expenditure variances** measure the difference between the actual amount of money paid and the amount of money that should have been paid for the actual quantity of materials or the actual number of hours of labour or variable overheads.

- **Usage and efficiency variances** are quantity variances. They measure the difference between the actual physical quantity of materials used or hours taken and the quantities that should have been used or taken for the actual volume of production. These physical differences are then converted into money values by applying the appropriate standard price or rate.

- The **idle time variance** is the number of hours of idle time valued at the standard rate per hour.

- The **total fixed production overhead variance** may be broken down into two parts as usual: an **expenditure variance** and a **volume variance**. The volume variance may in turn be split into an **efficiency variance** and a **capacity variance**.

- The **selling price variance** is the difference between what revenue should have been for the quantity sold and the actual revenue.

- The **sales volume variance** is the difference between the actual and budgeted sales volumes, valued at the standard profit or contribution margin per unit.

- An **operating statement/statement of variances** is a report, usually to senior management, at the end of a control period, reconciling budgeted profit for the period to actual profit.

- In a **standard marginal costing system**, there will be no fixed production overhead volume variance and the sales volume variance will be valued at standard contribution margin not standard profit margin.

Quick quiz

1   *Choose the appropriate words from those highlighted.*

If material price variances are extracted **at the time of receipt/as the material is used**, they will be brought to the attention of managers earlier than if they are extracted **at the time of receipt/as the material is used**.

And if variances are extracted **at the time of receipt/as material is used**, all stocks will be valued at **standard price/actual price**, which is administratively easier.

2   Idle time is a favourable efficiency variance. *True or false?*

3   *Fill in the blanks.*

Fixed production overhead volume variance = ... variance + ... variance

4   *Choose the appropriate word from those highlighted.*

Actual labour hours worked were higher than the budgeted labour hours for the period. The fixed overhead capacity variance will therefore be **adverse/ favourable**.

5   *Fill in the blank.*

Sales volume variance = (actual sales volume − budgeted sales volume) × ....

6   Which of the following statements about the fixed production overhead volume variance is true?

A   It is the same in a standard marginal costing system as in a standard absorption costing system.

B   It does not exist in a standard absorption costing system.

C   It does not exist in a standard marginal costing system.

D   It is made up of an expenditure variance and an efficiency variance.

Answers to quick quiz

1   at the time of receipt
    as the material is used
    at the time of receipt
    standard price

2   False. It is an adverse efficiency variance.

3   fixed production overhead capacity variance + fixed production overhead efficiency variance

4   favourable

5   Absorption costing system: standard profit per unit
    Marginal costing system: standard contribution per unit

6   C. This variance does not exist in a standard marginal costing system.

Now try the question below from the Exam Question Bank

Number	Level	Marks	Time
Q2	Introductory	n/a	50 mins

Chapter 3

FURTHER VARIANCE ANALYSIS

Topic list		Syllabus reference	Ability required
1	Materials mix and yield variances	(i)	Application/analysis
2	Labour mix and yield variances	(i)	Application/analysis
3	Planning and operational variances	(i)	Application/analysis

Introduction

Chapter 2 should have refreshed your memory on the basics of standard costing and those variances which you should have covered in your earlier studies. It also introduced you to the method of splitting the fixed production overhead volume variance into an efficiency variance and a capacity variance, and demonstrated how to calculate sales price and volume variances.

This chapter moves on to more advanced variance analysis and examines mix and yield variances. When a product requires **two or more materials** in its make-up the materials usage variance can be split into a **materials mix variance** and a **materials yield variance**. Likewise, labour efficiency variances can be split into a **labour mix variance** and a **labour yield variance**.

Don't be put off by these new terms. The **basic principle of variance calculation** covered in the previous chapter **still applies**: an actual result is compared with an original standard result.

In the last section of the chapter we will be moving away from this approach to variance calculation with a study of **planning and operational variances**.

Learning outcomes covered in this chapter

- **Calculate and interpret** material and labour variances
- **Calculate and interpret** planning and operational variances

Syllabus content covered in this chapter

- Material mix and yield variances
- Labour mix and yield variances
- Planning and operational variances

1 MATERIALS MIX AND YIELD VARIANCES

Pilot paper, 5/01

1.1 When a product requires **two or more raw materials** in its make-up, it is often possible to **sub-analyse the materials usage variance** into **materials mix** and **materials yield variances**.

1.2 Adding a greater proportion of one material (therefore a smaller proportion of a different material) might make the materials mix cheaper or more expensive. For example the standard mix of materials for a product might consist of the following.

		£
(²/₃) 2 kg of material A at £1.00 per kg		2.00
(¹/₃) 1 kg of material B at £0.50 per kg		0.50
		2.50

It may be possible to change the mix so that one kilogram of material A is used and two kilograms of material B. The new mix would be cheaper.

		£
(¹/₃) 1 kg of material A		1
(²/₃) 2 kg of material B		1
		2

1.3 By changing the proportions in the mix, the efficiency of the combined material usage may change. In our example, in making the proportions of A and B cheaper, at 1:2, the product may now require more than three kilograms of input for its manufacture, and the new materials requirement per unit of product might be 3.6 kilograms.

		£
(¹/₃) 1.2 kg of material A at £1.00 per kg		1.20
(²/₃) 2.4 kg of material B at £0.50 per kg		1.20
		2.40

1.4 In establishing a materials usage standard, management may therefore have to balance the cost of a particular mix of materials with the efficiency of the yield of the mix.

1.5 Once the standard has been established it may be possible to exercise control over the materials used in production by calculating and reviewing mix and yield variances.

> ### KEY TERMS
>
> A **materials mix variance** occurs when the materials are not mixed or blended in standard proportions. It is a measure of whether the actual mix is cheaper or more expensive than the standard mix.
>
> A **materials yield variance** occurs when there is a difference between the standard output for a given level of input and the actual output attained.

Calculating the variances

1.6 The mix variance for each material input is based on the following.

(a) The change in the material's weighting within the overall mix

(b) Whether the material's unit standard cost is greater or less than the standard weighted average cost of all material inputs.

A **yield variance** is calculated as the **difference between the standard output from what was actually input**, and the **actual output**, valued at the standard cost per unit of output.

When to calculate mix and yield variances

1.7 Mix and yield variances have no meaning, and should never be calculated, unless they are a guide to control action. They are **only appropriate in the following situations**.

(a) Where **proportions of materials in a mix are changeable and controllable**

(b) Where the **usage variance of individual materials is of limited value because of the variability of the mix**, and a combined yield variance for all the materials together is more helpful for control

1.8 It would be **totally inappropriate** to calculate a mix **variance where the materials in the 'mix' are discrete items**. A chair, for example, might consist of wood, covering material, stuffing and glue. These materials are separate components, and it would not be possible to think in terms of controlling the proportions of each material in the final product. The usage of each material must be controlled separately.

1.9 EXAMPLE: MATERIALS USAGE, MIX AND YIELD VARIANCES

A company manufactures a chemical, Dynamite, using two compounds Flash and Bang. The standard materials usage and cost of one unit of Dynamite are as follows.

		£
Flash	5 kg at £2 per kg	10
Bang	10 kg at £3 per kg	30
	15 kg	40

In a particular period, 80 units of Dynamite were produced from 500 kg of Flash and 730 kg of Bang.

Required

Calculate the materials usage, mix and yield variances.

1.10 SOLUTION

(a) **Usage variance**

	Flash	*Bang*
80 units of Dynamite should have used	400 kgs	800 kgs
but did use	500 kgs	730 kgs
Usage variance in kgs	100 kgs (A)	70 kgs (F)
× standard cost per kg	× £2	× £3
Usage variance in £	£200 (A)	£210 (F)
Total usage variance	£10 (F)	

The total usage variance can be analysed into mix and yield variances.

(b) **Mix variance**

The standard weighted average price of the input materials is £40/15 kg = £2.67 per kg.

Actual input = (500 + 730) kgs = 1,230 kgs

Standard mix of actual input

Flash 1/3 × 1,230 kgs =	410 kgs
Bang 2/3 × 1,230 kgs =	820 kgs
	1,230 kgs

Material	Actual input kg	Standard mix of actual input kg	Difference kg	×difference between w.av. price and std. price £	Mix variance £
Flash	500	410	90	(£2.67 − £2) 0.67	60 (F)
Bang	730	820	(90)	(£2.67 − £3) (0.33)	30 (F)
	1,230	1,230	-		90 (F)

The **total difference** or mix variance in **kgs** must **always** be **zero** as the mix variance measures the change in the relative proportions of the actual total input. The variance is calculated by comparing the expected mix of the total actual input with the actual mix of the total actual input: the difference between the two totals is zero.

The favourable total variance is due to the greater use in the mix of the relatively cheaper material, Flash. A favourable variance is shown on both Flash and Bang, thus demonstrating the savings that have been made and encouraging managers to use the cheaper material. However, this cheaper mix may have an adverse effect on the yield which is obtained from the mix, as we shall now see.

(c) **Yield variance**

Each unit of output (Dynamite) requires	5 kg	of Flash, costing	£10
	10 kg	of Bang, costing	£30
	15 kg		£40

1,230 kg should have yielded (÷ 15 kg)	82 units of Dynamite
but did yield	80 units of Dynamite
Yield variance in units	2 units (A)
× standard cost per unit of output	×£40
Yield variance in £	£80 (A)

The **adverse** yield variance is due to the **output from the input being less than standard**.

The mix variance and yield variance together add up to the usage variance, which is favourable, because the adverse yield from the mix did not negate the price savings which were made by using proportionately more of the cheaper material.

Exam focus point

There are a number of methods of splitting the total mix variance between the types of material (another is shown below). The method that you have learned above is preferable because it shows the favourable mix variances for each material, ie the savings made by switching to the cheaper material. From a behavioural point of view this rewards the manager for the savings made, subject to the effect on the yield.

In an exam you will not be penalised for the method used provided you can explain its behavioural consequences.

1.11 MIX VARIANCES: ALTERNATIVE SOLUTION

This approach compares actual input and the standard input for actual output.

Material	Actual input kg	Standard input kg	Difference kg	× difference between w av price and std. price £	Mix variance £
Flash	500	400 (80 × 5)	100	(£2.67 – £2) 0.67	67 (F)
Bang	730	800 (80 × 10)	(70)	(£2.67 – £3) (0.33)	23 (F)
					90 (F)

This approach has the same behavioural consequences as the one above. Note, however, that the total mix variance is not zero.

1.12 Have a go at the following question. Try it using both methods for the mix variance.

Question 1

The standard materials cost of product D456 is as follows.

		£
Material X	3 kg at £2.00 per kg	6
Material Y	5 kg at £3.60 per kg	18
	8 kg	24

During period 2, 2,000 kg of material X costing £4,100 and 2,400 kg of material Y costing £9,600 were used to produce 500 units of D456.

Required

Calculate price, mix and yield variances.

Answer

Price variances	£
2,000 kg of X should cost (× £2)	4,000
but did cost	4,100
Material X price variance	100 (A)

	£
2,400 kg of Y should cost (× £3.60)	8,640
but did cost	9,600
Material Y price variance	960 (A)

First method of mix variances

The standard weighted average price of the input materials is £24/8 kg = £3 per kg.

	kg
Total quantity used (2,000 + 2,400) kgs	4,400

		kg
Standard mix for actual use:	3/8 X	1,650
	5/8 Y	2,750
		4,400

Material	Actual input kg	Standard mix of actual input kg	Difference kg	× difference between w. av. price and std. price	£	Mix variance £
X	2,000	1,650	350	£(3 − 2)	1.00	350 (F)
Y	2,400	2,750	(350)	£(3 − 3.60)	(0.60)	210 (F)
	4,400	4,400	-			560 (F)

Alternative method of mix variances

The alternative method will produce the same total mix variance, but a different split between the mix variance for each material.

For an output of 500 units of D456:

Material	Actual input kg	Standard input kg	Difference kg	× difference between w.av. price and std. price	£	Mix variance £
X	2,000	1,500 (500 × 3)	500	£(3 − 2)	1.00	500 (F)
Y	2,400	2,500 (500 × 5)	(100)	£(3 − 3.60)	(0.60)	60 (F)
						560 (F)

Summary of mix variances

Both methods produce meaningful sub-analysis of the mix variance because they show the savings made by using more of the cheaper material X.

Yield variance

Each unit of D456 requires	3 kg	of X, costing	£6	
	5 kg	of Y, costing	£18	
	8 kg		£24	

4,400 kg should have yielded (÷ 8 kg)	550 units
but did yield	500 units
Yield variance in units	50 units (A)
× standard material cost per unit of output	× £24
Yield variance in £	£1,200 (A)

ATTENTION!

At the time of going to print both of these methods of calculating the mix variance were acceptable to the examiner. Watch out for articles in *Insider* for any changes to this guidance, however.

It is interesting to note, however, that a question in the May 2001 exam (see below) derived figures using the first method (although candidates were provided with an explanation of how the figures were derived).

Question 2

What do you see as the limitations of the calculation of materials mix and yield variances?

Answer

Here are some suggestions.

(a) A **change in the mix** of materials used will almost certainly have an **impact upon the yield**, but this will not be isolated from other causes of the yield variance, such as substandard materials quality.

(b) If a **favourable mix variance can be established**, without adverse effects upon yield or output quality, the **standard mix is obsolete**.

(c) Changes in actual unit costs of some ingredients may make a change in mix economically viable. An attempt **to optimise the price variance** may therefore result in an **adverse mix variance**.

(d) **Changes to the proportions of the input materials** are **assumed** to have **no impact on product quality**.

SUMMARY

Approach 1: compare actual input with standard mix of actual input

Approach 2: compare actual input with standard input for actual output.

For both approaches, value the mix variance for each material at the difference between budgeted weighted average price and standard price.

Deviations from standardised mix   5/01

1.13 In the May 2001 exam, candidates were given the percentage deviations for standardised mix for two months and the data used to calculate those deviations. They then had to calculate deviations for a third month and comment on the usefulness of such analysis for operational control.

1.14 The question stated that the deviations were shown in weight and were from the standard mix for the quantity input expressed as a percentage of the standardised weight for each ingredient. This sounds complicated but is actually referring to figures derived using our first method (think about it!). And because source data for the figures shown was provided, candidates could check their understanding of the method of calculation.

Try the question below, to see whether you could have coped with the exam question.

Question 3

Standard mix for one litre of product J

0.4 litres of ingredient O
0.2 litres of ingredient H
0.5 litres of ingredient N

Actual usage in control period 2

Ingredient 0	420 litres
Ingredient H	180 litres
Ingredient N	550 litres

Actual output	1,000 litres

Calculate the standard deviation from the standardised mix using the method of calculation described in Paragraph 1.14 above.

Answer

Quantity input = (420 + 180 + 550) = 1,150 litres

Standard mix for the quantity input

The standardised mix for the quantity input is the calculation we carry out in method one of calculating mix variances. You can check you have done it correctly by ensuring that the sum of the individual components equals total quantity input.

	Standardised mix for quantity input	*Litres*
O	$1,150 \times (0.4/1.1) =$	418.18
H	$1,150 \times (0.2/1.1) =$	209.09
N	$1,150 \times (0.5/1.1) =$	522.73
		1,150.00

Deviations – absolute

These are simply the differences between the actual input and the standard input calculated above, in other words the method one calculation of the mix in quantity.

	Actual input Litres	*Standard mix for actual input (see above)* Litres	*Deviation (or difference)* Litres
O	420	418.18	1.82 (A)
H	180	209.09	29.09 (F)
N	550	522.73	27.27 (A)
	1,150	1,150.00	-

Deviations as a %

O $(1.82/418.18) \times 100\% = 0.435\%$
H $(29.09/209.09) \times 100\% = 13.913\%$
N $(27.27/522.73) \times 100\% = 5.217\%$

2 LABOUR MIX AND YIELD VARIANCES

KEY TERMS

A **labour mix variance** (or **team composition variance**) can be calculated when more than one type or grade of labour is involved in making a product. It is a measure of whether the actual mix of labour grades is cheaper or more expensive than the standard mix.

A **labour yield variance** (or **labour output variance** or **team productivity variance**) can be calculated to see how productively people are working.

2.1 The calculations are the same as those required for materials mix and yield variances.

2.2 EXAMPLE: LABOUR MIX VARIANCES

Two grades of labour work together in teams to produce product X. The standard composition of each team is five grade A employees paid at £6 per hour and three grade B employees paid at £4 per hour. Output is measured in standard hours and expected output is 95 standard hours for 100 hours worked in total. During the last period, 2,280 standard hours of output were produced using 1,500 hours of grade A labour (costing £9,750) and 852 hours of grade B labour (costing £2,982).

Required

Calculate all possible labour variances.

2.3 SOLUTION

Initial working

Calculation of **standard rate per hour of output**

Labour grade

			£
A	5.00	hours × £6 =	30
B	3.00	hours × £4 =	12
	8.00	hours	42
Less 5%	0.40	hours	
	7.60	hours	

∴ Standard rate per hour of output = £42/7.6 = £5.5263 per standard hour

Direct labour total variance

		£
2,280 standard hours of output should have cost (× £5.5263)		12,600
but did cost		12,732
Direct labour total variance		132 (A)

Direct labour rate variance

		A		*B*
		£		£
Hours worked should have cost	(1,500 × £6)	9,000	(852 × £4)	3,408
but did cost		9,750		2,982
Direct labour rate variance		750 (A)		426 (F)
Total direct labour rate variance		£324 (A)		

Direct labour efficiency variance

		A		B
2,280 standard hours of output should take an input of	$(2,280 \div 0.95 \times {}^5/_8)$	1,500 hrs	$(2,280 \div 0.95 \times {}^3/_8)$	900 hrs
but did take		1,500 hrs		852 hrs
Efficiency variance in hours		-		48 hrs (F)
× standard rate per hour		× £6		× £4
		-		£192 (F)

The **labour efficiency variance** can be analysed further into the **team composition** variance (the **labour mix** variance) and the **team productivity** variance (the **labour yield** variance).

Team composition (labour mix) variance

Approach 1

The standard weighted rate per hour of labour is £42/8 = £5.25 per hour.

Total actual hours = 1,500 + 852 = 2,352 hours

Standard mix of actual input

		Hrs
A	$5/8 \times 2,352 =$	1,470
B	$3/8 \times 2,352 =$	882
		2,352

Labour grade	Actual hours	Std mix of actual hrs	Difference	× diff between w. av. price and std. price		Mix variance	
	Hrs	Hrs	Hrs	£		£	
A	1,500	1,470	30	£(5.25 – 6)	(0.75)	22.50	(A)
B	852	882	(30)	£(5.25 – 4)	1.25	37.50	(A)
	2,352	2,352	-			60.00	(A)

Approach 2

For an output of 2,280 standard hours:

Labour grade	Actual hours	Standard hours	Difference	×difference between w. av. price and std. price		Mix variance	
	Hrs	Hrs	Hrs	£		£	
A	1,500	1,500★	0	(£5.25 – 6)	(0.75)	0	
B	852	900★	(48)	(£5.25 – £4)	1.25	60	(A)
						60	(A)

★see efficiency variance above

The adverse mix variance resulted from using proportionately less of the cheaper grade B labour.

Team productivity (labour yield) variance

2,352 hours of work should have produced (× 0.95)	2,234.4 std hrs
but did produce	2,280.0 std hrs
Team productivity variance in hrs	45.6 std hrs (F)
× std rate per std hr	× £5.5263
Team productivity variance in £	£252 (F)

BPP PUBLISHING

3 PLANNING AND OPERATIONAL VARIANCES   Pilot paper, 5/01

3.1   So far in this text we have been looking at variances which are calculated using what we will call the **conventional approach** to variance analysis, whereby an **actual cost** is **compared** with an **original standard cost**. In this section of the chapter we will be examining **planning** and **operational variances**. They are not really alternatives to the conventional approach, they merely provide a much **more detailed analysis**.

3.2   Basically, the planning and operational approach attempts to **divide a total variance** (which has been calculated conventionally) into a group of **variances** which have arisen because of **inaccurate planning or faulty standards (planning variances)** and a group of **variances** which have been caused by **adverse or favourable operational performance** (**operational variances**, surprisingly enough!).

ATTENTION!

Planning and operational variances may seem confusing if you do not have a really good grasp of the conventional approach and so, before you go any further, make sure that you understand everything that we covered so far in this Text. Go back over any areas you are unsure about. Only when you are happy that you have mastered the basics should you begin on this section.

KEY TERMS

A **planning variance** (or **revision variance**) compares an original standard with a revised standard that should or would have been used if planners had known in advance what was going to happen.

An **operational variance** (or **operating variance**) compares an actual result with the revised standard.

Ex ante means original budget/standard.

Ex post means revised budget/standard.

3.3   Planning and operational variances are based on the principle that variances ought to be reported by taking as the **main starting point**, not the original standard, but a **standard** which can be seen, in hindsight, to be the **optimum** that should have been **achievable**.

3.4   Exponents of this approach argue that the monetary value of variances ought to be a realistic reflection of what the causes of the variances have cost the organisation. In other words they should show the cash (and profit) gained or lost as a consequence of operating results being different to what should have been achieved. Variances can be valued in this way by **comparing actual results with a realistic standard or budget**. Such variances are called **operational variances**.

3.5   **Planning variances** arise because the **original standard and revised more realistic standards are different** and have nothing to do with operational performance. In most cases, it is unlikely that anything could be done about planning variances: they are **not controllable by operational managers but by senior management**.

3.6   In other words the **cause of a total variance** might be one or both of the following.

- Adverse or favourable operational performance (**operational variance**)

- Inaccurate planning, or faulty standards (**planning variance**)

3.7   The CIMA *Official Terminology* defines an operational variance as 'A classification of variances in which non-standard performance is defined as being that which differs from an *ex post* standard. Operational variances can relate to any element of the standard product specification.'

The CIMA *Official Terminology* defines planning variances as 'A classification of variances caused by *ex ante* budget allowances being changed to an *ex post* basis. They are also known as revision variances.'

Calculating total planning and operational variances

3.8   We will begin by looking at how to split a total cost variance into its planning and operational components.

3.9   EXAMPLE: TOTAL COST PLANNING AND OPERATIONAL VARIANCES

At the beginning of 20X0, WB Ltd set a standard marginal cost for its major product of £25 per unit. The standard cost is recalculated once each year. Actual production costs during August 20X0 were £304,000, when 8,000 units were made.

With the benefit of hindsight, the management of WB Ltd realises that a more realistic standard cost for current conditions would be £40 per unit. The planned standard cost of £25 is unrealistically low.

Required

Calculate the planning and operational variances.

3.10   SOLUTION

With the benefit of hindsight, the **realistic standard should have been £40**. The variance caused by favourable or adverse **operating** performance should be calculated by comparing actual results against this realistic standard.

	£
Revised standard cost of actual production (8,000 × £40)	320,000
Actual cost	304,000
Total **operational** variance	16,000 (F)

The variance is favourable because the actual cost was lower than would have been expected using the revised basis.

The **planning** variance reveals the extent to which the original standard was at fault.

Revised standard cost	8,000 units × £40 per unit	320,000
Original standard cost	8,000 units × £25 per unit	200,000
Planning variance		120,000 (A)

It is an adverse variance because the original standard was too optimistic, overestimating the expected profits by understating the standard cost. More simply, it is adverse because the revised cost is much higher than the original cost.

	£
Planning variance	120,000 (A)
Operational variance	16,000 (F)
Total	104,000 (A)

If **traditional variance analysis** had been used, the total cost variance would have been the same, but **all the 'blame' would appear to lie on actual results** and operating inefficiencies (rather than some being due to faulty planning).

	£
Standard cost of 8,000 units (× £25)	200,000
Actual cost of 8,000 units	304,000
Total cost variance	104,000 (A)

Question 4

Suppose a budget is prepared which includes a raw materials cost per unit of product of £2 (2 kg of copper at £1 per kg). Due to a rise in world prices for copper during the year, the average market price of copper rises to £1.50 per kg. During the year, 1,000 units were produced at a cost of £3,250 for 2,200 kg of copper.

The planning and operational variances are

	Operational variance	*Planning variance*
A	£250 (A)	£1,000 (A)
B	£250 (A)	£1,100 (A)
C	£250 (F)	£1,000 (F)
D	£250 (A)	£1,000 (F)

Answer

The correct answer is A.

Operational variance

	£
Actual cost (for 1,000 units)	3,250
Revised standard cost (for 1,000 units) (2,000 kg × £1.50)	3,000
Total operational variance	250 (A)

Planning variance

	£
Revised standard cost (1,000 × 2 kg × £1.50)	3,000
Original standard cost (1,000 × 2 kg × £1)	2,000
Total planning variance	1,000 (A)

Operational price and usage variances

3.11 So far we have only considered planning and operational variances in total, without carrying out the usual two-way split. In Question 4, for instance, we identified a total operational variance for materials of £250 without considering whether this operational variance could be split between a usage variance and a price variance.

3.12 This is not a problem so long as you retain your grasp of knowledge you already possess. You know that a **price** variance measures the difference between the actual amount of money paid and the amount of money that should have been paid for that quantity of materials (or whatever). Thus, in our example:

	£
Actual price of actual materials (2,200 kg)	3,250
Revised standard price of actual materials (£1.50 × 2,200 kg)	3,300
Operational price variance	50 (F)

The variance is favourable because the materials were purchased more cheaply than would have been expected.

3.13 Similarly, a **usage** variance measures the difference between the actual physical quantity of materials used or hours taken and the quantities that should have been used or taken for the actual volume of production. Those physical differences are then converted into money values by applying the appropriate standard cost.

3.14 In our example we are calculating **operational variances,** so we are not interested in planning errors. This means that the **appropriate standard cost is the revised standard cost** of £1.50.

Actual quantity should have been	2,000 kgs
but was	2,200 kgs
Operational usage variance in kgs	200 kgs (A)
× revised standard cost per kg	× £1.50
Operational usage variance in £	£300 (A)

3.15 The two variances of course reconcile to the total variance as previously calculated.

	£
Operational price variance	50 (F)
Operational usage variance	(300) (A)
Total operational variance	250 (A)

Operational variances for labour and overheads

3.16 Precisely the same argument applies to the calculation of operational variances for labour and overheads, and the examples already given should be sufficient to enable you to do Question 5.

Question 5

A new product requires three hours of labour per unit at a standard rate of £6 per hour. In a particular month the budget is to produce 500 units. Actual results were as follows.

Hours worked	1,700
Production	540 units
Wages cost	£10,500

Within minutes of production starting it was realised that the job was extremely messy and the labour force could therefore claim an extra 25p per hour in 'dirty money'.

Required

What are the planning and operational variances?

	Planning	*Operational rate*	*Operational efficiency*
A	£405 (F)	£125 (F)	£500 (A)
B	£405 (A)	£125 (F)	£500 (A)
C	£405 (F)	£300 (A)	£500 (F)
D	£405 (A)	£300 (F)	£480 (A)

Answer

The correct answer is B.

Keep calm and calculate the *total* variance in the normal way to begin with. Then you will understand what it is that you have to analyse. Next follow through the workings shown above, substituting the figures in the exercise for those in the example.

Total labour variance	£
540 units should have cost (× 3 hrs × £6)	9,720
but did cost	10,500
	780 (A)

	£
Planning variance	
Revised standard cost (540 × 3 hrs × £6.25)	10,125
Original standard cost (540 × 3 hrs × £6.00)	9,720
	405 (A)

	£
Operational rate variance	
Actual cost of actual hrs	10,500
Revised standard cost of actual hrs (1,700 × £6.25)	10,625
	125 (F)

Operational efficiency variance	
540 units should have taken (× 3 hrs)	1,620 hrs
but did take	1,700 hrs
Operational efficiency variance in hours	80 hrs
× revised standard rate per hour	× £6.25
Operational efficiency variance in £	£500 (A)

Exam focus point

The pilot paper included a variance analysis question which contained planning and operational variances for labour. The calculations required were the same as those demonstrated in Question 4.

Planning variances and sub-variances

3.17 In the examples described so far, there has only been one 'planning error' in the standard cost. When two planning errors occur, there may be some difficulty in deciding how much of the total planning variance is due to each separate error.

3.18 EXAMPLE: TWO PLANNING ERRORS

A company estimates that the standard direct labour cost for a product should be £20 (4 hours × £5 per hour). Actual production of 1,000 units took 6,200 hours at a cost of £23,800. In retrospect, it is realised that the standard cost should have been 6 hours × £4 per hour = £24 per unit.

Required

Calculate the planning and operational variances.

3.19 SOLUTION

(a) **Operational variances**

(i)	1,000 units should take (× 6 hours)	6,000 hrs
	but did take	6,200 hrs
	Efficiency variance in hours	200 hrs (A)
	× revised standard cost per hour	× £4 (A)
	Efficiency variance in £	£800 (A)

		£
(ii)	6,200 hours should cost (× £4)	24,800
	but did cost	23,800
	Rate variance	1,000 (F)

(iii)	*Check:*		£
	Actual costs		23,800
	Revised standard cost (1,000 units × £24)		24,000
	Total operational variance (800 (A) + 1,000 (F))		200 (F)

(b) **Planning variance**

		£
Revised standard cost 1,000 units × 6 hours × £4		24,000
Original standard cost 1,000 units × 4 hours × £5		20,000
Planning variance		4,000 (A)

Commentary

Within the total planning variance, there are two separate variances.

- A **planning efficiency variance** of 1,000 units × (6 – 4) hours or 2,000 hours (A).
- A **planning rate variance** of £1 per hour (F).

The problem, however, is to put a **value** to these sub-variances. This can be done in either of **two ways**.

			£
(a)	Planning efficiency variance	2,000 hours (A) × original price of £5	10,000 (A)
	Planning rate variance	£1 per hour (F) × revised standard efficiency of 6,000 hours	6,000 (F)
	Total		4,000 (A)

			£
(b)	Planning efficiency variance	2,000 hours (A) × revised rate of £4	8,000 (A)
	Planning rate variance	£1 per hour (F) × original efficiency of 4,000 hours	4,000 (F)
	Total		4,000 (A)

3.20 Since the analysis can be done either way, it is **doubtful whether there is much value in splitting the total planning variance**. However, this point may be examinable and is worth learning. The following exercise provides an example of when there may be some point in carrying out the analysis.

Question 6

The standard materials cost of a product is 3 kg × £1.50 per kg = £4.50. Actual production of 10,000 units used 28,000 kg at a cost of £50,000. In retrospect it was realised that the standard materials cost should have been 2.5 kg per unit at a cost of £1.80 per kg (so that the *total* cost per unit was correct).

Required

Calculate the planning and operational variances in as much detail as possible, giving alternative analyses of planning variances.

Answer

As always, calculate the *total* materials variance first, to give you a point of reference. Then follow through the workings above.

Total materials variance	£
10,000 units should have cost (× £4.50)	45,000
but did cost	50,000
	5,000 (A)

Operational price variance	£
28,000 kg should cost (× £1.80)	50,400
but did cost	50,000
	400 (F)

BPP
PUBLISHING

Operational usage variance

10,000 units should use (× 2.5 kgs)	25,000 kgs
but did use	28,000 kgs
Variance in Kgs	3,000 kgs (A)
× standard rate per kg	× £1.80
	£5,400 (A)

Planning variance

	£
Either	
Planning price variance (5,000 kgs (F) × £1.50)	7,500 (F)
Planning usage variance (£0.30(A) × 25,000 kgs)	7,500 (A)
	-

	£
or	
Planning price variance (5,000 kgs (F) × £1.80)	9,000 (F)
Planning usage variance (£0.30 (A) × 30,000 kgs)	9,000 (A)
	-

Planning and operational sales variances

3.21 Our final calculations in this chapter deal with planning and operational sales variances.

3.22 EXAMPLE: PLANNING AND OPERATIONAL SALES VARIANCES

Dimsek Ltd budgeted to make and sell 400 units of its product, the role, in the four-week period no 8, as follows.

	£
Budgeted sales (100 units per week)	40,000
Variable costs (400 units × £60)	24,000
Contribution	16,000
Fixed costs	10,000
Profit	6,000

At the beginning of the second week, production came to a halt because stocks of raw materials ran out, and a new supply was not received until the beginning of week 3. As a consequence, the company lost one week's production and sales. Actual results in period 8 were as follows.

	£
Sales (320 units)	32,000
Variable costs (320 units × £60)	19,200
Contribution	12,800
Fixed costs	10,000
Actual profit	2,800

In retrospect, it is decided that the optimum budget, given the loss of production facilities in the third week, would have been to sell only 300 units in the period.

Required

Calculate appropriate planning and operational variances.

3.23 SOLUTION

The **planning** variance **compares the revised budget** with the **original budget**.

Revised sales volume, given materials shortage	300 units
Original budgeted sales volume	400 units
Planning variance in units of sales	100 units(A)
× standard contribution per unit	× £40
Planning variance in £	£4,000 (A)

Arguably, **running out of raw materials is an operational error** and so the loss of sales volume and contribution from the materials shortage is an opportunity cost that could have been avoided with better purchasing arrangements. The operational variances are variances calculated in the usual way, except that actual results are compared with the revised standard or budget. There is a sales volume variance which is an **operational variance**, as follows.

Actual sales volume	320 units
Revised sales volume	300 units
Operational sales volume variance in units	20 units (F)
(possibly due to production efficiency or marketing efficiency)	
× standard contribution per unit	× £40
	£800 (F)

These variances can be used as **control information** to reconcile budgeted and actual profit.

	£	£
Operating statement, period 8		
Budgeted profit		6,000
Planning variance	4,000 (A)	
Operational variance - sales volume	800 (F)	
		3,200 (A)
Actual profit in period 8		2,800

3.24 You will have noticed that in this example sales volume variances were **valued at contribution forgone**, and there were no fixed cost volume variances. This is because contribution forgone, in terms of lost revenue or extra expenditure incurred, is the nearest equivalent to **opportunity cost** which is readily available to management accountants (who assume linearity of costs and revenues within a relevant range of activity).

Question 7

KSO Ltd budgeted to sell 10,000 units of a new product during 20X0. The budgeted sales price was £10 per unit, and the variable cost £3 per unit.

Although actual sales in 20X0 were 10,000 units and variable costs of sales were £30,000, sales revenue was only £5 per unit. With the benefit of hindsight, it is realised that the budgeted sales price of £10 was hopelessly optimistic, and a price of £4.50 per unit would have been much more realistic.

Required

Calculate planning and operational variances.

Answer

The only variances are selling price variances.

Planning (selling price) variance

	Total
	£
Revised budget (10,000 × £4.50)	45,000
Original budget (10,000 × £10.00)	100,000
Planning variance	55,000 (A)

The original variance was too optimistic and so the planning variance is an adverse variance.

Operational (selling price) variance

	£
Actual sales (10,000 × £5)	50,000
Revised sales (10,000 × £4.50)	45,000
Operational (selling price) variance	5,000 (F)

The total difference between budgeted and actual profit of £50,000 (A) is therefore analysed as follows.

	£
Operational variance (selling price)	5,000 (F)
Planning variance	55,000 (A)
	50,000 (A)

The value of planning and operational variances

3.25 **Advantages of a system of planning and operational variances**

(a) The analysis highlights those variances which are **controllable** and those which are **non-controllable**.

(b) **Managers' acceptance** of the use of variances for performance measurement, and their **motivation**, is likely to increase if they know they will not be held responsible for poor planning and faulty standard setting.

(c) The **planning and standard-setting processes** should improve; standards should be more accurate, relevant and appropriate.

(d) Operational variances will provide a **'fairer' reflection of actual performance**.

3.26 **The limitations of planning and operational variances, which must be overcome if they are to be applied in practice.**

(a) It is difficult to **decide in hindsight** what the **realistic standard** should have been.

(b) It may become **too easy to justify all the variances as being due to bad planning**, so no operational variances will be highlighted.

(c) Establishing realistic revised standards and analysing the total variance into planning and operational variances can be a **time consuming** task, even if a spreadsheet package is devised.

(d) Even though the intention is to provide more meaningful information, **managers may be resistant** to the very idea of variances and refuse to see the virtues of the approach. Careful presentation and explanation will be required until managers are used to the concepts.

Exam focus point

The examiner has stressed that he wishes candidates to be able to discuss the usefulness and limitations of the techniques on the syllabus.

Management reports involving planning and operational variances

3.27 The format of a management report that includes planning and operational variances should be tailored to the information requirements of the managers who receive it.

3.28 From the **point of view of senior management** reviewing performance as a whole, a layout that identifies **all of the planning variances together**, and then **all of the operational variances** may be most illuminating. The difference due to planning is the responsibility of the planners, and the remainder of the difference is due to functional managers.

3.29 One possible layout is shown below.

X LTD OPERATING STATEMENT PERIOD 1

	£	£
Original budget contribution		X
Planning variances		
Material usage	X	
Material price	X	
Labour efficiency	X	
Labour idle time	X	
Labour rate	X	
Selling price	X̲	
		X̲
Revised budget contribution		X
Sales volume variance		X̲
Revised standard contribution from sales achieved		X̲
Operational variances	X	
Selling price	X	
Material usage	X	
Material price	X	
Labour efficiency	X	
Labour rate	X	
Variable overhead expenditure	X	
Variable overhead efficiency	X̲	
		X̲
Actual contribution		X
Less: fixed costs budget	X	
expenditure variance	X̲	
		X̲
Actual margin		X̲̲

Chapter roundup

- When two or more types of material are mixed together to produce a product it is possible to carry out further analysis on the usage variance. The **mix variance** explains how much of the usage variance was caused by a change in the relative proportions of the materials used. The **yield variance** shows how much of the usage variance was caused by using more or less material than the standard allowance.

- The purpose of a mix variance is to provide management with information to help in controlling the proportion of each item actually used. If it is not possible for managers to exercise control over the actual mix of material then there is little to be gained by calculating mix variances.

- If more than one type of labour is used in a product, the labour efficiency variance can be analysed further into a **labour mix (team composition) variance** and a **labour yield (team productivity or output) variance**.

- A planning and operational approach to variance analysis divides the total variance into those variances which have arisen because of inaccurate planning or faulty standards (**planning variances**) and those variances which have been caused by adverse or favourable operational performance, compared with a standard which has been revised in hindsight (**operational variances**).

Quick quiz

1   Which of the following statements about the materials mix variance is true?

    A   It should only be calculated if the proportions in the mix are controllable.
    B   In quantity, it is always the same as the usage variance.
    C   In quantity, it is always zero whatever method of calculation is used
    D   It can only be calculated for a maximum of three materials in the mix.

BPP PUBLISHING

2   *Fill in the blanks.*

Materials .... variance = materials mix variance + materials .... variance.

3   The labour mix variance is sometimes known as the team mix variance and the labour yield variance is sometimes known as the team yield variance. *True or false?*

4   In an operational and planning approach to variance analysis, which standards are used to calculate the operational variances?

Ex ante standards   ☐

Ex post standards   ☐

5   *Choose the correct words from those highlighted.*

A planning variance compares the **revised budget/original budget** with the **original budget/actual result**.

Answers to quick quiz

1   The correct answer is A.

2   Materials usage variance = materials mix variance + materials yield variance.

3   False. They are sometimes known as the team composition variance and the team productivity variance.

4   Ex post standards

5   revised budget
original budget

Now try the questions below from the Exam Question Bank

Number	Level	Marks	Time
Q3	Introductory	n/a	45 mins
Q4	Exam standard	25	45 mins
Q5	Exam standard	30	54 mins

Chapter 4

INTERPRETATION OF MANAGEMENT CONTROL INFORMATION

Topic list		Syllabus reference	Ability required
1	To investigate or not to investigate?	(i)	Application/analysis
2	Variance investigation models	(i)	Application/analysis
3	Composite variances	(i)	Application/analysis
4	Interpreting variances	(i)	Application/analysis
5	Benchmarking	(i)	Application/analysis

Introduction

You should now have absolutely no problem in calculating variances. But the **calculation of variances** in itself **does little to help management**. The fact that there was a labour efficiency variance of £500 in period 13 does not do much to assist management in their attempts to control their business. They need to know whether or not a variance should be investigated, why it might have occurred, what it means and whether its occurrence is linked to any other reported variance. They therefore **need to know how to investigate and interpret variances, and how to assess the interdependence between them**. This chapter will explain how this is done, and how other types of comparison may achieve control and improvement through a **benchmarking** exercise.

Learning outcomes covered in this chapter

- **Interpret** material, labour, variable overheads, fixed overheads and sales variances

- **Prepare** reports using a range of internal and external benchmarks and **interpret** the results

Syllabus content covered in this chapter

- Interpretation of variances; interrelationship, significance

- Benchmarking

1 TO INVESTIGATE OR NOT TO INVESTIGATE?

1.1 Before management decide whether or not to investigate a particular variance, there are a number of factors which should be considered.

1.2 **Materiality**

Small variations in a single period are bound to occur and **are unlikely to be significant**. Obtaining an 'explanation' is likely to be time-consuming and irritating for the manager concerned. The explanation will often be 'chance', which is not, in any case, particularly helpful. For such variations further investigation is not worthwhile.

1.3 Controllability

Controllability must also influence the decision whether to investigate further. If there is a general worldwide price increase in the price of an important raw material there is **nothing that can be done internally** to control the effect of this. If a central decision is made to award all employees a 10% increase in salary, staff costs in division A will increase by this amount and the variance is not controllable by division A's manager. Uncontrollable variances call for a **change in the plan**, not an investigation into the past.

1.4 Variance trend

If, say, an efficiency **variance** is £1,000 adverse in month 1, the obvious conclusion is that the process is **out of control** and that corrective action must be taken. This may be correct, but what if the same variance is £1,000 adverse every month? The **trend** indicates that the process is **in control** and the standard has been wrongly set. Suppose, though, that the same variance is consistently £1,000 adverse for each of the first six months of the year but that production has steadily fallen from 100 units in month 1 to 65 units by month 6. The variance trend in absolute terms is constant, but relative to the number of units produced, efficiency has got steadily worse.

1.5 Cost

The likely cost of an investigation needs to be weighed against the cost to the organisation of allowing the variance to continue in future periods.

1.6 Interrelationship of variances

Quite possibly, individual variances should not be looked at in isolation. One variance might be inter-related with another, and much of it might have occurred only because the other, inter-related, variance occurred too. When two variances are **interdependent (interrelated) one** will usually be **adverse** and the other **one favourable**. Here are some examples.

Interrelated variances	Explanation
Materials price and usage	If cheaper materials are purchased in order to obtain a favourable price variance, materials wastage might be higher and an adverse usage variance will occur. If the cheaper material is more difficult to handle, there might be an adverse labour efficiency variance too.
	If more expensive material is purchased, however, the price variance will be adverse but the usage variance might be favourable.
Labour rate and efficiency	If employees in a workforce are paid higher rates for experience and skill, using a highly skilled team might lead to an adverse rate variance and possible a favourable efficiency variance. In contrast, a favourable rate variance might indicate a larger-than-expected proportion of inexperienced workers which could result in an adverse labour efficiency variance, and perhaps poor materials handling and high rates of rejects and hence an adverse materials usage variance.

Interrelated variances	Explanation
Selling price and sales volume	We looked at this in Chapter 2.
Materials mix and yield variance	If the mix is cheaper than standard, there may be a resulting lower yield, so that a favourable mix variance might be offset by an adverse yield variance.
	Alternatively, a mix which is cheaper than standard might have no effect on yield, but the end product might be of sub-standard quality. Sales volumes might then be affected, or sales prices might have to be reduced to sell off the output that customers are not willing to buy at the normal price.

Because management accountants analyse total variances into component elements, ie materials price and usage, labour rate, idle time, efficiency, and so on, they should not lose sight of the overall 'integrated' picture of events, and any interdependence between variances should be reported whenever it is suspected to have occurred.

Question 1

There is likely to be interdependence between an adverse labour efficiency variance and

A   a favourable materials usage variance
B   an adverse fixed overhead expenditure variance
C   an adverse selling price variance
D   none of the above

Answer

The correct answer is A.

A higher paid and hence more skilled workforce could use materials most efficiently.

Exam focus point

'Interpretation of variances: interrelationship, significance' is a specific syllabus topic. You could be required to perform calculations *and* to analyse and explain your results.

1.7   **The performance standard used**

The **efficiency variance** reported in any control period, whether for materials or labour and overhead, will **depend on the efficiency level in the standard cost**.

(a)   If an **ideal standard** is used, **variances** will always be **adverse**.

(b)   If an **attainable standard** is used, or a **current** standard, we should expect **small variances around the standard** from one period to the next, which may not necessarily be significant.

(c)   Management might set a **target** standard **above the current** standard but **below the ideal** standard of efficiency. In such a situation, there will probably be adverse efficiency variances, though not as high as if ideal standards were used. However, if there is **support from the workforce** in trying to improve efficiency levels to the new standard, management would hope to see the **adverse efficiency variances gradually**

BPP PUBLISHING

diminish period by period, until the workforce eventually achieves 100% efficiency at the target standard level.

It is therefore necessary to make a judgement about what an adverse or favourable efficiency variance signifies, in relation to the 'toughness' of the standard set. **Trends** in efficiency variances, that is gradual improvements or deteriorations in efficiency, should be monitored, because these might be more informative than the variance in a single control period.

Management signals from variance trend information

1.8 **Variance analysis** is a means of assessing performance, but it is only a method of signalling to management areas of possible weakness where control action might be necessary. It does not provide a ready-made diagnosis of faults, nor does it provide management with a ready-made indication of what action needs to be taken. It merely **highlights items for possible investigation**.

1.9 **Individual variances should not be looked at in isolation**. As an obvious example, a favourable sales price variance is likely to be accompanied by an adverse sales volume variance: the increase in price has caused a fall in demand. We now know in addition that sets of variances should be scrutinised for a number of successive periods if their full significance is to be appreciated.

1.10 **Signals that may be extracted from variance trend information**

(a) Materials price variances may be favourable for a few months, then shift to adverse variances for the next few months and so on. This could indicate that prices are **seasonal** and perhaps stock could be built up in cheap seasons.

(b) Regular, perhaps fairly slight, increases in adverse price variances usually indicate the workings of general **inflation**. If desired, allowance could be made for general inflation when flexing the budget.

(c) Rapid large increases in adverse price variances may suggest a sudden **scarcity** of a resource. It may soon be necessary to seek out cheaper substitutes.

Question 2

What might be indicated by gradually improving labour efficiency variances? What about worsening trends in machine running expenses?

Answer

Gradually improving labour efficiency variances may signal the existence of a **learning curve** which has not been incorporated in the standard, or the success of a **productivity bonus scheme**. In either case opportunities should be sought to encourage the trend and the standard cost should be revised if it is to remain useful for control purposes.

Worsening trends in machine running expenses may show up that **equipment is deteriorating** and will soon need repair or even replacement.

1.11 These are just a few examples. Note that in each case it is suggested that the **variance trend be used as feedforward control information**, anticipating future problems before they occur.

Why might actual and standard performance differ?

1.12 Here are some common reasons.

(a) **Measurement errors**

In examination questions there is generally no question of the information that you are given being wrong. In practice, however, it may be extremely difficult to establish that 1,000 units of product A used 32,000 kg of raw material X. Scales may be **misread**, the **pilfering** or **wastage** of materials may go unrecorded, items may be wrongly classified (as material X3, say, when material X8 was used in reality), or employees may make **'cosmetic' adjustments** to their records to make their own performance look better than it really was.

Unless an investigation leads to an improvement in the accuracy of the recording system, it is **unlikely that there will be any benefit from the investigation** if the cause of the difference is found to be a measurement error.

(b) **Out of date standards**

(i) Price standards are likely to become out of data quickly when frequent changes to the costs of inputs occur or in periods of high **inflation**. In such circumstances an investigation of variances is likely to highlight a general change in market prices rather than efficiencies or inefficiencies in acquiring resources.

(ii) Standards may also be out of date where operations are subject to **technological development** or if **learning curve effects** have not been taken into account. **Investigation** of this type of variance **will provide feedback** on the inaccuracy of the standard and highlight the need to frequently review and update standards so that subsequent performance does not deviate from that expected.

(c) **Efficient or inefficient operations**

Such problems as spoilage or idle time, better quality material or more highly skilled labour are all likely to affect the efficiency of operations and hence cause variances. **Investigation** of variances in this category should highlight the causes of the inefficiency or efficiency and **lead to corrective action** to eliminate the inefficiency being repeated or action to compound the benefits of the efficiency.

(d) **Random or chance fluctuations**

(i) A **standard is an average figure**: really it represents the midpoint of a range of possible values and therefore **individual measurements** taken at specific times are **likely to deviate unpredictably within the predictable range**.

(ii) As long as the variance falls within this range, it will be classified as a random or chance fluctuation and will **not require investigating**.

2 VARIANCE INVESTIGATION MODELS

Rule-of-thumb model

2.1 This involves **deciding a limit** and if the size of a **variance is within the limit**, it should be considered **immaterial**. Only if it exceeds the limit is it considered materially significant, and worthy of investigation.

2.2 In practice many managers believe that this approach to deciding which variances to investigate is perfectly adequate. However, it has a number of **drawbacks**.

(a) Should variances be investigated if they exceed 10% of standard? Or 5%? Or 15%?

BPP PUBLISHING

(b) Should a **different fixed percentage be applied to favourable and unfavourable variances?**

(c) Suppose that the fixed percentage is, say, 10% and an important category of expenditure has in the past been very closely controlled so that adverse variances have never exceeded, say, 2% of standard. Now if adverse variances suddenly shoot up to, say, **8% or 9%** of standard, there might well be **serious excess expenditures incurred that ought to be controlled,** but with the fixed percentage limit at 10%, the variances would not be 'flagged' for investigation.

(d) **Unimportant categories** of low-cost expenditures might be loosely controlled, with variances commonly exceeding 10% in both a favourable and adverse direction. These would be regularly - and **unnecessarily - flagged for investigation**.

(e) Where actual expenditures have **normal and expected wide fluctuations** from period to period, but the 'standard' is a fixed expenditure amount, variances will be **flagged for investigation unnecessarily often**.

(f) There is **no attempt to consider the costs and potential benefits of investigating variances** (except insofar as the pre-set percentage is of 'material significance').

(g) The **past history of variances in previous periods is ignored**. For example, if the pre-set percentage limit is set at 10% and an item of expenditure has regularly exceeded the standard by, say, 6% per month for a number of months in a row, in all probability there is a situation that ought to warrant control action. Using the pre-set percentage rule, however, the variance would never be flagged for investigation in spite of the cumulative adverse variances.

2.3 Some of the difficulties can be overcome by **varying the pre-set percentage from account to account** (for example 5% for direct labour efficiency, 2% for rent and rates, 10% for salesmen's expenditure, 15% for postage costs, 5% for direct materials price, 3% for direct materials usage and so on). On the other hand, some difficulties, if they are significant, can only be overcome with a different cost-variance investigation model.

Statistical significance model

2.4 Historical data are used to **calculate** both a standard as **an expected average** and the **expected standard deviation** around this average when the process is under control. An **in-control process** (process being material usage, fixed overhead expenditure and so on) is one in which any resulting **variance is simply due to random fluctuations** around the expected outcome. An **out-of-control process**, on the other hand, is one in which **corrective action can be taken to remedy any variance**.

2.5 By assuming that variances that occur are normally distributed around this average, a **variance will be investigated if it is** *more* **than a distance from the expected average that the estimated normal distribution suggests is likely if the process is in control.** (Note that such a variance would be deemed significant.)

(a) A 95% or 0.05 significance level rule would state that variances should be investigated if they exceed 1.96 standard deviations from the standard.

(b) A 99% or 0.01 significance level rule would state that variances should be investigated if they exceed 2.58 standard deviations from the standard. This is less stringent than a 0.05 significance level rule.

(c) For simplicity, 1.96 and 2.58 standard deviations can be rounded up to 2 and 3 standard deviations respectively.

2.6 For example data could be collected and analysed to reveal the following pattern.

Standard hours per unit   6 hours
Standard deviation per unit   0.5 hours

Assume that a **0.05 significance level** rule is in use.

Suppose that 100 units are made and take 640 hours. The efficiency variance would be 40 hours (A). The standard deviation is 0.5 hours for one unit and $0.5 \times \sqrt{100} = 5$ hours for 100 units. Since 40 hours (A) is **8 standard deviations** from the standard of 600 hours, the efficiency variance should be **investigated**.

Question 3

Data has been collected and analysed and reveals that transport costs per month are £25,000, with a standard deviation of £2,000. A 0.01 significance rule is in use. Actual travel expenses are £28,750. Should the resulting variance be investigated?

Answer

Variance = £3,750 (A) = 1.875 standard deviations

The variance would not be investigated.

2.7 The statistical significance rule has two principal **advantages** over the rule of thumb approach.

(a) **Important costs** that normally vary by only a small amount from standard will be **signalled for investigation if variances increase significantly**.

(b) Costs that **usually fluctuate by large amounts will not be signalled** for investigation unless variances are extremely large.

2.8 The main **disadvantage** of the statistical significance rule is the problem of assessing standard deviations in expenditure.

Statistical control charts

2.9 By marking variances and control limits on a control chart, **investigation** is signalled not only when a particular **variance exceeds the control limit** (since it would be non-random and worth investigating) but also when the **trend of variances shows a progressively worsening movement** in actual results (even though the variance in any single control period has not yet overstepped the control limit).

2.10 The $\bar{x}$ **control chart** is based on the principle of the statistical significance model. For each cost item, a chart is kept of monthly variances and **tolerance limits are set at 1, 2 or 3 standard deviations**.

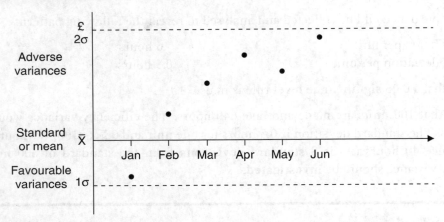

In this example, variances do not exceed the tolerance limits in any month, but the chart shows a worsening of variances over time, and so management might decide that an investigation is warranted, perhaps when it exceeds an inner warning limit.

2.11 Using a **cusum chart, the cumulative sum of variances** over a long period of time **is plotted**. If the variances are not significant, these 'sums' will simply fluctuate in a random way above and below the average to give a total or cumulative sum of zero. But if significant variances occur, the cumulative sum will start to develop a positive or negative drift, and when it exceeds a set tolerance limit, the situation must be investigated.

Cumulative sum of variances

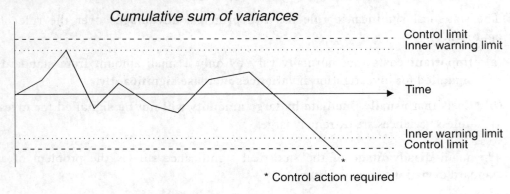

The **advantage** of the multiple period approach over the single period approach is that **trends are detectable earlier,** and control action would be introduced sooner than might have been the case if only current-period variances were investigated.

3 COMPOSITE VARIANCES

3.1 Suppose that a company makes a standard product, which uses six kilograms of material at £2 per kilogram. If actual output during a period is 100 units, which uses 640 kilograms at a cost of £2.30 per kilogram, the variances would be calculated as follows.

	£
640 kilograms should cost (× £2)	1,280
but did cost (× £2.30)	1,472
Price variance	192 (A)

100 units should use (× 6 kgs)	600 kg
but did use	640 kg
Usage variance in kgs	40 kg (A)
× standard cost per kg	× £2
Usage variance in £	£80 (A)

3.2 The **usage variance** would probably be **reported to the production manager**, and the **price variance** to the **purchasing manager**. Each would be held responsible for 'controlling' their respective variance item.

3.3 This traditional method of reporting fails to show that some of the price variance could have been avoided by the production manager. If the usage of materials had not been adverse, there would have been no need to buy the extra 40 kilograms of material, and the savings would have been 40 kg × £2.30 = £92. The purchasing manager could also have avoided the variance, of course, by buying all the materials at £2 per kilogram. This means that the **excess purchase price of the excess usage of materials could have been avoided by either the purchasing manager or the production manager**.

The name sometimes given to this **adverse price of adverse usage* is a composite variance**, and it may be shown in a diagram as follows.

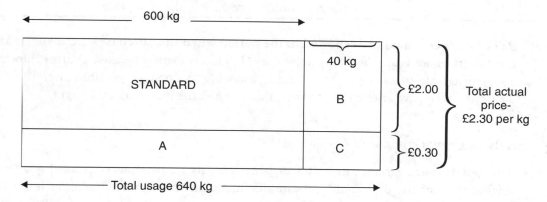

(* A **composite variance could also apply to labour rate and labour efficiency variances**.)

(a) The traditional price variance is A + C (£192 (A)).

(b) The traditional usage variance is B (£80(A)).

(c) However, the composite variance, C, is £0.30 per kg × 40 kg (A) = £12 (A), and so we might argue as follows.

   (i) The purchasing manager should be responsible for A + 2C (£204 (A)).
   (ii) The production manager should be responsible for B + C (£92 (A)).

   In other words, the composite variance should be reported to each of the managers jointly responsible for it.

4 INTERPRETING VARIANCES

Material price variances

4.1 An **adverse** price variance would suggest that the **managers responsible for buying decisions have paid too much for the materials**, and should be more careful in future. There are **reasons** why a large adverse or favourable price variance might occur, however, which are **outside the buying management's control**.

Reason	Comment
Inflation	This was discussed in Chapter 1.
Seasonal variations in prices	If material prices fluctuate seasonally, the standard price might be an average price for the year as a whole, on the assumption that it is impractical to buy a whole year's supply in the cheap season and store it until needed. In such a situation, price variances should be favourable for purchases in the cheap season and adverse for purchases in the more expensive season.
Rush orders	If buying managers are asked to make an order for immediate delivery, they might have to forgo a bulk purchase discount, or pay more for the quick supply lead time. The responsibility for the resulting adverse price variance should therefore belong to whoever made the rush order necessary in the first place.

4.2 **Price variances** should be **reported in the period when the purchases are made**, not when the materials are issued from stores and used. This is mainly because control information about price variances ought to be made available as soon as possible after the buying decision which gave rise to the variance, that is when the materials are bought.

Materials usage variances

4.3 A materials usage variance indicates that the quantity of materials consumed was larger or smaller than standard. It could indicate that materials **wastage** was higher or lower than it should have been or that the quantity of **rejects** was above or below standard. Wastage costs money, and should be kept to a minimum. The size of a materials usage variance, however, just like the size of a labour efficiency variance, **depends on the standard rate of usage** (or efficiency) and **whether the standard was attainable or ideal.**

In certain circumstances it could be worthwhile calculating mix and yield variances in order to carry out further analysis.

Labour rate variances

4.4 It might be tempting to think that the rate variance is something that operational managers can do little about, since rates of pay will be agreed at a senior level. A rate variance might, however, be due to **unexpected overtime working** (with overtime paid at a premium rate) or **productivity bonuses** added on to basic rates. To some extent, these should be **controllable by operational managers.**

Labour efficiency variances

4.5 The labour efficiency variance indicates that the actual production time needed to do the work was longer or less than expected. Inefficiency costs money: after all, if it takes three hours to make a unit of product instead of two hours, the unit cost of production will be higher and the profit from selling the unit will be less.

4.6 A standard time for labour to produce an item of work will normally take into account contingency allowances for down time and rest periods. Whether or not there is an allowance for these factors will depend on the type of performance standard used (ideal, attainable and so on). In a production industry based on batch production or jobbing work, the standard time will include an allowance for setting up times and clearing up times for each batch or job finished.

4.7 An **adverse** labour efficiency variance might indicate **poor labour productivity** in a period, for which a badly-motivated workforce or weak supervision might be to blame, but other causes of a variance might be as follows.

- Excessively **high down times,** due to a serious machine break down, or a bottleneck in production which left many of the workforce idle and waiting for work

- **Shorter batch runs** than expected, which increase the amount of setting up time and cleaning up time between batches, when no physical output is being produced

Overhead variances

4.8 Variances are supposed to provide management with control information. For example, an adverse material price variance of £100 tells management that the material used cost £100 more than it should have cost. But what about information provided by overhead variances? What control information can mangers get from the fact that there is an adverse fixed overhead capacity variance of £450 or that there is a favourable fixed overhead efficiency variance of £690? The information is not nearly so clear or understandable as that provided by labour and material variances, is it? But why is this?

Fixed overhead volume variance

4.9 Unlike expenditure variances or variable cost efficiency variances, the fixed overhead volume variance and its sub-divisions are **not a true reflection of the extra or lower cash spending** by an organisation as a result of the variance occurring. This is because the variances are valued in terms of overhead absorption rates; the estimates used in the calculation of these rates are often quite arbitrary but it is these absorption rates which determine the values assigned to the overhead variances.

4.10 **Together with the expenditure variance, the fixed overhead volume variance shows the under- or over-absorbed fixed overhead. Under/over absorption is simply a book balancing exercise,** however, which occurs as a result of the cost ascertainment process of absorption costing, and the level of under-/over-absorbed overhead depends on the accuracy of the original estimates used in calculating the absorption rates. The level of under/over absorption is not control information, it is simply a figure used to balance the books.

4.11 The fixed overhead efficiency and capacity variances are of **some relevance for control, however.** They **provide a measure of the difference between budgeted production volume and actual production volume,** and management should obviously be interested in whether budgeted output was achieved, and if not, why not.

4.12 Perhaps it would be more useful, however, if the losses or gains in output were valued in terms of contribution rather than in terms of absorption rates (which have arbitrary elements and were designed for quite a different purpose). The existence of a fixed overhead volume variance can therefore be important; it is only the monetary value given to the variance that can be misleading to managers.

Variable overhead efficiency variance

4.13 This arises because labour is either more or less efficient than standard. Variable production overheads tend to be incurred in direct proportion to production hours worked, and so if the workforce spends too much time on a job, it will incur not only more labour cost than it should, but also more variable overhead cost too.

Expenditure variances

4.14 The **fixed overhead expenditure variance** probably provides the **most useful** management information as the size of the variance can be said to be controllable.

(a) It does have its limitations, however. It is made up of a price component and a usage component. It can therefore vary if there are changes in charges (for example salary increases) or if quantities change (for example if more staff are taken on).

(b) For such variances to have any practical value as a control measure, the variances for each cost centre need to be calculated, and reported to the managers responsible. Within each overhead cost centre, the manager should be able to analyse the total variance into indirect materials cost variances, indirect labour cost variances and excess or favourable spending on other items, such as depreciation, postage and so on.

Selling price variance

4.15 This is perhaps the variance with the **most obvious meaning**. A selling price variance indicates by how much actual selling prices of products or services have exceeded or been less than standard.

Selling price variances will be **common**. Many companies sell their products to customers at a discount, with the size of the discount depending on the size of the order or who the customer is. (For example, regular customers might be given a minimum discount on their purchases, regardless of order quantity). The standard selling price might ignore discounts altogether, or it might have an allowance for the average expected discount. In either event, the actual sales prices and standard sales prices will usually differ.

Sales volume variance

4.16 A sales volume variance will result in **higher-than-expected sales revenue if it is favourable, but there will be an off-setting increase in the cost of sales**. Similarly, an adverse sales volume variance will result in lower-than-expected sales revenue, but there will be an offsetting reduction in the cost of sales.

The **net effect** of a sales volume variance is an **increase or reduction in profitability**, which is valued in terms of profit margin when a standard absorption costing system is in use and in terms of contribution margin, when a standard marginal costing system is in use.

Summary

4.17

Variance	Favourable	Adverse
Material price	Unforeseen discounts received Greater care in purchasing Change in material standard	Price increase Careless purchasing Change in material standard
Material usage	Material used of higher quality than standard More efficient use of material Errors in allocating material to jobs	Defective material Excessive waste or theft Stricter quality control Errors in allocating material to jobs
Labour rate	Use of workers at a rate of pay lower than standard	Wage rate increase
Idle time	**The idle time variance is always adverse**	Machine breakdown Illness or injury to worker
Labour efficiency	Output produced more quickly than expected because of worker motivation, better quality materials etc Errors in allocating time to jobs	Lost time in excess of standard Output lower than standard set because of lack of training, sub-standard materials etc Errors in allocating time to jobs
Fixed overhead expenditure	Savings in costs incurred More economical use of services	Increase in cost of services used Excessive use of services Change in type of service used

Overhead expenditure variances ought to be traced to the individual cost centres where the variances occurred.

Variance	Favourable	Adverse
Fixed overhead efficiency	See labour efficiency	See labour efficiency
Fixed overhead capacity	Actual time worked greater than budget (eg overtime working)	Excessive idle time Shortage of plant capacity

Question 4

M Ltd absorbs fixed production overhead at a predetermined rate based on budgeted output. Extracts from the variance analysis for April are as follows.

Fixed production overhead expenditure variance	£6,000 (F)
Fixed production overhead efficiency variance	£8,000 (A)
Fixed production overhead capacity variance	£7,000 (F)

Consider the following statements concerning production in April.

Statement

1 The fixed production overhead was over-absorbed by £5,000
2 Production output was higher than budget
3 Labour hours worked were higher than budget
4 Labour hours worked were more than the standard allowance for the actual output

Which of these statements are consistent with the reported variances?

A Statements 1 and 4 only
B Statements 2 and 3 only
C Statements 1, 2 and 3 only
D Statements 1, 3 and 4 only

Answer

The correct answer is D.

Statement 1 is correct because over-absorbed fixed overhead is represented by a favourable total overhead variance.

If the production output was higher than budget, the volume variance, ie the sum of the efficiency and capacity variances would be favourable. Statement 2 is incorrect.

If labour hours were higher than budget then the capacity variance would be favourable. Statement 3 is correct.

If labour takes longer than the standard time allowance then the efficiency variance is adverse. Statement 4 is correct.

Question 5

Jot down ideas for answering the following questions.

(a) Explain the problems concerning control of operations that a manufacturing company can be expected to experience in using a standard costing system during periods of rapid inflation.

(b) Suggest three methods by which the company could try to overcome the problems to which you have referred in answer to (a) above, indicating the shortcomings of each method.

Answer

(a) (i) Inflation should be budgeted for in standard prices. But **how** can the rate of inflation and the timing of inflationary increases be accurately **estimated**? Who decides **how much inflationary 'allowance'** should be added to each manager's expenditure budget?

(ii) How can actual expenditure be judged against a **realistic 'standard' price level**. Ideally, there would be an external price index (for example, one published by the government's Central Statistical Office) but even external price indices are not reliable guides to the prices an organisation ought to be paying.

(iii) The existence of inflation tends to **eliminate the practical value of price variances** as a pointer to controlling spending.

(iv) Inflation affects operations more directly. Usually costs go up before an organisation can put up the prices of its own products to customers. Inflation therefore tends to **put pressure on a company's cash flows**.

(v) To provide useful and accurately-valued variances (accurate efficiency variances as well as reliable price variances) the **standard costs ought to be revised frequently**. This would be an administrative burden on the organisation.

(vi) If the organisation uses standard costs for pricing or stock valuation, frequent revisions of the standard would be necessary to keep prices ahead of costs or stocks sensibly valued.

(b) To overcome the problems, we could suggest the following.

(i) **Frequent revision** of the standard costs. **Problem** - the administrative burden.

(ii) **Incorporating estimates** of the rate of inflation and the timing of inflation into budget expenditure allowances and standard costs. **Problem** - accurate forecasting.

(iii) Constructing **internal indices** of material prices to measure what actual price levels should have been. **Problem** - the administrative burden of constructing and maintaining the index.

(iv) A **determined effort** by management to **keep costs down**, and resist unnecessary spending. Cost control can minimise the damaging effects of price inflation. **Problem** - obtaining the cooperation of all management and employees in cost control efforts.

5 BENCHMARKING

5.1 We have seen how standard costing achieves control by the comparison of actual results with a pre-determined standard.

5.2 **Benchmarking is another type of comparison exercise through which an organisation attempts to improve performance.** The idea is to seek the best available performance against which the organisation can monitor its own performance.

> ### KEY TERM
>
> CIMA's *Official Terminology* defines **benchmarking** as 'The establishment, through data gathering, of targets and comparators, through whose use relative levels of performance (and particularly areas of underperformance) can be identified. By the adoption of identified best practices it is hoped that performance will improve.'

5.3 CIMA lists four types of benchmarking.

Type	Description
Internal benchmarking	A method of comparing one operating unit or function with another within the same industry
Functional benchmarking	Internal functions are compared with those of the best external practitioners of those functions, regardless of the industry they are in (also known as **operational** or **generic** benchmarking)
Competitive benchmarking	Information is gathered about direct competitors, through techniques such as reverse engineering★
Strategic benchmarking	A type of competitive benchmarking aimed at strategic action and organisational change

★ **Reverse engineering**: buying a competitor's product and dismantling it, in order to understand its content and configuration

5.4 From this list you can see that a benchmarking exercise **does not necessarily have to involve the comparison of operations with those of a competitor.** Indeed, it might be difficult to persuade a direct competitor to part with any information which is useful for comparison purposes. Functional benchmarking, for example, does not always involve direct competitors. For instance a railway company may be identified as the 'best' in terms of on-board catering, and an airline company that operates on different routes could seek opportunities to improve by sharing information and comparing their own catering operations with those of the railway company.

5.5 A 1994 survey of the *The Times* Top 1,000 companies (half of which were in manufacturing) revealed that the business functions most subjected to benchmarking in the companies using the technique were **customer services, manufacturing, human resources and information services.**

Obtaining information

5.6 **Financial information** about competitors is **easier** to acquire than non-financial information. Information about **products** can be obtained from **reverse engineering, product literature, media comment** and **trade associations**. Information about **processes** (how an organisation deals with customers or suppliers) is more **difficult** to find.

5.7 Such information can be obtained from **group companies** or possibly **non-competing organisations in the same industry** (such as the train and airline companies mentioned in Paragraph 5.4).

Why use benchmarking?

For setting standards

5.8 Benchmarking allows **attainable standards** to be established following the examination of both **external and internal information**. If these standards are **regularly reviewed** in the light of information gained through benchmarking exercises, they can become part of a programme of **continuous improvement** (a topic covered in Chapter 9) by becoming increasingly demanding.

Other reasons

5.9 Anna Green, in her article *The Borrowers* in the October 1996 edition of Pass magazine, explains the **benefits** of benchmarking.

   (a) Its flexibility means that it can be used in both the public and private sector and by people at different levels of responsibility.

   (b) Cross comparisons (as opposed to comparisons with similar organisations) are more likely to expose radically different ways of doing things.

   (c) It is an effective method of implementing change, people being involved in identifying and seeking out different ways of doing things in their own areas.

   (d) It identifies the processes to improve.

   (e) It helps with cost reduction.

   (f) It improves the effectiveness of operations.

   (g) It delivers services to a defined standard.

   (h) It provides a focus on planning.

'Most importantly benchmarking establishes a desire to achieve continuous improvement and helps develop a culture in which it is easier to admit mistakes and make changes.'

Case examples

Two examples can be given of the successful application of benchmarking. One is *British Steel*, which started using benchmarking in 1988, comparing its overall performance against other major steel companies and obtaining detailed data from measurement against other steel plants. At present British Steel benchmarks costs, customer service, quality, reliability and responsiveness.

The second example is *British Airways* which has 'used benchmarking since 1987 to help transform itself from a stodgy, state-controlled enterprise to a leading world airline'. BA staff analyse their own business processes and identify the weakest elements, and then visit direct competitors with checklists and questions. Problems are often found to be shared and competitors are willing to pool information in pursuit of solutions.

5.10 Benchmarking works, it is claimed, for the following reasons.

   (a) The comparisons are carried out by the managers who have to live with any changes implemented as a result of the exercise.

   (b) Benchmarking focuses on improvement in key areas and sets targets which are challenging but 'achievable'. What is *really* achievable can be discovered by examining what others have achieved: managers are thus able to accept that they are not being asked to perform miracles.

5.11 Benchmarking has other advantages: it can provide **early warning of competitive disadvantage** and should lead to a greater incidence of **teamworking** and **cross-functional learning**.

Question 6

We've looked at the advantages of benchmarking. Can you think of any disadvantages?

Answer

- Difficulties in deciding which activities to benchmark
- Identifying the 'best in class' for each activity
- Persuading other organisations to share information
- Successful practices in one organisation may not transfer successfully to another
- The danger of drawing incorrect conclusions from inappropriate comparisons

Chapter roundup

- Before investigating variances management should bear in mind **materiality**, **controllability**, **variance trend**, **cost**, **interrelationships** and **performance standards**.

- Individual variances should not be looked at in isolation since one variance might be **interrelated** with another, and much of the variance might have occurred only because the other, interrelated variance occurred too.

- The **efficiency variance** reported in any control period will depend on the efficiency level in the standard cost.

- **Actual and standard performance might differ** because of measurement errors, out of date standards, efficient or inefficient operations and/or random or chance fluctuations.

- **Variance investigation models** involve the **rule-of-thumb** model, the **statistical significance model** and **statistical control charts**.

- An in-control process is one in which any resulting variance is simply due to random fluctuations around the expected outcome. An out-of-control process is one in which corrective action can be taken to remedy any variance.

- **Inflation** will affect price variances.

- **Benchmarking** is an attempt to identify best practices and by comparison of operations to achieve improved performance.

Quick quiz

1 Favourable variances are never worthy of investigation because they result in profit increases. *True or false?*

2 Which of the following is not a reason why actual and standard performance might differ?

    A   Measurement errors
    B   Realistic standards
    C   Efficient or inefficient operations
    D   Random or chance fluctuations

3 *Choose the correct words from those highlighted.*

    A **cusum/cumus** chart plots **individual/the cumulative sum of** variances **over a period of time/on a one-off basis**.

BPP PUBLISHING

4   The following variances were reported for period 1.

Direct labour rate   £2,800 adverse
Direct labour efficiency   £1,350 favourable

Which of the following statements are consistent with these variances?

A   Direct labour achieved levels of efficiency which were higher than standard,   Consistent
     and were accordingly paid bonuses at higher rates than standard   Not consistent

B   The original standard labour rate was unrealistically low because it   Consistent
     failed to take account of rapid wage inflation   Not consistent

C   The production manager elected to use more skilled labour at a higher   Consistent
     hourly rate of pay than budgeted   Not consistent

5   If ideal standards are used, reported efficiency variances will tend to be favourable. *True or false?*

6   *Match the type of benchmarking to the descriptions.*

Type of benchmarking

Internal; functional; competitive; strategic

Descriptions

(a) Information is gathered about direct competitors

(b) Internal functions are compared with those of the best external practitioners of those functions,
     regardless of the industry they are in

(c) One operating unit or function is compared with another within the same industry

(d) A type of competitive benchmarking aimed at strategic action and organisational change

Answers to quick quiz

1   False

2   B. Out of date standards would cause a difference.

3   A cusum chart plots the cumulative sum of variances over a period of time.

4   All of the statements are consistent with the reported variances.

5   False. They will tend to be adverse.

6   Internal benchmarking   (c)
     Functional benchmarking   (b)
     Competitive benchmarking   (a)
     Strategic benchmarking   (d)

Now try the question below from the Exam Question Bank

Number	Level	Marks	Time
Q6	Exam standard	25	45 mins

Part B
Budgeting

Chapter 5

BUDGETS

Topic list	Syllabus reference	Ability required
1 Budgetary planning and control systems	(ii)	Comprehension/analysis
2 The preparation of budgets	(ii)	Comprehension/analysis
3 The sales budget	(ii)	Comprehension/analysis
4 Production and related budgets	(ii)	Comprehension/analysis
5 Cash budgets	(ii)	Comprehension/analysis
6 The master budget	(ii)	Comprehension/analysis
7 Monitoring procedures	(ii)	Comprehension/analysis
8 Alternative approaches to budgeting	(ii)	Comprehension/analysis
9 Budgeting in an uncertain environment	(ii)	Comprehension/analysis

Introduction

This chapter begins a new topic, **budgeting**. You will meet the topic at all stages of your future examination studies and so it is vital that you get a firm grasp of it now.

You may recognise much of this chapter from your management accounting fundamentals studies for Paper 2; you have already covered most of the topics in this chapter at a basic level and so we have included a couple of deemed knowledge boxes on the most straightforward areas.

The chapter begins by explaining the **reasons for operating a budgetary planning and control system** and then explains some of the **key terms and techniques** associated with budgeting.

You should have already covered **budget preparation** (including the preparation of cash budgets) but we will look at some more complex examples.

Section 7 explains how the budgeting process does not stop once the master budget has been prepared but is a **constant task** of the management accountant.

The chapter concludes with a review of a number of **alternative approaches to budgeting**.

Learning outcomes covered in this chapter

- **Explain** why organisations prepare plans
- **Explain and interpret** the effect of amendments to budget/plan assumptions
- **Discuss** alternative approaches to budgeting

Syllabus content covered in this chapter

- Planning
- Incremental budgeting
- Rolling budgets
- Zero-based budgeting
- Activity-based budgeting

1   BUDGETARY PLANNING AND CONTROL SYSTEMS

> **KEY TERM**
>
> The **budget** is 'a quantitative statement for a defined period of time, which may include planned revenues, expenses, assets, liabilities and cash flows. A budget provides a focus for the organisation, aids the co-ordination of activities and facilitates planning'.
>
> (CIMA *Official Terminology*)

1.1   There is, however, little point in an organisation simply preparing a budget for the sake of preparing a budget. A beautifully laid out budgeted profit and loss account filed in the cost accountant's file and never looked at again is worthless. The organisation should gain from both the actual preparation process and from the budget once it has been prepared.

1.2   Budgets are therefore not prepared in isolation and then filed away but are the fundamental components of what is known as the **budgetary planning and control system**. A budgetary planning and control system is essentially a system for ensuring **communication**, **coordination** and **control** within an organisation. Communication, coordination and control are general objectives: more information is provided by an inspection of the specific objectives of a budgetary planning and control system.

Objective	Comment
Ensure the achievement of the organisation's objectives	Objectives are set for the organisation as a whole, and for individual departments and operations within the organisation. Quantified expressions of these objectives are then drawn up as targets to be achieved within the timescale of the budget plan.
Compel planning	This is probably the most important feature of a budgetary planning and control system. Planning forces management to look ahead, to set out detailed plans for achieving the targets for each department, operation and (ideally) each manager and to anticipate problems. It thus prevents management from relying on ad hoc or uncoordinated planning which may be detrimental to the performance of the organisation.
Communicate ideas and plans	A formal system is necessary to ensure that each person affected by the plans is aware of what he or she is supposed to be doing. Communication might be one-way, with managers giving orders to subordinates, or there might be a two-way dialogue and exchange of ideas.
Coordinate activities	The activities of different departments or sub-units of the organisation need to be coordinated to ensure maximum integration of effort towards common goals. This concept of coordination implies, for example, that the purchasing department should base its budget on production require–ments and that the production budget should in turn be based on sales expectations. Although straightforward in concept, coordination is remarkably difficult to achieve, and there is often '**sub-optimality**' and conflict between departmental plans in the budget so that the efforts of each department are not fully integrated into a combined plan to achieve the company's best targets.

Objective	Comment
Provide a framework for responsibility accounting	Budgetary planning and control systems require that managers of **budget centres** are made responsible for the achievement of budget targets for the operations under their personal control.
Establish a system of control	A budget is a **yardstick** against which actual performance is measured and assessed. Control over actual performance is provided by the comparisons of actual results against the budget plan. Departures from budget can then be investigated and the reasons for the departures can be divided into **controllable** and **uncontrollable** factors.
Motivate employees to improve their performance	The interest and commitment of employees can be retained via a system of feedback of actual results, which lets them know how well or badly they are performing. The identification of controllable reasons for departures from budget with managers responsible provides an incentive for improving future performance.

2   THE PREPARATION OF BUDGETS

2.1   Having seen why organisations prepare budgets, we will now turn our attention to the mechanics of budget preparation. We will begin by defining and explaining a number of terms.

Planning

> **KEY TERM**
>
> **Planning** is described in the *Official Terminology* as 'The establishment of objectives, and the formulation, evaluation and selection of the policies, strategies, tactics and action required to achieve them. Planning comprises long-term/strategic planning, and short-term operation planning. The latter is usually for a period of up to one year'.

2.2   The overall planning process therefore covers both the long and short term.

Type of planning	Detail
Strategic/corporate /long-range planning	Covers periods longer than one year and involves 'The formulation, evaluation and selection of strategies for the purpose of preparing a long-term plan of action to attain objectives. (CIMA *Official Terminology*).
Budgetary/short-term tactical planning	Involves preparing detailed plans, which generally cover one year, for an organisation's functions, activities and departments. Works within the framework set by the strategic plans and converts those strategic plans into action.
Operation planning	Planning on a very short-term or day-to-day basis and is concerned with planning how an organisation's resources will be used. Works within the framework set by the budgetary plans and converts the budgetary plans into action.

The budget period

> **KEY TERM**
>
> The **budget period** is 'The period for which a budget is prepared and used, which may then be sub-divided into control periods'. (CIMA *Official Terminology*)

2.3 Except for capital expenditure budgets, the budget period is commonly the accounting year (sub-divided into 12 or 13 control periods).

The budget manual

> **KEY TERM**
>
> The **budget manual** is a collection of instructions governing the responsibilities of persons and the procedures, forms and records relating to the preparation and use of budgetary data.

2.4

Likely contents of a budget manual	Examples
An explanation of the objectives of the budgetary process	• The purpose of budgetary planning and control • The objectives of the various stages of the budgetary process • The importance of budgets in the long-term planning and administration of the enterprise
Organisational structures	• An organisation chart • A list of individuals holding budget responsibilities
Principal budgets	• An outline of each • The relationship between them
Administrative details of budget preparation	• Membership, and terms of reference of the budget committee • The sequence in which budgets are to be prepared • A timetable
Procedural matters	• Specimen forms and instructions for their completion • Specimen reports • Account codes (or a chart of accounts) • The name of the budget officer to whom enquiries must be sent

The responsibility for preparing budgets

2.5 Managers responsible for preparing budgets should ideally be the managers (and their subordinates) who are responsible for carrying out the budget, selling goods or services and authorising expenditure. Examples are as follows.

(a) The **sales manager** should draft the **sales budget** and **selling overhead** cost centre budgets.

(b) The **purchasing manager** should draft the **material purchases** budget.

(c)   The **production manager** should draft the **direct production** cost budgets.

(d)   Various **cost centre managers** should prepare the individual production, administration and distribution cost centre budgets for their own cost centre.

(e)   The **cost accountant** will **analyse** the budgeted overheads to determine the overhead absorption rates for the next budget period.

Budget committee

2.6   The **coordination** and **administration** of budgets is usually the responsibility of a **budget committee** (with the managing director as chairman).

(a)   The budget committee is assisted by a **budget officer** who is usually an accountant. Every part of the organisation should be represented on the committee, so there should be a representative from sales, production, marketing and so on.

(b)   **Functions of the budget committee**

- **Coordination** of the preparation of budgets, which includes the issue of the budget manual

- **Issuing of timetables** for the preparation of functional budgets

- **Allocation of responsibilities** for the preparation of functional budgets

- **Provision of information** to assist in the preparation of budgets

- **Communication of final budgets** to the appropriate managers

- **Comparison** of actual results with budget and the investigation of variances

- **Continuous assessment** of the budgeting and planning process, in order to improve the planning and control function

Budget preparation

2.7   Let us now look at the steps involved in the preparation of a budget. The procedures will differ from organisation to organisation, but the step-by-step approach described in this chapter is indicative of the steps followed by many organisations. The preparation of a budget may take weeks or months, and the budget committee may meet several times before the functional budgets are co-ordinated and the master budget is finally agreed.

> **KEY TERM**
>
> The CIMA *Official Terminology* defines a **departmental/functional budget** as 'A budget of income and/or expenditure applicable to a particular function.
>
> A function may refer to a department or a process. Functional budgets frequently include:
>
> - Production cost budget (based on a forecast of production and plant utilisation)
> - Marketing cost budget, sales budget
> - Personnel budget
> - Purchasing budget
> - Research and development budget'

The principal budget factor

2.8   The first task in the budgetary process is to identify the **principal budget factor**. This is also known as the **key** budget factor or **limiting** budget factor.

> ### KEY TERM
>
> The **principal budget factor** is the factor which limits the activities of an organisation.

2.9   **Likely principal budget factors**

(a)   The **principal budget factor** is usually **sales demand**: a company is usually restricted from making and selling more of its products because there would be no sales demand for the increased output at a price which would be acceptable/profitable to the company.

(b)   Other possible factors

- Machine capacity
- Distribution and selling resources
- The availability of key raw materials
- The availability of cash.

2.10   Once this factor is defined then the remainder of the budgets can be prepared. For example, if sales are the principal budget factor then the production manager can only prepare his budget after the sales budget is complete.

2.11   Management may not know what the limiting budget factor is until a draft budget has been attempted. The first draft budget will therefore usually begin with the preparation of a draft sales budget.

Knowledge brought forward

Steps in the preparation of a budget

Step 1   Identification of **principal/key/limiting budget factor**

Step 2   Preparation of a **sales budget,** assuming that sales is the principal budget factor (in units and in sales value for each product, based on a sales forecast)

Step 3   Preparation of a **finished goods stock budget** (to determine the planned change in finished goods stock levels)

Step 4   Preparation of a **production budget** (calculated as sales ± budgeted change in finished goods stock, in units)

Step 5   Preparation of **budgets for production resources**

- Materials usage
- Machine usage
- Labour

Step 6   Preparation of a **raw materials stock budget** (to determine the planned change in raw materials stock levels)

Step 7   Preparation of a **raw materials purchases budget** (calculated as usage ± budgeted change in raw materials stock)

Step 8   Preparation of **overhead cost budgets** (such as production, administration, selling and distribution and R&D)

> *Step 9* Calculation of **overhead absorption rates** (if absorption costing is used)
>
> *Step 10* Preparation of a **cash budget** (and others as required, **capital expenditure** and **working capital** budgets)
>
> *Step 11* Preparation of a **master budget** (budgeted P&L account and budgeted balance sheet)

2.12 Remember that it is **unlikely** that the execution of the **above steps** will be **problem-free** as data from one budget becomes an input in the preparation of another budget. For example, the materials purchases budget will probably be used in preparing the creditors budget. The creditors budget will then become an input to the cash budget, and so on. The budgets must therefore be **reviewed in relation to one another**. Such a review may indicate that some budgets are out of balance with others and need modifying so that they will be compatible with other conditions, constraints and plans. The budget officer must identify such inconsistencies and bring them to the attention of the manager concerned.

2.13 Alternatively, there may have been a **change in one of the organisational policies,** such as a change in selling prices, which will need to be **incorporated into the budget**. The revision of one budget may lead to the revision of all budgets. This process must continue until all budgets are acceptable and co-ordinated with each other.

2.14 If such changes are made manually, the process can be very time consuming and costly. Computer **spreadsheets** can help immensely.

Question 1

A company that manufactures and sells a range of products, with sales potential limited by market share, is considering introducing a system of budgeting.

Required

(a) List (in order of preparation) the functional budgets that need to be prepared.

(b) State which budgets will comprise the master budget.

(c) Consider how the work outlined in (a) and (b) can be coordinated in order for the budgeting process to be successful.

Answer

(a) The **sequence of budget preparation** will be roughly as follows.

- Sales budget. (The market share limits demand and so sales is the principal budget factor. All other activities will depend upon this forecast.)

- Finished goods stock budget (in units)

- Production budget (in units)

- Production resources budgets (materials, machine hours, labour)

- Overhead budgets for production, administration, selling and distribution, research and development and so on

Other budgets required will be the capital expenditure budget, the working capital budget (debtors and creditors) and, very importantly, the cash budget.

(b) The **master budget** is the summary of all the functional budgets. It often includes a summary profit and loss account and balance sheet.

(c) Procedures for preparing budgets can be contained in a **budget manual** which shows which budgets must be prepared when and by whom, what each functional budget should contain and detailed directions on how to prepare budgets including, for example, expected price increases, rates of interest, rates of depreciation and so on.

The formulation of budgets can be coordinated by a **budget committee** comprising the senior executives of the departments responsible for carrying out the budgets: sales, production, purchasing, personnel and so on.

The budgeting process may also be assisted by the use of a **spreadsheet/computer budgeting package**.

3 THE SALES BUDGET

3.1 We have already established that, for many organisations, the principal budget factor is sales volume. The sales budget is therefore **often the primary budget** from which the majority of the other budgets are derived.

3.2 Before the sales budget can be prepared a sales forecast has to be made. A **forecast** is an estimate of what is likely to occur in the future. A budget, in contrast, is a plan of what the organisation is aiming to achieve and what it has set as a target. We will be looking at forecasting techniques in detail in the next chapter.

3.3 On the basis of the sales forecast and the production capacity of the organisation, a sales budget will be prepared. This may be subdivided, possible subdivisions being by product, by sales area, by management responsibility and so on.

3.4 Once the sales budget has been agreed, related budgets can be prepared.

4 PRODUCTION AND RELATED BUDGETS

4.1 If the principal budget factor was production capacity then the production budget would be the first to be prepared. To assess whether production is the principal budget factor, the **production capacity available** must be determined, taking account of a number of factors.

- **Available labour**, including idle time, overtime and standard output rates per hour
- **Availability of raw materials** including allowances for losses during production
- **Maximum machine hours available**, including expected idle time and expected output rates per machine hour

It is, however, normally sales volume that is the constraint and therefore the production budget is usually prepared after the sales budget and the finished goods stock budget.

4.2 The production budget will show the quantities and costs for each product and product group and will tie in with the sales and stock budgets. This co-ordinating process is likely to show any shortfalls or excesses in capacity at various times over the budget period.

4.3 If there is likely to be a **shortfall** then consideration should be given to how this can be avoided. Possible **options** include the following.

- Overtime working
- Subcontracting
- Machine hire
- New sources of raw materials

A significant shortfall means that production capacity is, in fact, the limiting factor.

4.4 If **capacity exceeds sales volume** for a length of time then consideration should be given to **product diversification**, a **reduction in selling price** (if demand is price elastic) and so on.

4.5 Once the production budget has been finalised, the labour, materials and machine budgets can be drawn up. These budgets will be based on budgeted activity levels, planned stock positions and projected labour and material costs.

4.6 EXAMPLE: THE PRODUCTION BUDGET AND DIRECT LABOUR BUDGET

Landy Ltd manufactures two products, A and B, and is preparing its budget for 20X3. Both products are made by the same grade of labour, grade Q. The company currently holds 800 units of A and 1,200 units of B in stock, but 250 of these units of B have just been discovered to have deteriorated in quality, and must therefore be scrapped. Budgeted sales of A are 3,000 units and of B 4,000 units, provided that the company maintains finished goods stocks at a level equal to three months' sales.

Grade Q labour was originally expected to produce one unit of A in two hours and one unit of B in three hours, at an hourly rate of £2.50 per hour. In discussions with trade union negotiators, however, it has been agreed that the hourly wage rate should be raised by 50p per hour, provided that the times to produce A and B are reduced by 20%.

Required

Prepare the production budget and direct labour budget for 20X3.

4.7 SOLUTION

The expected time to produce a unit of A will now be 80% of 2 hours = 1.6 hours, and the time for a unit of B will be 2.4 hours. The hourly wage rate will be £3, so that the direct labour cost will be £4.80 for A and £7.20 for B (thus achieving a saving for the company of 20p per unit of A produced and 30p per unit of B).

(a) **Production budget**

		Product A			Product B	
		Units	Units		Units	Units
Budgeted sales			3,000			4,000
Closing stocks	($^3/_{12}$ of 3,000)	750		($^3/_{12}$ of 4,000)	1,000	
Opening stocks (minus stocks scrapped)		800			950	
(Decrease)/increase in stocks			(50)			50
Production			2,950			4,050

(b) **Direct labour budget**

	Grade Q	Cost
	Hours	£
2,950 units of product A	4,720	14,160
4,050 units of product B	9,720	29,160
Total	14,440	43,320

It is assumed that there will be no idle time among grade Q labour which, if it existed, would have to be paid for at the rate of £3 per hour.

The standard hour

> **KEY TERM**
>
> A **standard hour** or standard minute is 'The amount of work achievable at standard efficiency levels in an hour or minute'. (CIMA *Official Terminology*)

4.8 This is a useful concept in budgeting for labour requirements. For example, budgeted **output of different products or jobs** in a period could be converted into standard hours of production, and a labour budget constructed accordingly.

4.9 Standard hours are particularly useful when management wants to monitor the production levels of a variety of dissimilar units. For example product A may take five hours to produce and product B, seven hours. If four units of each product are produced, instead of saying that total output is eight units, we could state the production level as $(4 \times 5) + (4 \times 7)$ standard hours = 48 standard hours.

4.10 EXAMPLE: DIRECT LABOUR BUDGET BASED ON STANDARD HOURS

Truro Ltd manufactures a single product, Q, with a single grade of labour. Its sales budget and finished goods stock budget for period 3 are as follows.

Sales	700 units
Opening stocks, finished goods	50 units
Closing stocks, finished goods	70 units

The goods are inspected only when production work is completed, and it is budgeted that 10% of finished work will be scrapped.

The standard direct labour hour content of product Q is three hours. The budgeted productivity ratio for direct labour is only 80% (which means that labour is only working at 80% efficiency).

The company employs 18 direct operatives, who are expected to average 144 working hours each in period 3.

Required

(a) Prepare a production budget.

(b) Prepare a direct labour budget.

(c) Comment on the problem that your direct labour budget reveals, and suggest how this problem might be overcome.

4.11 SOLUTION

(a) **Production budget**

	Units
Sales	700
Add closing stock	70
	770
Less opening stock	50
Production required of 'good' output	720
Wastage rate	10%

Total production required $\quad 720 \times \dfrac{100\,\star}{90} = 800$ units

($\star$ Note that the required adjustment is 100/90, not 110/100, since the waste is assumed to be 10% of total production, not 10% of good production.)

(b) Now we can prepare the **direct labour budget**.

Standard hours per unit	3
Total standard hours required = 800 units × 3 hours	2,400 hours
Productivity ratio	80%

Actual hours required $\quad 2,400 \times \dfrac{100}{80} = 3,000$ hours

(c) If we look at the **direct labour budget** against the information provided, we can identify the problem.

	Hours
Budgeted hours available (18 operatives × 144 hours)	2,592
Actual hours required	3,000
Shortfall in labour hours	408

The (draft) budget indicates that there will not be enough direct labour hours to meet the production requirements.

(d) **Overcoming insufficient labour hours**

(i) **Reduce the closing stock** requirement below 70 units. This would reduce the number of production units required.

(ii) Persuade the workforce to do some **overtime** working.

(iii) Perhaps **recruit** more direct labour if long-term prospects are for higher production volumes.

(iv) **Improve** the **productivity** ratio, and so reduce the number of hours required to produce the output.

(v) If possible, **reduce** the **wastage** rate below 10%.

4.12 EXAMPLE: THE MATERIAL PURCHASES BUDGET

Tremor Ltd manufactures two products, S and T, which use the same raw materials, D and E. One unit of S uses 3 litres of D and 4 kilograms of E. One unit of T uses 5 litres of D and 2 kilograms of E. A litre of D is expected to cost £3 and a kilogram of E £7.

Budgeted sales for 20X2 are 8,000 units of S and 6,000 units of T; finished goods in stock at 1 January 20X2 are 1,500 units of S and 300 units of T, and the company plans to hold stocks of 600 units of each product at 31 December 20X2.

Stocks of raw material are 6,000 litres of D and 2,800 kilograms of E at 1 January, and the company plans to hold 5,000 litres and 3,500 kilograms respectively at 31 December 20X2.

The warehouse and stores managers have suggested that a provision should be made for damages and deterioration of items held in store, as follows.

Product S :	loss of 50 units
Product T :	loss of 100 units
Material D :	loss of 500 litres
Material E :	loss of 200 kilograms

Required

Prepare a material purchases budget for the year 20X2.

4.13 SOLUTION

To calculate material purchase requirements, it is first of all necessary to calculate the budgeted production volumes and material usage requirements.

	Product S		*Product T*	
	Units	Units	Units	Units
Sales		8,000		6,000
Provision for losses		50		100
Closing stock	600		600	
Opening stock	1,500		300	
(Decrease)/increase in stock		(900)		300
Production budget		7,150		6,400

| | | Material D | Material E | |
	Litres	Litres	Kg	Kg
Usage requirements				
To produce 7,150 units of S		21,450		28,600
To produce 6,400 units of T		32,000		12,800
Usage budget		53,450		41,400
Provision for losses		500		200
		53,950		41,600
Closing stock	5,000		3,500	
Opening stock	6,000		2,800	
(Decrease)/increase in stock		(1,000)		700
Material purchases budget		52,950		42,300

	Material D	Material E
Cost per unit	£3 per litre	£7 per kg
Cost of material purchases	£158,850	£296,100
Total purchases cost		£454,950

Question 2

J Ltd purchases a basic commodity and then refines it for resale. Budgeted sales of the refined product are as follows.

	April	May	June
Sales in kg	9,000	8,000	7,000

- The basic raw material costs £3 per kg.
- Material losses are 10% of finished output.
- The target month-end raw material stock level is 5,000 kg plus 25% of the raw material required for next month's budgeted production.
- The target month-end stock level for finished goods is 6,000 kg plus 25% of next month's budgeted sales.

What are the budgeted raw material purchases for April?

A   8,500 kg   B   9,350 kg   C   9,444.25 kg   D   9,831.25 kg

Answer

The correct answer is B.

	March kg	April kg	May kg
Required finished stock:			
Base stock	6,000	6,000	6,000
+ 25% of next month's sales	2,250	2,000	1,750
= Required stock	8,250	8,000	7,750
Sales for month		9,000	8,000
		17,000	15,750
Less: opening stock		8,250	8,000
Required finished production		8,750	7,750
+ 10% losses = raw material required		9,625	8,525
Required material stock:			
Base stock	5,000.00	5,000.00	
+ 25% of material for next month's production	2,406.25	2,131.25	
= Required closing material stock	7,406.25	7,131.25	
Production requirements		9,625.00	
		16,756.25	
Less: opening stock		7,406.25	
Required material purchases		9,350.00	

Using stock control formulae in budget preparation

4.14 In the previous example, you were simply told the stock levels. In an exam, however, you may also be required to use stock control formulae to determine stock levels.

Knowledge brought forward

Stock control formulae to learn

- Reorder level = maximum usage × maximum lead time

- Minimum level = reorder level – (average usage × average lead time)

- Maximum level = reorder level + reorder quantity – (minimum usage × minimum lead time)

- Economic order quantity (EOQ) = $\sqrt{\dfrac{2CoD}{Ch}}$

Question 3

The following information relates to material R.
Cost per kg = £100
Cost of ordering, per order = £500
Annual cost of holding 1 kg of R, as a % of cost = 10%

	Maximum	Average	Minimum
Usage each week (kgs)	3,500	2,800	2,000
Lead time (wks)	5 wks	2 wks	?

A year consists of 48 weeks.

What is the reorder level?

A   17,500 kgs
B   3,500 kgs
C   5 weeks
D   2,800 kgs

Answer

The correct answer is A.

Reorder level   = maximum usage × maximum lead time

                 = 3,500 × 5 = 17,500 kgs

Question 4

What is the EOQ for material R described in Question 3?

A   2,592 kgs
B   13,440,000 kgs
C   3,666 kgs
D   2,800 kgs

Answer

The correct answer is C.

$$EOQ = \sqrt{\frac{2CoD}{Ch}} = \sqrt{\frac{2 \times £500 \times (2,800 \times 48)}{£100 \times 10\%}} = 3,666 \text{ kgs.}$$

Question 5

What is the minimum level for material R described in Question 3?

A   3,500 kgs
B   2,800 kgs
C   2,000 kgs
D   11,900 kgs

Answer

The correct answer is D.

Minimum level	= reorder level – (average usage × average lead time)
	= 17,500 – (2,800 × 2)
	= 11,900 kgs

4.15   Now work through the following example which incorporates stock control formulae into a budgeting question.

4.16   EXAMPLE: BUDGETS AND STOCK CONTROL FORMULAE

The following data relate to the JIP, the product produced by Giring Ltd.

Budgeted data

	1 October to 1 December 20X5			1 January to 31 March 20X6		
Sales division	1	2	3	1	2	3
Sales of JIP (£'000)	54	342	228	60	360	240
Stocks of JIP						
opening (units)	90	320	260	100	350	250
maximum (units)	150	500	350	150	500	350

Standard cost data

Direct materials	Me1	10 kgs at £3 per kilo
	Me2	5 kgs at £2 per kilo
Direct wages	S	5 hours at £4 per hour
	SS	2 hours at £5 per hour

Production overhead is absorbed as a labour hour rate, that is £12 per hour in respect of S and £10 per hour in respect of SS.

Administration and selling overhead is recovered at 20% of production cost.

Profit is calculated at 10% of selling price.

Direct materials data

	Materials	
	Me1	Me2
Maximum consumption per week (kgs)	3,600	1,800
Minimum consumption per week (kgs)	2,400	1,200
Reorder quantity (kgs)	20,000	12,000
Stock at 30 September 20X5 (kgs)	24,500	13,650
Stock at 31 December 20X5 (kgs)	23,000	14,400
Lead time from suppliers (weeks)		
Maximum	6	5
Minimum	4	3

A major sales campaign is planned in the budget period beginning 1 April 20X6. In anticipation of an increase in sales, an advertising campaign will commence in the previous quarter. The production director has requested that stocks of raw materials be increased to maximum level by 1 April 20X6 and the sales director has requested that stocks of finished goods be increased to maximum level by 1 April 20X6.

Required

Prepare the following budgets for the three months ending 31 March 20X6.

(a) Production
(b) Purchases
(c) Production cost

4.17 SOLUTION

Working: Calculation of standard cost and profit per unit

		£ per unit
Direct materials	Me1	30
	Me2	10
Direct wages	S	20
	SS	10
Production overhead	S - 5 hours × £12	60
	SS - 2 hours × £10	20
Total production cost		150
Administration and selling overhead - 20%		30
		180
Profit - 10% of selling price		20
Selling price		200

(a) **Product JIP - Production Budget for three months ending 31 March 20X6**

		Units	Units
Sales units	- Division 1	300	
	- Division 2	1,800	
	- Division 3	1,200	
			3,300
Add required closing stock	- Division 1	150	
	- Division 2	500	
	- Division 3	350	
			1,000
			4,300
Less opening stock	- Division 1	100	
	- Division 2	350	
	- Division 3	250	
			700
Required production			3,600

(b) Maximum stock = reorder level + reorder quantity – (minimum usage × minimum lead time)

		Me1 kgs	Me2 kgs
Reorder level = Maximum usage × Maximum lead time			
Me1 = 3,600 × 6		21,600	
Me2 = 1,800 × 5			9,000
Reorder quantity		20,000	12,000
		41,600	21,000
Minimum usage × minimum lead time			
Me1 = 2,400 × 4		9,600	
Me2 = 1,200 × 3			3,600
Maximum stocks		32,000	17,400

BPP PUBLISHING

Direct materials - Purchases budget for the three months ending 31 March 20X6

	Me1 kgs	*Me2* kgs
Required closing stocks (maximum level)	32,000	17,400
Production requirements		
Me1 3,600 × 10kg	36,000	
Me2 3,600 × 5kg		18,000
	68,000	35,400
Less opening stock 31 December 20X5	23,000	14,400
Purchases	45,000	21,000
× standard price (£3/£2)	£135,000	£42,000

(c) **Production cost budget for the three months ending 31 March 20X6**

		£'000	£'000
Direct materials	- Me1 3,600 × £30	108	
	- Me2 3,600 × £10	36	
			144
Direct wages	- S 3,600 × £20	72	
	- SS 3,600 × £10	36	
			108
Production overhead	- S 3,600 × £60	216	
	- SS 3,600 × £20	72	
			288
Total production cost			540

Non-production overheads

4.18 In the modern business environment, an increasing proportion of overheads are not directly related to the volume of production, such as administration overheads and research and development costs.

4.19 **Key decisions in the budgeting process for non production overheads**

(a) Deciding which fixed costs are committed (will be incurred no matter what) and which fixed costs will depend on management decisions.

(b) Deciding what factors will influence the level of variable costs. Administration costs for example may be partly governed by the number of orders received.

5 CASH BUDGETS

The usefulness of cash budgets

5.1 The cash budget is one of the most important planning tools that an organisation can use. It shows the **cash effect of all plans made within the budgetary process** and hence its preparation can lead to a **modification of budgets** if it shows that there are insufficient cash resources to finance the planned operations.

5.2 It can also give management an indication of **potential problems** that could arise and allows them the opportunity to take action to avoid such problems. A cash budget can show **four positions**. Management will need to take appropriate action depending on the potential position.

Cash position	Appropriate management action
Short-term surplus	• Pay creditors early to obtain discount • Attempt to increase sales by increasing debtors and stocks • Make short-term investments
Short-term deficit	• Increase creditors • Reduce debtors • Arrange an overdraft
Long-term surplus	• Make long-term investments • Expand • Diversify • Replace/update fixed assets
Long-term deficit	• Raise long-term finance (such as via issue of share capital) • Consider shutdown/disinvestment opportunities

5.3 A cash budgeting question in an examination could ask you to recommend appropriate action for management to take once you have prepared the cash budget. Ensure your advice takes account both of whether there is a surplus or deficit and whether the position is long or short term.

Exam focus point

The pilot paper contained a multiple choice question on cash budgets. Information was provided about cash sales and debtor payment patterns and candidates were required to calculate one month's sales receipts.

What to include in a cash budget

5.4 A cash budget is prepared to show the expected receipts of cash and payments of cash during a budget period.

5.5 **Sources of cash receipts**

- Cash sales
- Payments by debtors (credit sales)
- The sale of fixed assets
- The issue of new shares or loan stock and less formalised loans
- The receipt of interest and dividends from investments outside the business

Remember that bad debts will **never be received in cash** and doubtful debts may not be received so you have to adjust if necessary for such items.

5.6 Although all the **receipts** in Paragraph 5.5 would affect a cash budget they would **not all appear in the profit and loss account**.

(a) The issue of new shares or loan stock is a balance sheet item.

(b) The cash received from an asset affects the balance sheet, and the profit or loss on the sale of an asset, which appears in the profit and loss account, is not the cash received but the difference between cash received and the written down value of the asset at the time of sale.

5.7 **Reasons for paying cash**

- Purchase of stocks
- Purchase of capital items

- Payroll costs or other expenses
- Payment of interest, dividends or taxation

5.8 **Not all payments** are **profit and loss account items**. The purchase of capital equipment and the payment of VAT affect the balance sheet. Some costs in the profit and loss account such as profit or loss on sale of fixed assets or depreciation are not cash items but are costs derived from accounting conventions.

5.9 In addition, the **timing** of cash receipts and payments **may not coincide** with the recording of profit and loss account transactions. For example, a dividend might be declared in the results for year 6 and shown in the profit and loss account for that year, but paid in cash in year 7.

5.10 Cash budgets are most effective if they are treated as **rolling budgets**. We will be looking at rolling budgets in more detail later in this chapter.

Knowledge brought forward

Steps in the preparation of a cash budget

- Set up a proforma cash budget.

		Month 1 £	Month 2 £	Month 3 £
Cash receipts:	Receipts from debtors	X	X	X
	Loan etc	X	X	X
		X	X	X
Cash payments:	Payments to creditors	X	X	X
	Wages etc	X	X	X
		X	X	X
Opening balance		X	X	X
Net cash flow (receipts - payments)		X	X	X
Closing balance		X	X	X

- Enter the figures that can be entered straightaway (receipts or payments that you are told occur in a specific month)
- Sort out cash receipts from debtors.
    - Establish budgeted sales month by month.
    - Establish the length of credit period taken by debtors, using the following formula to calculate it if necessary.

$$\frac{\text{Debtors collection period}}{\text{(no of days credit)}} = \frac{\text{average (or year - end) debtors during period}}{\text{total credit sales in period}} \times \text{no of days in period}$$

    - Hence determine when budgeted sales revenue will be received as cash (by considering cash receipts from total debtors, ignoring any provision for doubtful debts).
    - Establish when opening debtors will pay.
- Establish when any other cash income will be received.
- Sort out cash payments to creditors.
    - Establish production quantities and materials usage quantities each month.
    - Establish materials stock changes and hence the quantity and cost of materials purchases each month.
    - Establish the length of credit period taken from suppliers, using the following formula to calculate it if necessary.

$$\frac{\text{Creditors payment period}}{\text{(no of days credit)}} = \frac{\text{average (or year - end) creditors during period}}{\text{total purchases on credit in period}} \times \text{no of days in period}$$

    - Hence calculate when cash payments to suppliers will be made and when the amount due to opening creditors will be paid.
- Establish when any other cash payments (excluding non-cash items such as depreciation) will be made.

5.11 EXAMPLE: PROFIT AND LOSS ACCOUNT AND CASH BUDGET

Penny Ltd operates a retail business. Purchases are sold at cost plus $33\frac{1}{3}\%$.

(a)

	Budgeted sales in month	Labour cost in month	Expenses incurred in month
	£	£	£
January	40,000	3,000	4,000
February	60,000	3,000	6,000
March	160,000	5,000	7,000
April	120,000	4,000	7,000

(b) It is management policy to have sufficient stock in hand at the end of each month to meet half of next month's sales demand.

(c) Creditors for materials and expenses are paid in the month after the purchases are made/expenses incurred. Labour is paid in full by the end of each month. Labour costs and expenses are treated as period costs in the P & L account.

(d) Expenses include a monthly depreciation charge of £2,000.

(e) (i) 75% of sales are for cash.
    (ii) 25% of sales are on one month's credit.

(f) The company will buy equipment costing £18,000 for cash in February and will pay a dividend of £20,000 in March. The opening cash balance at 1 February is £1,000.

Required

(a) Prepare a cash budget for February and March.
(b) Prepare a profit and loss account for February and March.

5.12 SOLUTION

(a) CASH BUDGET

	February	March
Receipts	£	£
Receipts from sales	55,000 (W1)	135,000 (W2)
Payments		
Trade creditors	37,500 (W3)	82,500 (W3)
Expense creditors	2,000 (W4)	4,000 (W4)
Labour	3,000	5,000
Equipment purchase	18,000	-
Dividend	–	20,000
Total payments	60,500	111,500
Receipts less payments	(5,500)	23,500
Opening cash balance b/f	1,000	(4,500)★
Closing cash balance c/f	(4,500)★	19,000

Workings

			£
1	**Receipts in February**	75% of Feb sales (75% × £60,000)	45,000
		25% of Jan sales (25% × £40,000)	10,000
			55,000

			£
2	**Receipts in March**	75% of Mar sales (75% × £160,000)	120,000
		25% of Feb sales (25% × £60,000)	15,000
			135,000

3   **Purchases**

			January £		February £
For Jan sales	(50% of £30,000)		15,000		
For Feb sales	(50% of £45,000)		22,500	(50% of £45,000)	22,500
For Mar sales			–	(50% of £120,000)	60,000
			37,500		82,500

These purchases are paid for in February and March.

4   **Expenses**

Cash expenses in January (£4,000 – £2,000) and February (£6,000 – £2,000) are paid in February and March respectively. Depreciation is not a cash item.

(b)   PROFIT AND LOSS ACCOUNT

	February £	February £	March £	March £
Sales		60,000		160,000
Cost of purchases (75%)		45,000		120,000
Gross profit		15,000		40,000
Less: Labour	3,000		5,000	
Expenses	6,000		7,000	
		9,000		12,000
Net profit		6,000		28,000

> **ATTENTION!**
>
> (a)   The asterisks show that the **cash balance at the end of February** is **carried forward** as the **opening cash balance for March**.
>
> (b)   The fact that **profits** are made in February and March **disguises** the fact that there is a **cash shortfall** at the end of February.
>
> (c)   Steps should be taken either to ensure that an **overdraft facility** is available for the cash shortage at the end of February, or to **defer certain payments** so that the overdraft is avoided.
>
> (d)   Some payments must be made on due dates (payroll, taxation and so on) but it is possible that other payments can be delayed, depending on the requirements of the business and/or the goodwill of suppliers.

Cash budgets and an opening balance sheet

5.13   You might be given a cash budget question in which you are required to analyse an opening balance sheet to decide how many outstanding debtors will pay what they owe in the first few months of the cash budget period, and how many outstanding creditors must be paid.

5.14   EXAMPLE: CASH BUDGETS AND OPENING BALANCE SHEET

A balance sheet as at 31 December 20X4 shows the following details.

Debtors	£150,000
Trade creditors	£60,000

You are given the following information.

(a)   Debtors are allowed two months to pay.

(b)   1½ months' credit is taken from trade creditors.

(c) Sales and materials purchases were both made at an even monthly rate throughout 20X4.

Required

Ascertain the months of 20X5 in which the debtors will eventually pay and the creditors will be paid.

5.15 SOLUTION

(a) Since debtors take two months to pay, the £150,000 of debtors in the balance sheet represents credit sales in November and December 20X4, who will pay in January and February 20X5 respectively. Since sales in 20X4 were at an equal monthly rate, the cash budget should plan for receipts of £75,000 each month in January and February from the debtors in the opening balance sheet.

(b) Similarly, since creditors are paid after 1½ months, the balance sheet creditors will be paid in January and the first half of February 20X5, which means that budgeted payments will be as follows.

	£
In January (purchases in 2nd half of November and 1st half of December 20X4)	40,000
In February (purchases in 2nd half of December 20X4)	20,000
Total creditors in the balance sheet	60,000

(The balance sheet creditors of £60,000 represent 1½ months' purchases, so that purchases in 20X4 must be £40,000 per month, which is £20,000 per half month.)

Bad debts and provisions for doubtful debts

5.16 These may complicate the calculation of cash received from credit customers. Suppose that Wolf Ltd had debtors on 1 January 20X4 and 31 December 20X4 as follows.

	1 Jan	31 Dec
	£	£
Debtors in total	36,000	42,000
Less provision for doubtful debts	(6,000)	(10,000)
Debtors reported in balance sheet	30,000	32,000

During 20X4 the value of sales amounted to £200,000 and the provision for doubtful debts was increased by £4,000 (from £6,000 to £10,000).

What was the amount of cash received from customers in 20X4?

5.17 The cash receipts are calculated from the total debtors, ignoring the provision for doubtful debts. The provision is made just in case some customers default on payment but they have not defaulted yet.

	£
Debtors at the beginning of the year	36,000
Sales during the year	200,000
	236,000
Debtors at the end of the year	(42,000)
Cash received during the year	194,000

Changing stock levels

5.18 A further problem may arise if a business plans to build up or reduce its stock level over the budget period. This makes it more difficult to calculate amounts paid to suppliers.

5.19 EXAMPLE: CALCULATING THE AMOUNTS PAID TO SUPPLIERS

At 31 December 20X5 ESP Ltd held stocks which cost £60,000. The period of credit allowed by suppliers is one month and trade creditors at 31 December 20X5 amounted to £30,000. It is company policy to hold stocks equal to the cost of sales in the next two months and, until the end of 20X5, the monthly cost of sales was £30,000.

From 1 January 20X6 the company expects to increase its monthly sales by 20%. The policy on stock levels will remain unchanged, and suppliers will continue to allow one month's credit.

Required

Calculate the cash payments to trade creditors each month in 20X6.

5.20 SOLUTION

(a) We must first calculate the volume of purchases each month. In January 20X6 the stock levels must be increased from £60,000 to 120% of £60,000 = £72,000 (ie two months' cost of sales at the new volume of sales). In addition, monthly consumption of stocks will rise 20% from £30,000 to £36,000.

	£
In January, purchases must be as follows.	
Value of stock required at 31 January	72,000
Stock used up/sold in January	36,000
Total stock needed	108,000
Value of stock as at 1 January	(60,000)
Purchases required in January	48,000

Purchases from February onwards must then be enough to replace the stocks used up (£36,000 per month).

(b) Having calculated purchases, we can now establish **when** payments will be made, **allowing for one month's credit** from suppliers.

Month of purchase	Cost of purchases £	Month of payment
December 20X5 (opening balance sheet)	30,000	January
January 20X6	48,000	February
February	36,000	March
March	36,000	April

Monthly payments of £36,000 become regularly established from March 20X6 onwards.

Question 6

X Ltd will begin trading on 1 January 20X3. The following sales revenue is budgeted for January to March 20X3.

January	February	March
£13,000	£17,000	£10,000

Five per cent of sales will be for cash. The remainder will be credit sales. A discount of 5% will be offered on all cash sales. The payment pattern for credit sales is expected to be as follows.

Invoices paid in the month after sale	75%
Invoices paid in the second month after sale	23%
Bad debts	2%

Invoices are issued on the last day of each month.

The amount budgeted to be received from customers in March 20X3 is

A   £15,428   B   £15,577.50   C   £15,928   D   £16,065.50

Answer

The correct answer is A.

	Received in March £
Cash sales (5% × £10,000) × 95%	475.00
February sales (£17,000 × 95%) × 75%	12,112.50
January sales (£13,000 × 95%) × 23%	2,840.50
	15,428.00

Question 7

You are presented with the following cash budget for your organisation for the period January to June 20X2.

CASH BUDGET

	January £	February £	March £	April £	May £	June £
Cash receipts						
Cash sales	44,000	52,000	56,000	60,000	64,000	72,000
Credit sales	48,000	60,000	66,000	78,000	84,000	90,000
	92,000	112,000	122,000	138,000	148,000	162,000
Cash payments						
Purchases	60,000	80,000	90,000	110,000	130,000	140,000
Wages						
75%	12,000	15,000	18,000	21,000	24,000	27,000
25%	3,000	4,000	5,000	6,000	7,000	8,000
Overheads	10,000	15,000	15,000	15,000	20,000	20,000
Dividends			20,000			
Capital						
expenditure			30,000			40,000
	85,000	114,000	178,000	152,000	181,000	235,000
b/f	15,000	22,000	20,000	(36,000)	(50,000)	(83,000)
Net cash flow	7,000	(2,000)	(56,000)	(14,000)	(33,000)	(73,000)
c/f	22,000	20,000	(36,000)	(50,000)	(83,000)	(156,000)

Prior to the preparation of the cash budget, the managing director had been pleased with the functional budgets because they showed sales increasing by more than 100% in the period under review. In order to achieve this he had arranged a bank overdraft with a ceiling of £50,000 to accommodate the increased stock levels and wage bill for overtime worked.

Required

Comment upon the cash budget in the light of your managing director's comments and offer advice.

Answer

The overdraft arrangements are quite inadequate to service the cash needs of the business over the six-month period. If the figures are realistic then action should be taken now to avoid difficulties in the near future. The following are **possible courses of action**.

(a)　Activities could be curtailed.

(b)　Other sources of cash could be explored, for example a long-term loan to finance the capital expenditure and a factoring arrangement to provide cash due from debtors more quickly.

(c)　Efforts to increase the speed of debt collection could be made.

(d)　Payments to creditors could be delayed.

(e)　The dividend payments could be postponed (the figures indicate that this is a small company, possibly owner-managed).

(f)　Staff might be persuaded to work at a lower rate in return for, say, an annual bonus or a profit-sharing agreement.

(g)　Extra staff might be taken on to reduce the amount of overtime paid.

(h)　The stockholding policy should be reviewed; it may be possible to meet demand from current production and minimise cash tied up in stocks.

5.21 This question has demonstrated the use of a cash budget for feedforward control, which you will learn more about in Chapter 7.

6 THE MASTER BUDGET

6.1 When all the functional budgets and the cash budget have been prepared, they are **summarised** and a **budgeted profit and loss account, balance sheet** and **cash flow** are prepared. This master budget provides the overall picture of the planned performance for the budget period.

6.2 It is this master budget which is **submitted** to senior managers or directors for their approval. If the master budget is **approved** as an acceptable plan for the forthcoming budget period then it acts as an **instruction and authorisation** to budget managers, to allow them to take action to achieve their budgets.

6.3 If the master budget is not approved as an acceptable plan then it will be returned to the budget committee for amendment. The **amended** master budget will then be reviewed again by senior management. Thus, budgeting is an **iterative process** and it may be necessary to perform many iterations before an acceptable, workable budget is adopted and approved.

7 MONITORING PROCEDURES

7.1 The budgeting process does not stop once the budgets have been agreed. **Actual results should be compared on a regular basis with the budgeted results.** The frequency with which such comparisons are made depends very much on the organisation's circumstances and the sophistication of its control systems but it should occur at least **monthly**. Management should receive a report detailing the differences and should investigate the reasons for the differences. If the **differences** are **within the control** of management, **corrective action** should be taken to bring the reasons for the difference under control and to ensure that such inefficiencies do not occur in the future. We will look at this procedure in more detail in Chapter 7.

7.2 The differences may have occurred, however, because the budget was **unrealistic** to begin with or because the actual conditions did not reflect those anticipated (or could have possibly been anticipated). This would therefore **invalidate** the remainder of the budget.

7.3 Because the original budget was unrealistic or because of changes in anticipated conditions, the budget committee may need to reappraise the organisation's future plans and may need to adjust the budget to take account of such changes. The **revised budget** then represents a revised statement of formal operating plans for the remaining portion of the budget period.

ATTENTION!

The important point to note is that the budgetary process does not end for the current year once the budget period has begun: budgeting should be seen as a **continuous and dynamic process**.

8   ALTERNATIVE APPROACHES TO BUDGETING

Incremental budgeting

8.1   The **traditional approach** to budgeting is to **base next year's budget on the current year's results plus an extra amount for estimated growth or inflation next year.** This approach is known as **incremental budgeting** since it is concerned mainly with the increments in costs and revenues which will occur in the coming period.

8.2   Incremental budgeting is a reasonable procedure if current operations are as effective, efficient and economical as they can be. It is also appropriate for budgeting for costs such as staff salaries, which may be estimated on the basis of current salaries plus an increment for inflation and are hence administratively fairly easy to prepare.

Question 8

Can incremental budgeting be used to budget for rent? What about for advertising expenditure?

Answer

Incremental budgeting is appropriate for budgeting for rent, which may be estimated on the basis of current rent plus an increment for the annual rent increase. Advertising expenditure, on the other hand, is not so easily quantifiable and is more discretionary in nature. Using incremental budgeting for advertising expenditure could allow slack (unnecessary expenditure) and wasteful spending to creep into the budget.

8.3   In general, however, it is an **inefficient form of budgeting** as it **encourages slack** and **wasteful spending** to creep into budgets. Past inefficiencies are perpetuated because cost levels are rarely subjected to close scrutiny.

8.4   To ensure that inefficiencies are not concealed, however, alternative approaches to budgeting have been developed. One such approach is **zero base budgeting (ZBB)**.

Zero base budgeting

The principles of ZBB

8.5   ZBB rejects the assumption inherent in incremental budgeting that this year's activities will continue at the same level or volume next year, and that next year's budget can be based on this year's costs plus an extra amount, perhaps for expansion and inflation.

KEY TERM

Zero base budgeting is 'A method of budgeting which requires each cost element to be specifically justified, as though the activities to which the budget relates were being undertaken for the first time. Without approval the budget allowance is zero.'

(CIMA *Official Terminology*)

8.6   In reality, however, managers do not have to budget from zero, but can **start from their current level of expenditure and work downwards,** asking what would happen if any particular aspect of current expenditure and current operations were removed from the budget. In this way, every aspect of the budget is examined in terms of its cost and the benefits it provides and the selection of better alternatives is encouraged.

Implementing ZBB

8.7 The implementation of ZBB involves a number of steps but of greater importance is the **development of a questioning attitude** by all those involved in the budgetary process. Existing practices and expenditures must be challenged and searching questions asked.

- Does the activity need to be carried out?
- What would be the consequences if the activity was not carried out?
- Is the current level of provision adequate?
- Are there alternative ways of providing the function?
- How much should the activity cost?
- Is the expenditure worth the benefits achieved?

8.8 **The three steps of ZBB**

Step 1. Define **decision packages**, comprehensive **descriptions of specific organisational activities (decision units) which management can use to evaluate the activities and rank them in order of priority against other activities.** There are two types.

(a) **Mutually exclusive packages** contain **alternative methods of getting the same job done.** The best option among the packages must be selected by comparing costs and benefits and the other packages are then discarded.

(b) **Incremental packages divide one aspect of an activity into different levels of effort.** The 'base' package will describe the minimum amount of work that must be done to carry out the activity and the other packages describe what additional work could be done, at what cost and for what benefits.

EXAMPLE

Suppose that a cost centre manager is preparing a budget for maintenance costs. He might first consider two mutually exclusive packages. Package A might be to keep a maintenance team of two men per shift for two shifts each day at a cost of £60,000 per annum, whereas package B might be to obtain a maintenance service from an outside contractor at a cost of £50,000. A cost-benefit analysis will be conducted because the quicker repairs obtainable from an in-house maintenance service might justify its extra cost. If we now suppose that package A is preferred, the budget analysis must be completed by describing the incremental variations in this chosen alternative.

- The **'base' package** would describe the minimum requirement for the maintenance work. This might be to pay for one man per shift for two shifts each day at a cost of £30,000.

- **Incremental package 1** might be to pay for two men on the early shift and one man on the late shift, at a cost of £45,000. The extra cost of £15,000 would need to be justified, for example by savings in lost production time, or by more efficient machinery.

- **Incremental package 2** might be the original preference, for two men on each shift at a cost of £60,000. The cost-benefit analysis would compare its advantages, if any, over incremental package 1; and so on.

Question 9

What might the base package and incremental packages for a personnel department cover?

	Base	*Incremental*
A	Recruitment	Training
B	Dismissal	Recruitment
C	Training	Pension administration
D	Pension administration	Recruitment

Answer

The correct answer is A.

The base package might cover the recruitment and dismissal of staff. Incremental packages might cover training, pension administration, trade union liaison, staff welfare and so on.

Step 2. **Evaluate and rank each activity (decision package)** on the basis of its benefit to the organisation. This can be a lengthy process. Minimum work requirements (those that are essential to get a job done) will be given high priority and so too will work which meets legal obligations. In the accounting department these would be minimum requirements to operate the payroll, purchase ledger and sales ledger systems, and to maintain and publish a satisfactory set of accounts.

Step 3. **Allocate resources** in the budget according to the funds available and the evaluation and ranking of the competing packages.

The advantages and limitations of ZBB

8.9 **Advantages** of ZBB

- It is possible to identify and **remove inefficient or obsolete operations.**
- It forces employees to **avoid wasteful expenditure**.
- It can **increase motivation**.
- It **responds to changes in the business environment**.
- ZBB **documentation provides** an in-depth **appraisal of an organisation's operations.**
- It **challenges the status quo.**
- In summary, ZBB should result in a **more efficient allocation of resources**.

8.10 The major **disadvantage** of ZBB is the **volume of extra paperwork** created. The assumptions about costs and benefits in each package must be continually updated and new packages developed as soon as new activities emerge. The following problems might also occur.

(a) **Short-term benefits** might be **emphasised** to the detriment of long-term benefits.

(b) It may give the impression **that all decisions have to be made in the budget.** Management must be able to meet unforeseen opportunities and threats at all times, however, and must not feel restricted from carrying out new ideas simply because they were not approved by a decision package, cost benefit analysis and the ranking process.

(c) It may be a **call for management skills** both in constructing decision packages and in the ranking process **which the organisation does not possess.** Managers may therefore have to be trained in ZBB techniques.

(d) The organisation's **information systems may not be capable of providing suitable information.**

(e) **The ranking process can be difficult.** Managers face three common problems.

(i)   A large number of packages may have to be ranked.

(ii)   It can be difficult to rank packages which appear to be equally vital, for legal or operational reasons.

(iii) It is difficult to rank activities which have qualitative rather than quantitative benefits - such as spending on staff welfare and working conditions.

8.11   In summary, perhaps the **most serious drawback to ZBB is that it requires a lot of management time and paperwork.** One way of obtaining the benefits of ZBB but of overcoming the drawbacks is to apply it selectively on a rolling basis throughout the organisation. This year finance, next year marketing, the year after personnel and so on. In this way all activities will be thoroughly scrutinised over a period of time.

Question 10

What might the base and incremental packages cover in your department if your organisation used ZBB?

Using ZBB

8.12   ZBB is not particularly suitable for direct manufacturing costs, which are usually budgeted using standard costing, work study and other management planning and control techniques. ZBB is best applied to **support expenses**, that is expenditure incurred in departments which exist to support the essential production function. These support areas include marketing, finance, quality control, personnel, data processing, sales and distribution. In many organisations, these expenses make up a large proportion of the total expenditure. These activities are less easily quantifiable by conventional methods and are more **discretionary** in nature. We return to the problem of budgeting for discretionary costs later in this section.

8.13   ZBB can also be successfully applied to **service industries** and **non-profit-making organisations** such as local and central government, educational establishments, hospitals and so on, and in any organisation where alternative levels of provision for each activity are possible and costs and benefits are separately identifiable.

Question 11

You work for a large multinational company which manufactures weedkillers. It has been decided to introduce zero base budgeting in place of the more traditional incremental budgeting. The manager of the research and development department has never heard of zero base budgeting.

Required

Write a report to the manager of the research and development department which explains the following.

(a)   How zero base budgeting techniques differ from traditional budgeting
(b)   How ZBB may assist in planning and controlling discretionary costs
(c)   How ZBB will help to control budgetary slack

Answer

REPORT

To: R&D manager
From: Management accountant   Date: 01.01.X3
Subject: Zero base budgeting

(a) The **traditional approach** to budgeting works from the premise that last year's activities will continue at the same level or volume, and that next year's budget can be based on last year's costs plus an extra amount to allow for expansion and inflation. The term 'incremental' budgeting is often used to describe this approach.

   Zero base budgeting (ZBB) quite literally works from a zero base. The approach recognises that every activity has a cost and insists that there must be quantifiable benefits to justify the spending. ZBB expects managers to choose the best method of achieving each task on a cost-benefit basis. Activities must be ranked in order of priority.

(b) **Discretionary cost** is 'expenditure whose value is a matter of policy', that is, it is not vital to the continued existence of an organisation in the way that, say, raw materials are to a manufacturing business. ZBB was developed originally to help management with the difficult task of allocating resources in precisely such areas. Research and development is a frequently cited example; others are advertising and training.

   Within a research and development department ZBB will establish priorities by ranking the projects that are planned and in progress. Project managers will be forced to consider the benefit obtainable from their work in relation to the costs involved. The result may be an overall increase in R&D expenditure, but only if it is justified.

   It is worth mentioning that when R&D costs are subsequently being monitored care is needed in interpreting variances. A favourable expenditure variance may not be a good thing: it may mean that not enough is being spent on R&D activity.

(c) **Budgetary slack** may be defined as the **difference between the minimum necessary costs and the costs built into the budget or actually incurred**. One of the reasons why, under traditional budgeting, an extra amount is added to last year's budget may be because managers are overestimating costs to avoid being blamed in the future for overspending and to make targets easier to achieve. Slack is a protective device and it is self-fulfilling because managers will subsequently ensure that their actual spending rises to meet the (overestimated) budget, in case they are blamed for careless budgeting.

   In an R&D department a further incentive to include slack is the nature of the work. Managers may well have 'pet' projects in which their personal interest is so strong that they tend to ignore the benefit or lack of benefit to the organisation which is funding them.

   The ZBB approach, as described in (a) above, clearly will not accept this approach: all expenditure has (in theory) to be justified in cost-benefit terms in its entirety in order to be included in next year's budget. In practice it is more likely that managers will start from their current level of expenditure as usual, but ZBB requires them to work downwards, asking what would happen if any particular element of current expenditure and current operations were removed from the budget.

Programme planning and budgeting systems

8.14 A programme planning and budgeting system (PPBS) sets a budget in terms of **programmes** (groups of activities with common objectives). By focusing on objectives, the budget is therefore **orientated towards the ultimate output of the organisation**. This contrasts with the traditional approach to budgeting, which focuses on inputs (such as material and labour).

8.15 Such an approach is therefore particularly useful for **public sector** and **non-profit seeking** organisations, such as government departments, schools, hospitals and charities, to ensure that expenditure is **focused** on programmes and activities that generate the most **beneficial results**. This is of particular value at a time when there is increasing public demand for

accountability by such organisations: donors to charities have recently expressed concern over the high proportion of donations used to pay administrative expenses. PPBS allows people (taxpayers and donors) to see where their money is going and how it has been spent.

8.16 **Disadvantages of using traditional budgeting for public sector and non-profit seeking organisations**

(a) Activities often span several years but the emphasis is on annual figures.

(b) It is difficult to incorporate into a budget report planned or actual achievements (number of sufferers helped, level of education and so on) as these achievements tend to be non-financial in nature.

(c) Costs relating to a particular objective are spread across a number of cost categories. For example, the costs relating to an objective of a police force to protect people and property from traffic hazards might be allocated to a variety of traditional cost categories – personnel, transport, administration, training and so on. It would be impossible to tell how much was spent, or authorised, to achieve that objective.

(d) There is no evidence as to how effectively or efficiently resources are being used.

8.17 PPBS would overcome these problems as the emphasis would be on objectives and the best use of resources to achieve effectiveness over the medium to long term.

8.18 **PPBS approach**

Step 1. Review long-term objectives (such as, for a police force, protect persons and property and deal with offenders).

Step 2. Set out the programmes of activities needed to achieve the objectives (such as police patrol on foot, police patrol in vehicles and so on).

Step 3. Evaluate the alternative programmes in terms of costs and benefits and select the most appropriate programmes.

Step 4. Analyse the programmes selected, finding out (for example) what would happen to the level of achievement of objectives if resources allocated to a particular programme were reduced by, say, 10%.

Discretionary costs

Budgeting for discretionary costs

8.19 It is much easier to set budgets for **engineered costs** (costs for which there is a **demonstrable relationship between the input** to a process and the **output** of that process) than for **discretionary costs** (costs for which there is **no clear relationship between the input and output of a process**, often because the **output is difficult to measure**, in terms of quantity and/or quality). It is obviously easier to budget for direct material costs (engineered cost) than for the cost of the accounts department (discretionary cost).

8.20 **Budgeting for discretionary costs** can be made **easier** by **converting them into engineered costs**.

- Develop suitable output measures
- Understand how input impacts on output

8.21 For example, by analysing the work undertaken to process an invoice for payment, an **average time** for dealing with an invoice can be established and the relationship between the number of invoices processed and the resources required to do this ascertained.

The analysis required for **activity based costing** (see Chapter 10) will also add to an understanding of the relationship between the inputs and outputs of a process.

8.22 If a discretionary cost cannot be converted into an engineered cost, ZBB or PPBS will be needed.

Control of discretionary costs

8.23 Discretionary costs **cannot be controlled on the basis of outputs** because of the difficulty is specifying outputs in financial terms. In order to set minimum standards of performance, some measure of output is needed, however. An accounts department may be required to pay invoices within two weeks of receipt, for example.

8.24 **Inputs** can be **controlled**, however, if the **budget** acts as a device to ensure financial resources allocated to the activity are not exceeded.

Rolling budgets

> **KEY TERM**
>
> CIMA's *Official Terminology* defines a **rolling budget** as 'A budget continuously updated by adding a further accounting period (month or quarter) when the earliest accounting period has expired.'

8.25 Rolling budgets are also called **continuous budgets**. They are particularly **useful** when an organisation is facing a **period of uncertainty** so that it is difficult to prepare accurate forecasts. For example it may be difficult to estimate the level of inflation for the forthcoming period.

8.26 Rolling budgets are an attempt to prepare **targets and plans** which are **more realistic** and **certain**, particularly with a regard to price levels, by shortening the period between preparing budgets.

8.27 Instead of preparing a **periodic budget annually** for the full budget period, budgets would be prepared, say, every one, two or three months (four, six, or even twelve budgets each year). Each of these budgets would plan for the next twelve months so that the current budget is extended by an extra period as the current period ends: hence the name rolling budgets. **Cash budgets** are usually prepared on a rolling basis.

8.28 Suppose, for example, that a rolling budget is prepared every three months. The first three months of the budget period would be planned in great detail, and the remaining nine months in lesser detail, because of the greater uncertainty about the longer-term future.

(a) The first continuous budget would show January to March Year 1 in detail, and April to December Year 1 in less detail.

(b) At the end of March, the first three months of the budget would be removed and a further three months would be added at the end for January to March Year 2.

(c) The remaining nine months for April to December Year 1 would be updated in the light of current conditions, adding more detail to the earliest three months, April to June Year 1.

8.29 The detail in the first three months would be principally important for the following.

- **Planning** working capital and short-term resources (cash, materials, labour and so on)

- **Control**: the budget for each control period should provide a more reliable yardstick for comparison with actual results.

Question 12

What advantages and disadvantages of rolling budgets can you think of?

Answer

The **advantages** are as follows.

(a) They reduce the element of uncertainty in budgeting. If a high rate of inflation or major changes in market conditions or any other change is likely which cannot be quantified with accuracy, rolling budgets concentrate detailed planning and control on short-term prospects where the degree of uncertainty is much smaller.

(b) They force managers to reassess the budget regularly, and to produce budgets which are up to date in the light of current events and expectations.

(c) Planning and control will be based on a recent plan instead of an annual budget that might have been made many months ago and which is no longer realistic.

(d) There is always a budget which extends for several months ahead. For example, if rolling budgets are prepared quarterly there will always be a budget extending for the next 9 to 12 months. If rolling budgets are prepared monthly there will always be a budget for the next 11 to 12 months. This is not the case when annual budgets are used.

The **disadvantages** of rolling budgets can be a deterrent to using them.

(a) A system of rolling budgets calls for the routine preparation of a new budget at regular intervals during the course of the one financial year. This involves more time, effort and money in budget preparation.

(b) Frequent budgeting might have an off-putting effect on managers who doubt the value of preparing one budget after another at regular intervals, even when there are major differences between the figures in one budget and the next.

Activity based budgeting (ABB)

8.30 This is a method of budgeting based on an **activity framework** which utilises **cost driver data** in the budget setting and variance feedback process. It is an important recent development in budgeting and you will learn more about it when you have been introduced to the principles of activity based costing (ABC) later in this text.

9 BUDGETING IN AN UNCERTAIN ENVIRONMENT

Budgets for worst possible, best possible and most likely outcomes

9.1 When some future events are uncertain and the performance of the organisation depends on how these future events turn out, one way of budgeting is to prepare three budgets.

(a) The **most likely outcome budget**, which will start off as the **master budget**.

(b) A budget for the **worst possible or pessimistic outcome**. The 'worst possible' should be for a **realistic** worst outcome, based on the assumption that key events or outcomes which are uncertain at the time of budgeting will turn out for the worst.

(c) A budget for the **best possible outcome**.

9.2 EXAMPLE: MOST LIKELY, PESSIMISTIC AND OPTIMISTIC BUDGETS

Suppose that Netcord Ltd is a company which makes and sells tennis rackets. Its sales for the past few years, and its profits, have been constant as follows.

	£
Sales	1,500,000
Variable costs	500,000
Contribution	1,000,000
Fixed costs	800,000
Profit	200,000

In preparing a budget for the next year, there is uncertainty about several key points.

(a) Netcord Ltd has tendered for two contracts, each to supply an overseas customer. The sales value of contract A is £500,000, that of contract B £300,000. For each of these orders, variable costs (including selling and shipping costs) would be 40% of sales value. Total fixed costs would be unaffected by the order. The company hopes to win both orders, but thinks it more likely that it will win contract A but not contract B.

(b) A new product, a model of squash racket, is due to be launched next year. Expected sales are £30,000 per month, with variable costs of 50% of sales, and fixed costs of £5,000 per month. The most likely launch date for the new product is in mid-year (ie six months into the year) but it could be launched as early as the end of month 4 or as late as the end of month 9.

(c) Although it is expected that sales price and costs will not go up, there is a reasonable possibility that variable costs on the current product range will go up by 10%.

Required

Prepare a most likely, a pessimistic and an optimistic budget.

9.3 SOLUTION

The most likely, optimistic and pessimistic assumptions are shown.

Most likely	**Optimistic**	**Pessimistic**
Win contract A	Win contract A	Don't win contract A
Don't win contract B	Win contract B	Don't win contract B
New product after 6 months	New product after 4 months	New product after 9 months
No change in costs	No change in costs	Variable costs up 10%

	Most likely		Optimistic		Pessimistic	
	£'000	£'000	£'000	£'000	£'000	£'000
Normal sales, current product	1,500		1,500		1,500	
Variable costs	500		500		550	
Contribution		1,000		1,000		950
Overseas contracts						
Sales	500		800		0	
Variable costs (40%)	200		320		0	
Contribution		300		480		0
Squash rackets						
Sales	180		240		90	
Variable costs (50%)	90		120		45	
Contribution		90		120		45
Total contribution		1,390		1,600		995
Fixed costs						
Squash rackets	30		40		15	
Other	800		800		800	
		830		840		815
Profit		560		760		180

The 'most likely' budget will probably be adopted as the master budget, but the management of Netcord Ltd could **use the three budgets** as follows.

(a) To **assess the likely effect of actual outcomes** (for example winning contract A).

(b) To **identify by how much each uncertain outcome might affect profits**, and do whatever they can to **try to avoid the worst outcome** if profits would be particularly badly affected.

In this example, it is fairly clear that winning contract A is the most important 'uncertain outcome' and management might wish to think about ways in which they can improve their chances of winning it.

9.4 The most likely/worst possible/best possible (or **three tier**) **approach** to budgeting is best suited to situations where there are only a **few uncertain outcomes**. When there are a **large number of outcomes** which cannot be predicted with any reasonable confidence, having just three budgets will probably be too simplistic and not really helpful to management. In such circumstances, **spreadsheet** packages can be used. We look at this topic at the end of the next chapter.

Chapter roundup

- The **objectives** of a budgetary planning and control system are as follows.

  - To ensure the achievement of the organisation's objectives
  - To compel planning
  - To communicate ideas and plans
  - To coordinate activities
  - To provide a framework for responsibility accounting
  - To establish a system of control
  - To motivate employees to improve their performance

- A **budget** is a quantified plan of action for a forthcoming accounting period.

- The **budget manual** is a collection of instructions governing the responsibilities of persons and the procedures, forms and records relating to the preparation and use of budgetary data.

- Managers responsible for preparing budgets should ideally be the managers responsible for carrying out the budget.

- The **budget committee** is the coordinating body in the preparation and administration of budgets.

- The **principal budget factor** should be identified at the beginning of the budgetary process, and the budget for this is prepared before all the others.

- Once prepared, the **subsidiary budgets** must be reviewed to ensure they are consistent with one another.

- **Cash budgets** show the expected receipts and payments during a budget period and are a vital management planning and control tool.

- The **master budget** is a summary of the functional (subsidiary) budgets and cash budget and includes a budgeted profit and loss account and a budgeted balance sheet.

- The budgeting process does not end for the forthcoming year once the budget period has begun: budgeting should be seen as a **continuous and dynamic process.**

- The principle behind **zero base budgeting** is that the budget for each cost centre should be prepared from 'scratch' or zero. Every item of expenditure must be justified to be included in the budget for the forthcoming period.

- There is a three-step approach to ZBB.

  ° Define **decision packages**   ° Evaluate and rank packages   ° Allocate resources

- ZBB is particularly useful for budgeting for discretionary costs.

- **PPBS** is particularly useful for public sector and non-profit seeking organisations.

- **Rolling budgets** (continuous budgets) are budgets which are continuously updated by adding a further period (say a month or a quarter) and deducting the earliest period.

- **Cash budgets** are usually prepared on a rolling basis.

- In an uncertain environment, the **three tier approach** to budgeting can be used.

Quick quiz

1   Which of the following is not an objective of a system of budgetary planning and control?

    A   To establish a system of control
    B   To coordinate activities
    C   To compel planning
    D   To motivate employees to maintain current performance levels

2   Sales is always the principal budget factor and so it is always the first budget to be prepared. *True or false?*

Part B: Budgeting

3   *Choose the appropriate words from those highlighted.*

A **forecast/budget** is an **estimate/guarantee** of **what is likely to occur in the future/has happened in the past**.

A **forecast/budget** is a **quantified plan/unquantified plan/guess** of what the organisation is aiming to **achieve/spend**.

4   *Fill in the blanks.*

When preparing a production budget, the quantity to be produced is equal to sales .... opening stock .... closing stock.

5   *Fill in the blanks.*

Reorder level = ... × ....

6   Which of the following should be included in a cash budget?

	Include	Do not include
Funds from the issue of share capital		
Revaluation of a fixed asset		
Receipt of dividends from outside the business		
Depreciation of production machinery		
Bad debts written off		
Repayment of a bank loan		

7   What are the three components of the master budget?

1   ....
2   ....
3   ....

8   Match the description to the type of budget.

Types of budget

Incremental budget; rolling budget; zero base budget

Description

(a)   Next year's budget is based on the current year's results plus an extra amount for estimated growth or inflation next year.

(b)   Each item in the budget is specifically justified, as though each activity were being undertaken for the first time.

(c)   The budget is continuously updated by adding a further accounting period when the earliest accounting period has expired.

Answers to quick quiz

1   D. The objective is to motivate employees to *improve* their performance.

2   False. The budget for the principal budget factor must be prepared first, but sales is not always the principal budget factor.

3   A forecast is an estimate of what is likely to occur in the future.

    A budget is a quantified plan of what the organisation is aiming to achieve.

4   When preparing a production budget, the quantity to be produced is equal to sales minus opening stock plus closing stock.

5   Reorder level = maximum usage × maximum lead time

6

	Include	*Do not include*
Funds from the issue of share capital	✓	
Revaluation of a fixed asset		✓
Receipt of dividends from outside the business	✓	
Depreciation of production machinery		✓
Bad debts written off		✓
Repayment of a bank loan	✓	

7   Budgeted cash flow, budgeted profit and loss account and budgeted balance sheet.

8   Incremental budget (a); rolling budget (c); zero base budget (b).

Now try the question below from the Exam Question Bank

Number	Level	Marks	Time
Q7	Introductory	30	54 mins

Chapter 6

PREPARING FORECASTS FOR BUDGETARY PLANS

Topic list	Syllabus reference	Ability required
1 Forecasting using historical data	(ii)	Application/evaluation
2 Linear regression analysis	(ii)	Application/evaluation
3 Scatter diagrams and correlation	(ii)	Application/evaluation
4 Sales forecasting	(ii)	Application/evaluation
5 Regression and forecasting	(ii)	Application/evaluation
6 The components of time series	(ii)	Application/evaluation
7 Finding the trend	(ii)	Application/evaluation
8 Finding the seasonal variations	(ii)	Application/evaluation
9 Time series analysis and forecasting	(ii)	Application/evaluation
10 Using spreadsheet packages to build business models	(ii)	Application/evaluation
11 Forecasting problems	(ii)	Application/evaluation

Introduction

In Chapter 5 we saw how to prepare budgets but we have not yet looked at where the figures which go into the budgets come from. As we will see in this chapter, to produce a budget calls for the **preparation of forecasts of costs and revenues**. Various quantitative techniques can assist with these **'number-crunching' aspects of budgeting.** This chapter aims to provide an understanding of those techniques. Note that the techniques will be described within their budgetary context.

It has been said that **budgeting is more a test of forecasting skill than anything else** and there is a certain amount of truth in such a comment. Forecasts need to be made of sales volumes and prices, wage rates and earnings, material availability and prices, rates of inflation, the cost of bought-in services and the cost of overhead items such as power. However, it is not sufficient to simply add a percentage to last year's budget in the hope of achieving a realistic forecast.

A budget should be **realistic** and so it will be based to some extent on forecasts prepared. In formulating a budget, however, management will be trying to establish some control over the conditions that will apply in the future.

Much of this chapter will be revision from your 3c Business Mathematics paper, but work through all of the material slowly and carefully to ensure that you have a thorough knowledge of quantitative forecasting techniques.

Learning outcomes covered in this chapter

- **Calculate** future sales and costs using forecasting techniques and **evaluate** the results

Syllabus content covered in this chapter

- Time series and regression

- 'What-if?' analysis

1 FORECASTING USING HISTORICAL DATA

1.1 Numerous techniques have been developed for using past costs incurred as the basis for forecasting future values. These techniques range from simple arithmetic and visual methods to advanced computer-based statistical systems. With all techniques, however, there is the **presumption that the past will provide guidance to the future**. Before using any extrapolation techniques, the **past data** must therefore be critically examined to **assess their appropriateness for the intended purpose**. The following checks should be made.

(a) The **time period** should be long enough to include any periodically paid costs but short enough to ensure that averaging of variations in the level of activity has not occurred.

(b) The **data** should be examined to ensure that any non-activity level factors affecting costs were roughly the same in the past as those forecast for the future. Such factors might include changes in technology, changes in efficiency, changes in production methods, changes in resource costs, strikes, weather conditions and so on. Changes to the past data are frequently necessary.

(c) The **methods of data collection** and the accounting policies used should not introduce bias. Examples might include depreciation policies and the treatment of by-products.

(d) Appropriate choices of **dependent** and **independent variables** must be made.

1.2 The two forecasting methods which we are going to look at (the scatter diagram method and linear regression analysis) are based on the assumption that a **linear relationship** links levels of cost and levels of activity.

Knowledge brought forward

Linear relationships

- A **linear relationship** can be expressed in the form of an equation which has the general form $Y = a + bX$

  where   Y is the **dependent** variable, depending for its value on the value of X

           X is the **independent** variable, whose value helps to determine the corresponding value of y

           a is a **constant**, a fixed amount

           b is a constant, being the **coefficient of X** (that is, the number by which the value of X should be multiplied to derive the value of Y)

- If there is a linear relationship between total costs and level of activity, Y = total costs, X = level of activity, a = fixed cost (the cost when there is no activity level) and b = variable cost per unit.

- The graph of a linear equation is a **straight line** and is determined by two things, the **gradient** (or slope) of the straight line and the point at which the straight line crosses the Y axis (the **intercept**).

  ○ Gradient = b in the equation $Y = a + bX = (Y_2 - Y_1)/(X_2 - X_1)$ where (X_1, Y_1), (X_2, Y_2) are two points on the straight line

  ○ Intercept = a in the equation $Y = a + bX$

---

2 LINEAR REGRESSION ANALYSIS

2.1 You will have learned simple linear regression analysis in your Paper 3c studies. However, 'regression' is specifically mentioned in the Paper 8 syllabus therefore we will start from basics in this Text.

2.2 **Linear regression analysis**, also known as the **'least squares technique'**, is a **statistical method** of estimating costs using historical data from a number of previous accounting periods. The analysis is used to derive a **line of best fit which has the general form**

Y = a + bX where

Y, the dependent variable = total cost
X, the independent variable = the level of activity
a, the intercept of the line on the Y axis = the fixed cost
b, the gradient of the line = the variable cost per unit of activity.

2.3 Historical data is collected from previous periods and adjusted to a common price level to remove inflationary differences. This provides a number of readings for activity levels (X) and their associated costs (Y). Then, by substituting these readings into the formulae below for a and b, estimates of the fixed cost and variable cost per unit are provided.

FORMULA PROVIDED IN THE EXAM

$$\text{If } Y = a + bX, b = \frac{n\sum XY - \sum X \sum Y}{n\sum X^2 - (\sum X)^2} \text{ and } a = \overline{Y} - b\overline{X}$$

where $\overline{X}, \overline{Y}$ are the average values of X and Y and n is the number of pairs of data for X and Y.

These formulae are provided in the exam. An example will help to illustrate this technique.

2.4 EXAMPLE: LEAST SQUARES METHOD

The transport department of Norwest Council operates a large fleet of vehicles. These vehicles are used by the various departments of the Council. Each month a statement is prepared for the transport department comparing actual results with budget. One of the items in the transport department's monthly statement is the cost of vehicle maintenance. This maintenance is carried out by the employees of the department. To facilitate control, the transport manager has asked that future statements should show vehicle maintenance costs analysed into fixed and variable costs.

Data from the six months from January to June year 2 inclusive are given below.

Year 2	Vehicle maintenance cost £	Vehicle running hours
January	13,600	2,100
February	15,800	2,800
March	14,500	2,200
April	16,200	3,000
May	14,900	2,600
June	15,000	2,500

Required

Analyse the vehicle maintenance costs into fixed and variable costs, based on the data given, utilising the least squares method.

2.5 SOLUTION

If Y = a + bX, where Y represent costs and X represents running hours (since costs depend on running hours) then b= (nΣXY − ΣXΣY)/ (nΣX² − (ΣX)²), when n is the number of pairs of data, which is 6 in this problem.

X '000 hrs	Y £'000	XY	X²
2.1	13.6	28.56	4.41
2.8	15.8	44.24	7.84
2.2	14.5	31.90	4.84
3.0	16.2	48.60	9.00
2.6	14.9	38.74	6.76
2.5	15.0	37.50	6.25
15.2	90.0	229.54	39.10

Variable cost per hour, b = (6(229.54) − (15.2)(90.00))/(6(39.1) − (15.2)²)

= (1,377.24 − 1,368)/(234.6 − 231.04) = 9.24/3.56 = £2.60

Fixed costs (in £'000), a = $\overline{Y} - b\overline{X}$ = (ΣY/n) − (bΣX/n) = (90/6) − (2.6(15.2)/6) = 8.41 approx, say £8,400

Question 1

You are given the following data for output at a factory and costs of production over the past five months.

Month	Output '000 units x	Costs £'000 y
1	20	82
2	16	70
3	24	90
4	22	85
5	18	73

Required

(a) Calculate an equation to determine the expected cost level for any given output volume.

(b) Prepare a budget for total costs if output is 22,000 units.

Answer

(a) *Workings*

X	Y	XY	X²	Y²
20	82	1,640	400	6,724
16	70	1,120	256	4,900
24	90	2,160	576	8,100
22	85	1,870	484	7,225
18	73	1,314	324	5,329
ΣX = 100	ΣY = 400	ΣXY = 8,104	ΣX² = 2,040	ΣY² = 32,278

n = 5 (There are five pairs of data for x and y values)

b = (nΣXY − ΣXΣY)/(nΣX² − (ΣX)²) = ((5 × 8,104) − (100 × 400))/ ((5 × 2,040) − 100²)

= (40,520 − 40,000)/(10,200 − 10,000) = 520/200 = 2.6

a = $\overline{Y} - b\overline{X}$ = (400/5) − (2.6 ÷ (100/5)) = 28

Y = 28 + 2.6X

where Y = total cost, in thousands of pounds and X = output, in thousands of units.

(b) If the output is 22,000 units, we would expect costs to be 28+ 2.6 × 22 = 85.2 = £85,200.

The conditions suited to the use of linear regression analysis

2.6 **Conditions which should apply if linear regression analysis is to be used to estimate costs**

(a) A **linear cost function should be assumed**. This assumption can be tested by measures of reliability, such as the correlation coefficient and the coefficient of determination (which ought to be reasonably close to 1). We will be looking at these concepts later in the chapter.

(b) When calculating a line of best fit, there will be a range of values for X. In Question 1, the line Y = 28 + 2.6X was predicted from data with output values ranging from X = 16 to X = 24. Depending on the degree of correlation between X and Y, we might safely use the estimated line of best fit to forecast values for Y, provided that the value of X remains within the range 16 to 24. We would be on less safe ground if we used the equation to predict a value for Y when X = 10, or 30, or any other value outside the range 16 to 24, because we would **have to assume that costs behave in the same way outside the range of x values used to establish the line in the first place.**

> **KEY TERMS**
>
> - **Interpolation** means using a line of best fit to predict a value within the two extreme points of the observed range.
>
> - **Extrapolation** means using a line of best fit to predict a value outside the two extreme points.

(c) The **historical data** for cost and output should be **adjusted to a common price level** (to overcome cost differences caused by inflation) and the historical data should also be **representative of current technology, current efficiency levels and current operations** (products made).

(d) As far as possible, **historical data should be accurately recorded** so that variable costs are properly matched against the items produced or sold, and fixed costs are properly matched against the time period to which they relate. For example, if a factory rental is £120,000 per annum, and if data is gathered monthly, these costs should be charged £10,000 to each month instead of £120,000 in full to a single month.

(e) Management should either be **confident that conditions** which have existed in the past **will continue into the future or amend the estimates** of cost produced by the linear regression analysis to **allow for expected changes** in the future.

(f) As with any forecasting process, the **amount of data available is very important**. Even if correlation is high, if we have fewer than about ten pairs of data, we must regard any forecast as being somewhat unreliable.

(g) It must be assumed that the **value of one variable, Y, can be predicted or estimated from the value of one other variable, X.**

Question 2

The relationship between total operating cost and quantity produced (in a manufacturing company) is given by the linear regression model TC = 5,000 + 500Q, where TC = total operating cost (in £) per annum and Q = quantity produced per annum (kg).

What reservations might you have about relying on the above model for budgetary planning purposes?

Answer

(a) The reliability of the model is unknown if we do not know the correlation coefficient. A low correlation would suggest that the model may be unreliable.

(b) The model is probably valid only over a certain range of quantity produced. Outside this range, the relationship between the two variables may be very different.

(c) The model is based on past data, and assumes that what has happened in the past will happen in the future.

(d) The model assumes that a linear relationship exists between the quantity produced per annum and the total operating costs per annum. It is possible that a non-linear relationship may exist.

(e) The fixed costs of £5,000 per annum may be misleading if they include an element of allocated costs.

---

3   SCATTER DIAGRAMS AND CORRELATION

The scatter diagram method of forecasting

3.1   By this method of cost estimation, cost and activity data are plotted on a graph. A **'line of best fit'** is then drawn. This line should be drawn through the middle of the plotted points as closely as possible so that the distance of points above the line are equal to distances below the line. Where necessary costs should be adjusted to the same indexed price level to allow for inflation.

Scatter diagram method of estimating costs

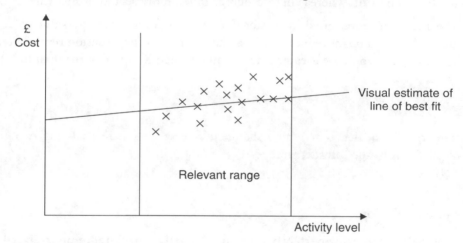

3.2   The fixed cost is the intercept of the line of best fit on the vertical axis. Suppose the fixed cost is £500 and that one of the plotted points (which is very close to the line or actually on it) represents output of 100 units and total cost of £550. The variable cost of 100 units is therefore calculated as £(550 − 500) = £50 and so the variable cost per unit is £0.50. The equation of the line of best fit is therefore *approximately* Y = 500 + 0.5X.

3.3   If the company to which this data relate wanted to forecast total costs when output is 90 units, a forecast based on the equation would be 500 + (0.5 × 90) = £545. Alternatively the **forecast could be read directly from the graph using the line of best fit.**

3.4   The disadvantage of the scatter diagram method is that the cost line is drawn by visual judgement and so is a **subjective approximation.**

 BPP PUBLISHING

Correlation

3.5   (a)   (b)

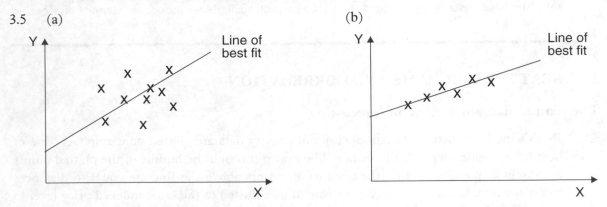

In the scatter diagrams above, you should agree that a line of best fit is more likely to reflect the 'real' relationship between X and Y in (b) than in (a). In (b), the pairs of data are all close to the line of best fit, whereas in (a), there is much more scatter around the line.

In the situation represented in scatter diagram (b), forecasting the value of Y from a given value for X would be more likely to be accurate than in the situation represented in (a). This is because there would be greater correlation between X and Y in (b) than in (a).

KEY TERM

Correlation is the degree to which change in one variable is related to change in another - in other words, the interdependence between variables.

Degrees of correlation

3.6   Two variables might be **perfectly correlated**, **partly correlated**, **uncorrelated** or subject to **non-linear correlation**.

3.7   **Perfect correlation**

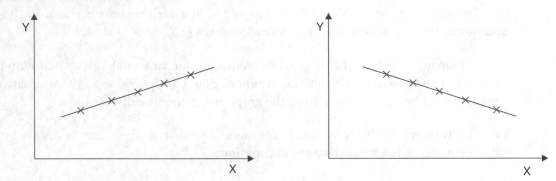

All the pairs of values lie on a straight line. An **exact linear relationship** exists between the two variables.

3.8 Partial correlation

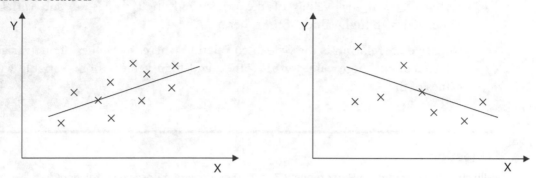

In the left hand diagram, although there is no exact relationship, **low values of X tend to be associated with low values of Y, and high values of X with high values of Y.**

In the right hand diagram, there is no exact relationship, but **low values of X tend to be associated with high values of Y and vice versa.**

3.9 No correlation

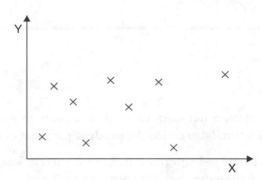

The values of these two variables are not correlated with each other.

3.10 Non-linear or curvilinear correlation

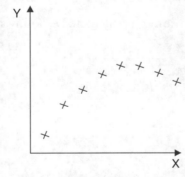

There is a relationship between X and Y since the points are on an obvious curve but it is not a linear relationship.

Positive and negative correlation

3.11 Correlation, whether perfect or partial, can be **positive** or **negative**.

BPP PUBLISHING

KEY TERMS

- **Positive correlation** is the type of correlation where low values of one variable are associated with low values of the other, and high values of one variable are associated with high values of the other.

- **Negative correlation** is the type of correlation where low values of one variable are associated with high values of the other, and high values of one variable with low values of the other.

Question 3

Which of the diagrams in Paragraphs 3.7 to 3.10 demonstrate positive correlation?

A   The left hand diagrams in Paragraphs 3.7 and 3.8
B   The right hand diagrams in Paragraphs 3.7 and 3.8
C   The diagrams in Paragraphs 3.7 and 3.8
D   None of them

Answer

The correct answer is A.

Measures of correlation

The coefficient of correlation, r

3.12   The **degree of correlation between two variables** can be measured using the **Pearsonian coefficient of correlation** (also called the **product moment correlation coefficient**).

    r has a value between –1 (perfect negative correlation) and +1 (perfect positive correlation). If r = 0 then the variables are uncorrelated.

FORMULA TO LEARN

The **coefficient of correlation**, r, is calculated as follows.

$$r = \frac{n\sum XY - \sum X \sum Y}{\sqrt{[n\sum X^2 - (\sum X)^2][n\sum Y^2 - (\sum Y)^2]}}$$

ATTENTION!

You are not provided with this formula in the exam.

3.13   Look back at the example in Paragraph 2.4. Suppose that we wanted to know the correlation between vehicle maintenance costs and vehicle running hours. We can use a lot of the calculation in Paragraph 2.5 to determine r.

$$r = \frac{6(229.54) - (15.2)(90.0)}{\sqrt{[6(39.1) - (15.2)^2][6\sum y^2 - (90.0)^2]}} = \frac{1,377.24 - 1,368}{\sqrt{(234.6 - 231.04)(6\sum y^2 - 8,100)}}$$

All we need to calculate is $\sum Y^2$.

| Y (£'000) | 13.60 | 15.80 | 14.50 | 16.20 | 14.90 | 15.00 | *Total* 90.00 |
| Y^2 | 184.96 | 249.64 | 210.25 | 262.44 | 222.01 | 225.00 | 1,354.30 |

$$r = \frac{9.24}{\sqrt{(3.56)(6 \times (1,354.30) - 8,100)}} = 0.96$$

3.14 A **fairly high degree of positive correlation** between X (vehicle running hours) and Y (vehicle maintenance cost) is indicated here **because r is quite close to +1.**

The coefficient of determination, r^2

> ### KEY TERM
>
> The **coefficient of determination** is a measure of the proportion of the change in the value of one variable that can be explained by variations in the value of the other variable.

3.15 In our example, $r^2 = (0.96)^2 = 0.9216$, and so 92% of variation in the value of Y (cost) can be explained by a linear relationship with X (running hours). This leaves only 8% of variations in y to be predicted from other factors. It is therefore **likely that vehicle** running hours could be used with a high degree of confidence to predict costs during a period.

Correlation and causation

3.16 If two variables are well correlated this may be due to pure chance or there may be a reason for it. The **larger the number of pairs of data,** the **less likely it is that the correlation is due to chance,** though that possibility should never be ignored.

3.17 **If there is a reason, it may not be causal.** Monthly net income is well correlated with monthly credit to a person's bank account, for the logical (rather than causal) reason that for most people the one equals the other. **Even if there is a causal explanation** for a correlation, it **does not follow that variations in the value of one variable cause variations in the value of the other.** Sales of ice cream and of sunglasses are well correlated, not because of a direct causal link but because the weather influences both variables.

3.18 Having said this, it is of course possible that where two variables are correlated, there is a direct causal link to be found.

The interactions of r^2 and r with linear regression

3.19 The successful application of linear regression models depends on X and Y being closely linearly related. r measures the strength of the linear relationship between two variables but **what numerical value of r is suggestive of sufficient linearity in data to allow one to proceed with linear regression?** The lower the value of r, the less chance of forecasts made using linear regression being adequate.

3.20 If there is a perfect linear relationship between the two variables ($r = \pm 1$), we can predict y from any given value of X with great confidence. If correlation is high (for example r = 0.9), the actual values will all be quite close to the regression line and so predictions should not be far out. If correlation is below about 0.7, predictions will only give a very rough guide to the likely value of Y.

3.21 If r = 0.75, say, you may feel that the linear relationship between the two variables is fairly strong. But r^2 = 56.25% indicates that only just over half of the variations in the dependent variable can be explained by a linear relationship with the independent variable. The low figure could be because a non-linear relationship is a better model for the data or because extraneous factors need to be considered. It is a **common rule of thumb that $r^2 \geq 80\%$ indicates that linear regression may be applied for the purpose of forecasting.**

4   SALES FORECASTING

4.1 The sales budget is frequently the first budget prepared since **sales is usually the principal budget factor,** but before the sales budget can be prepared a sales forecast has to be made. Sales forecasting is complex *and* difficult and involves the consideration of a number of factors including the following.

- Past sales patterns
- The economic environment
- Results of market research
- Anticipated advertising during the budget period
- Competition
- Changing consumer taste
- New legislation
- Distribution and quality of sales outlets and personnel
- Pricing policies and discounts offered
- Legislation
- Environmental factors

4.2 As well as bearing in mind those factors, management can use a number of forecasting methods, often combining them to reduce the level of uncertainty.

Method	Detail
Sales personnel	They can be asked to provide estimates.
Market research	Especially relevant for new products or services.
Mathematical models	Set up so that repetitive computer simulations can be run which permit managers to review the results that would be obtained in various circumstances.
Mathematical techniques	See later in this chapter.

5   REGRESSION AND FORECASTING

5.1 The same regression techniques as those considered earlier in the chapter can be used to **calculate a regression line (a trend line) for a time series.** A time series is simply a series of figures or values recorded over time (such as total annual costs for the last ten years). The determination of a trend line is particularly useful in forecasting. (We will be looking at time series and trend lines in more detail in the next section.)

5.2 The **years (or days or months) become the X variables in the regression formulae** by **numbering them from 0 upwards.**

5.3   EXAMPLE: REGRESSION AND FORECASTING

Sales of product B over the seven year period from year 1 to year 7 were as follows.

Year	Year 1	Year 2	Year 3	Year 4	Year 5	Year 6	Year 7
Sales of B ('000 units)	22	25	24	26	29	28	30

There is high correlation between time and the volume of sales.

Required

Calculate the trend line of sales, and forecast sales in year 8 and year 9.

5.4 SOLUTION

Workings

Year	X	Y	XY	X²
1	0	22	0	0
2	1	25	25	1
3	2	24	48	4
4	3	26	78	9
5	4	29	116	16
6	5	28	140	25
7	6	30	180	36
	$\Sigma X = 21$	$\Sigma Y = 184$	$\Sigma XY = 587$	$\Sigma X^2 = 91$

n = 7

Where $Y = a + bX$

$b = ((7 \times 587) - (21 \times 184))/((7 \times 91) - (21 \times 21)) = 245/196 = 1.25$

$a = (184/7) - ((1.25 \times 21)/7) = 22.5357$, say 22.5

$Y = 22.5 + 1.25X$ where X = 0 in year 1, X = 1 in year 2 and so on.

Using this trend line, predicted sales in year 8 (X = 7) would be $22.5 + 1.25 \times 7 = 31.25 = 31,250$ units.

Similarly, for year 9 (X = 8) predicted sales would be $22.5 + 1.25 \times 8 = 32.50 = 32,500$ units.

6 THE COMPONENTS OF TIME SERIES

KEY TERM

A **time series** is a series of figures or values recorded over time.

6.1 Examples of time series

- Output at a factory each day for the last month
- Monthly sales over the last two years
- The Retail Prices Index each month for the last ten years

KEY TERM

A graph of a time series is called a **historigram**.

6.2 (Note the 'ri'; this is not the same as a histogram.) For example, consider the following time series.

Year	Year 0	Year 1	Year 2	Year 3	Year 4	Year 5	Year 6
Sales (£'000)	20	21	24	23	27	30	28

The historigram is as follows.

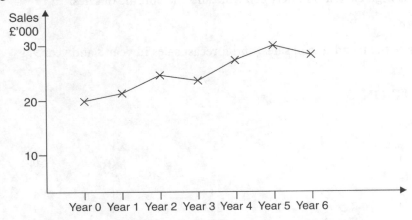

The horizontal axis is always chosen to represent time, and the vertical axis represents the values of the data recorded.

6.3 Components of a time series

- A **trend**

- **Seasonal variations** or fluctuations

- Cycles, or **cyclical variations**

- Non-recurring, **random variations**, caused by unforeseen circumstances such as a change in government, a war, technological change or a fire

The trend

> **KEY TERM**
>
> The **trend** is the underlying long-term movement over time in values of data recorded.

6.4 In the following examples of time series, there are three types of trend.

Year	Output per labour hour Units	Cost per unit £	Number of employees
4	30	1.00	100
5	24	1.08	103
6	26	1.20	96
7	22	1.15	102
8	21	1.18	103
9	17	1.25	98
	(A)	(B)	(C)

(a) In time series **(A)** there is a **downward trend** in the output per labour hour. Output per labour hour did not fall every year, because it went up between year 5 and year 6, but the long-term movement is clearly a downward one.

(b) In time series **(B)** there is an **upward trend** in the cost per unit. Although unit costs went down in year 7 from a higher level in year 6, the basic movement over time is one of rising costs.

(c) In time series **(C)** there is **no clear movement** up or down, and the number of employees remained fairly constant. The trend is therefore a static, or level one.

Seasonal variations

> ### KEY TERM
>
> **Seasonal variations** are short-term fluctuations in recorded values, due to different circumstances which affect results at different times of the year, on different days of the week, at different times of day, or whatever.

6.5 Here are two examples of seasonal variations.

(a) Sales of ice cream will be higher in summer than in winter.

(b) The telephone network may be heavily used at certain times of the day (such as mid-morning and mid-afternoon) and much less used at other times (such as in the middle of the night).

6.6 **Seasonal** is a term which may appear to refer to the seasons of the year, but its meaning in time series analysis is somewhat broader, as the examples given above show.

> ### Exam focus point
>
> The pilot paper contained a straightforward multiple choice question which provided the regression equation for sales units together with quarterly seasonal variations. The requirement was to use this information to prepare a sales forecast for a given period.

6.7 EXAMPLE: A TREND AND SEASONAL VARIATIONS

The number of customers served by a company of travel agents over the past four years is shown in the following historigram.

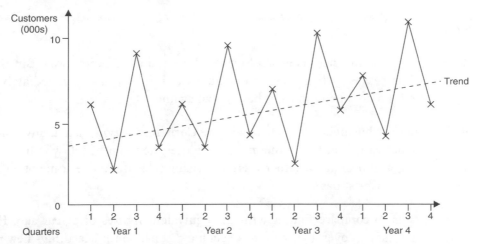

In this example, there would appear to be large seasonal fluctuations in demand, but there is also a basic upward trend.

Cyclical variations

6.8 Cyclical variations are **medium-term changes in results caused by circumstances which repeat in cycles**. In business, cyclical variations are commonly associated with economic cycles, successive booms and slumps in the economy. Economic cycles may last a few years. Cyclical variations are longer term than seasonal variations.

Summarising the components

6.9 In practice a time series could incorporate all of the four features we have been looking at and, to make reasonably accurate forecasts, the four features often have to be isolated. We can begin the process of isolating each feature by summarising the components of a time series as follows.

The **actual time series, Y = T + S + C + R**

where	Y	= the actual time series	C	= the cyclical component
	T	= the trend series	R	= the random component
	S	= the seasonal component		

6.10 Though you should be aware of the cyclical component, it is unlikely that you will be expected to carry out any calculation connected with isolating it. The mathematical model which we will use, the **additive model**, therefore excludes any reference to C and is **Y = T + S + R**.

> **KEY TERM**
>
> The **additive model** expresses a time series as $Y = T + S + R$.

We will begin by looking at how to find the trend in a time series.

7 FINDING THE TREND

7.1 Look at these monthly sales figures.

Year 6	August	September	October	November	December
Sales (£'000)	0.02	0.04	0.04	3.20	14.60

7.2 It looks as though the business is expanding rapidly - and so it is, in a way. But when you know that the business is a Christmas card manufacturer, then you see immediately that the January sales will no doubt slump right back down again.

7.3 It is obvious that the business will do better in the Christmas season than at any other time - that is the seasonal variation. Using the monthly figures, how can he tell whether or not the business is doing well overall - whether there is a rising sales trend over time other than the short-term rise over Christmas?

7.4 One possibility is to compare figures with the equivalent figures of a year ago. However, many things can happen over a year to make such a comparison misleading - new products might now be manufactured and prices will probably have changed.

7.5 In fact, there are a number of ways of overcoming this problem of distinguishing trend from seasonal variations. One such method is called **moving averages**. This method attempts to **remove seasonal (or cyclical) variations from a time series by a process of averaging so as to leave a set of figures representing the trend**.

7.6 A **moving average** is an average of the results of a fixed number of periods. Since it is an average of several time periods, it is **related to the mid-point of the overall period.**

7.7 EXAMPLE: MOVING AVERAGES

Year	Sales
	Units
0	390
1	380
2	460
3	450
4	470
5	440
6	500

Required

Take a moving average of the annual sales over a period of three years.

7.8 SOLUTION

(a) Average sales in the three year period year 0 – year 2 were (390 + 380 + 460)/3 = 1,230/3 = 410. This average relates to the middle year of the period, year 1.

(b) Similarly, average sales in the three year period year 1 – year 3 were (380 + 460 + 450)/3 = 1,290/3 = 430. This average relates to the middle year of the period, year 2.

(c) The average sales can also be found for the periods year 2 - year 4, year 3 - year 5 and year 4 - year 6, to give the following.

Year	Sales	Moving total of 3 years sales	Moving average of 3 years sales (÷ 3)
0	390		
1	380	1,230	410
2	460	1,290	430
3	450	1,380	460
4	470	1,360	453
5	440	1,410	470
6	500		

Note the following points.

(i) The **moving average series has five figures** relating to years 1 to 5. The **original series had seven figures** for years 0 to 6.

(ii) There is an upward trend in sales, which is more noticeable from the series of moving averages than from the original series of actual sales each year.

7.9 The above example averaged over a three-year period. Over what period should a moving average be taken? The answer to this question is that the **moving average which is most appropriate will depend on the circumstances and the nature of the time series.**

(a) A moving average which takes an **average of the results in many time periods will represent results over a longer term** than a moving average of two or three periods.

(b) On the other hand, with a moving average of results in many time periods, the **last figure in the series will be out of date by several periods**. In our example, the most recent average related to year 5. With a moving average of five years' results, the final figure in the series would relate to year 4.

(c) When there is a **known cycle** over which seasonal variations occur, such as all the days in the week or all the seasons in the year, the **most suitable moving average would be one which covers one full cycle.**

Moving averages of an even number of results

7.10 In the previous example, **moving averages were taken of the results in an** *odd* **number of time periods,** and the **average then related to the mid-point of the overall period.**

7.11 If a **moving average** were taken of results in an **even number of time periods,** the basic technique would be the same, but the mid-point of the overall period would not relate to a single period. For example, suppose an average were taken of the following four results.

Spring	120	
Summer	90	average 115
Autumn	180	
Winter	70	

The average would relate to the mid-point of the period, between summer and autumn.

7.12 The trend line average figures need to relate to a particular time period; otherwise, seasonal variations cannot be calculated. To overcome this difficulty, we take a **moving average of the moving average.** An example will illustrate this technique.

7.13 EXAMPLE: MOVING AVERAGES OVER AN EVEN NUMBER OF PERIODS

Calculate a moving average trend line of the following results of Linden Ltd.

Year	Quarter	Volume of sales '000 units
5	1	600
	2	840
	3	420
	4	720
6	1	640
	2	860
	3	420
	4	740

7.14 SOLUTION

A moving average of four will be used, since the volume of sales would appear to depend on the season of the year, and each year has four quarterly results. The moving average of four does not relate to any specific period of time; therefore a second moving average of two will be calculated on the first moving averages.

Year	Quarter	Actual volume of sales '000 units (A)	Moving total of 4 quarters' sales '000 units (B)	Moving average of 4 quarters' sales '000 units (B ÷ 4)	Mid-point of 2 moving averages Trend line '000 units (C)
5	1	600			
	2	840			
			2,580	645.0	
	3	420			650.00
			2,620	655.0	
	4	720			657.50
			2,640	660.0	
6	1	640			660.00
			2,640	660.0	
	2	860			662.50
			2,660	665.0	
	3	420			
	4	740			

7.15 By taking a mid point (a moving average of two) of the original moving averages, we can relate the results to specific quarters (from the third quarter of year 5 to the second quarter of year 6).

8 FINDING THE SEASONAL VARIATIONS

8.1 Once a trend has been established we can find the seasonal variations. As we saw earlier, the additive model for time series analysis is $Y = T + S + R$. We can therefore write $Y - T = S + R$. In other words, if we deduct the trend series from the actual series, we will be left with the seasonal and residual components of the time series. If we assume that the random component is relatively small, and hence negligible, the **seasonal component can be found as $S = Y - T$, the de-trended series.**

8.2 The actual and trend sales for Linden Ltd (as calculated in Paragraph 7.14) are set out below. The **difference between the actual results for any one quarter (Y) and the trend figure for that quarter (T)** will be the seasonal variation for that quarter.

Year	Quarter	Actual	Trend	Seasonal variation
5	1	600		
	2	840		
	3	420	650.00	−230.00
	4	720	657.50	62.50
6	1	640	660.00	−20.00
	2	860	662.50	197.50
	3	420		
	4	740		

8.3 Suppose that seasonal variations for the third and fourth quarters of year 6 and the first and second quarters of year 7 are −248.75, 62.50, −13.75 and 212.50 respectively. The variation between the actual result for a particular quarter and the trend line average is not the same from year to year, but an **average of these variations can be taken**.

Year	Q_1	Q_2	Q_3	Q_4
5			−230.00	62.50
6	−20.00	197.50	−248.75	62.50
7	−13.75	212.50		
Total	−33.75	410.00	−478.75	125.00
Average (÷ 2)	−16.875	205.00	−239.375	62.50

8.4 Variations around the basic trend line should cancel each other out, and add up to zero. At the moment, they do not. We therefore **spread the total of the variations** (11.25) **across the four quarters** (11.25 ÷ 4) **so that the final total of the variations sum to zero.**

	Q_1	Q_2	Q_3	Q_4	Total
Estimated quarterly variations	− 16.8750	205.0000	−239.3750	62.5000	11.250
Adjustment to reduce variations to 0	−2.8125	−2.8125	−2.8125	−2.8125	−11.250
Final estimates of quarterly variations	−19.6875	202.1875	−242.1875	59.6875	0
These might be rounded as follows	Ql: −20,	Ql: 202,	Ql:-242,	Ql: 60,	Total: 0

Seasonal variations using the proportional model

8.5 The method of estimating the seasonal variations in the above example was to use the differences between the trend and actual data. This model **assumes that the components of the series are independent** of each other, so that an increasing trend does not affect the seasonal variations and make them increase as well, for example.

BPP PUBLISHING

The alternative is to use the **proportional model** whereby each actual figure is expressed as a proportion of the trend. Sometimes this method is called the **multiplicative model**.

> **KEY TERM**
>
> The **proportional (multiplicative) model** summarises a time series as $Y = T \times S \times R$ (or $Y = T \star S \star R$).

8.6 The **trend component** will be the **same whichever model is used** but the values of the **seasonal and random components** will **vary according to the model being applied**.

8.7 The example in Paragraph 7.13 can be reworked on this alternative basis. The trend is calculated in exactly the same way as before but we need a different approach for the seasonal variations. The proportional model is $Y = T \times S \times R$ and, just as we calculated $S = Y - T$ for the additive model (Paragraph 7.13) we can calculate $S = Y/T$ for the proportional model.

Year	Quarter	Actual (Y)	Trend (T)	Seasonal percentage (Y/T)
5	1	600		
	2	840		
	3	420	650.00	0.646
	4	720	657.50	1.095
6	1	640	660.00	0.970
	2	860	662.50	1.298
	3	420		
	4	740		

8.8 Suppose that seasonal variations for the next four quarters are 0.628, 1.092, 0.980 and 1.309 respectively. The summary of the seasonal variations expressed in proportional terms is therefore as follows.

Year	Q_1 %	Q_2 %	Q_3 %	Q_4 %
5			0.646	1.095
6	0.970	1.298	0.628	1.092
7	0.980	1.309		
Total	1.950	2.607	1.274	2.187
Average	0.975	1.3035	0.637	1.0935

8.9 **Instead of summing to zero**, as **with the additive approach**, the **averages should sum (in this case) to 4.0, 1.0 for each of the four quarters.** They actually sum to 4.009 so 0.00225 has to be deducted from each one.

	Q_1	Q_2	Q_3	Q_4
Average	0.97500	1.30350	0.63700	1.09350
Adjustment	−0.00225	−0.00225	−0.00225	−0.00225
Final estimate	0.97275	1.30125	0.63475	1.09125
Rounded	0.97	1.30	0.64	1.09

8.10 Note that the **proportional model is better than the additive model when the trend is increasing or decreasing over time**. In such circumstances, seasonal variations are likely to be increasing or decreasing too. The additive model simply adds absolute and unchanging seasonal variations to the trend figures whereas the proportional model, by multiplying increasing or decreasing trend values by a constant seasonal variation factor, takes account of changing seasonal variations.

9 TIME SERIES ANALYSIS AND FORECASTING

9.1 By extrapolating a trend and then adjusting for seasonal variations, forecasts of future values can be made.

9.2 **Making forecasts of future values**

Step 1. Find a trend line using moving averages or using linear regression analysis (see Section 5).

Step 2. Use the trend line to forecast future trend line values.

Step 3. **Adjust these values by the average seasonal variation applicable to the future period, to determine the forecast for that period.** With the additive model, add (or subtract for negative variations) the variation. With the multiplicative model, multiply the trend value by the variation proportion.

9.3 Extending a trend line outside the range of known data, in this case forecasting the future from a trend line based on historical data, is known as **extrapolation**.

9.4 EXAMPLE: FORECASTING

The sales (in £'000) of swimwear by a large department store for each period of three months and trend values found using moving averages are as follows.

Quarter	Year 4		Year 5		Year 6		Year 7	
	Actual	Trend	Actual	Trend	Actual	Trend	Actual	Trend
	£'000	£'000	£'000	£'000	£'000	£'000	£'000	£'000
First			8		20	40	40	57
Second			30	30	50	45	62	
Third			60	31	80	50	92	
Fourth	24		20	35	40	54		

Using the additive model, seasonal variations have been determined as follows.

Quarter 1	Quarter 2	Quarter 3	Quarter 4
−£18,250	+£2,750	+£29,750	−£14,250

Required

Predict sales for the last quarter of year 7 and the first quarter of year 8, stating any assumptions.

9.5 SOLUTION

We might guess that the trend line is rising steadily, by $(57 - 40)/4 = 4.25$ per quarter in the period 1st quarter year 6 to 1st quarter year 7 (57 being the prediction in 1st quarter year 7 and 40 the prediction in 1st quarter year 6). Since the trend may be levelling off a little, a quarterly increase of +4 in the trend will be assumed.

		Trend	Seasonal variation	Forecast
1st quarter	Year 7	57		
4th quarter	Year 7 (+ (3 × 4))	69	−14.25	54.75
1st quarter	Year 8 (+ (4 × 4))	73	−18.25	54.75

Rounding to the nearest thousand pounds, the forecast sales are £55,000 for each of the two quarters.

9.6 Note that you could actually plot the trend line figures on a graph, extrapolate the trend line into the future and read off forecasts from the graph using the extrapolated trend line.

9.7 If we had been using the proportional model, with an average variation for (for example) quarter 4 of 0.8, our prediction for the fourth quarter of year 7 would have been $69 \times 0.8 = 55.2$, say £55,000.

Question 4

The trend in a company's sales figures can be described by the linear regression equation Y = 780 + 4X, where X is the month number (with January year 3 as month 0) and Y is sales in thousands of pounds. The average seasonal variation for March is 106%.

The forecast sales for March year 5 (to the nearest £'000) are

A £890,000   B £933,000   C £937,000   D £941,000

Answer

The correct answer is C.

X = 26

Forecast = $1.06 \times [780 + (4 \times 26)] = 937.04 = £937,040$ or about £937,000.

10 USING SPREADSHEET PACKAGES TO BUILD BUSINESS MODELS

KEY TERM

A **spreadsheet** is 'The term commonly used to describe many of the modelling packages available for microcomputers, being loosely derived from the likeness to a "spreadsheet of paper" divided into rows and columns'.　　　(CIMA *Computing Terminology*)

10.1 It is a type of general purpose software package with **many business applications**, not just accounting ones. It **can be used to build a model**, in which data is presented in these **rows and columns**, and it is up to the model builder to determine what data or information should be presented in it, how it should be presented and how the data should be manipulated by the spreadsheet program. The most widely used spreadsheet packages are Lotus 1-2-3 and Excel.

10.2 The idea behind a spreadsheet is that the model builder should **construct a model as follows**.

(a) Identify what data goes into each row and column and by **inserting text** (for example, column headings and row identifications).

(b) **Specify how the numerical data in the model should be derived**. Numerical data might be derived using one of the following methods.

(i) **Insertion into the model via keyboard input**.

(ii) **Calculation from other data in the model** by means of a formula specified within the model itself. The model builder must insert these formulae into the spreadsheet model when it is first constructed.

(iii) **Retrieval from data on a disk file** from another computer application program or module.

Exam focus point

The pilot paper required an explanation of how a spreadsheet could be set up to provide flexible budget control reports. You should be prepared to discuss how the principles of spreadsheet modelling can be applied in a variety of management accounting applications.

The advantages of spreadsheets

10.3   The uses of spreadsheets are really only limited by your imagination, and by the number of rows and columns in the spreadsheet, but some of the more **common accounting applications** are listed below.

- Balance sheets
- Cash flow analysis/forecasting
- General ledger
- Inventory records
- Job cost estimates
- Market share analysis and planning

- Profit projections
- Profit statements
- Project budgeting and control
- Sales projections and records
- Tax estimation

10.4   The great value of spreadsheets derives from their **simple format** of rows, columns and worksheets of data, and the ability of the data **users to have direct access themselves** to their spreadsheet model via their own PC. For example, an accountant can construct a cash flow model with a spreadsheet package on the PC on his desk: he can **create** the model, **input** the data, **manipulate** the data and **read or print the output** direct. He will also have fairly **instant access** to the model whenever it is needed, in just the time it takes to load the model into his PC. Spreadsheets therefore bring computer modelling within the everyday reach of data users.

The disadvantages of spreadsheets

10.5   Spreadsheets have disadvantages if they are not properly used.

(a)   A **minor error in the design** of a model at any point can **affect the validity of data** throughout the spreadsheet. Such errors can be very difficult to trace.

(b)   Even if it is properly designed in the first place, it is very **easy to corrupt** a model by accidentally changing a cell or inputting data in the wrong place.

(c)   It is possible to **become over-dependent on them**, so that simple one-off tasks that can be done in seconds with a pen and paper are done on a spreadsheet instead.

(d)   The possibility for experimentation with data is so great that it is possible to **lose sight of the original intention** of the spreadsheet.

(e)   Spreadsheets **cannot take account of qualitative factors** since they are invariably difficult to quantify. Decisions should not be made on the basis of quantitative information alone.

In summary, spreadsheets should be seen as a **tool in planning and decision making**. The user must make the decision.

'What if' analysis

10.6   Once a model has been constructed the consequences of changes in any of the variables may be tested by asking **'what if' questions, a form of sensitivity analysis**. For example, a spreadsheet may be used to develop a cash flow model, such as that shown below.

	A	B	C	D
		Month 1	Month 2	Month 3
1		Month 1	Month 2	Month 3
2	Sales	1,000	1,200	1,440
3	Cost of sales	(650)	(780)	(936)
4	Gross profit	350	420	504
5				
6	Receipts:			
7	Current month	600	720	864
8	Previous month	-	400	480
9		-	-	-
10		600	1,120	1,344
11	Payments	(650)	(780)	(936)
12		(50)	340	408
13	Balance b/f	-	(50)	290
14	Balance c/f	(50)	290	698

10.7 Typical 'what if' questions for sensitivity analysis

(a) What if the cost of sales is 68% of sales revenue, not 65%?

(b) What if payment from debtors is received 40% in the month of sale, 50% one month in arrears and 10% two months in arrears, instead of 60% in the month of sale and 40% one month in arrears?

(c) What if sales growth is only 15% per month, instead of 20% per month?

10.8 Using the spreadsheet model, the answers to such questions can be obtained simply and quickly, using the editing facility in the program. The information obtained should **provide management with a better understanding of what the cash flow position in the future might be**, and **what factors are critical to ensuring that the cash position remains reasonable**. For example, it might be found that the cost of sales must remain less than 67% of sales value to achieve a satisfactory cash position.

Exam focus point

'What if?' analysis is specifically mentioned on your Paper 8 syllabus. Although we have discussed the analysis in the context of spreadsheets, it can obviously be performed manually - but much more slowly and probably inaccurately!

Question 5

(a) Write out the formulae that would appear in column C of the spreadsheet shown above.

(b) Comment on the effect on the cash balances if *all* of the 'what if' conditions listed in Paragraph 10.7 applied. Perform the calculations manually, then if you have access to a spreadsheet package, you could use it to check your answer.

(c) Which cells in column C would have to be changed, and how, if the 'what if' conditions applied?

(d) How could the design of the spreadsheet model be improved to facilitate sensitivity analysis?

Answer

(a)

C2:	B2*1.2		C10:	@ SUM(C7..C9)
C3:	C2*0.65		C11:	C3
C4:	C2 + C3		C12:	C10 + C11
C7:	C2*0.6		C13:	B14
C8:	B2*0.4		C14:	C12 + C13

Note that the figures are entered into each cell as either positive or negative and so C4, for example, is calculated by *adding* 1,200 and -780.

(b)

A	B		C		D
	Month 1		Month 2		Month 3
Sales	1,000	(+15%)	1,150	(+15%)	1,323
Cost of sales (68%)	680		782		900
Gross profit	320		368		423
Receipts					
Current month (40%)	400		460		529
Previous month (50%)	–		500		575
Two months in arrears (10%)	–		–		100
	400		960		1,204
Payments	(680)		(782)		(900)
	(280)		178		304
Balance b/f	–		(280)		(102)
Balance c/f	(280)		(102)		202

The cash position would be substantially worse if all of the 'what if' conditions occurred simultaneously. Although the cash balance would become positive during month 3, the closing balance would be much lower. If these conditions were to apply then management would need to make arrangements to finance a large short-term deficit during months 1 and 2.

(c)   C2:   B2*1.15
      C3:   C2*0.68
      C7:   C2*0.4
      C8:   B2*0.5
      C9:   Blank (but D9 would have B2*0.1)

(d)   It would be much easier to conduct sensitivity analysis if the items that are variable were allocated specific cells outside the body of the cash flow table. For example rows 15 - 19 could contain the following.

	A	B
15	Cost of sales/Sales	0.68
16	Receipts - current month	0.40
17	- 1 month in arrears	0.50
18	- 2 months in arrears	0.10
19	Sales growth	1.15

The formulae in row C would then read as follows.

C2   B2*B19
C3   C2*B15
C7   C2*B16
C8   B2*B17
C9   A2*B18

(Note that B17, for example, is an absolute cell address whereas C2 is a relative cell address.)

Further sensitivity analysis could be conducted simply by changing the values in cells B15 - B19, rather than having to rewrite each column each time a variable is changed.

Analysing relationships

10.9   One of the major **assumptions** in **linear regression analysis** is that there is a **linear relationship** between the dependent and independent variables.

10.10 The relationship might be **curvilinear,** however. A curvilinear relationship can be expressed in the form $Y = aX^b$ (where Y is the dependent variable, X is the independent variable and a and b are constants).

Question 6

You have already encountered this equation in an earlier chapter. Can you remember where?

Answer

It is the equation of a learning curve.

10.11 Before the advent of computers and spreadsheet packages, if we knew that a linear relationship did not exist between, say, cumulative sales (Y) and time (X), we would have needed to use logarithms to find the value of b. ('a' would be sales in the first time period.)

Nowadays, fortunately, a **spreadsheet** package can be used to carry out a series of **repetitive calculations** (substituting the given value of a and the given values of X into $Y = aX^b$ and changing the value of b until the results with a particular value of b are close to the given values of Y).

10.12 The resulting equation can then be used for **forecasting** purposes.

11 FORECASTING PROBLEMS

11.1 All forecasts are subject to error, but the likely errors vary from case to case.

- The **further into the future** the forecast is for, the **more unreliable** it is likely to be.
- The **less data** available on which to base the forecast, the **less reliable** the forecast.
- The **pattern** of trend and seasonal variations **may not continue** in the future.
- **Random variations** may upset the pattern of trend and seasonal variation.

11.2 There are a number of changes that also may make it difficult to forecast future events.

Type of change	Examples
Political and economic changes	Changes in interest rates, exchange rates or inflation can mean that future sales and costs are difficult to forecast.
Environmental changes	The opening of high-speed rail links might have a considerable impact on some companies' markets.
Technological changes	These may mean that the past is not a reliable indication of likely future events. For example new faster machinery may make it difficult to use current output levels as the basis for forecasting future production output.
Technological advances	Advanced manufacturing technology is changing the cost structure of many firms. Direct labour costs are reducing in significance and fixed manufacturing costs are increasing. This causes forecasting difficulties because of the resulting changes in cost behaviour patterns, breakeven points and so on.
Social changes	Alterations in taste, fashion and the social acceptability of products can cause forecasting difficulties.

Chapter roundup

- This chapter has considered the quantitative methods the management accountant can use to obtain information for inclusion in budgets.

- **Linear regression analysis** (least squares technique) involves determining a **line of best fit.**

- **Scatter diagrams** can be used to estimate the fixed and variable components of costs.

- **Correlation** describes the extent to which the values of two variables are related. Two variables might be **perfectly** correlated, **partly** correlated or **uncorrelated**. The correlation may be **positive** or **negative**. The degree of correlation between two variables can be measured using the **Pearsonian coefficient of correlation**, **r**. The **coefficient of determination** indicates the variations in the dependent variable that can be explained by variations in the independent variable.

- A **time series** is a series of figures or values recorded over time. A time series has four components: a **trend**, **seasonal variations**, **cyclical variations** and **random variations**. **Trend** values can be determined by a process of **moving averages**. **Seasonal variations** can be estimated using the **additive** model or the **proportional** (**multiplicative**) model.

- **Forecasts** can be made by calculating a **trend line** (using moving averages or linear regression), using the trend line to forecast future trend line values, and adjusting these values by the **average seasonal variation** applicable to the future period.

- **Spreadsheet packages** can be used to build business models to assist the forecasting and planning process.

- **'What if' analysis** involves changing the values of the forecast variables to see the effect on the forecast outcome. The information provided helps managers to better understand the sensitivity of the forecast to the value of the variables.

- Management should have reasonable confidence in their estimates and forecasts. The assumptions on which the forecasts/estimates are based should be properly understood and the methods used to make a forecast or estimate should be in keeping with the nature, quantity and reliability of the data on which the forecast or estimate will be based. There is no point in using a 'sophisticated' technique with unreliable data; on the other hand, if there is a lot of accurate data about historical costs, it would be a waste of the data to use the scatter diagram method for cost estimating.

Quick quiz

1   In the equation Y = a + bX, which is the dependent variable?

    A   Y
    B   a
    C   b
    D   X

2   *Fill in the missing words.*

    Extrapolation involves using a .... of best .... to predict a value .... the two extreme points of the observed range.

3   Between sales of suntan cream and sales of cold drinks, one would expect (assuming spending money to be unlimited)

    A   positive, but spurious, correlation
    B   negative, but spurious, correlation
    C   positive correlation indicating direct causation
    D   negative correlation indicating direct causation

BPP PUBLISHING

4   Which of the following statements is/are true of the coefficient of determination?

	True	False
(a)		
(b)		
(c)		

(a)   It is the square of the Pearsonian coefficient of correlation

(b)   It can never quite equal 1

(c)   If it is high, this proves that variations in one variable cause variations in the other

5   *Choose the appropriate words from those highlighted.*

When using **regression analysis/analytical regression** for forecasting, the X variables are the **years (or days or months)/the level of sales (or costs)**.

6   What are the four components of a time series?

A   Trend, seasonal variations, cyclical variations, relative variations

B   Trend, systematic variations, cyclical variations, relative variations

C   Trend, systematic variations, seasonal variations, random variations

D   Trend, seasonal variations, cyclical variations, random variations

7   The multiplicative model expresses a time series as $Y = T + S + R$. *True or false?*

8   A time series for weeks 1 to 12 has been analysed into a trend and seasonal variations, using the additive model. The trend value is $84 + 0.7w$, where w is the week number. The actual value for week 9 is 88.7. What is the seasonal variation for week 9?

A   90.3

B   −1.6

C   1.6

D   6.3

Answers to quick quiz

1   A

2   Line; fit; outside.

3   A. When cold drinks sell well, so will suntan cream. Neither sales level causes the other; both are caused by the weather.

4   Statement (a) is true. The coefficient of determination is r^2
Statement (b) is false. r can reach 1 or −1, so r^2 can reach 1
Statement (c) is false. Correlation does not prove a causal link

5   regression analysis
years (or days or months)

6   D

7   False. The multiplicative model expresses a time series as $Y = T \times S \times R$

8   B. For week 9, the trend value is $84 + (0.7 \times 9) = 90.3$

The seasonal variation is actual − trend = 88.7 − 90.3, = −1.6, indicating that the value for week 9 is below what one might expect from the trend.

Now try the question below from the Exam Question Bank

Number	Level	Marks	Time
Q8	Introductory	n/a	25 mins

Chapter 7

BUDGETARY CONTROL AND PERFORMANCE MEASUREMENT

Topic list	Syllabus reference	Ability required
1 Fixed and flexible budgets	(ii)	Analysis/application
2 Preparing flexible budgets	(ii)	Analysis/application
3 Flexible budgets and budgetary control	(ii)	Analysis/application
4 Budget centres and budgetary control reports	(ii)	Analysis/application
5 Feedback and feedforward control mechanisms	(ii)	Analysis/application
6 Behavioural implications of budgeting	(ii)	Analysis/application
7 Participation and performance evaluation	(ii)	Analysis/application
8 The use of budgets as targets	(ii)	Analysis/application
9 The management accountant and motivation	(ii)	Analysis/application
10 The balanced scorecard	(ii)	Evaluation

Introduction

You should now be able to prepare **forecasts** using mathematical techniques and have a firm grasp of the budgeting process. This chapter continues the budgeting theme and looks at budgetary control.

Budgetary control is basically the comparison of actual results with budgeted results. Variances are calculated to identify the differences between actual and budgeted results and these differences are reported to management so that appropriate **action** can be taken.

Such a system relies upon a system of **flexible** (as opposed to **fixed**) **budgets**. Flexible budgets are vital for both planning and control and this chapter shows how they are constructed and their use in the overall budgetary control process. The topic should be familiar to you from your Paper 2 studies and so we will be concentrating on just the most complex areas.

The chapter then moves on to consider the **behavioural implications** of operating a budgetary control system. There has been a great deal of research into the behavioural implications of budgeting and, as in all studies of human behaviour, it is difficult to draw concrete conclusions. There is, however, one point which is agreed: **budgeting is more than a mathematical technique.**

The chapter concludes with a discussion of another aspect of performance evaluation: **the balanced scorecard.**

Learning outcomes covered in this chapter

- **Evaluate** performance using fixed and flexible budget reports
- **Discuss** the behavioural implications of planning and budgeting
- **Evaluate** the balanced scorecard

Syllabus content covered in this chapter

- Fixed and flexible budgeting
- Behavioural implications
- Balanced scorecard

1 FIXED AND FLEXIBLE BUDGETS   **Pilot paper**

1.1   The master budget prepared before the beginning of the budget period is known as the **fixed** budget. By the term 'fixed', we do not mean that the budget is kept unchanged. Revisions to a fixed master budget will be made if the situation so demands. The term 'fixed' means the following.

(a)   The budget is prepared on the basis of an estimated volume of production and an estimated volume of sales, but no plans are made for the event that actual volumes of production and sales may differ from budgeted volumes.

(b)   When actual volumes of production and sales during a control period (month or four weeks or quarter) are achieved, a fixed budget is not adjusted (in retrospect) to represent a new target for the new levels of activity.

1.2   The major purpose of a fixed budget lies in its use at the planning stage, when it seeks to define the broad objectives of the organisation.

KEY TERM

A **flexible budget** is 'A budget which, by recognising different cost behaviour patterns, is designed to change as volume of activity changes'.   (CIMA *Official Terminology*)

1.3   **Two uses of flexible budgets**

(a)   **At the planning stage**. For example, suppose that a company expects to sell 10,000 units of output during the next year. A master budget (the fixed budget) would be prepared on the basis of these expected volumes. However, if the company thinks that output and sales might be as low as 8,000 units or as high as 12,000 units, it may prepare **contingency** flexible budgets, at volumes of, say 8,000, 9,000, 11,000 and 12,000 units, and then assess the possible outcomes. This is an example of the use of **'what if?' analysis** that you studied in Chapter 6.

(b)   **Retrospectively**. At the end of each control period, flexible budgets can be used to compare actual results achieved with what results should have been under the circumstances. Flexible budgets are an essential factor in budgetary control.

(i)   Management needs to know about how good or bad actual performance has been. To provide a measure of performance, there must be a yardstick (budget/standard) against which actual performance can be measured.

(ii)   Every business is dynamic, and actual volumes of output cannot be expected to conform exactly to the fixed budget. Comparing actual costs directly with the fixed budget costs is meaningless.

(iii)   For useful control information, it is necessary to compare actual results at the actual level of activity achieved against the results that should have been expected at this level of activity, which are shown by the flexible budget.

2 PREPARING FLEXIBLE BUDGETS

Knowledge brought forward

The preparation of flexible budgets

- The first step in the preparation of a flexible budget is the determination of **cost behaviour patterns**, which means deciding whether costs are fixed, variable or semi-variable.

- Fixed costs will remain constant as activity levels change.

- For non-fixed costs, divide each cost figure by the related activity level. If the cost is a **linear variable cost**, the cost per unit will remain constant. If the cost is a **semi-variable cost**, the unit rate will reduce as activity levels increase.

- Split semi-variable costs into their fixed and variable components using the **high-low method** or the **scattergraph method**.

- Calculate the **budget cost allowance** for each cost item as budget cost allowance = budgeted fixed cost* + (number of units produced/sold × variable cost per unit)**.

   * nil for totally variable cost   ** nil for fixed cost

2.1 EXAMPLE: FIXED AND FLEXIBLE BUDGETS

Suppose that Gemma Ltd expects production and sales during the next year to be 90% of the company's output capacity, that is, 9,000 units of a single product. Cost estimates will be made using the high-low method and the following historical records of cost.

Units of output/sales	Cost of sales
9,800	£44,400
7,700	£38,100

The company's management is not certain that the estimate of sales is correct, and has asked for flexible budgets to be prepared at output and sales levels of 8,000 and 10,000 units. The sales price per unit has been fixed at £5.

Required

Prepare appropriate budgets.

2.2 SOLUTION

If we assume that within the range 8,000 to 10,000 units of sales, all costs are fixed, variable or mixed (in other words there are no stepped costs, material discounts, overtime premiums, bonus payments and so on) the fixed and flexible budgets would be based on the estimate of fixed and variable cost.

		£
Total cost of 9,800 units	=	44,400
Total cost of 7,700 units	=	38,100
Variable cost of 2,100 units	=	6,300

The variable cost per unit is £3.

		£
Total cost of 9,800 units	=	44,400
Variable cost of 9,800 units (9,800 × £3)	=	29,400
Fixed costs (all levels of output and sales)	=	15,000

2.3   The fixed budgets and flexible budgets can now be prepared as follows.

	Flexible budget *8,000 units* £	*Fixed budget* *9,000 units* £	*Flexible budget* *10,000 units* £
Sales (× £5)	40,000	45,000	50,000
Variable costs (× £3)	24,000	27,000	30,000
Contribution	16,000	18,000	20,000
Fixed costs	15,000	15,000	15,000
Profit	1,000	3,000	5,000

2.4   Have a go at the following question. It is more complicated than the last example because it includes inflation. You will need to recall your studies of index numbers from Paper 3(c) *Business Mathematics.*

Question 1

Rice and Faull Ltd has recorded the following total costs during the last five years.

Year	Output volume Units	Total cost £	Average price level index
0	65,000	145,000	100
1	80,000	179,000	112
2	90,000	209,100	123
3	60,000	201,600	144
4	75,000	248,000	160

The expected costs in year 5 when output is 85,000 units and the average price level index is 180 will be

A   £165,000   B   £185,625   C   £207,850   D   £297,000

Answer

The correct answer is D

Price levels should be adjusted to a common basis, say index level 100.

(a)

	Output	Total cost £	Cost at price level index = 100 £
High level	90,000 units	209,100 × (100/123)	= 170,000
Low level	60,000 units	201,600 × (100/144)	= 140,000
Variable cost	30,000 units		= 30,000

The variable cost is therefore £1 per unit.

(b)   Use the variable cost to determine the fixed cost.

	£
Total cost of 90,000 units (Index 100)	170,000
Variable cost of 90,000 units (× £1)	90,000
Fixed costs (Index 100)	80,000

(c)   Costs in year 5 for 85,000 units will be as follows.

	£
Variable costs (Index 100)	85,000
Fixed costs (Index 100)	80,000
Total costs (Index 100)	165,000

At year 5 price levels (Index 180) = £165,000 ×(180/100) = £297,000

> ### Exam focus point
>
> The pilot paper included a multiple choice question which required the use of the high-low method to analyse a semi-variable cost. The budget cost allowance had to be determined for a given output, but inflation was not involved on this occasion.

The need for flexible budgets

2.5 We have seen that flexible budgets may be prepared in order to plan for variations in the level of activity above or below the level set in the fixed budget. It has been suggested, however, that since many cost items in modern industry are fixed costs, the value of flexible budgets in planning is dwindling.

(a) In many manufacturing industries, plant costs (depreciation, rent and so on) are a very large proportion of total costs, and these tend to be fixed costs.

(b) Wage costs also tend to be fixed, because employees are generally guaranteed a basic wage for a working week of an agreed number of hours.

(c) With the growth of service industries, labour (wages or fixed salaries) and overheads will account for most of the costs of a business, and direct materials will be a relatively small proportion of total costs.

2.6 Flexible budgets are nevertheless necessary, and even if they are not used at the planning stage, they must be used for budgetary control variance analysis.

3 FLEXIBLE BUDGETS AND BUDGETARY CONTROL

> ### KEY TERM
>
> The CIMA *Official Terminology* defines **budgetary control** as 'The establishment of budgets relating the responsibilities of executives to the requirements of a policy, and the continuous comparison of actual with budgeted results, either to secure by individual action the objectives of that policy or to provide a basis for its revision'.

3.1 In other words, individual managers are held responsible for investigating differences between budgeted and actual results, and are then expected to take corrective action or amend the plan in the light of actual events.

3.2 It is therefore vital to ensure that valid comparisons are being made. Consider the following example.

3.3   Penny Ltd manufactures a single product, the Darcy. Budgeted results and actual results for
       May are as follows.

	Budget	Actual	Variance	
Production and sales of the Darcy (units)	7,500	8,200		
	£	£	£	
Sales revenue	75,000	81,000	6,000	(F)
Direct materials	22,500	23,500	1,000	(A)
Direct labour	15,000	15,500	500	(A)
Production overhead	22,500	22,800	300	(A)
Administration overhead	10,000	11,000	1,000	(A)
	70,000	72,800	2,800	(A)
Profit	5,000	8,200	3,200	(F)

Note. (F) denotes a favourable variance and (A) an unfavourable or adverse variance.

3.4   In this example, the variances are meaningless for the purposes of control. All costs were
       higher than budgeted but the volume of output was also higher; it is to be expected that
       actual variable costs would be greater those included in the fixed budget. However, it is not
       possible to tell how much of the increase is due to **poor cost control** and how much is due
       to the **increase in activity**.

3.5   Similarly it is not possible to tell how much of the increase in sales revenue is due to the
       increase in activity. Some of the difference may be due to a difference between budgeted
       and actual selling price but we are unable to tell from the analysis above.

3.6   For control purposes we need to know the answers to questions such as the following.

       •   Were actual costs higher than they should have been to produce and sell 8,200 Darcys?
       •   Was actual revenue satisfactory from the sale of 8,200 Darcys?

3.7   Instead of comparing actual results with a fixed budget which is based on a different level of
       activity to that actually achieved, the correct approach to budgetary control is to compare
       actual results with a budget which has been **flexed** to the actual activity level achieved.

3.8   Suppose that we have the following estimates of the behaviour of Penny Ltd's costs.

       (a)   Direct materials and direct labour are variable costs.

       (b)   Production overhead is a semi-variable cost, the budgeted cost for an activity level of
              10,000 units being £25,000.

       (c)   Administration overhead is a fixed cost.

       (d)   Selling prices are constant at all levels of sales.

3.9 The **budgetary control analysis** should therefore be as follows.

	Fixed budget	*Flexible budget*	*Actual results*	*Variance*
Production and sales (units)	7,500	8,200	8,200	
	£	£	£	£
Sales revenue	75,000	82,000 (W1)	81,000	1,000 (A)
Direct materials	22,500	24,600 (W2)	23,500	1,100 (F)
Direct labour	15,000	16,400 (W3)	15,500	900 (F)
Production overhead	22,500	23,200 (W4)	22,800	400 (F)
Administration overhead	10,000	10,000 (W5)	11,000	1,000 (A)
	70,000	74,200	72,800	1,400 (F)
Profit	5,000	7,800	8,200	400 (F)

Workings

1 Selling price per unit = £75,000 ÷ 7,500 = £10 per unit
  Flexible budget sales revenue = £10 × 8,200 = £82,000

2 Direct materials cost per unit = £22,500 ÷ 7,500 = £3
  Budget cost allowance = £3 × 8,200 = £24,600

3 Direct labour cost per unit = £15,000 ÷ 7,500 = £2
  Budget cost allowance = £2 × 8,200 = £16,400

4 Variable production overhead cost per unit
  = £(25,000 − 22,500)/(10,000 − 7,500)
  = £2,500/2,500 = £1 per unit
  ∴ Fixed production overhead cost = £22,500 − (7,500 × £1) = £15,000
  ∴ Budget cost allowance = £15,000 + (8,200 × £1) = £23,200

5 Administration overhead is a fixed cost and hence budget cost allowance = £10,000

3.10 **Comment**

(a) In selling 8,200 units, the expected profit should have been, not the fixed budget profit of £5,000, but the flexible budget profit of £7,800. Instead actual profit was £8,200 ie £400 more than we should have expected.

One of the reasons for this improvement is that, given output and sales of 8,200 units, the cost of resources (material, labour etc) was £1,400 lower than expected. (A comparison of the fixed budget and the actual costs in Paragraph 3.3 appeared to indicate that costs were not being controlled since all of the variances were adverse).

In Chapter 2 you saw how these total cost variances can be analysed to reveal how much of the variance is due to lower resource prices and how much is due to efficient resource usage.

(b) The sales revenue was, however, £1,000 less than expected because a lower price was charged than budgeted.

We know this because flexing the budget has eliminated the effect of changes in the volume sold, which is the only other factor that can affect sales revenue. You have probably already realised that this variance of £1,000 (A) is a **selling price variance**.

The lower selling price could have been caused by the increase in the volume sold (to sell the additional 700 units the selling price had to fall below £10 per unit). We do not know if this is the case but without flexing the budget we could not know that a different selling price to that budgeted had been charged. Our initial analysis in Paragraph 3.3 had appeared to indicate that sales revenue was ahead of budget.

3.11 The difference of £400 between the flexible budget profit of £7,800 at a production level of 8,200 units and the actual profit of £8,200 is due to the net effect of cost savings of £1,400 and lower than expected sales revenue (by £1,000).

3.12 The difference between the original budgeted profit of £5,000 and the actual profit of £8,200 is the total of the following.

(a) The savings in resource costs/lower than expected sales revenue (a net total of £400 as indicated by the difference between the flexible budget and the actual results).

(b) The effect of producing and selling 8,200 units instead of 7,500 units (a gain of £2,800 as indicated by the difference between the fixed budget and the flexible budget). This is the **sales volume contribution variance**.

3.13 A **full variance analysis statement** would be as follows.

	£	£
Fixed budget profit		5,000
Variances		
Sales volume	2,800 (F)	
Selling price	1,000 (A)	
Direct materials cost	1,100 (F)	
Direct labour cost	900 (F)	
Production overhead cost	400 (F)	
Administration overhead cost	1,000 (A)	
		3,200 (F)
Actual profit		8,200

3.14 If management believes that any of the variances are large enough to justify it, they will investigate the reasons for their occurrence to see whether any corrective action is necessary. You learned about identifying the significance of variances in Chapter 4.

Exam focus point

A narrative question in the pilot paper required a critical discussion of the format of an operating statement that was presented in the question. Basically, the statement was inadequate because it used a fixed budget comparison. Candidates were expected to discuss why this was inappropriate and to suggest and explain the use of a flexible budgeting system.

Question 2

Flower Ltd budgeted to sell 200 units and produced the following budget.

	£	£
Sales		71,400
Variable costs		
Labour	31,600	
Material	12,600	
		44,200
Contribution		27,200
Fixed costs		18,900
Profit		8,300

Actual sales turned out to be 230 units, which were sold for £69,000. Actual expenditure on labour was £27,000 and on material £24,000. Fixed costs totalled £10,000.

Required

Prepare a flexible budget that will be useful for management control purposes.

Answer

	Budget 200 units £	Bu Budget per unit £	Flexed budget 230 units	Actual 230 units £	Variance
Sales	71,400	357	82,110	69,000	13,110 (A)
Variable costs					
Labour	31,600	158	36,340	27,000	9,340 (F)
Material	12,600	63	14,490	24,000	9,510 (A)
	44,200	221	50,830	51,000	
Contribution	27,200	136	31,280	18,000	13,280 (A)
Fixed costs	18,900		18,900	10,000	8,900 (F)
Profit	8,300		12,380	8,000	4,380 (A)

Flexible budgets, control and computers

3.15 The production of flexible budget control reports is an area in which computers can provide invaluable assistance to the cost accountant, calculating flexed budget figures using fixed budget and actual results data and hence providing detailed variance analysis. For control information to be of any value it must be produced quickly: speed is one of the many advantages of computers.

Exam focus point

The pilot paper contained a ten-mark part of a question which required an explanation of how a spreadsheet could be set up to produce a flexed budget and variance calculations.

3.16 In all the flexible budgets we have discussed so far, the budgets have been flexed according to the volume of output in units. Later in this text you will learn about activity based budgeting (ABB), which may identify other appropriate bases for flexing the budget. These alternative bases are known as cost drivers.

4 BUDGET CENTRES AND BUDGETARY CONTROL REPORTS

KEY TERM

A **budget centre** is defined in CIMA *Official Terminology* as 'A section of an entity for which control may be exercised and budgets prepared'.

4.1 Budgetary control is based around a system of budget centres. Each budget centre will have its own budget and a manager will be responsible for managing the budget centre and ensuring that the budget is met.

Budgetary control reports

4.2 If the **budget holders** (managers of budget centres) are to attempt to meet budgets they must receive regular budgetary control reports so that they can monitor the budget centre's operations and take any necessary control action.

5 FEEDBACK AND FEEDFORWARD CONTROL MECHANISMS

Feedback

5.1 The term 'feedback' is used to describe both the process of reporting back control information to management and the control information itself. In a business organisation, it is information produced from within the organisation (**management control reports**) with the purpose of helping management and other employees with control decisions.

(a) **Single loop feedback**, normally expressed as feedback, is the feedback of relatively small variations between actual and plan in order that corrective action can bring performance in line with planned results. This implies that the existing plans will not change. This type of feedback is associated with budgetary control and standard costing.

(b) **Double loop feedback**, also known as **higher level feedback**, ensures that plans, budgets, organisational structures and the control systems themselves are revised to meet changes in conditions.

(c) Feedback will most often be **negative:** targets were missed and this was **not** what was required. It may, however, be **positive:** targets were missed, but other targets were hit which were better than those we were aiming at. Negative feedback would result in control action to get back onto target. Positive feedback means that the target should be moved.

Feedforward control

5.2 Most control systems make use of a comparison between results of the current period (historical costs) and the planned results. Past events are therefore used as a means of controlling or adjusting future activity.

5.3 Consider, however, a **cash budget**. This is used to identify likely peaks and troughs in cash balances, and if it seems probable that, say, a higher overdraft facility will be needed later in the year, control action will be taken in advance of the actual need, to make sure that the facility will be available. This is an example of **feedforward control**, that is, control based on comparing original targets or actual results with a **forecast** of future results. You saw an example of a cash budget being used for feedforword control in Chapter 5.

5.4 The 'information revolution', which has arisen from computer technology, management information systems theory and the growing use of quantitative techniques has widened the scope for the use of this control technique. Forecasting models can be constructed which enable regular revised forecasts to be prepared about what is now likely to happen in view of changes in key variables (such as sales demand, wage rates and so on). You studied forecasting in Chapter 6.

5.5 If regular forecasts are prepared, managers will have both the current forecast and the original plan to guide their action. The original plan may or may not be achievable in view of the changing circumstances. The current forecast indicates what is expected to happen in view of these circumstances.

5.6 **Examples of control comparisons**

Step 1. **Current forecast versus plan.** What action must be taken to get back to the plan, given the differences between the current forecast and the plan? Is any control action worthwhile?

Step 2. If **control action** is **planned,** the current forecast will need to be amended to take account of the effects of the control action and a **revised forecast** prepared.

Step 3. The next comparison should then be **revised forecast versus plan** to determine whether the plan is now expected to be achieved.

Step 4. A comparison between the **original current forecast** and the **revised forecast** will show what the expected effect of the control action will be.

Step 5. At the **end of a control period**, actual results will be analysed and two comparisons may be made.

- **Actual results versus the revised forecast.** Why did differences between the two occur?

- **Actual results so far in the year versus the plan.** How close are actual results to the plan?

Step 6. At the same time, a **new current forecast** should be prepared, and the cycle of comparisons and control action may begin again.

It is in this way that costs are constantly controlled and monitored.

6 BEHAVIOURAL IMPLICATIONS OF BUDGETING

6.1 The purpose of a budgetary control system is to assist management in planning and controlling the resources of their organisation by providing appropriate control information. The information will only be valuable, however, if it is interpreted correctly and used purposefully by managers *and* employees.

6.2 The correct use of control information therefore depends not only on the content of the information itself, but also on the behaviour of its recipients. This is because control in business is exercised by people. Their attitude to control information will colour their views on what they should do with it and a number of behavioural problems can arise.

(a) The **managers who set the budget** or standards are **often not the managers** who are then made **responsible for achieving budget targets.**

(b) The **goals of the organisation as a whole,** as expressed in a budget, **may not coincide with the personal aspirations of individual managers**.

(c) **Control is applied at different stages by different people**. A supervisor might get weekly control reports, and act on them; his superior might get monthly control reports, and decide to take different control action. Different managers can get in each others' way, and resent the interference from others.

Motivation

6.3 Motivation is what makes people behave in the way that they do. It comes from individual attitudes, or group attitudes. Individuals will be motivated by personal desires and interests. These may be in line with the objectives of the organisation, and some people 'live for their jobs'. Other individuals see their job as a chore, and their motivations will be unrelated to the objectives of the organisation they work for.

6.4 It is therefore vital that the goals of management and the employees harmonise with the goals of the organisation as a whole. This is known as **goal congruence**. Although obtaining goal congruence is essentially a behavioural problem, **it is possible to design and run a budgetary control system which will go some way towards ensuring that goal congruence is achieved**. Managers and employees must therefore be favourably disposed towards the budgetary control system so that it can operate efficiently.

6.5 The management accountant should therefore try to ensure that employees have positive attitudes towards **setting budgets, implementing budgets** (that is, putting the organisation's plans into practice) and feedback of results (**control information**).

Poor attitudes when setting budgets

6.6 **If managers are involved in preparing a budget,** poor attitudes or hostile behaviour towards the budgetary control system can begin at the **planning stage.**

(a) Managers may **complain that they are too busy** to spend much time on budgeting.

(b) They may **build 'slack' into their expenditure estimates**.

(c) They may argue that **formalising a budget plan on paper is too restricting** and that managers should be allowed flexibility in the decisions they take.

(d) They may set budgets for their budget centre and **not coordinate** their own plans with those of other budget centres.

(e) They may **base future plans on past results**, instead of using the opportunity for formalised planning to look at alternative options and new ideas.

6.7 On the other hand, **managers may not be involved in the budgeting process**. Organisational goals may not be communicated to them and they might have their budget decided for them by senior management or administrative decision. It is **hard for people to be motivated to achieve targets set by someone else.**

Poor attitudes when putting plans into action

6.8 Poor attitudes also arise **when a budget is implemented**.

(a) Managers might **put in only just enough effort** to achieve budget targets, without trying to beat targets.

(b) A formal budget might **encourage rigidity and discourage flexibility**.

(c) **Short-term planning** in a budget **can draw attention away from the longer-term consequences** of decisions.

(d) There might be **minimal cooperation and communication** between managers.

(e) Managers will often try to make sure that they **spend up to their full budget allowance, and do not overspend,** so that they will not be accused of having asked for too much spending allowance in the first place.

Poor attitudes and the use of control information

6.9 The **attitude of managers towards the accounting control information** they receive **might reduce the information's effectiveness**.

(a) Management accounting control reports could well be seen as having a relatively **low priority** in the list of management tasks. Managers might take the view that they have more pressing jobs on hand than looking at routine control reports.

(b) Managers might **resent control information**; they may see it as **part of a system of trying to find fault with their work**. This resentment is likely to be particularly strong when budgets or standards are imposed on managers without allowing them to participate in the budget-setting process.

(c) If budgets are seen as **pressure devices** to push managers into doing better, control reports will be resented.

(d) Managers **may not understand the information** in the control reports, because they are unfamiliar with accounting terminology or principles.

(e) Managers might have a **false sense of what their objectives should be**. A production manager might consider it more important to maintain quality standards regardless of cost. He would then dismiss adverse expenditure variances as inevitable and unavoidable.

(f) **If there are flaws in the system of recording actual costs**, managers will dismiss control information as unreliable.

(g) **Control information** might be **received weeks after the end of the** period to which it relates, in which case managers might regard it as out-of-date and no longer useful.

(h) Managers might be **held responsible for variances outside their control**.

6.10 It is therefore obvious that accountants and senior management should try to implement systems that are acceptable to budget holders and which produce positive effects.

Pay as a motivator

6.11 Many researchers agree that **pay can be an important motivator**, when there is a formal link between higher pay (or other rewards, such as promotion) and achieving budget targets. Individuals are likely to work harder to achieve budget if they know that they will be rewarded for their successful efforts. There are, however, problems with using pay as an incentive.

(a) A serious problem that can arise is that **formal reward and performance evaluation systems can encourage dysfunctional behaviour**. Many investigations have noted the tendency of managers to pad their budgets either in anticipation of cuts by superiors or to make the subsequent variances more favourable. And there are numerous examples of managers making decisions in response to performance indices, even though the decisions are contrary to the wider purposes of the organisation.

(b) The targets must be challenging, but fair, otherwise individuals will become dissatisfied. **Pay can be a demotivator as well as a motivator!**

7 PARTICIPATION AND PERFORMANCE EVALUATION

Participation

7.1 It has been argued that **participation** in the budgeting process **will improve motivation** and so will improve the quality of budget decisions and the efforts of individuals to achieve their budget targets (although obviously this will depend on the personality of the individual, the nature of the task (narrowly defined or flexible) and the organisational culture).

7.2 There are basically two ways in which a budget can be set: from the **top down** (imposed budget) or from the **bottom up** (participatory budget).

BPP PUBLISHING

Imposed style of budgeting

> **KEY TERM**
>
> An **imposed/top-down budget** is 'A budget allowance which is set without permitting the ultimate budget holder to have the opportunity to participate in the budgeting process'.
>
> (CIMA *Official Terminology*)

7.3 In this approach to budgeting, **top management prepare a budget with little or no input from operating personnel** which is then imposed upon the employees who have to work to the budgeted figures.

7.4 **The times when imposed budgets are effective**

- In newly-formed organisations
- In very small businesses
- During periods of economic hardship
- When operational managers lack budgeting skills
- When the organisation's different units require precise coordination

7.5 There are, of course, advantages and disadvantages to this style of setting budgets.

(a) **Advantages**

- Strategic plans are likely to be incorporated into planned activities.
- They enhance the coordination between the plans and objectives of divisions.
- They use senior management's awareness of total resource availability.
- They decrease the input from inexperienced or uninformed lower-level employees.
- They decrease the period of time taken to draw up the budgets.

(b) **Disadvantages**

(i) Dissatisfaction, defensiveness and low morale amongst employees. It is hard for people to be motivated to achieve targets set by somebody else.

(ii) The feeling of team spirit may disappear.

(iii) The acceptance of organisational goals and objectives could be limited

(iv) The feeling of the budget as a punitive device could arise.

(v) Managers who are performing operations on a day to day basis are likely to have a better understanding of what is achievable.

(vi) Unachievable budgets could result if consideration is not given to local operating and political environments. This applies particularly to overseas divisions.

(vii) Lower-level management initiative may be stifled.

Participative style of budgeting

> **KEY TERM**
>
> **Participative/bottom-up budgeting** is 'A budgeting system in which all budget holders are given the opportunity to participate in setting their own budgets'.
>
> (CIMA *Official Terminology*)

7.6 In this approach to budgeting, **budgets are developed by lower-level managers who then submit the budgets to their superiors.** The budgets are based on the lower-level managers' perceptions of what is achievable and the associated necessary resources.

Question 3

In what circumstances might participative budgets *not* be effective?

A   In centralised organisations
B   In well-established organisations
C   In very large businesses
D   During periods of economic affluence

Answer

The correct answer is A.

An imposed budget is likely to be most effective in a centralised organisation.

As well as in the circumstances in B, C and D, participative budgets are also effective when operational management have strong budgeting skills and when the organisation's different units act autonomously.

7.7 **Advantages of participative budgets**

- They are based on information from employees most familiar with the department.
- Knowledge spread among several levels of management is pulled together.
- Morale and motivation is improved.
- They increase operational managers' commitment to organisational objectives.
- In general they are more realistic.
- Co-ordination between units is improved.
- Specific resource requirements are included.
- Senior managers' overview is mixed with operational level details.
- Individual managers' aspiration levels are more likely to be taken into account.

7.8 **Disadvantages of participative budgets**

- They consume more time.
- Changes implemented by senior management may cause dissatisfaction.
- Budgets may be unachievable if managers are not qualified to participate.
- They may cause managers to introduce budgetary slack and budget bias.
- They can support 'empire building' by subordinates.
- An earlier start to the budgeting process could be required.
- Managers may set 'easy' budgets to ensure that they are achievable.

Negotiated style of budgeting

KEY TERM

A **negotiated budget** is 'A budget in which budget allowances are set largely on the basis of negotiations between budget holders and those to whom they report'.

(CIMA *Official Terminology*)

7.9 At the two extremes, budgets can be dictated from above or simply emerge from below but, in practice, different levels of management often agree budgets by a process of negotiation.

In the imposed budget approach, operational managers will try to negotiate with senior managers the budget targets which they consider to be unreasonable or unrealistic. Likewise senior management usually review and revise budgets presented to them under a participative approach through a process of negotiation with lower level managers. **Final budgets are therefore most likely to lie between what top management would really like and what junior managers believe is feasible.** The budgeting process is hence a **bargaining process** and it is this bargaining which is of vital importance, **determining whether the budget is an effective management tool or simply a clerical device.**

Performance evaluation

7.10 A very important **source of motivation to perform well** (to achieve budget targets, perhaps, or to eliminate variances) is, not surprisingly, being **kept informed about how actual results are progressing, and how actual results compare with target.** Individuals should not be kept in the dark about their performance.

7.11 The information fed back about actual results should have the qualities of good information.

Question 4

Cast your mind back to your earlier studies. Which of the following is not a quality of good information?

A   Relevant
B   Complete
C   Timely
D   Cheap

Answer

The correct answer is D.

Good information is not necessarily cheap. The cost of providing it should be less than the value of the benefits it provides, however.

Here are the qualities of good information.

- Relevance
- Accuracy
- Inspires confidence
- Timely
- Cost of provision less than the value of benefits provided

- Completeness
- Clarity
- Appropriately communicated (channel and recipient)
- Manageable volume

7.12 **Features of feedback**

(a) Reports should be **clear** and **comprehensive**.

(b) The 'exception principle' should be applied so that **significant variances** are highlighted for investigation.

(c) Reports should identify the **controllable** costs and revenues, which are the items that can be directly influenced by the manager who receives the report. It can be demotivating if managers feel that they are being held responsible for items which are outside their control and which they are unable to influence.

(d) Reports should be **timely**, which means they must be produced in good time to allow the individual to take control action before any adverse results get much worse.

(e) Information should be **accurate** (although only accurate enough for its purpose as there is no need to go into unnecessary detail for pointless accuracy).

(f) Reports should be communicated to the manager who has **responsibility** and **authority** to act on the matter.

7.13 Surprisingly research evidence suggests that **all too often accounting performance measures lead to a lack of goal congruence**. Managers seek to improve their performance on the basis of the indicator used, even if this is not in the best interests of the organisation as a whole. For example, a production manager may be encouraged to achieve and maintain high production levels and to reduce costs, particularly if his or her bonus is linked to these factors. Such a manager is likely to be highly motivated. But the need to maintain high production levels could lead to high levels of slow-moving stock, resulting in an adverse effect on the company's cash flow.

7.14 The **impact of an accounting system on managerial performance** depends ultimately on how the information is used. Research by Hopwood has shown that there are three distinct ways of using budgetary information to evaluate managerial performance.

Style of evaluation	Comment
Budget constrained	'The manager's performance is primarily evaluated upon the basis of his ability to continually meet the budget on a short-term basis. This criterion of performance is stressed at the expense of other valued and important criteria and the manager will receive unfavourable feedback from his superior if, for instance, his actual costs exceed the budgeted costs, regardless of other considerations.'
Profit conscious	'The manager's performance is evaluated on the basis of his ability to increase the general effectiveness of his unit's operations in relation to the long-term purposes of the organisation. For instance, at the cost centre level one important aspect of this ability concerns the attention which he devotes to reducing long-run costs. For this purpose, however, the budgetary information has to be used with great care in a rather flexible manner.'
Non-accounting	'The budgetary information plays a relatively unimportant part in the superior's evaluation of the manager's performance.'

7.15 A summary of the effects of the three styles of evaluation is as follows.

	Style of evaluation		
	Budget constrained	*Profit conscious*	*Non-accounting*
Involvement with costs	HIGH	HIGH	LOW
Job-related tension	HIGH	MEDIUM	MEDIUM
Manipulation of the accounting reports (**bias**)	EXTENSIVE	LITTLE	LITTLE
Relations with the supervisor	POOR	GOOD	GOOD
Relations with colleagues	POOR	GOOD	GOOD

Research has shown no clear preference for one style over another.

Budgetary slack

KEY TERM

Budgetary slack is the difference between the minimum necessary costs and the costs built into the budget or actually incurred.

7.16 In the process of preparing budgets, managers might **deliberately overestimate costs and underestimate sales**, so that they will not be blamed in the future for overspending and poor results.

In controlling actual operations, managers must then **ensure that their spending rises to meet their budget**, otherwise they will be 'blamed' for careless budgeting.

7.17 A typical situation is for a manager to **pad the budget** and waste money on non-essential expenses so that he uses all his budget allowances. The reason behind his action is the fear that unless the allowance is fully spent it will be reduced in future periods thus making his job more difficult as the future reduced budgets will not be so easy to attain. Because inefficiency and slack are allowed for in budgets, achieving a budget target means only that costs have remained within the accepted levels of inefficient spending.

7.18 **Conversely**, it has been noted that, after a run of mediocre results, some managers **deliberately overstate revenues and understate cost estimates**, no doubt feeling the need to make an immediate favourable impact by promising better performance in the future. They may merely delay problems, however, as the managers may well be censured when they fail to hit these optimistic targets.

8 THE USE OF BUDGETS AS TARGETS

8.1 Once decided, budgets become targets. As targets, they can motivate managers to achieve a high level of performance. But **how difficult should targets be**? And how might people react to targets of differing degrees of difficulty in achievement?

(a) There is likely to be a **demotivating** effect where an **ideal standard** of performance is set, because adverse efficiency variances will always be reported.

(b) A **low standard of efficiency** is also **demotivating**, because there is no sense of achievement in attaining the required standards, and there will be no impetus for employees to try harder to do better than this.

(c) A **budgeted level of attainment** could be 'normal': that is, the **same as the level that has been achieved in the past**. Arguably, this level will be **too low**. It might **encourage budgetary slack**.

8.2 It has been argued that **each individual has a personal 'aspiration level'**. This is a level of performance in a task with which the individual is familiar, which the individual undertakes for himself to reach. This aspiration level might be quite challenging and if individuals in a work group all have similar aspiration levels it should be possible to incorporate these levels within the official operating standards.

8.3 Some care should be taken, however, in applying this.

(a) If a manager's **tendency to achieve success is stronger than the tendency to avoid failure**, budgets with **targets of intermediate levels of difficulty** are the most **motivating**, and stimulate a manager to better performance levels. Budgets which are either too easy to achieve or too difficult are de-motivating, and managers given such targets achieve relatively low levels of performance.

(b) A manager's **tendency to avoid failure might be stronger than the tendency to achieve success**. (This is likely in an organisation in which the budget is used as a pressure device on subordinates by senior managers). Managers might then be discouraged from trying to achieve budgets of intermediate difficulty and tend to avoid taking on such tasks, resulting in poor levels of performance, worse than if budget targets were either easy or very difficult to achieve.

8.4 It has therefore been suggested that in a situation where budget targets of an intermediate difficulty *are* motivating, such targets ought to be set if the purpose of budgets is to motivate; however, although budgets which are set for **motivational purposes** need to be stated in terms of **aspirations rather than expectations**, budgets for planning and decision purposes need to be stated in terms of the best available estimate of expected actual performance. The **solution** might therefore be to have **two budgets**.

(a) A **budget for planning and decision making based on reasonable expectations**.

(b) A second **budget for motivational purposes**, with **more difficult targets of performance** (that is, targets of an intermediate level of difficulty).

These two budgets might be called an **'expectations budget'** and an **'aspirations budget'** respectively.

9 THE MANAGEMENT ACCOUNTANT AND MOTIVATION

9.1 We have seen that budgets serve many purposes, but in some instances their purposes can conflict and have an effect on management behaviour. Management and the management accountant therefore require strategies and methods for dealing with the resulting tensions and conflict. For example, should targets be adjusted for uncontrollable and unforeseeable environmental influence? But what is then the effect on motivation if employees view performance standards as changeable?

9.2 **Can performance measures** and the related budgetary control system ever **motivate managers** towards achieving the organisation's goals?

(a) Accounting measures of performance **can't provide a comprehensive assessment** of what a person has achieved for the organisation.

(b) It is unfair as it is usually **impossible to segregate controllable and uncontrollable components of performance**.

(c) Accounting **reports tend to concentrate on short-term achievements**, to the exclusion of the long-term effects.

(d) Many accounting **reports try to serve several different purposes**, and in trying to satisfy several needs actually satisfy none properly.

9.3 The management accountant does not have the authority to do much on his or her own to improve hostile or apathetic attitudes to control information. There has to be support, either from senior management or from budget centre managers. However, the management accountant can do quite a lot to improve and then maintain the standard of a budgetary control reporting system.

(a) **How senior management can offer support**

   (i) Making sure that a **system of responsibility accounting is adopted**. We will discuss this in the next chapter.

   (ii) Allowing **managers to have a say in formulating their budgets**.

   (iii) Offering **incentives** to managers who meet budget targets.

   (iv) **Not regarding budgetary control information as a way of apportioning blame.**

(b) **Budget centre managers should accept their responsibilities.** In-house training courses could be held to encourage a collective, cooperative and positive attitude amongst managers.

(c) **How the management accountant can improve** (or maintain) the **quality of the budgetary control system**

   (i) **Develop a working relationship with operational managers,** going out to meet them and discussing the control reports.

   (ii) **Explain the meaning of budgets and control reports.**

   (iii) **Keep accounting jargon in these reports to a minimum.**

   (iv) Make **reports clear and to the point,** for example using the principle of reporting by exception.

   (v) Provide control information with a **minimum of delay.**

   (vi) **Make control information as useful as possible,** by distinguishing between directly attributable and controllable costs over which a manager should have influence and apportioned or fixed costs which are unavoidable or uncontrollable.

   (vii) Make sure that **actual costs are recorded accurately.**

   (viii) Ensure that **budgets are up-to-date**, either by having a system of rolling budgets, or else by updating budgets or standards as necessary, and ensuring that standards are 'fair' so that control information is realistic.

ATTENTION!

There are no ideal solutions to the conflicts caused by the operation of a budgetary control system. Management and the management accountant have to develop their own ways of dealing with them, taking into account their organisation, their business and the personalities involved.

Question 5

Discuss the behavioural aspects of participation in the budgeting process and any difficulties you might envisage.

Answer

The level of participation in the budgeting process can vary from zero participation to a process of group decision making. There are a number of behavioural aspects of participation to consider.

(a) **Communication.** Managers cannot be expected to achieve targets if they do not know what those targets are. Communication of targets is made easier if managers have participated in the budgetary process from the beginning.

(b) **Motivation**. Managers are likely to be better motivated to achieve a budget if they have been involved in compiling it, rather than having a dictatorial budget imposed on them.

(c) **Realistic targets**. A target must be achievable and accepted as realistic if it is to be a motivating factor. A manager who has been involved in setting targets is more likely to accept them as realistic. In addition, managers who are close to the operation of their departments may be more aware of the costs and potential savings in running it.

(d) **Goal congruence**. One of the best ways of achieving goal congruence is to involve managers in the preparation of their own budgets, so that their personal goals can be taken into account in setting targets.

Although participative budgeting has many advantages, difficulties might also arise.

(a) **Pseudo-participation**. Participation may not be genuine, but merely a pretence at involving managers in the preparation of their budgets. Managers may feel that their contribution is being ignored, or that the participation consists of merely obtaining their agreement to a budget which has already been decided. If this is the case then managers are likely to be more demotivated than if there is no participation at all.

(b) **Coordination**. If participative budgeting is well managed it can improve the coordination of the preparation of the various budgets. There is, however, a danger that too many managers will become involved so that communication becomes difficult and the process become complex.

(c) **Training**. Some managers may not possess the necessary skill to make an effective contribution to the preparation of their budgets. Additional training may be necessary, with the consequent investment of money and time. It may also be necessary to train managers to understand the purposes and advantages of participation.

(d) **Slack**. If budgets are used in a punitive fashion for control purposes then managers will be tempted to build in extra expenditure to provide a 'cushion' against overspending. It is easier for them to build in slack in a participative system.

10 THE BALANCED SCORECARD

10.1 So far in our discussion we have focussed on performance measurement and control from a financial point of view. Another approach, originally developed by Kaplan and Norton, is the use of what is called a 'balanced scorecard' consisting of a **variety of indicators both financial and non-financial.**

KEY TERM

The **balanced scorecard approach** is 'An approach to the provision of information to management to assist strategic policy formulation and achievement. It emphasises the need to provide the user with a set of information which addresses all relevant areas of performance in an objective and unbiased fashion. The information provided may include both financial and non-financial elements, and cover areas such as profitability, customer satisfaction, internal efficiency and innovation.' (CIMA *Official Terminology*)

10.2 The balanced scorecard focuses on **four different perspectives,** as follows.

Perspective	Question	Explanation
Customer	What do existing and new customers value from us?	Gives rise to targets that matter to customers: cost, quality, delivery, inspection, handling and so on.
Internal	What processes must we excel at to achieve our financial and customer objectives?	Aims to improve internal processes and decision making.
Innovation and learning	Can we continue to improve and create future value?	Considers the business's capacity to maintain its competitive position through the acquisition of new skills and the development of new products.
Financial	How do we create value for our shareholders?	Covers traditional measures such as growth, profitability and shareholder value but set through talking to the shareholder or shareholders direct.

Performance targets are set once the key areas for improvement have been identified, and the balanced scorecard is the **main monthly report**.

10.3 The scorecard is '**balanced**' in the sense that managers are required to **think in terms of all four perspectives**, to **prevent improvements being made in one area at the expense of** another.

10.4 The types of measure which may be monitored under each of the four perspectives include the following. The list is not exhaustive but it will give you an idea of the possible scope of a balanced scorecard approach. The measures selected, particularly within the internal perspective, will vary considerably with the type of organisation and its objectives.

Perspective	Measures	
Customer	• New customers acquired	• On-time deliveries
	• Customer complaints	• Returns
Internal	• Quality control rejects	• Speed of producing management information
	• Average set-up time	
Innovation and learning	• Labour turnover rate	
	• Percentage of revenue generated by new products and services	
	• Average time taken to develop new products and services	
Financial	• Return on capital employed	• Revenue growth
	• Cash flow	• Earnings per share

10.5 Broadbent and Cullen (in Berry, Broadbent and Otley, ed, *Management Control*, 1995) identify the following **important features** of this approach.

- It looks at both **internal and external matters** concerning the organisation.
- It is **related to the key elements of a company's strategy**.
- **Financial and non-financial measures** are linked together.

10.6 The balanced scorecard approach may be particularly useful for performance measurement in organisations which are unable to use simple profit as a performance measure. For example the **public sector** has long been forced to use a **wide range of performance indicators,** which can be formalised with a balanced scorecard approach.

Question 6

To which perspective of the balanced scorecard could the measure 'training days per employee' be most appropriately applied?

A   Customer
B   Internal
C   Innovation and learning
D   Financial

Answer

The correct answer is C.

Problems

10.7   As with all techniques, problems can arise when it is applied.

Problem	Explanation
Conflicting measures	Some measures in the scorecard such as research funding and cost reduction may naturally conflict. It is often difficult to determine the balance which will achieve the best results.
Selecting measures	Not only do appropriate measures have to be devised but the number of measures used must be agreed. Care must be taken that the impact of the results is not lost in a sea of information.
Expertise	Measurement is only useful if it initiates appropriate action. Non-financial managers may have difficulty with the usual profit measures. With more measures to consider this problem will be compounded.
Interpretation	Even a financially-trained manager may have difficulty in putting the figures into an overall perspective.

BPP
PUBLISHING

Chapter roundup

- **Fixed budgets** remain unchanged regardless of the level of activity; **flexible budgets** are designed to flex with the level of activity. Comparison of a fixed budget with the actual results for a different level of activity is of little use for control purposes. Flexible budgets should be used to show what cost and revenues should have been for the actual level of activity.

- Budgetary control is based around a system of **budget centres**. Each centre has its own budget which is the responsibility of the **budget holder**.

- **Feedback** describes both the process of reporting back control information to management and the control information itself.

- **Feedforward control** is based on comparing original targets or actual results with a **forecast** of future results.

- Used correctly a budgetary control system can **motivate** but it can also produce undesirable **negative reactions**.

- There are basically two ways in which a budget can be set: from the top down (imposed budget) or from the **bottom up** (**participatory** budget). Many writers refer to a third style (negotiated).

- There are three ways of using budgetary information to evaluate managerial performance (**budget constrained style**, **profit conscious style**, **non-accounting style**).

- In certain situations it is useful to prepare an **expectations budget** and an **aspirations budget**.

- Management and the management accountant require strategies and methods for dealing with the **tensions** and **conflict** resulting from the **conflicting purposes** of a budget.

- The **balanced scorecard approach** to the provision of information focuses on four different perspectives: customer, financial, internal, innovation and learning.

Quick quiz

1   *Fill in the blanks.*

A flexible budget is a budget which, by recognising ...., is designed to .... as the level of activity changes.

2   An extract of the costs incurred at two different activity levels is shown. Classify the costs according to their behaviour patterns and show the budget cost allowance for an activity of 1,500 units.

		1,000 units £	2,000 units £	Type of cost	Budget cost allowance for 1,500 units £
(a)	Fuel	3,000	6,000	....	....
(b)	Photocopying	9,500	11,000	....	....
(c)	Heating	2,400	2,400	....	....
(d)	Direct wages	6,000	8,000	....	....

3   Feedforward control is based on comparing original targets or actual results with a forecast of future results. *True or false?*

4   *Match the descriptions to the budgeting style.*

Description

(a)   Budget allowances are set without the involvement of the budget holder

(b)   All budget holders are involved in setting their own budgets

(c)   Budget allowances are set on the basis of discussions between budget holders and those to whom they report

Budgeting style

Negotiated budgeting
Participative budgeting
Imposed budgeting

5   *Choose the appropriate words from those highlighted.*

An **expectations/aspirations** budget would be most useful for the purposes of planning and decision making based on reasonable expectations, whereas an **aspirations/expectations** budget is more appropriate for improving motivation by setting targets of an intermediate level of difficulty.

6   In the context of a balanced scorecard approach to performance measurement, to which of the four perspectives does each measure relate?

Performance measure	*Perspective*
(a) Time taken to develop new products	....
(b) Percentage of on-time deliveries	....
(c) Average set-up time	....
(d) Return on capital employed	....

Answers to quick quiz

1   cost behaviour patterns
     flex or change

2   (a)   Variable £4,500

     (b)   Semi-variable £10,250

     (c)   Fixed £2,400

     (d)   Semi-variable £7,000

3   True

4   (a)   Imposed budgeting

     (b)   Participative budgeting

     (c)   Negotiated budgeting

5   expectations
     aspirations

6   (a)   Learning

     (b)   Customer

     (c)   Internal

     (d)   Financial

Now try the questions below from the Exam Question Bank

Number	Level	Marks	Time
Q9	Exam standard	25	45 mins
Q10	Exam standard	25	45 mins
Q11	Exam standard	25	45 mins

Chapter 8

COST AND PROFIT CENTRES. TRANSFER PRICING

Topic list		Syllabus reference	Ability required
1	Responsibility accounting	(ii)	Comprehension/analysis
2	The basic principles of transfer pricing	(ii)	Comprehension
3	The use of market price as a basis for transfer prices	(ii)	Analysis
4	Cost-based approaches to transfer pricing	(ii)	Analysis

Introduction

In this chapter we will be studying another aspect of control information and performance measurement which is concerned with monitoring the performance of separate parts of the same organisation. We will be looking in outline at a system of **responsibility accounting** and particularly at the operation of **cost centres** and **profit centres** within such a system.

Within the context of profit centres we will learn how to determine the price of those products or services which are transferred between the centres. The price of these 'internal sales' is known as the **transfer price**.

We will be reviewing the principles of transfer pricing and looking at the merits and disadvantages of a number of different transfer pricing systems.

Learning outcomes covered in this chapter

- **Explain** why it is necessary to identify controllable and uncontrollable costs

- **Compare** and **contrast** cost and profit centres

- **Explain** the principles of transfer pricing

- **Compare** and **contrast** transfer pricing systems

Syllabus content covered in this chapter

- Controllable and uncontrollable costs

- Cost and profit centres

- Principles of transfer pricing

- Transfer pricing systems

1 RESPONSIBILITY ACCOUNTING

1.1 When performance is measured in terms of accounting results the name given to the procedure is **responsibility accounting.**

KEY TERM

Responsibility accounting is a system of accounting that segregates revenues and costs into areas of personal responsibility in order to monitor and assess the performance of each part of an organisation.

1.2 There are three types of responsibility accounting unit, or responsibility centre: cost centre, profit centre and investment centre. Your Paper 8 syllabus requires you to be able to compare and contrast cost centres and profit centres.

KEY TERM

A **responsibility centre** is 'A department or organisational function whose performance is the direct responsibility of a specific manager'. (CIMA *Official Terminology*)

1.3 A system of **cost centres** would be used where the manager of each centre is able to control the costs incurred in the centre. A cost centre is either unable to earn a measurable revenue, or the manager has no control over the revenue that is earned.

KEY TERM

A **cost centre** is 'A production or service location, function, activity or item of equipment for which costs are accumulated'. (CIMA *Official Terminology*)

Question 1

Can you think of an example of a cost centre for each of the categories mentioned in CIMA's definition?

Answer

Here are some suggestions.

Production location	Any type of production department
Service location	Canteen
Function	Sales representative
Activity	Inspection
Item of equipment	Mainframe computer

1.4 In order to be monitored as a **profit centre**, the centre must be capable of earning a measurable revenue, over which the manager is able to exercise control. It must also be possible for the manager to control the costs incurred in the centre. The manager's performance can therefore be monitored according to the profit generated by the profit centre.

KEY TERM

A **profit centre** is 'A part of a business accountable for both costs and revenues'.
(CIMA *Official Terminology*)

1.5 The revenue earned in a profit centre need not necessarily be a result of sales external to the organisation. **Transfer pricing** is used when divisions of an organisation need to charge other divisions of the same organisation for goods and services they provide to them. For example, subsidiary A of X plc might make a component that is used as part of a product made by subsidiary B of X plc, but that can also be sold to the external market, including makers of rival products to subsidiary B's product. Therefore there will be two sources of revenue for A.

(a) External sales revenue from sales made to other organisations

(b) Internal sales revenue from sales made to other responsibility centres within the same organisation, valued at the transfer price

1.6 The following table should help to summarise the differences between a cost centre and a profit centre.

Type of responsibility centre	Manager has control over ...	Principal performance measurement
Cost centre	Controllable costs	Variance analysis Efficiency measures
Profit centre	Controllable costs Sales volumes Sales prices (including transfer prices)	Profit

Controllable costs and uncontrollable costs

1.7 Managers of responsibility centres should only be held accountable for costs over which they have some influence. From a motivation point of view this is important because it can be very demoralising for managers who feel that their performance is being judged on the basis of something over which they have no influence. It is also important from a control point of view in that control reports should ensure that information on costs is reported to the manager who is able to take action to control them.

> **KEY TERM**
>
> A **controllable cost** is 'A cost which can be influenced by its budget holder'.
>
> (CIMA *Official Terminology*)

1.8 Responsibility accounting attempts to associate costs, revenues, assets and liabilities with the managers most capable of controlling them. As a system of accounting, it therefore distinguishes between controllable and uncontrollable costs.

(a) Most **variable costs** within a department are thought to be **controllable in the short term** because managers can influence the efficiency with which resources are used, even if they cannot do anything to raise or lower price levels.

(b) Many **fixed costs are uncontrollable** (or committed) **in the short term**, although some fixed costs **may be discretionary**.

Question 2

Which of the following is an example of a discretionary cost?

A   Material costs
B   Advertising expenditure
C   Cost of heating and lighting
D   Salaries

Answer

The correct answer is B.

A discretionary cost is a cost whose amount, within a particular time period, is determined by, and can be altered by, the budget holder.

(c)   **Many fixed costs are directly attributable** to a department or profit centre in that although they are fixed (in the short term) within the relevant range of output, a drastic reduction in the department's output, or closure of the department entirely, would reduce or remove these costs.

(d)   A cost which is not controllable by a junior **manager** or supervisor might be controllable by a senior **manager.** For example, there may be high direct labour costs in a department caused by excessive overtime working. The supervisor may feel obliged to continue with the overtime in order to meet production schedules, but his senior may be able to reduce costs by deciding to hire extra full-time staff, thereby reducing the requirements for overtime.

(e)   A cost which is not controllable by a manager in **one department** may be controllable by a manager in **another department.** For example, an increase in material costs may be caused by buying at higher prices than expected (controllable by the purchasing department) or by excessive wastage and spoilage (controllable by the production department).

ATTENTION!

You can see from these descriptions that there are no clear cut rules as to which costs are controllable and which are uncontrollable. Each situation and cost must be reviewed separately and a decision taken according to the effect on the control value of the information and its behavioural impact.

Centralisation and decentralisation

1.9   The degree of authority delegated by top management to lower-level management will fall between two extremes.

Description of organisation	Detail	Disadvantages
Centralised	Head office has complete control over all activities. All decisions are made at the top level.	• Top management involved in day to day management rather than strategic planning • Lower-level managers probably make better quality decisions (they have knowledge of local conditions) more quickly
Decentralised	Lower-level managers have full control over activities and decisions.	• Dysfunctional decision making and difficult to retain goal congruence (see Paragraph 2.2 below) • Top management may lose control • Costs of duplication of activities (eg accounts department) • Lack of lower-level management expertise

1.10 Cost and revenue centres are used in the weakest form of decentralisation, investment centres (the managers of which are responsible for costs, revenues and investment) in the strongest form.

2 THE BASIC PRINCIPLES OF TRANSFER PRICING Pilot paper

> **KEY TERM**
>
> A **transfer price** is 'The price at which goods or services are transferred between different units of the same company'. (CIMA *Official Terminology*)

Some problems with transfer pricing

Divisional autonomy

2.1 Transfer prices are particularly appropriate for **profit centres** because if one profit centre does work for another the size of the transfer price will affect the costs of one profit centre and the revenues of another.

2.2 However, a danger with profit centre accounting is that the business organisation will **divide into a number of self-interested segments**, each acting at times against the wishes and interests of other segments. Decisions might be taken by profit centre managers in the best interests of their own part of the business, but against the best interests of other profit centres and possibly the organisation as a whole.

2.3 A task of **head office** is therefore to try to **prevent dysfunctional decision making** by individual profit centres. To do this, head office must reserve some power and authority for itself and so **profit centres cannot be allowed to make entirely autonomous decisions**.

2.4 Just how much authority head office decides to keep for itself will vary according to individual circumstances. **A balance** ought to be kept **between divisional autonomy** to provide incentives and motivation, and **retaining centralised authority** to ensure that the organisation's profit centres are all working towards the same target, the benefit of the organisation as a whole (in other words, **retaining goal congruence** among the organisation's separate divisions).

Divisional performance measurement

2.5   Profit centre managers tend to put their own profit performance above everything else. Since profit centre performance is measured according to the profit they earn, no profit centre will want to do work for another and incur costs without being paid for it. Consequently, profit centre managers are likely to dispute the size of transfer prices with each other, or disagree about whether one profit centre should do work for another or not. Transfer prices **affect behaviour and decisions** by profit centre managers.

Corporate profit maximisation

2.6   When there are disagreements about how much work should be transferred between divisions, and how many sales the division should make to the external market, there is presumably a **profit-maximising level of output and sales for the organisation as a whole**. However, unless each profit centre also maximises its own profit at this same level of output, there will be inter-divisional disagreements about output levels and the profit-maximising output will not be achieved.

Aims of a system of transfer pricing

2.7   Ideally a transfer price should be set at a level that overcomes these problems.

(a)   The transfer price should provide an 'artificial' selling price that enables the **transferring division to earn a return for its efforts**, and the **receiving division to incur a cost for benefits received**.

(b)   The transfer price should be set at a level that enables **profit centre performance** to be **measured 'commercially'**. This means that the transfer price should be a fair commercial price.

(c)   The transfer price should, if possible, encourage profit centre managers to agree on the **amount** of goods and services to be **transferred**, which will also be at a level that is **consistent with the aims of the organisation as a whole** (such as maximising company profit).

2.8   Transfer prices are therefore a way of promoting **divisional autonomy**, ideally without prejudicing the measurement of **divisional performance**, whilst at the same time encouraging **goal congruence**.

2.9   The method of transfer pricing used should therefore meet three criteria.

- **Equity** (provides a fair measure of divisional performance)
- **Neutrality** (avoids the distortion of business decision making)
- **Administrative simplicity**

3   THE USE OF MARKET PRICE AS A BASIS FOR TRANSFER PRICES

Market price as the transfer price

3.1   If an **external market price exists** for transferred goods, profit centre managers will be aware of the price they could obtain or the price they would have to pay for their goods on the external market, and they would inevitably **compare** this price **with the transfer price**.

3.2 EXAMPLE: TRANSFERRING GOODS AT MARKET VALUE

A company has two profit centres, A and B. A sells half of its output on the open market and transfers the other half to B. Costs and external revenues in an accounting period are as follows.

	A £	B £	Total £
External sales	8,000	24,000	32,000
Costs of production	12,000	10,000	22,000
Company profit			10,000

Required

What are the consequences of setting a transfer price at market value?

3.3 SOLUTION

If the transfer price is at market price, A would be happy to sell the output to B for £8,000, which is what A would get by selling it externally instead of transferring it.

	A £	A £	B £	B £	Total £
Market sales		8,000		24,000	32,000
Transfer sales		8,000		-	
		16,000		24,000	
Transfer costs		-		8,000	
Own costs	12,000		10,000		22,000
		12,000		18,000	
Profit		4,000		6,000	10,000

The **transfer sales of A are self-cancelling with the transfer costs of B** so that the total profits are unaffected by the transfer items. The transfer price simply spreads the total profit of £10,000 between A and B.

Consequences

(a)   A earns the same profit on transfers as on external sales. B must pay a commercial price for transferred goods, and both divisions will have their profit measured in a fair way.

(b)   A will be indifferent about selling externally or transferring goods to B because the profit is the same on both types of transaction. B can therefore ask for and obtain as many units as it wants from A.

Adjusted market price: using market value less savings

3.4   **Internal transfers** are often **cheaper** than external sales, with **savings** in selling and administration costs, bad debt risks and possibly transport/delivery costs. It would therefore seem reasonable for the **buying division to expect a discount** on the external market price. The transfer price might be slightly less than market price, so that **A and B could share the cost savings** from internal transfers compared with external sales. It should be possible to reach agreement on this price and on output levels with a minimum of intervention from head office.

The merits and disadvantages of market value transfer prices

3.5   A market-based transfer price therefore seems to be the **ideal** transfer price because the buying division is likely to benefit from a better quality of service, greater flexibility, and dependability of supply. Both divisions may benefit from cheaper costs of administration, selling and transport. A market price as the transfer price would therefore result in decisions which would be in the best interests of the company or group as a whole.

3.6 **Disadvantages of market value as a transfer price**

(a) The **market price may be a temporary one**, induced by adverse economic conditions, or dumping, or the market price might depend on the volume of output supplied to the external market by the profit centre.

(b) A transfer price at market value might, under some circumstances, **act as a disincentive to use up any spare capacity** in the divisions. A price based on incremental cost, in contrast, might provide an incentive to use up the spare resources in order to provide a marginal contribution to profit.

(c) Many products **do not have an equivalent market price** so that the price of a similar, but not identical, product might have to be chosen. In such circumstances, the option to sell or buy on the open market does not really exist.

(d) There might be an **imperfect external market** for the transferred item, so that if the transferring division tried to sell more externally, it would have to reduce its selling price.

4 COST-BASED APPROACHES TO TRANSFER PRICING

4.1 Cost-based approaches to transfer pricing are often used in practice, because in practice the following conditions are common.

(a) There is **no external market** for the product that is being transferred.

(b) Alternatively, although there is an external market it is an **imperfect** one because the market price is affected by such factors as the amount that the company setting the transfer price supplies to it, or because there is only a limited external demand.

In either case there will **not be a suitable market price** upon which to base the transfer price.

Actual cost versus standard cost

4.2 EXAMPLE: TRANSFERS AT STANDARD OR ACTUAL COST

A company has two profit centres, A and B. A sells half its output externally. It transfers the other half of its output to B. Cost and revenue details in an accounting period are as follows.

	A	B	Total
	£	£	£
External sales	8,000	24,000	32,000
Standard cost of production in the division	10,000	11,000	21,000
Cost variances in the division	2,000 (A)	1,000 (F)	1,000 (A)
Profit			10,000

If the **transfer price is at actual cost**, A in our example would have 'sales' to B of £6,000 ((£10,000 + £2,000) × 50%). This would be a cost to B as follows.

BPP PUBLISHING

	A		B		Company as a whole
	£	£	£	£	£
Open market sales		8,000		24,000	32,000
Transfer sales		6,000		–	
Total sales, inc transfers		14,000		24,000	
Transfer costs			6,000		
Own costs and variances	12,000		10,000		22,000
Total costs, inc transfers		12,000		16,000	
Profit		2,000		8,000	10,000

4.3 There are two main **drawbacks with this actual cost transfer price**.

(a) **All of the inefficiencies (adverse variances) on A's work for B are transferred to B.** This would mean that there is no incentive for the manager of A to control costs, since all the inefficiencies on internal work are passed to B. Furthermore the manager of centre B would be charged with excess costs over which it would not be possible to exercise any control. Similarly, if A had managed to generate favourable variances, all of the resulting savings would be passed to B and A would receive no recognition.

(b) **A makes no profit on the work transferred internally.** The manager of centre A would prefer to sell output on the open market to earn a profit, rather than transfer to B, regardless of whether or not transfers to B would be in the best interests of the company as a whole. Centre A needs a profit on its transfers in order to be motivated to supply B.

4.4 The problem of transferring adverse and favourable variances could be overcome through the use of **standard cost** instead of actual cost. However the use of standard cost would still suffer from the disadvantage that **A makes no profit on the work transferred internally.**

Transfers at standard cost plus

4.5 One way to **ensure that A makes a profit** would be to use a **'standard cost plus'** system, where a profit margin is added to the standard cost to determine the transfer price. In this way A's profits would reflect all its own efficiencies and inefficiencies, since variances would not be transferred, and A would also receive a profit on internal transfers.

Question 3

Suppose that, in our example, the transfer price is set at 'standard cost plus 25%'. The profits for centres A and B will be

	Profit centre A	Profit centre B
A	£1,500	£8,500
B	£2,250	£7,750
C	£3,500	£6,500
D	£6,000	£4,000

Answer

The correct answer is B.

The value of the transfers will be ((£10,000 x 50%) + 25%) = £6,250

	A		B		Company as a whole
	£	£	£	£	£
Open market sales		8,000		24,000	32,000
Transfer sales		6,250		–	
Total sales, inc transfers		14,250		24,000	
Transfer costs			6,250		
Own costs and variances	12,000		10,000		22,000
Total costs, inc transfers		12,000		16,250	
Profit		2,250		7,750	10,000

Note that the total profit does not change, but the split between A and B has altered.

4.6 Profit centre A now gains some profit at the expense of B. However, A makes a bigger profit on external sales in this case because the profit mark-up of 25% is less than the profit mark-up on open market sales. But as we discussed earlier there may be certain **savings on internal transfers**. The lower mark-up enables A and B to share these savings and thus tends to **encourage internal transfers**.

Question 4

If the entire cost of A's overspending of £2,000 is now borne by division A, why has A's profit increased by £250 instead of falling by £2,000 when compared with using actual cost for the transfer price?

Answer

A was already bearing 50% of its overspending (£1,000). Furthermore, A is now earning a 25% margin on its standard costs transferred of £5,000 (£1,250).

	£
Profit margin on £5,000 standard costs transferred	1,250
Less remainder of overspending now borne by A	1,000
Increase in A's profit	250

Transfer prices based on standard variable cost

4.7 A variable cost approach entails charging the standard variable cost that has been incurred by the supplying division to the receiving division. Suppose that A's cost per unit is £15, of which £6 is fixed and £9 is variable.

	A		B		Company as a whole
	£	£	£	£	£ £
Market sales		8,000		24,000	32,000
Transfer sales		3,000*		-	
Total sales, inc transfers		11,000		24,000	
Transfer costs			3,000		-
Own costs and variances	12,000		10,000		22,000
Total costs, inc transfers		12,000		13,000	22,000
(Loss)/Profit		(1,000)		11,000	10,000

*Transfer value = 9/15 × (£10,000 × 50%)

4.8 This result is **deeply unsatisfactory for the manager of division** A who could make an additional £5,000 (£(8,000 – 3,000)) profit if no goods were transferred to division B (assuming that there is demand for the additional units externally). For the company overall, however, this action would cause a large fall in profit, because division B could make no sales at all.

4.9 The problem is that with a transfer price at variable cost the **supplying division does not cover its fixed costs.**

Fixed costs and transfer pricing

4.10 There are a number of ways in which the problem in Paragraph 4.9 can be overcome.

(a) **Each division** can be given a **share of the overall contribution** earned by the organisation. It will be necessary to decide what the shares should be centrally, however, **undermining divisional autonomy**.

(b) A **two-part charging system** can be used. Transfer prices are set at standard variable cost and once a year there is a **transfer of a fixed fee to the supplying division**, representing an allowance for its fixed costs. This method risks sending the message to the supplying division that it need not control its fixed costs, however, because the company will subsidise any inefficiencies. On the other hand, if fixed costs are incurred because spare capacity is kept available for the needs of other divisions, it is reasonable to expect those other divisions to pay a fee if they 'booked' that capacity in advance but later failed to utilise it. But the main problem with this approach is that it is likely to **conflict with divisional autonomy**.

Transfers at actual cost plus

4.11 One transfer pricing option that we have not yet considered is the use of actual cost plus a profit margin.

Question 5

What problems can you envisage with the use of 'actual cost plus' as a basis for transfer prices?

Answer

The use of actual cost suffers from the disadvantages discussed earlier, in terms of all efficiencies and inefficiencies being transferred. 'Actual cost plus' can in fact create an **incentive for the transferring division to overspend**. Not only does the division get to transfer out its own excess costs, but it also earns a profit margin on the excess!

Chapter roundup

- **Responsibility accounting** is a system where the performance of different parts of an organisation is monitored in terms of accounting results.

- The manager of a **cost centre** is responsible for controlling the costs of the centre, but cannot earn or control any revenues.

- The manager of a **profit centre** is responsible for controlling the centre's costs and revenues, and hence the profits of the centre.

- **Controllable costs** are those which can be influenced by the budget holder. **Uncontrollable costs** cannot be so influenced.

- A **transfer price** is the price at which goods or services are transferred from one responsibility centre to another.

- A market based transfer price might be adjusted downwards to allow for savings made on internal transfers compared with external sales.

- Use of **actual costs** in a transfer price **transfers all efficiencies and inefficiencies** between profit centres.

- The addition of a profit margin to standard cost helps to **create a profit incentive** for the transferring centre.

Quick quiz

1   *Fill in the blanks.*

Type of responsibility centre	*Manager has control over ......*
Cost centre	(a) ....
Profit centre	(b) ....
	(c) ....
	(d) ....

2   Controllable costs are those which cannot be influenced by the budget holder. *True or false?*

3   *Choose the appropriate words from those highlighted.*

A **cost/market** based transfer price might be adjusted **upwards/downwards** to make allowance for **extra costs/savings** made on **internal/external** transfers compared with external sales.

4   Which of the following is not a disadvantage of the use of market value as transfer price?

A   Market price might be a permanent one.
B   In some circumstances, acts as a disincentive to use up any spare capacity.
C   An equivalent market price may not exist.
D   There may be an imperfect external market.

5   The use of 'actual cost plus' as the basis for a transfer price can create an incentive for the transferring division to overspend. *True or false?*

Answers to quick quiz

1 (a) Controllable costs

(b)-(d) Controllable costs, sales volumes, sales prices (including transfer prices)

2 False. They can be influenced by the budget holder.

3 A market based transfer price might be adjusted downwards to make allowance for savings made on internal transfers compared with external sales.

4 A. The disadvantage is that the market price might be a temporary one.

5 True

Now try the question below from the Exam Question Bank

Number	Level	Marks	Time
Q12	Introductory	n/a	20 mins

Part C
Allocation and management of resources

Chapter 9

THE MODERN BUSINESS ENVIRONMENT

Topic list		Syllabus reference	Ability required
1	The changing business environment	(iii)	Comprehension
2	Advanced manufacturing technology (AMT)	(iii)	Comprehension
3	Production management strategies	(iii)	Analysis
4	Just-in-time (JIT) systems	(iii)	Analysis
5	Synchronous manufacturing	(iii)	Comprehension
6	Total quality management (TQM)	(iii)	Comprehension
7	Costs of quality and cost of quality reports	(iii)	Application/analysis
8	World class manufacturing (WCM)	(iii)	Comprehension

Introduction

The end of the twentieth century has seen **significant changes in the business environment** in which both manufacturing and service organisations operate.

- Most organisations are now competing in a highly-competitive global market

- Product life cycles have reduced because of technological innovations and increasingly discriminating customer demands

- Customer satisfaction has become an overriding priority.

Organisations have therefore adopted new **management approaches**, have changed their **manufacturing systems** and have invested in **new technology**, and it is these changes that we will be looking at in this chapter.

Learning outcomes covered in this chapter

- **Describe** the modern business environment

- **Compare** and **contrast** alternative production and management strategies

- **Explain** total quality management

- **Prepare** and **discuss** cost of quality reports

Syllabus content covered in this chapter

- Modern business environment

- Resource planning systems: MRP I, MRP II and ERP

- Just-in-time

- Total quality management

1 THE CHANGING BUSINESS ENVIRONMENT

Exam focus point

The examiner has confirmed that topics previously examined in the old syllabus Paper 10 *Management Accounting Applications* are likely to appear in optional questions or in small parts of a question before they appear in compulsory questions. The topics in this chapter were included in the *Management Accounting Applications* syllabus and so are unlikely to appear in Section B in the first couple of sittings of this paper.

Changing competitive environment

For manufacturing organisations

1.1 **Before the 1970s, barriers of communication** and **geographical distance** limited the extent to which overseas organisations could compete in domestic markets. Cost increases could often be passed on to customers and so there were **few efforts to maximise efficiency and improve management practices,** or to reduce costs. **During the 1970s,** however, **overseas competitors** gained access to domestic markets by **establishing global networks for acquiring raw materials and distributing high-quality, low-priced goods**. To succeed, organisations had to compete against the best companies in the world.

For service organisations

1.2 **Prior to the 1980s,** many service organisations (such as the utilities, the financial services and airlines industries) were either **government-owned monopolies** or were **protected by a highly-regulated, non-competitive environment. Improvements in quality and efficiency** of operations or levels of profitability were not expected, and costs increases were often covered by increasing service prices. Cost systems to measure costs and profitability of individual services were not deemed necessary.

The competitive environment for service organisations changed radically in the **1980s,** however, following **privatisation** of government-owned monopolies and **deregulation**. The resulting intense competition and increasing product range has led to the **requirement for cost management and management accounting information systems** which allow service organisations to assess the costs and profitability of services, customers and markets.

Changing product life cycles

1.3 Today's **competitive environment,** along with high levels of **technological innovation** and **increasingly discriminating and sophisticated customer demands,** constantly **threaten a product's life cycle.**

KEY TERM

Product life cycle is 'The period which begins with the initial product specification, and ends with the withdrawal from the market of both the product and its support. It is characterised by defined stages including research, development, introduction, maturity, decline and abandonment'. (CIMA *Official Terminology*)

1.4 Organisations can no longer rely on years of high demand for products and so, to compete effectively, they need to continually **redesign their products** and to **shorten the time it takes to get them to the market place.**

1.5 In many organisations today, **up to 90% of a product's life cycle cost is determined by decisions made** early within the cycle, **at the design stage. Management accounting systems that monitor spending and commitment to spend during the early stages of a product's life cycle** are therefore becoming **increasingly important.**

Changing customer requirements

1.6 Successful organisations in today's competitive environment make **customer satisfaction** their **priority** and concentrate on the following **key success factors.**

Key success factor	Detail
Cost efficiency	
Quality	Focusing on total quality management (TQM), covered in Section 6
Time	Providing a speedier response to customer requests, ensuring 100% on-time delivery and reducing the time taken to develop and bring new products to market
Innovation	Developing a steady stream of innovative new products and having the flexibility to respond to customer requirements

1.7 They are also taking on board **new management approaches.**

Approach	Detail
Continuous improvement	A facet of TQM, being a continuous search to reduce costs, eliminate waste and improve the quality and performance of activities that increase customer satisfaction or value
Employee empowerment	Providing employees with the information to enable them to make continuous improvements without authorisation from superiors
Total value-chain analysis	Ensuring that all the factors which add value to an organisation's products - the value chain of research and development, design, production, marketing, distribution and customer service - are coordinated within the overall organisational framework

Changing manufacturing systems

1.8 Traditionally, manufacturing industries have fallen into a few broad groups according to the **nature of the production process** and **materials flow.**

Type of production	Description
Jobbing industries	Industries in which **items are produced individually**, often for a specific customer order, as a 'job'. Such a business requires versatile equipment and highly skilled workers to give it the flexibility to turn its hand to a variety of jobs. The jobbing factory is typically laid out on a **functional** basis with, say, a milling department, a cutting department, finishing, assembly and so on.
Batch processing	Involves the manufacture of **standard goods in batches**. 'Batch production is often carried out using **functional** layouts but with a greater number of more **specialised machines**. With a functional layout batches move by different and complex routes through various specialised departments travelling over much of the factory floor before they are completed.' (Drury, *Management and Cost Accounting*)

Type of production	Description
Mass or flow production	Involves the **continuous production of standard items** from a sequence of continuous or repetitive operations. This sort of production often uses a **product-based** layout whereby product A moves from a milling machine to a cutting machine to a paint-spraying machine, product B moves from a sawing machine to a milling machine to an oven and then to finishing and so on.
	The point is that there is no separate 'milling department' or 'assembly department' to which all products must be sent to await their turn on the machines: each product has its own dedicated machine.

1.9 In recent years, however, a new type of manufacturing system known as **group technology** (or **repetitive manufacturing**) has emerged. The system involves a **flexible or cellular arrangement of machines** which **manufacture groups of products having similar manufacturing requirements.** By grouping together facilities required to produce similar products, some of the **benefits associated with flow production systems** (lower throughput times, easier scheduling, reduced set-up times and reduced work in progress) are possible to achieve. Moreover, the increase in **customer demand for product diversity can be satisfied** by such a manufacturing system.

Dedicated cell layout

1.10 The modern development in this sphere is to merge the flexibility of the functional layout with the speed and productivity of the product layout. **Cellular** manufacturing involves a **U-shaped flow** along which are arranged a number of different machines that are used to make products with similar machining requirements.

1.11 The machines are operated by workers who are **multi-skilled** (can operate each machine within the cell rather than being limited to one operation such as 'lathe-operator', 'grinder', or whatever) and are able to perform routine preventative maintenance on the cell machines. The aim is to facilitate **just-in-time** production (see Section 4) and obtain the associated improvements in **quality** and reductions in **costs**.

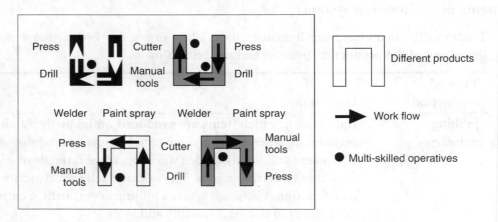

BPP PUBLISHING

Case example

In January 1994 the *Financial Times* carried a good example of this approach in an article about the Paddy Hopkirk car accessory factory in Bedfordshire.

> One morning the factory was just an untidy sprawl of production lines surrounded by piles of crates holding semi-finished components. Two days later, when the workforce came to work (after Christmas), the machines has been brought together in tightly grouped 'cells'. The piles of components had disappeared, and the newly cleared floor space was neatly marked with colour-coded lines mapping out the flow of materials.

> Overnight there were dramatic differences. In the first full day, productivity on some lines increased by up to 30%, the space needed for some processes had been halved, and work in progress had been cut considerably. The improved layout had allowed some jobs to be combined, freeing up operators for development elsewhere in the factory.

1.12 As we saw earlier, **to compete effectively** organisations need to **continually redesign their products** and to **shorten the time it takes to get them to the market place. Manufacturing processes** must therefore be **sufficiently flexible** both to accommodate new product design rapidly and to satisfy the demand for greater product diversity.

2 ADVANCED MANUFACTURING TECHNOLOGY (AMT)

2.1 Organisations need to be able to compete in today's fast-moving, sophisticated world markets. As noted above, they need to be innovative and flexible and be able to deal with short product life cycles. They need to be able to offer greater product variety whilst maintaining or reducing their costs. They may want to reduce set-up times and inventories and have the greatest possible manufacturing flexibility. AMT helps them to do this.

KEY TERM

Advanced manufacturing technology (AMT) encompasses automatic production technology, computer-aided design and manufacturing, flexible manufacturing systems and a wide array of innovative computer equipment.

Computer-aided design (CAD)

2.2 Computer-aided design allows new products to be designed (and old ones modified) on a computer screen.

(a) The effects of **changing product specifications** (for example to test stress and find weaknesses or to optimise usage of materials) can be explored.

(b) **Designs can be assessed in terms of cost and simplicity**. A simple design is likely to produce a more reliable product and a simple product is easier to manufacture, thereby reducing the possibility of production errors. Quality and cost reduction can therefore be incorporated into a product at the design stage.

(c) **Databases can be used** to match part requirements of the new design with existing product parts, thereby allowing a reduction in product parts required and a minimisation of stockholdings.

BPP PUBLISHING

Computer-aided manufacturing (CAM)

2.3 Computer-aided manufacturing refers to the control of the physical production process by computers.

Feature	Detail
Robots	Typically comprise computer controlled arms and attachments that can perform tasks like welding, bolting parts together and moving them about.
Computer numerically controlled (CNC) machines	Programmable machine tools for punching holes, cutting and so on. Manufacturing configurations and set-up instructions are stored on computer programs and so can be changed almost immediately via a keyboard. Flexibility and a reduction in set-up times are thus major advantages of CAM. Moreover, computers can repeat the same operation in an identical manner time and time again, without tiring or error, unlike human operators, with obvious advantages for both quality control and production control.
Automated guided vehicles (AGV)	Used for materials handling, often in place of the traditional conveyor belt approach.
Automated storage and retrieval systems (ASRS)	Also used for materials handling.

2.4 The **ultimate aim** of CAM is a **set-up time of zero**. Although this may not be achievable (in the near future at least), CAM has provided, and still is providing, the **possibility** of economic **production in smaller and smaller batch sizes** with the result that the production schedule is becoming more and more driven by customer requirements.

Flexible manufacturing systems (FMS)

2.5 A flexible manufacturing system (FMS) is a **highly-automated manufacturing system**, which is computer controlled and capable of producing a broad 'family' of parts in a flexible manner. **It is characterised by small batch production, the ability to change quickly from one job to another and very fast response times,** so that output can be produced quickly in response to specific orders that come in.

2.6 The sophistication of flexible manufacturing systems varies from one system to another, but **features** can include the following.

- A **JIT system** (discussed later in this chapter)

- Full **computer-integrated manufacturing (CIM)** (the integration of many or all of the elements of AMT into one coherent system) or perhaps just **islands of automation (IAs)** (a series of automated sub-systems within the factory)

- **Computerised materials handling systems (MHS)**

- **Automated storage and retrieval systems (ASRS)** for raw materials and parts

Electronic data interchange (EDI)

2.7 It is not simply within the manufacturing functions of an organisation that technology has made an impact. Electronic data interchange facilitates communication between an organisation and its customers and suppliers by the electronic transfer of information.

3 PRODUCTION MANAGEMENT STRATEGIES

3.1 In Section 1 we looked at the various methods of organising the production process. In this section and the next we shall now look at **various production management strategies** and **resource planning systems** that are used to **manage the production process**.

Traditional approach

3.2 The traditional approach to **determining materials requirements** is **to monitor the level of stocks** constantly so that once they fall to a preset level they can be reordered. The problem with this approach is that **relationships between different stock lines** are **ignored** whereas, in reality, the demand for a particular item of stock is interdependent on the assemblies and subassemblies of which it forms a part. The computer techniques we will look at below overcome this problem by integrating interrelationships into the stock ordering process.

Materials requirement planning (MRP I)

3.3 MRP I is a computerised information, planning and control system that can be used in a traditional manufacturing environment as well as with AMT. MRP I uses information from a master production schedule which details how many finished goods items are needed, and when, and works back from this to determine the requirements for parts and materials in the earlier stages of the production process. MRP I systems are chiefly used in a batch manufacturing environment.

3.4 **The aims of MRP I**

- Minimising stock levels
- Avoiding the high costs of rush orders
- Minimum disruption to production

3.5 MRP I is therefore concerned with **maximising efficiency in the timing of orders for raw materials or parts that are placed with external suppliers** and **efficient scheduling of the manufacturing and assembly of the end product.**

Manufacturing resource planning (MRP II)

3.6 MRP I evolved into MRP II. MRP II **plans production jobs and also calculates resource needs such as labour and machine hours.** It therefore attempts to integrate materials requirement planning, factory capacity planning, shopfloor control, management accounting, purchasing and even marketing into a **single complete (and computerised) manufacturing control system**. Most MRP II systems are a collection of computer programs that permit the sharing of information with and between departments in an organisation.

3.7 MRP II is used by many companies for manufacturing planning, but with the advent of JIT manufacturing (see Section 4) it has been **criticised** as a planning system.

> 'The primary criticism of the MRP II approach is that **by modelling the reality of manufacturing plant, it builds in all the bad habits**. It takes account of long leadtimes, shopfloor queues, large batch sizes, scrap and quality problems. Instead of accommodating these things, it should be driving towards their elimination. Poor productivity is built into MRPII and planned into the production process.'
>
> (Brian Maskell, *Management Accounting,* January 1989 (with BPP's emphasis))

BPP PUBLISHING

Many world class manufacturers in Japan have therefore taken an alternative approach to dealing with complex production scheduling and purchasing by attempting to simplify their production processes.

3.8 Even so, MRP II has advantages as a system for planning and controlling manufacturing systems, especially when JIT methods are unsuitable.

Enterprise resource planning (ERP)

KEY TERM

Enterprise resource planning (ERP) systems are accounting-orientated information systems for identifying and planning the enterprise-wide resources needed to take, make, distribute and account for customer orders.

(*S Shankarnarayanan* 'ERP Systems - Using IT to gain competitive advantage')

3.9 A 1990 article in the *Financial Times (Passport to Business Integration,* Paul Taylor) described ERP as an umbrella term for integrated business software systems that power a corporate information structure, thus helping companies to control their inventory, purchasing, manufacturing, finance and personnel operations.

3.10 Originally, ERP systems were simple extensions of MRP II systems, but their scope has now widened. They allow an organisation to automate and integrate most of its business processes, share common data and practices across the whole enterprise and produce and access information in a real-time environment. ERP may also incorporate transactions with an organisation's suppliers.

They help large national and multinational companies in particular to manage geographically dispersed and complex operations. For example, an organisation's UK sales office may be responsible for marketing, selling and servicing a product assembled in the US using parts manufactured in France and Hong Kong. ERP enables the organisation to understand and manage the demand placed on the plant in France.

Optimised production technology (OPT)

3.11 One further innovation deserves a brief mention. (Bear in mind though that a new TLA (Three-letter Acronym) seems to gain favour every few months.) OPT also requires detailed information about stock levels, product structures, routings, set-up times and operation times for each procedure of each product but it *also* **seeks to optimise the use of bottleneck resources.**

'The OPT philosophy contends that the **primary goal of manufacturing is to make money**. Three important criteria are identified to evaluate progress towards achieving this goal. These are throughput, inventory and operating expenses. The goal is to **maximise throughput** while simultaneously **maintaining or decreasing inventory and operating expenses**.

The OPT approach determines what prevents throughput [of products through the production process] from being higher by **distinguishing between bottleneck and non-bottleneck resources**. A bottleneck might be a machine whose capacity limits the throughput of the whole production process. The aim is to identify bottlenecks and remove them or, of this is not possible, ensure that they are fully utilised at all times. Non-bottleneck resources should be scheduled and operated based on constraints within the system, and should not be used to produce more than the bottlenecks can absorb.

With the OPT approach, it is vitally important to schedule all non-bottleneck resources within the manufacturing system based on the constraints of the system (ie the bottlenecks). For example, if only 70% of the output of a non-bottleneck resource can be absorbed by the following bottleneck resource then 30% of the utilisation of the non-bottleneck is simply concerned with increasing inventory. It can therefore be argued that by operating at the 70% level, the non-bottleneck resource is achieving 100% efficiency.'

(Drury, *Management and Cost Accounting (with BPP's emphasis)*)

Question 1

Answer this question without looking back over the preceding sections.

Which of the following has not been discussed in this chapter?

A   MPT
B   MRP
C   OPT
D   ERP

Answer

The correct answer is A.

4   JUST-IN-TIME (JIT) SYSTEMS   Pilot paper

4.1   'Traditional' responses to the problems of improving manufacturing capacity and reducing unit costs of production might be described as follows.

- Longer production runs
- Economic batch quantities
- Fewer products in the product range
- More overtime
- Reduced time on preventive maintenance, to keep production flowing

In general terms, longer production runs and large batch sizes should mean less disruption, better capacity utilisation and lower unit costs.

4.2   Just-in-time systems challenge such 'traditional' views of manufacture.

KEY TERMS

Just-in-time (JIT) is 'A system whose objective is to produce or to procure products or components as they are required by a customer or for use, rather than for stock. A JIT system is a 'pull' system, which responds to demand, in contrast to a 'push' system, in which stocks act as buffers between the different elements of the system, such as purchasing, production and sales.'

Just-in-time production is 'A system which is driven by demand for finished products whereby each component on a production line is produced only when needed for the next stage'.

Just-in-time purchasing is 'A system in which material purchases are contracted so that the receipt and usage of material, to the maximum extent possible, coincide'.

(CIMA *Official Terminology*)

4.3   Although described as a technique in the *Official Terminology*, JIT is more of a **philosophy or approach to management** since it encompasses a **commitment to continuous improvement** and the **search for excellence** in the design and operation of the production management system.

4.4   JIT has the following **essential elements**.

Element	Detail
JIT purchasing	Parts and raw materials should be purchased as near as possible to the time they are needed, using **small frequent deliveries against bulk contracts**.
Close relationship with suppliers	In a JIT environment, the responsibility for the **quality of goods lies with the supplier**. A **long-term commitment** between supplier and customer should therefore be established: the supplier is guaranteed a demand for his products since he is the sole supplier and he is able to plan to meet the customer's production schedules. If an organisation has confidence that suppliers will deliver material of 100% quality, on time, so that there will be no rejects, returns and hence no consequent production delays, **usage of materials can be matched with delivery of materials and stocks can be kept at near zero levels**.
Uniform loading	All parts of the productive process should be operated at a speed which matches the rate at which the final product is demanded by the customer. Production runs will therefore be shorter and there will be smaller stocks of finished goods because output is being matched more closely to demand (and so storage costs will be reduced).
Set-up time reduction	Machinery set-ups are **non-value-added activities** (see below) which should be reduced or even eliminated.
Machine cells	Machines or workers should be **grouped by product or component** instead of by the type of work performed. The **non-value-added activity of materials movement** between operations is therefore **minimised by** eliminating space between work stations. Products can flow from machine to machine without having to wait for the next stage of processing or returning to stores. **Lead times and work in progress are thus reduced**.
Quality	Production management should seek to **eliminate scrap and defective units** during production, and to avoid the need for reworking of units since this stops the flow of production and leads to late deliveries to customers. Product quality and production quality are important 'drivers' in a JIT system.
Pull system (Kanban)	The use of a Kanban, or signal, to ensure that products/components are only produced when needed by the next process. Nothing is produced in anticipation of need, to then remain in stock, consuming resources.

Element	Detail
Preventative maintenance	Production systems must be reliable and prompt, without unforeseen delays and breakdowns. Machinery must be kept fully maintained, and so preventative maintenance is an important aspect of production.
Employee involvement	Workers within each machine cell should be trained to operate each machine within that cell and to be able to perform routine preventative maintenance on the cell machines (ie to be **multiskilled and flexible**).

Value added

4.5 JIT aims to eliminate all **non-value-added costs**. Value is only added while a product is actually being processed. Whilst it is being inspected for quality, moving from one part of the factory to another, waiting for further processing and held in store, value is not being added. Non value-added activities should therefore be eliminated.

KEY TERM

'A **value-added** cost is incurred for an activity that cannot be eliminated without the customer's perceiving a deterioration in the performance, function, or other quality of a product. The cost of a picture tube in a television set is value-added.

The costs of those activities that can be eliminated without the customer's perceiving deterioration in the performance, function, or other quality of a product are non-value-added. The costs of handling the materials of a television set through successive stages of an assembly line may be non-value-added. Improvements in plant layout that reduce handling costs may be achieved without affecting the performance, function, or other quality of the television set.'

(Horngren)

Question 2

Which of the following is a value-added activity?

A   Setting up a machine so that it drills holes of a certain size
B   Repairing faulty production work
C   Painting a car, if the organisation manufactures cars
D   Storing materials

Answer

The correct answer is C.

The other activities are non-value-adding activities.

Case example

The following extract from an article in the *Financial Times* illustrates how 'just-in-time' some manufacturing processes can be. The emphasis is BPP's.

'Just-in-time manufacturing is down to a fine art at *Nissan Motor Manufacturing (UK)*. **Stockholding of some components is just ten minutes** - and the holding of all parts bought in Europe is less than a day.

Nissan has moved beyond just-in-time to **synchronous supply** for some components, which means manufacturers deliver these components directly to the production line minutes before they are needed.

These manufacturers do not even receive an order to make a component until the car for which it is intended has started along the final assembly line. Seat manufacturer *Ikeda Hoover*, for example, has about 45 minutes to build seats to specification and deliver them to the assembly line a mile away. It delivers 12 sets of seats every 20 minutes and they are mounted in the right order on an overhead conveyor ready for fitting to the right car.

Nissan has **close relationships with this dozen or so suppliers** and deals exclusively with them in their component areas. It involves them and even their own suppliers in discussions about future needs and other issues. These companies have generally established their own manufacturing units close to the Nissan plant.

Other parts from further afield are collected from manufacturers by *Nissan* several times a day at fixed times. This is more efficient than having each supplier making individual haulage arrangements.'

Problems associated with JIT

4.6   JIT should not be seen as a panacea for all the endemic problems associated with Western manufacturing. It might not even be appropriate in all circumstances.

(a)   It is **not always easy to predict patterns of demand**.

(b)   JIT makes the organisation **far more vulnerable to disruptions in the supply chain**.

(c)   JIT, originated by Toyota, was designed at a time when all of Toyota's manufacturing was done within a 50 km radius of its headquarters. Wide geographical spread, however, makes this difficult.

Case examples

- The Kobe earthquake in Japan in 1995 severely disrupted industry in areas unaffected by the actual catastrophe. Plants that had not been hit by the earthquake were still forced to shut down production lines less than 24 hours after the earthquake struck because they held no buffer stocks which they could use to cover the shortfall caused by non delivery by the Kobe area suppliers.

- In October 1991 the workforce at the French state-owned car maker *Renault's* gear-box production plant at Cléon went on strike. The day afterwards a British plant had to cease production. Within two weeks *Renault* was losing 60% of its usual daily output a day. The weaknesses were due to the following.

    ° Sourcing components from one plant only

    ° Heavy dependence on in-house components

    ° Low inventory

    ° The fact '...that Japanese-style management techniques depend on stability in labour relations, something in short supply in the French public sector'.

(Financial Times, 31 October 1991)

Question 3

Batch sizes within a JIT manufacturing environment may well be smaller than those associated with traditional manufacturing systems.

What costs might be associated with this feature of JIT?

1   Increased set-up costs

2   Opportunity cost of lost production capacity as machinery and the workforce reorganise for a different product

3   Additional materials handling costs

4   Increased administrative costs

A   None of the above
B   1, 2, 3 and 4
C   1 only
D   2 and 3 only

Answer

The correct answer is B.

Modern versus traditional stock control systems

4.7   There is no reason for the newer approaches to supersede the old entirely. A restaurant, for example, might find it preferable to use the traditional economic order quantity approach for staple non-perishable food stocks, but adopt JIT for perishable and 'exotic' items. In a hospital a stock-out could, quite literally, be fatal, and JIT would be quite unsuitable.

> ### Exam focus point
>
> There is a fairly straightforward optional question worth 25 marks in the pilot paper which, if you have worked through carefully and fully understood this section, you should have no trouble in answering.

5   SYNCHRONOUS MANUFACTURING

> ### KEY TERM
>
> **Synchronous manufacturing** is a manufacturing philosophy which aims to ensure that all operations within an organisation are performed for the common good of the organisation and that nothing is done unless it improves the bottom line.

5.1   It therefore requires managers to **focus on areas of operations which offer the greatest possibilities for global improvements** (such as at a bottleneck resource) rather than improving the process everywhere in the system, which is the JIT philosophy.

5.2   Proponents of synchronous manufacturing **regard JIT as unfocused**. They claim that it fails to identify capacity restraints in advance but waits until a problem occurs, which disrupts the entire processing system. Synchronous manufacturing, on the other hand, attempts to **detect problems before they happen** so that the production process and hence throughput are unaffected. According to advocates of synchronous manufacturing, **JIT** fails to focus effectively on bottleneck resources, with the result that **throughput may not be optimal**.

5.3   Synchronous manufacturing aims to **develop a production schedule that takes account of the constraints within the processing system**. This involves a detailed analysis of the plant's capabilities and the manufacturing environment with the aim of identifying the system's constraints. Time buffers are then built into the system at strategic points throughout the plant so as to avoid disruption and to ensure that the planned production schedule is met.

6 TOTAL QUALITY MANAGEMENT (TQM)

6.1 The modern business environment is remarkably different from the business environment of a decade or so ago. One change has been the **switch in emphasis away from quantity towards quality.** Consumers and **customers** have become **more sophisticated and discerning** in their requirements. They are no longer satisfied with accepting the late delivery of the same old unreliable products from an organisation which does not appear to care for its customers. They want new products, superior on-time delivery performance and an immediate response to their requests. Many organisations are therefore turning to quality to help them to survive the competitive modern business environment. **By developing new products quickly and supplying them on time at a consistently high level of quality such organisations are likely to become the success stories of the 1990s.**

Question 4

In your opinion, what organisations are likely to become the success stories of the first decade of the new Millennium? Why?

Total quality management

6.2 **Quality** means 'the **degree of excellence of a thing**' - how well made it is, or how well performed if it is a service, how well it serves its purpose, and how it measures up against its rivals. These criteria imply two things.

- That quality is something that **requires care on the part of the provider**.
- That quality is largely **subjective** - it is in the eye of the beholder, the **customer**.

6.3 The **management** of quality is the process of:

(a) Establishing **standards of quality** for a product or service

(b) Establishing **procedures or production methods** which ought to ensure that these required standards of quality are met in a suitably high proportion of cases

(c) **Monitoring** actual quality

(d) Taking **control action** when actual quality falls below standard

6.4 Take the postal service as an example. The postal service might establish a standard that 90% of first class letters will be delivered on the day after they are posted, and 99% will be delivered within two days of posting.

(a) Procedures would have to be established for ensuring that these standards could be met (attending to such matters as frequency of collections, automated letter sorting, frequency of deliveries and number of staff employed).

(b) Actual performance could be monitored, perhaps by taking samples from time to time of letters that are posted and delivered.

(c) If the quality standard is not being achieved, management should take control action (employ more postmen or advertise the use of postcodes again).

6.5 Quality management becomes **total (Total Quality Management (TQM)) when it is applied to everything a business does.**

KEY TERM

Total quality management (TQM) is 'an integrated and comprehensive system of planning and controlling all business functions so that products or services are produced which meet or exceed customer expectations. TQM is a philosophy of business behaviour, embracing principles such as employee involvement, continuous improvement at all levels and customer focus, as well as being a collection of related techniques aimed at improving quality such as full documentation of activities, clear goal setting and performance measurement from the customer perspective.'

(CIMA *Official Terminology*)

Get it right, first time

6.6 One of the basic principles of TQM is that the **cost of preventing mistakes is less than the cost of correcting them** once they occur. The aim should therefore be **to get things right first time**. Every mistake, delay and misunderstanding, directly costs an organisation money through **wasted time and effort,** including time taken in pacifying customers. The **lost potential for future sales because of poor customer service must also be taken into account.**

Continuous improvement

6.7 A second basic principle of TQM is dissatisfaction with the *status quo*: the belief that it is **always possible to improve** and so the aim should be to '**get it more right next time**'.

Quality assurance procedures

6.8 Because TQM embraces every activity of a business, quality assurance procedures **cannot be confined to the production process** but must also cover the work of sales, distribution and administration departments, the efforts of external suppliers, and the reaction of external customers.

Quality assurance of goods inwards

6.9 The quality of output depends on the quality of input materials, and so quality control should include **procedures for acceptance and inspection of goods inwards and measurement of rejects**. Each supplier can be given a 'rating' for the quality of the goods they tend to supply, and preference with purchase orders can be given to well-rated suppliers. This method is referred to as 'vendor rating'.

6.10 Where a **quality assurance scheme** is in place the supplier guarantees the quality of goods supplied and allows the customers' inspectors access while the items are being manufactured. The **onus is on the supplier to carry out the necessary quality checks**, or face cancellation of the contract.

6.11 Suppliers' quality assurance schemes are being used increasingly, particularly where extensive sub-contracting work is carried out, for example in the motor industries. One such scheme is **BS EN ISO 9000** certification. A company that gains registration has a certificate testifying that it is operating to a structure of written policies and procedures which are designed to ensure that it can consistently deliver a product or service to meet customer requirements.

BPP PUBLISHING

Inspection of output

6.12 This will take place at various key stages in the production process and will provide a continual check that the production process is under control. The aim of inspection is *not* really to sort out the bad products from the good ones after the work has been done. The **aim is to satisfy management that quality control in production is being maintained.**

6.13 The **inspection of samples** rather than 100% testing of all items will keep inspection costs down, and smaller samples will be less costly to inspect than larger samples. The greater the confidence in the reliability of production methods and process control, the smaller the samples will be.

Monitoring customer reaction

6.14 Some sub-standard items will inevitably be produced. Checks during production will identify some bad output, but other items will reach the customer who is the ultimate judge of quality. **Complaints ought to be monitored** in the form of letters of complaint, returned goods, penalty discounts, claims under guarantee, or requests for visits by service engineers. Some companies actually survey customers on a regular basis.

Employees and quality

6.15 Employees often have a poor attitude towards quality, as a system imposed 'from outside' by non-operational staff and as an implication of lack of trust in workers to maintain quality standards or to apply a control system with objectivity themselves.

6.16 **Attitudes to quality control and the management of it** have, however, been **undergoing changes**.

(a) As the pace of change in the environment has increased so attention to quality and a commitment to quality standards has become a **vital factor for organisational adaptation and survival**.

(b) It is being recognised that **workers can be motivated by a positive approach to quality**: producing quality work is a tangible and worthwhile objective. Where responsibility for quality checking has been given to the worker himself (encouraging self-supervision), **job satisfaction may be increased**: it is a kind of job enrichment, and also a sign of trust and respect, because imposed controls have been removed.

(c) **Non-aversive ways of implementing quality control** have been devised. **Cultural orientation** (the deep 'belief' in quality, filtered down to all operatives) can be enlisted. **Inter-group competition** to meet and beat quality standards, for example, might be encouraged. **Quality circles** may be set up, perhaps with responsibility for implementing improvements which they identify.

6.17 Problems can therefore be overcome by **changing people's attitudes** rather than teaching them new tricks. The key issue is to instil **understanding of, and commitment to, working practices that lead to quality**.

Case example

As part of its TQM programme *BICC Cables* reorganised its factory from its traditional process-based operation into a dedicated product layout. It then launched two separate but related training and development activities, teamwork training and JIT training.

'To implement (JIT) working it was decided to use a firm of consultants in the first manufacturing cell to ensure a comprehensively structured introduction, with our own people working alongside them, and then to implement JIT in the other three cells ourselves.

We decided to create a **game** to convey JIT principles, and all employees in the first cell participated in it. This was followed by a series of **training/information sessions**, during which the importance of bottleneck management and inventory control was emphasised.

Employees rapidly gained an understanding of JIT and learnt the basic lessons that lots of work in progress was not necessary for the factory to be productive and that people did not always have to be busy to be effective. As in the game, we installed '**Kanbans**' on the shopfloor to limit and control the flow of inventory. When the Kanban is full, it acts as a signal to the previous process not to transfer any more work and, if required, to stop the previous process.

This was a difficult idea to take on. In effect we went **against traditional practice** by asking people to stop processes even though there was work to be done and to make themselves available for other work. This focuses attention on where effort needs to be applied to get products dispatched.

This cycle of training and implementation was repeated in the remaining three cells until the complete factory unit was operating along the JIT lines. The use of Kanbans has significantly reduced work in progress, and space has been released which has been used to accommodate new machines.'

6.18 Workers themselves are frequently the best source of information about how (or how not) to improve quality. **Empowerment** therefore has two key aspects.

(a) Allowing workers to have the **freedom to decide how to do** the necessary work, using the skills they possess and acquiring new skills as necessary to be an effective team member.

(b) Making workers **responsible** for achieving production targets and for quality control.

Design for quality

6.19 A TQM environment aims to get it right first time, and this means that **quality, not faults, must be designed into the organisation's products and operations from the outset**.

Quality control happens at various stages in the process of designing a product or service.

(a) At the **product design stage**, quality control means trying to design a product or service so that its specifications provide a suitable balance between price and quality (of sales and delivery, as well as manufacture) which will make the product or service competitive.

(b) **Production engineering** is the **process of designing the methods for making a product** (or service) **to the design specification**. It sets out to make production methods as efficient as possible, and to avoid the manufacture of sub-standard items.

(c) **Information systems** should be designed to get the required information to the right person at the right time; **distribution systems** should be designed to get the right item to the right person at the right time; and so on.

Quality control and inspection

6.20 A distinction should be made between **quality control** and **inspection**.

(a) **Quality control** involves setting controls for the process of manufacture or service delivery. It is a aimed at **preventing the manufacture of defective items** or the provision of defective services.

(b) **Inspection** is a technique of **identifying when defective items are being produced at an unacceptable level.** Inspection is usually carried out at three main points.
   (i) Receiving inspection - for raw materials and purchased components
   (ii) Floor or process inspection for WIP
   (iii) Final inspection or testing for finished goods

Question 5

Read the following extract from an article in the *Financial Times* in April 1993, and then list the features and methods of a quality information system that *Lloyds Bank* might have devised to collect information on the impact of the 'service challenge' described here.

'If you telephone a branch of *Lloyds Bank* and it rings five times before there is a reply; if the person who answers does not introduce him or herself by name during the conversation; if you are standing in a queue with more people in it than the number of tills, then something is wrong.'

'If any of these things happen then the branch is breaching standards of customer service set by the bank since last July ... the "service challenge" was launched in the bank's 1,888 branches last summer after being tested in 55 branches in 1990 ...'

'*Lloyds* already has evidence of the impact. Customers were more satisfied with pilot branches in 1991 than with others.'

Answer

A wide variety of answers is possible. The article goes on to explain how the bank is actually going about monitoring the impact of the initiative.

(a)   It has devised a 100 point scale showing average satisfaction with branch service.

(b)   It conducts a 'first impressions' survey of all new customers.

(c)   There is also a general survey carried out every six months which seeks the views of a weighted sample of 350 customers per branch.

(d)   A survey company telephones each branch anonymously twice a month to test how staff respond to enquiries about products.

(e)   A quarter of each branch's staff answer a monthly questionnaire about the bank's products to test their knowledge.

(f)   Groups of employees working in teams in branches are allowed to set their own additional standards. This is to encourage participation.

(g)   Branches that underperform are more closely watched by 24 managers who monitor the initiative.

---

7   COSTS OF QUALITY AND COST OF QUALITY REPORTS   Pilot paper

7.1   When we talk about quality-related costs you should remember that a concern for **good quality saves money**; it is **poor quality that costs money.**

7.2   **Cost of quality reports highlight the total cost to an organisation of producing products or services that do not conform with quality requirements.** Four categories of cost should be reported: prevention costs, appraisal costs, internal failure costs and external failure costs.

KEY TERMS

The **cost of quality** is 'The difference between the actual cost of producing, selling and supporting products or services and the equivalent costs if there were no failures during production or usage'. The cost of quality can be analysed into the following.

Cost of conformance is 'The cost of achieving specified quality standards.

- **Cost of prevention** - the costs incurred prior to or during production in order to prevent substandard or defective products or services from being produced

- **Cost of appraisal** - costs incurred in order to ensure that outputs produced meet required quality standards'

Cost of non-conformance is 'The cost of failure to deliver the required standard of quality.

- **Cost of internal failure** - the costs arising from inadequate quality which are identified before the transfer of ownership from supplier to purchaser

- **Cost of external** - the cost arising from inadequate quality discovered after the transfer of ownership from supplier to purchaser'   (CIMA *Official Terminology*)

Quality-related cost	Example
Prevention costs	Quality engineering
	Design/development of quality control/inspection equipment
	Maintenance of quality control/inspection equipment
	Administration of quality control
	Training in quality control
Appraisal costs	Acceptance testing
	Inspection of goods inwards
	Inspection costs of in-house processing
	Performance testing
Internal failure costs	Failure analysis
	Re-inspection costs
	Losses from failure of purchased items
	Losses due to lower selling prices for sub-quality goods
	Costs of reviewing product specifications after failures
External failure costs	Administration of customer complaints section
	Costs of customer service section
	Product liability costs
	Cost of repairing products returned from customers
	Cost of replacing items due to sub-standard products/marketing errors

Exam focus point

Quality costs were examined in the objective testing section of the pilot paper.

7.3   The **cost of conformance** is a **discretionary** cost which is incurred with the intention of **eliminating the costs of internal and external failure**. The **cost of non-conformance**, on the other hand, can **only be reduced by increasing the cost of conformance**. The **optimal investment in conformance costs** is when **total costs of quality reach a minimum** (which may be below 100% quality conformance).

7.4 Shown below is a typical cost of quality report. **Some figures** in the report, such as the contribution forgone due to sales lost because of poor quality, may have to be **estimated,** but it is better to include an estimate rather than omit the category from the report.

The report has the following **uses**.

(a) By expressing each cost category as a percentage of sales revenue, **comparisons** can be made with previous periods, divisions within the group or other organisations, thereby highlighting problem areas. A comparison of the proportion of external failure costs to sales revenue with the figures for other organisations, for example, can provide some idea of the level of customer satisfaction.

(b) It can be used to make senior management aware of **how much is being spent** on quality-related costs.

(c) It can provide an indication of **how total quality costs could be reduced by a more sensible division of costs between the four categories.** For example, an increase in spending on prevention costs should reduce the costs of internal and external failure and hence reduce total spending.

COST OF QUALITY REPORT
YEAR ENDING 31 DECEMBER 20X0

	£'000	£'000	Cost as % of annual turnover (£10 million)
Prevention costs			
Design of quality control equipment	80		
Quality control training	80		
		160	1.6
Appraisal costs			
Inspection of goods inwards	90		
Inspection of WIP	100		
		190	1.9
Internal failure costs			
Scrap	150		
Rework	200		
		350	3.5
External failure costs			
Returns	500		
Contribution forgone on lost sales	400		
Handling customer complaints	100		
		1,000	10.0
		1,700	17.0

7.5 Although cost of quality reports provide a useful summary of the costs, effort and progress of quality, **non-financial quality measures** may be more appropriate for **lower levels of management**. Here are some examples of such measures.

- Number of customer complaints
- Number of warranty claims
- Number of defective units delivered to customers as a percentage of total units delivered

Standard costing in a total quality environment   5/01

7.6 It has been argued that **traditional variance analysis** is **unhelpful** and **potentially misleading** in the modern organisation, and causes managers to **focus their attention on the wrong issues**.

7.7 **Standard costing** concentrates on **quantity** and ignores other factors contributing to an organisation's effectiveness. In a **total quality** environment, however, quantity is not an issue, **quality** is. Effectiveness in such an environment therefore centres on high quality output (produced as a result of high quality input); the cost of failing to achieve the required level of effectiveness is not measured in variances, but in terms of the **internal and external failure costs** which would not be identified by traditional standard costing analysis.

7.8 **Standard costing** might measure, say, **labour efficiency** in terms of individual tasks and the level of **output**. In a **total quality environment**, labour is most likely to be viewed as a number of **multi-task teams** who are responsible for completion of a part of the production process. The effectiveness of such a team is more appropriately measured in terms of **re-working** required, **returns** from customers, **defects** identified in subsequent stages of production and so on.

7.9 In a **TQM** environment there are likely to be **minimal rate variances** if the workforce are paid a guaranteed weekly wage. Fixed price contracts, with suppliers guaranteeing levels of quality, are often a feature, especially if a JIT system is also in place, and so there are likely to be **few, if any, material price and usage variances.**

7.10 So **can standard costing and TQM exist together?**

(a) Predetermined standards conflict with the TQM philosophy of continual improvement.

(b) Continual improvements should alter quantities of inputs, prices and so on, whereas standard costing is best used in a stable, standardised, repetitive environment.

(c) Standard costs often incorporate a planned level of scrap in material standards. This is at odds with the TQM aim of 'zero defects'.

7.11 On the other hand, variance analysis can contribute towards the aim of improved product quality. Can you think how? The following question tests this point.

Question 6

AB plc has been receiving an increasing number of customer complaints about a general weakness in the quality of its products in recent months. The company believes that its future success is dependent on product quality and it is therefore determined to improve it.

Required

Describe the contribution that variance analysis can make towards the aim of improved product quality.

Answer

Variance analysis can be used to enhance product quality and to keep track of quality control information. This is because variance analysis measures both the planned use of resources and the actual use of resources in order to compare the two.

As variance analysis is generally expressed in terms of purely quantitative measures, such as quantity of raw materials used and price per unit of quantity, issues of quality would appear to be excluded from the reporting process. Quality would appear to be an excuse for spending more time, say, or buying more expensive raw materials.

Variance analysis, as it currently stands, therefore needs to be **adapted** to take account of quality issues.

(i) Variance analysis reports should routinely include **measures such as defect rates**. Although zero defects will be most desirable, such a standard of performance may not be reached at first. However there should be an expected rate of defects: if this is exceeded then management attention is directed to the excess.

(ii) The **absolute number of defects** should be measured *and* **their type**. If caused by certain materials and components this can shed light on, say, a favourable materials price variance which might have been caused by substandard materials being purchased more cheaply. Alternatively, if the defects are caused by shoddy assembly work this can shed light on a favourable labour efficiency variance if quality is being sacrificed for speed.

(iii) It should also be possible to provide **financial measures for the cost of poor quality**. These can include direct costs such as the wages of inspection and quality control staff, the cost of time in rectifying the defects, and the cost of the materials used in rectification.

(iv) Measures could be built into materials price and variance analysis, so that the **materials price variance** as currently reported includes a **factor reflecting the quality of materials purchased**.

8 WORLD CLASS MANUFACTURING (WCM)

8.1 World class manufacturing (WCM) is a term much in vogue at present. It was coined in the mid-1980s to **describe the fundamental changes taking place in manufacturing companies** we have been examining. WCM is a very broad term.

> **KEY TERM**
>
> 'World Class Manufacturing (WCM) describes the manufacture of high-quality products reaching customers quickly (or the delivery of a prompt and quality service) at a low cost to provide high performance and customer satisfaction.'
>
> Peter J Clarke ('The old and the new in management accounting', *Management Accounting*, June 1995)

8.2 In essence, however, WCM can be taken to have four key elements.

Key element	Description
A new approach to product quality	Instead of a policy of trying to detect defects or poor quality in production as and when they occur, WCM sets out to **identify the root causes of poor quality, eliminate them, and achieve zero defects, that is 100% quality,** thereby incorporating the principles of **TQM.**
Just-in-time manufacturing	See Section 4
Managing people	WCM aims to utilise the skills and abilities of the work force to the full. Employees are given **training** in a variety of skills, so that they can **switch from one task to another**. They are also given more **responsibility** for production scheduling and quality. A **team approach** is encouraged, with strong trust between management and workers.
Flexible approach to customer requirements	The WCM policy is to **develop close relationships** with customers in order to know what their requirements are, supply them on time, with short delivery lead times and change the product mix quickly and develop new products or modify existing products as customer needs change.

8.3 A WCM manufacturer will have a clear **manufacturing strategy** aimed at issues such as quality and reliability, short lead times (the time from start to finish of production), flexibility and customer satisfaction. But to compete, the world class manufacturer must appreciate that it is **not just in manufacturing that he must excel**. A **clear understanding** of the relationship between all of the factors which add value to an organisation's products (the **value chain**) is vital.

8.4   The value chain is made up of the following.

- Research and development
- Design
- Production
- Marketing

- Distribution
- Customer service
- Customers

8.5   To improve quality, reduce costs and increase innovation, the manufacturer must ensure that the **functions within the value chain are coordinated** within the overall organisational framework.

Case example

In January 1993 the *Financial Times* reported the findings of a comparative study of 18 UK and Japanese companies by *Andersen Consulting* and Cambridge University. All of the companies were suppliers of components to the motor industry. The overall finding was that **most of the UK companies lag far behind the 'world class' productivity and quality standards set by the best Japanese companies**. Specific points mentioned included the following.

(a)   UK plants had an average of 2.5 **defects** per 100 components, compared with 2.5 per 10,000 for the best Japanese plants.

(b)   The UK plants typically needed **twice as many employees** to produce the same number of parts.

(c)   The world class plants were making a **more complex and rapidly changing mix of products** than their rivals.

(d)   The world class plants **involved more of their employees** more intensively in problem-solving. In such plants **team leaders** were pivotal, developing the skills of team members as well as taking responsibility for quality and management issues.

(e)   The **organisation of** the production process in world class firms was highly significant. 'It starts with integrating every production step into an uninterrupted flow - so parts travel the minimum distance and hardly wait for the next operation.' Thereafter, 'the discipline governing the flow comes from short set-up times and small lots produced just-in-time, thus eliminating waste and work in progress.' Random interruptions and variability such as machine breakdowns, supplier hiccups or defective parts are eliminated.

(f)   The 'world class' firms had a **tightly integrated supply chain**, marked by minimal stock, frequent deliveries of small volumes of parts, lack of disruption and stable supply volumes. The discipline of the system came from short lead times between order and delivery and building to customer order rather than to accumulate stock.

Chapter roundup

- Changes to the **competitive environment**, **product life cycles** and **customer requirements** have had a significant impact on the modern business environment.

- Different approaches for **organising a manufacturing process include jobbing industries, batch processing and mass production**.

- **Cellular manufacturing** involves a U-shaped flow along which are arranged a number of different machines that are used to make products with similar machining requirements.

- **Advanced manufacturing technology (AMT)** is a general expression encompassing **computer-aided design (CAD), computer-aided manufacturing (CAM)** and **flexible manufacturing systems (FMS)**. An FMS is a highly-automated manufacturing system which is computer controlled and capable of producing a broad 'family' of parts in a flexible manner.

- The **production management strategies** linked to AMT are materials requirement planning (MRPI), manufacturing resource planning (MRPII), enterprise resource planning (ERP), optimised production technology (OPT) and just-in-time (JIT).

- **JIT** aims for zero inventory and perfect quality and operates by demand-pull. It consists of **JIT purchasing** and **JIT production** and results in lower investment requirements, space savings, greater customer satisfaction and increased flexibility.

- **Synchronous manufacturing** aims to ensure that all operations within an organisation are performed for the common good of the organisation.

- In the context of **Total Quality Management** 'quality' means getting it right first time, and improving continuously.

- **Quality costs** can be analysed into **prevention, appraisal, internal failure** and **external failure** costs and should be detailed in a **cost of quality report.**

- **World class manufacturing (WCM)** aims for high quality, fast production, and the flexibility to respond to customer needs.

Quick quiz

1   *Match the type of production with one of the descriptions (1) to (4).*

Jobbing industries	(1)	Merges the flexibility of the functional layout with the speed and productivity of the product layout
Batch processing	(2)	Uses a product-based layout
Mass/flow production	(3)	Factory is typically laid out on a functional basis
Cellular manufacturing	(4)	Uses functional layout but with a high number of specialised machines

2   *Choose four possible features of a FMS from the list below.*

| CNC machines | Robots | CIM | ASRS |
| Computerised MHS | JIT system | AGV | CAD |

3   *Choose the correct words from those highlighted.*

   Materials requirement planning/manufacturing requirement planning/materials resource planning/manufacturing resource planning is concerned with maximising efficiency in the timing of orders for raw materials or parts that are placed with external suppliers and efficient scheduling of the manufacturing and assembly of the end product.

4   *Fill in the blanks in this list of the nine essential elements of JIT.*

   (a)   JIT ....
   (b)   Close relationship with ....
   (c)   Uniform ....
   (d)   Set-up time ....

(e)   .... cells

(f)   ....

(g)   .... (Kanban)

(h)   .... maintenance

(i)   .... involvement

5   The cost of inspecting a product for quality is a value-added cost. *True or false?*

6   *Which of the following is/are correct?*

(a)   Cost of conformance = cost of prevention + cost of internal failure
(b)   Cost of conformance = cost of internal failure + cost of external failure
(c)   Cost of non-conformance = cost of internal failure + cost of external failure
(d)   Cost of conformance = cost of appraisal + cost of prevention
(e)   Cost of non-conformance = cost of prevention + cost of appraisal
(f)   Cost of non-conformance = cost of appraisal + cost of external failure

7   *Match the cost to the correct cost category.*

Costs

(a)   Administration of quality control
(b)   Product liability costs
(c)   Acceptance testing
(d)   Losses due to lower selling prices for sub-quality goods

Cost categories

•   Prevention costs
•   Appraisal costs
•   Internal failure costs
•   External failure costs

Answers to quick quiz

1   Jobbing industries   - description (3)
    Batch processing   - description (4)
    Mass/flow production   - description (2)
    Cellular manufacturing   - description (1)

2   JIT system   Computerised MHS
    CIM   ASRS

3   Materials requirement planning

4   (a)   JIT purchasing
    (b)   Close relationships with suppliers
    (c)   Uniform loading
    (d)   Set-up time reduction
    (e)   Machine cells
    (f)   Quality
    (g)   Pull system (Kanban)
    (h)   Preventative maintenance
    (i)   Employee involvement

5   False

6   (c) and (d) are correct.

7   (a)   Prevention costs
    (b)   External failure costs
    (c)   Appraisal costs
    (d)   Internal failure costs

Now try the question below from the Exam Question Bank

Number	Level	Marks	Time
Q13	Pilot paper	25	45 mins

Chapter 10

ACTIVITY BASED COSTING

Topic list		Syllabus reference	Ability required
1	The reasons for the development of ABC	(iii)	Comprehension
2	Definition of ABC	(iii)	Comprehension
3	Outline of an ABC system	(iii)	Comprehension
4	Absorption costing versus ABC	(iii)	Comprehension
5	Merits and criticisms of ABC	(iii)	Comprehension
6	Activity based budgeting	(iii)	Analysis/evaluation

Introduction

In the previous chapter we looked at the modern business environment and the impact that it has had on organisations.

In this chapter we will be considering one of the **management accounting techniques for allocating and managing resources** (in this case overheads) which has emerged in response to the modern developments we looked at in Chapter 9.

Learning outcomes covered in this chapter

* **Explain** activity based costing

* **Evaluate** performance using fixed and flexible budget reports

* **Discuss** alternative approaches to budgeting

Syllabus content covered in this chapter

* Activity based costing

* Activity based budgeting

1 THE REASONS FOR THE DEVELOPMENT OF ABC

1.1 The traditional cost accumulation system of **absorption costing** was developed in a time when most organisations produced only a **narrow range of products** and when **overhead costs were only a very small fraction of total costs**, direct labour and direct material costs accounting for the largest proportion of the costs. Errors made in attributing overheads to products were not too significant.

1.2 Nowadays, however, with the advent of **advanced manufacturing technology (AMT)**, **overheads** are likely to be far **more important** and in fact direct labour may account for as little as 5% of a product's cost. It therefore now appears difficult to justify the use of direct labour or direct material as the basis for absorbing overheads or to believe that errors made in attributing overheads will not be significant.

1.3 Many resources are used in **non-volume related support activities,** (which have increased due to AMT) such as setting-up, production scheduling, inspection and data processing. These support activities assist the efficient manufacture of a wide range of products and are **not, in general, affected by changes in production volume.** They tend to **vary in the long term according to the range and complexity** of the products manufactured rather than the volume of output.

1.4 The wider the range and the more complex the products, the more support services will be required. Consider, for example, factory X which produces 10,000 units of one product, the Alpha, and factory Y which produces 1,000 units each of ten slightly different versions of the Alpha. Support activity costs in the factory Y are likely to be a lot higher than in factory X but the factories produce an identical number of units. For example, factory X will only need to set-up once whereas Factory Y will have to set-up the production run at least ten times for the ten different products. Factory Y will therefore incur more set-up costs for the same volume of production.

1.5 **Traditional costing systems,** which assume that all products consume all resources in proportion to their production volumes, tend to **allocate too great a proportion of overheads to high volume products** (which cause relatively little diversity and hence use fewer support services) and **too small a proportion of overheads to low volume products** (which cause greater diversity and therefore use more support services). **Activity based costing (ABC) attempts to overcome this problem.**

2 DEFINITION OF ABC

Pilot paper

> **KEY TERM**
>
> **Activity based costing (ABC)** is 'An approach to the costing and monitoring of activities which involves tracing resource consumption and costing final outputs. Resources are assigned to activities and activities to cost objects based on consumption estimates. The latter utilise cost drivers to attach activity costs to outputs'.   (CIMA *Official Terminology*)

2.1 The **major ideas** behind activity based costing are as follows.

(a) **Activities cause costs.** Activities include ordering, materials handling, machining, assembly, production scheduling and despatching.

(b) **Producing products creates demand for the activities.**

(c) **Costs** are **assigned** to a product **on the basis of the product's consumption of the activities.**

3 OUTLINE OF AN ABC SYSTEM

5/01

3.1 An ABC system operates as follows.

Step 1. Identify an organisation's major activities.

Step 2. Identify the **factors which determine the size of the costs of an activity/cause the costs of an activity.** These are known as **cost drivers.**

BPP PUBLISHING

KEY TERM

A **cost driver** is 'Any factor which causes a change in the cost of an activity, eg the quality of parts received by an activity is a determining factor in the work required by that activity and therefore affects the resources required. An activity may have multiple cost drivers associated with it.' (CIMA *Official Terminology*)

Look at the following examples.

Costs	Possible cost driver
Ordering costs	Number of orders
Materials handling costs	Number of production runs
Production scheduling costs	Number of production runs
Despatching costs	Number of despatches

For those **costs that vary with production levels in the short term**, ABC uses **volume-related cost drivers** such as labour or machine hours. The cost of oil used as a lubricant on the machines would therefore be added to products on the basis of the number of machine hours, since oil would have to be used for each hour the machine ran.

Step 3. Collect the **costs associated with each cost driver** into what are known as **cost pools**.

Step 4. Charge costs to products on the basis of their usage of the activity. A product's usage of an activity is measured by the number of the activity's cost driver it generates.

Question 1

Which of the following definitions best describes a cost driver?

A   Any activity which causes an increase in costs
B   A collection of costs associated with a particular activity
C   A cost that varies with production levels
D   Any factor which causes a change in the cost of an activity

Answer

The correct answer is D.

Transactions analysis

3.2   Miller and Vollman ('The Hidden Factory', *Harvard Business Review*, 1985) provided a useful system for analysing the activities which cause overheads to be incurred.

Types of transaction	Detail
Logistical transactions	Those activities concerned with organising the flow of resources throughout the manufacturing process.
Balancing transactions	Those activities which ensure that demand for and supply of resources are matched.
Quality transactions	Those activities which relate to ensuring that production is at the required level of quality.

Types of transaction	Detail
Change transactions	Those activities associated with ensuring that customers' requirements (delivery date, changed design and so on) are met.

Note that the primary driver of these activities is not usually production volume. For example, the level of change transactions might be determined by the number of customers and the number of different product types, rather than by production volume.

4 ABSORPTION COSTING VERSUS ABC 5/01

4.1 The following example illustrates the point that traditional cost accounting techniques result in a misleading and inequitable division of costs between low-volume and high-volume products, and that ABC can provide a more meaningful allocation of costs.

4.2 EXAMPLE: ACTIVITY BASED COSTING

Suppose that Cooplan Ltd manufactures four products, W, X, Y and Z. Output and cost data for the period just ended are as follows.

	Output units	Number of production runs in the period	Material cost per unit £	Direct labour hours per unit	Machine hours per unit
W	10	2	20	1	1
X	10	2	80	3	3
Y	100	5	20	1	1
Z	100	5	80	3	3
		14			

Direct labour cost per hour	£5

Overhead costs	£
Short run variable costs	3,080
Set-up costs	10,920
Expediting and scheduling costs	9,100
Materials handling costs	7,700
	30,800

Required

Prepare unit costs for each product using conventional costing and ABC.

4.3 SOLUTION

Using a **conventional absorption costing approach** and an absorption rate for overheads based on either direct labour hours or machine hours, the product costs would be as follows.

	W £	X £	Y £	Z £	Total £
Direct material	200	800	2,000	8,000	
Direct labour	50	150	500	1,500	
Overheads *	700	2,100	7,000	21,000	
	950	3,050	9,500	30,500	44,000

	W	X	Y	Z
Units produced	10	10	100	100
Cost per unit	£95	£305	£95	£305

* £30,800 ÷ 440 hours = £70 per direct labour or machine hour.

Using **activity based costing** and assuming that the number of production runs is the cost driver for set-up costs, expediting and scheduling costs and materials handling costs and that machine hours are the cost driver for short-run variable costs, unit costs would be as follows.

	W	X	Y	Z	Total
	£	£	£	£	£
Direct material	200	800	2,000	8,000	
Direct labour	50	150	500	1,500	
Short-run variable overheads (W1)	70	210	700	2,100	
Set-up costs (W2)	1,560	1,560	3,900	3,900	
Expediting, scheduling costs (W3)	1,300	1,300	3,250	3,250	
Materials handling costs (W4)	1,100	1,100	2,750	2,750	
	4,280	5,120	13,100	21,500	44,000
Units produced	10	10	100	100	
Cost per unit	£428	£512	£131	£215	

Workings

1	£3,080 ÷ 440 machine hours =	£7 per machine hour
2	£10,920 ÷ 14 production runs =	£780 per run
3	£9,100 ÷ 14 production runs =	£650 per run
4	£7,700 ÷ 14 production runs =	£550 per run

Summary

Product	Conventional costing Unit cost	ABC Unit cost	Difference per unit	Difference in total
	£	£	£	£
W	95	428	+ 333	+3,330
X	305	512	+ 207	+2,070
Y	95	131	+ 36	+3,600
Z	305	215	− 90	−9,000

The figures suggest that the **traditional volume-based absorption costing system is flawed.**

(a) It **underallocates overhead costs to low-volume products** (here, W and X) and **over-allocates overheads to higher-volume products** (here Z in particular).

(b) It **underallocates overhead costs to smaller-sized products** (here W and Y with just one hour of work needed per unit) and **over allocates overheads to larger products** (here X and particularly Z).

ABC versus traditional costing methods

4.4 Both traditional absorption costing and ABC systems adopt the two stage allocation process.

Allocation of overheads

4.5 **ABC** establishes **separate cost pools for support activities** such as despatching. As the costs of these activities are assigned directly to products through cost driver rates, **reapportionment of service department costs is avoided.**

Absorption of overheads

4.6 The principal difference between the two systems is the way in which overheads are absorbed into products.

 (a) **Absorption costing** most commonly uses two **absorption bases** (labour hours and/or machine hours) to charge overheads to products.

 (b) **ABC** uses **many cost drivers** as absorption bases (number of orders, number of despatches and so on).

4.7 **Absorption rates** under **ABC** should therefore be **more closely linked to the causes of overhead costs.**

Cost drivers

4.8 The **principal idea** of ABC is to **focus attention on what causes costs to increase,** ie the **cost drivers**.

 (a) Those **costs that do vary with production volume,** such as power costs, should be traced to products using production **volume-related cost drivers** as appropriate, such as direct labour hours or direct machine hours.

 Overheads which do not **vary** with output but **with some other activity** should be traced to products using **transaction-based cost drivers,** such as number of production runs and number of orders received.

 (b) Traditional costing systems allow overheads to be related to products in rather more arbitrary ways producing, it is claimed, less accurate product costs.

Question 2

A company manufactures two products, L and M, using the same equipment and similar processes. An extract of the production data for these products in one period is shown below.

	L	M
Quantity produced (units)	5,000	7,000
Direct labour hours per unit	1	2
Machine hours per unit	3	1
Set-ups in the period	10	40
Orders handled in the period	15	60

Overhead costs	£
Relating to machine activity	220,000
Relating to production run set-ups	20,000
Relating to handling of orders	45,000
	285,000

Required

Calculate the production overheads to be absorbed by one unit of each of the products using the following costing methods.

(a) A traditional costing approach using a direct labour hour rate to absorb overheads
(b) An activity based costing approach, using suitable cost drivers to trace overheads to products

Answer

(a) **Traditional costing approach**

	Direct labour hours
Product L = 5,000 units × 1 hour	5,000
Product M = 7,000 units × 2 hours	14,000
	19,000

$$\therefore \text{ Overhead absorption rate} = \frac{£285,000}{19,000}$$

		=	£15 per hour

Overhead absorbed would be as follows.

Product L	1 hour × £15	=	£15 per unit
Product M	2 hours × £15	=	£30 per unit

(b) **ABC approach**

		Machine hours
Product L	= 5,000 units × 3 hours	15,000
Product M	= 7,000 units × 1 hour	7,000
		22,000

Using ABC the overhead costs are absorbed according to the **cost drivers**.

	£			
Machine-hour driven costs	220,000	÷	22,000 m/c hours	= £10 per m/c hour
Set-up driven costs	20,000	÷	50 set-ups	= £400 per set-up
Order driven costs	45,000	÷	75 orders	= £600 per order

Overhead costs are therefore as follows.

		Product L £		Product M £
Machine-driven costs	(15,000 hrs × £10)	150,000	(7,000 hrs × £10)	70,000
Set-up costs	(10 × £400)	4,000	(40 × £400)	16,000
Order handling costs	(15 × £600)	9,000	(60 × £600)	36,000
		163,000		122,000
Units produced		5,000		7,000
Overhead cost per unit		£32.60		£17.43

These figures suggest that product M absorbs an unrealistic amount of overhead using a direct labour hour basis. Overhead absorption should be based on the activities which drive the costs, in this case machine hours, the number of production run set-ups and the number of orders handled for each product.

Exam focus point

ABC's appearance in the pilot paper was limited to a multiple choice question which asked for the most appropriate definition of the technique.

When should ABC be introduced?

4.9 ABC should only be introduced if the **additional information** it provides will **result in action that will increase** the organisation's overall **profitability**. This is most likely to **occur** in situations such as the following, when the **ABC analysis differs significantly from the absorption costing analysis**.

- Production overheads are high in relation to direct costs, especially direct labour.
- Overhead resource consumption is not just driven by production volume.
- There is wide variety in the product range.
- The overhead resource input varies significantly across the product range.

Analysis of activities

4.10 ABC attempts to relate the incidence of costs to the level of activities undertaken. A **hierarchy of cost**, showing five levels of activity, has been suggested.

Type of activities	Costs are dependent on ….	Examples
Unit level	Volume of production	Machine power
Batch level	Number of batches	Set-up costs
Product level	Existence of a product group/line	Product management
Facility level	Organisation simply being in business	Rent and rates

4.11 The difference between a unit product cost determined using absorption costing and one determined using ABC will depend on the proportion of overhead cost which falls into each of the categories above.

(a) If most overheads are related to unit level and facility level activities, the costs will be similar.

(b) If the overheads tend to be associated with batch or product level activities they will be significantly different.

5 MERITS AND CRITICISMS OF ABC 5/01

5.1 As you will have discovered when you attempted the question above, there is nothing difficult about ABC. Once the necessary information has been obtained it is similar to traditional absorption costing. This simplicity is part of its appeal. Further merits of ABC are as follows.

(a) The **complexity of manufacturing has increased,** with wider product ranges, shorter product life cycles and more complex production processes. **ABC recognises this complexity with its multiple cost drivers.**

(b) In a more competitive environment, companies must be able to assess product profitability realistically. **ABC facilitates a good understanding of what drives overhead costs.**

(c) In modern manufacturing systems, overhead functions include a lot of non-factory-floor activities such as product design, quality control, production planning and customer services. **ABC is concerned with all overhead costs** and so it takes management accounting beyond its 'traditional' factory floor boundaries.

(d) By controlling the incidence of the cost driver, the level of the **cost** can be **controlled**.

Criticisms of ABC

5.2 It has been suggested by critics that **activity based costing has some series flaws.**

(a) Some measure of (arbitrary) cost apportionment may still be required at the cost pooling stage for items like rent, rates and building depreciation.

(b) Can a single cost driver explain the cost behaviour of all items in its associated pool?

(c) Unless costs are caused by an activity that is measurable in quantitative terms and which can be related to production output, cost drivers will not be usable. What drives the cost of the annual external audit, for example?

(d) ABC is sometimes introduced because it is fashionable, not because it will be used by management to provide meaningful product costs or extra information. If management is not going to use ABC information, an absorption costing system may be simpler to operate.

6 ACTIVITY BASED BUDGETING 5/01

6.1 You may remember in Part B, when we were looking at alternative approaches to budgeting and flexible budgets, that mention was made of activity based budgeting. Now that you have studied the underlying technique of activity based costing we can cover the topic in detail.

KEY TERM

Activity based budgeting is 'A method of budgeting based on an activity framework and utilising cost driver data in the budget-setting and variance feedback processes.'

(CIMA *Official Terminology*)

6.2 At its **simplest**, activity based budgeting (ABB) is merely the **use of costs determined using** ABC **as a basis for preparing budgets**. Implementing ABC leads to the realisation that the **business as a whole** needs to be **managed** with far more reference to the behaviour of activities and cost drivers identified. For example, traditional budgeting may make managers 'responsible' for activities which are driven by factors beyond their control: the cost of setting-up new personnel records and of induction training would traditionally be the responsibility of the personnel manager even though such costs are driven by the number of new employees required by managers other than the personnel manager.

6.3 More **formally**, therefore, ABB involves **defining the activities** that underlie the financial figures in each function and using the level of activity to decide **how much resource should be allocated**, how well it is being **managed** and to explain **variances** from budget.

6.4 **Claimed results of using ABB**

(a) Different activity levels will provide a foundation for the base package and incremental packages of ZBB.

(b) The organisation's overall strategy and any actual or likely changes in that strategy will be taken into account because ABB attempts to manage the business as the sum of its interrelated parts.

(c) Critical success factors (an activity in which a business must perform well if it is to succeed) will be identified and performance measures devised to monitor progress towards them.

(d) The focus is on the whole of an activity, not just its separate parts, and so there is more likelihood of getting it right first time. For example, what is the use of being able to produce goods in time for their despatch date if the budget provides insufficient resources for the distribution manager who has to deliver them.

Flexed budgets using ABC data

6.5 Suppose the budget for a production department for a given period is as follows.

	£
Wages	220,000
Materials	590,000
Equipment	20,000
Power, heat and light	11,000
	841,000

This budget gives little indication of the link between the level of activity in the department and the costs incurred, however.

6.6   Suppose the activities in the department have been identified as sawing, hammering, finishing, reworking and production reporting. The budget might therefore be restated as follows.

Activities	Cost driver	Budgeted cost per unit of cost driver £	Budgeted no of cost drivers	Budget £
Sawing	Number of units sawed	50.00	5,000	250,000
Hammering	Number of units hammered together	10.00	35,000	350,000
Finishing	Number of sq metres finished	0.50	400,000	200,000
Reworking	Number of items reworked	12.40	2,500	31,000
Production reporting	Number of reports	400.00	25	10,000
				841,000

6.7   **Advantages of this approach**

(a)   Costs classified as fixed in the first budget can now be seen to be variable and hence can be more readily controlled.

(b)   The implications of increases/decreases in levels of activity are immediately apparent. For example, if acceptable quality levels were raised so that an additional 200 units per annum were reworked, budgeted costs would increase by 200 × £12.40 = £2,480.

6.8   A **flexible budget** would be prepared as follows.

	Actual no of cost drivers	Budgeted cost per unit of cost driver £	Flexed budget £	Actual cost £	Variance £	
Sawing	6,000	50.00	300,000	297,000	3,000	(F)
Hammering	40,000	10.00	400,000	404,000	4,000	(A)
Finishing	264,400	0.50	132,200	113,200	19,000	(F)
Reworking	4,500	12.40	55,800	56,100	300	(A)
Production reporting	30	400.00	12,000	13,700	1,700	(A)
			900,000	884,000	16,000	(F)

Chapter roundup

- An alternative to the traditional method of accounting for costs - absorption costing - is **activity based costing (ABC)**. ABC involves the identification of the factors (**cost drivers**) which cause the costs of an organisation's major activities. Support overheads are charged to products on the basis of their usage of an activity.

- When using ABC, for costs that vary with production levels in the short term, the cost driver will be volume related (labour or machine hours). Overheads that vary with some other activity (and not volume of production) should be traced to products using transaction-based cost drivers such as production runs or number of orders received.

- Although ABC has obvious merits, a number of criticisms have been raised.

- At its simplest, **activity based budgeting (ABB)** is merely the use of costs determined using ABC as a basis for preparing budgets. More formally, activity based budgeting involves defining the activities that underlie the financial figures in each function and using the level of activity to decide how much resource should be allocated, how well it is being managed and to explain divergences from budget.

Quick quiz

1   *Choose the correct words from those highlighted.*

Traditional costing systems tend to allocate **too great/too small** a proportion of overheads to high volume products and **too great/too small** a proportion of overheads to low volume products.

2   *Fill in the blanks.*

The major ideas behind ABC are as follows.

(a)   Activities cause ....

(b)   Producing products creates demand for the ....

(c)   Costs are assigned to a product on the basis of the product's consumption of the ....

3   *Match the most appropriate cost driver to each cost.*

Costs	*Cost driver*
(a) Set-up costs	Number of machine hours
(b) Short-run variable costs	Number of production runs
(c) Materials handling and despatch	Number of orders executed

4   ABC recognises the complexity of modern manufacturing by the use of multiple cost pools. *True or false?*

Answers to quick quiz

1   Too great
    Too small

2   (a)   Costs
    (b)   Activities
    (c)   Activities

3   (a)   Number of production runs
    (b)   Number of machine hours
    (c)   Number of orders executed

4   False. Complexity is recognised by the use of multiple cost drivers.

Now try the question below from the Exam Question Bank

Number	Level	Marks	Time
Q14	Introductory	n/a	45 mins

Chapter 11

COST REDUCTION

Topic list	Syllabus reference	Ability required
1 Cost control and cost reduction	(iii)	Analysis
2 Planning for cost reduction	(iii)	Analysis
3 The scope of cost reduction campaigns	(iii)	Analysis
4 Methods of cost reduction - improving efficiency	(iii)	Analysis
5 Methods of cost reduction - material costs	(iii)	Analysis
6 Methods of cost reduction - labour costs	(iii)	Analysis
7 Other aspects of cost reduction	(iii)	Analysis
8 Value analysis	(iii)	Analysis
9 The scope of value analysis	(iii)	Analysis
10 Carrying out a value analysis	(iii)	Analysis
11 Functional analysis	(iii)	Analysis

Introduction

In this chapter we begin by considering how costs can be managed using fairly standard, common sense ways of **reducing costs** (such as using better quality materials and setting more challenging standards for efficiency). We then move on to two particular approaches to cost management. **Value analysis** looks at how a product can be modified and improved without reducing the **cost, exchange, use or esteem values** of the product to the customer or user. **Functional analysis**, on the other hand, uses the **functions** of a product or service as the basis for cost management.

Learning outcomes covered in this chapter

* **Compare** and **contrast** value analysis and functional analysis

Syllabus content covered in this chapter

* Cost reduction programmes
* Value and functional cost analysis

1   COST CONTROL AND COST REDUCTION

1.1   Cost reduction should not be confused with cost control.

KEY TERM

Cost control is about regulating the costs of operating a business and keeping costs within acceptable limits.

BPP
PUBLISHING

The limits will usually be standard costs or target cost limits. If actual costs differ from planned costs by an excessive amount, cost control action will be necessary.

You might like to think of cost control as an exercise in good housekeeping; the wasteful use of valuable resources is avoided and efficiency and cost consciousness are encouraged.

Cost reduction, in contrast, is a planned and positive approach to reducing expenditure and starts with an assumption that current cost levels, or planned cost levels, are too high, even though cost control might be good and efficiency levels high.

> ## KEY TERM
>
> **Cost reduction** is 'The reduction in unit cost of goods or services without impairing suitability for the use intended'.　　　　　　　　　(CIMA *Official Terminology*)

1.2　Cost control action ought to lead to a reduction in excessive spending (for example when material wastage is higher than budget.) A cost reduction programme, on the other hand, aims to reduce expected actual cost levels to below current budgeted or standard levels by purchasing new equipment, changing methods of working and so on. So whereas **cost control aims to reduce costs to budget or standard level, cost reduction aims to reduce costs to below budget or standard level**, as budgets and standards do not necessarily reflect the cost and conditions which minimise costs.

2　PLANNING FOR COST REDUCTION

2.1　**Basic approaches to cost reduction**

(a)　**Crash programmes to cut spending levels.** Management might decide on an immediate programme to reduce spending to a minimum. Some current projects might be abandoned, capital expenditures deferred, employees made redundant and so on. The absence of careful planning might make such crash programmes look like panic measures. What's more, they might be too little and too late, or misdirected. For example, decisions by a company to reduce the size of its internal audit section might cut staff costs in the short term but increase costs in the longer term.

(b)　**Planned programmes to reduce costs.** Many companies tend to introduce crash programmes for cost reduction in times of crisis and ignore the problem completely in times of prosperity. A far better approach is to have continual assessments of the organisation's products, production methods, internal administration systems and so on.

Cost reduction exercises should therefore be planned campaigns to cut expenditure; they should preferably be continuous and long-term, so that short-term cost reductions are not soon reversed and 'forgotten'.

2.2　**Major difficulties with introducing cost reduction programmes**

(a)　There may be **resistance from employees** to the pressure to reduce costs, usually because the nature and purpose of the campaign has not been properly explained to them, and because they feel threatened by the change.

(b)　The programme may be limited to a small area of the business with the result that **costs are reduced in one cost centre, only to reappear as an extra cost in another**.

(c)　Cost reduction campaigns are **often introduced as a rushed, desperate measure** instead of a carefully organised, well thought-out exercise.

Question 1

Before looking for ways in which costs can be reduced it is useful to consider the reasons why unnecessary costs occur. Can you think of any examples?

Answer

- Lack of information, for example about new materials, products or processes
- Lack of ideas
- Incorrect beliefs, for example that quantities are too small to justify mass production techniques
- Changed circumstances, for example a failure to take advantage of better processes

3 THE SCOPE OF COST REDUCTION CAMPAIGNS

3.1 The scope of a cost reduction **campaign should embrace the activities of the entire company**.

3.2 A cost reduction campaign should have a **long-term aim as well as short-term objectives.**

(a) In the **short term** only **variable costs,** for the most part, are susceptible to cost reduction efforts. Many fixed costs (for example rent) are unavoidable.

(b) Some fixed costs are **avoidable in the short term** (for example advertising or sales promotion expenditure). These are called **discretionary fixed costs**.

(c) In the **long term most costs can be either reduced or avoided**. This includes fixed cost as well as variable cost expenditure items.

4 METHODS OF COST REDUCTION - IMPROVING EFFICIENCY 5/01

4.1 One way of reducing costs is to improve the efficiency of material usage, the productivity of labour, or the efficiency of machinery.

4.2 **Improved materials usage** might be achieved by reducing levels of wastage.

Question 2

Which of the following will not result in a reduction in wastage?

A Changing the specifications for cutting materials.
B Identifying poor quality output at an earlier stage in operational processes.
C Using a better quality of materials.
D Using more expensive materials

Answer

The correct answer is D.

More expensive materials are not necessarily of better quality.

4.3 **Improving labour productivity**

- Giving pay incentives for better productivity
- Changing work methods to eliminate unnecessary procedures
- Improving the methods for achieving cooperation between groups or departments
- Introducing standards where they did not exist before

Case example

A case study (the *Midland Bank International Division*) was reported in the February 1997 edition of *Management Accounting*. In this example, clerical standards were introduced into 15 departments, including over 1,000 clerical staff, and it was suggested that by establishing standards for routine office work, clerical efficiency would be improved.

4.4 Improving the efficiency of equipment usage

(a) Making better use of equipment resources. For example, if an office PC is only in use for 50% of its available time, it might be possible to put another application on to it, and so improve office productivity.

(b) Achieving a better balance between preventive maintenance and machine 'down-time' for repairs.

Question 3

A machine may be maintained at one of four levels, 1, 2, 3 and 4. The monthly costs of the maintenance work, and the monthly hours of production lost, are as follows.

Level	Maintenance cost £	Hours lost (cost £350/hour)
1	4,000	14
2	5,200	10
3	6,700	6
4	7,200	4

Which level of maintenance should be chosen.

A Level 1
B Level 2
C Level 3
D Level 4

Answer

The correct answer is D.

Level	Maintenance cost £	Cost of hours lost £	Total cost £
1	4,000	4,900	8,900
2	5,200	3,500	8,700
3	6,700	2,100	8,800
4	7,200	1,400	8,600

Level 4 gives the lowest total monthly cost.

4.5 Once improved standards of efficiency have been set, as a means of reducing costs, it is important that cost *control* should be applied by management.

5 METHODS OF COST REDUCTION - MATERIAL COSTS   5/01

5.1 Other ways of reducing materials costs

(a) A company could **obtain lower prices for purchases** of materials and components. Bulk purchase discounts might be obtainable at favourable rates or a system of putting all major purchase contracts out to tender might help to reduce prices.

(b) A company could **improve stores control and cut stores costs**. You should be aware of the concept of the economic order quantity, which is the size of order that will minimise the combined costs of ordering items for stock and stockholding costs. Stockholding costs might be reduced by dealing with problems of obsolescence, deterioration of items in store or theft.

(c) **Alternative materials** such as cheaper substitute materials could be used.

Question 4

Standardisation of parts and components might offer enormous cost reduction potential for some manufacturing industries. Can you think why this might be the case?

Answer

(a) If a manufacturer has fewer types of components to manufacture, he will be able to increase the length of production runs, thereby reducing production costs. (Non-standard parts tend to be produced in small runs, and unit costs will be higher as a consequence.)

(b) Standardisation helps to cut purchasing cost because there will be fewer items to buy and stock. The company can purchase in bulk, and so perhaps obtain bulk purchase discounts. It may also be possible to buy standard parts from more than one supplier, and so purchasing will be more competitive.

6 METHODS OF COST REDUCTION - LABOUR COSTS   5/01

6.1 Methods of reducing labour costs

- Improving efficiency or productivity, which was mentioned earlier
- Improving work methods following a work study or O & M programme (see below)
- **Replacing people with machinery**

Work study

> **KEY TERMS**
>
> **Work study** is a way of raising productivity by reorganising work. There are two main parts to work study: method study and work measurement.
>
> - **Method study** involves systematically recording and critically examining existing and proposed ways of doing work in order to develop and apply easier and more effective methods, and reduce costs.
>
> - **Work measurement** involves establishing the time for a qualified worker to carry out a specified job at a specified level of performance

6.2 Main objectives of a work study

(a) Analysis, design and improvement of work systems, work places and work methods

(b) Establishment of standards so as to be able to determine requirements in labour and equipment, assess performance, plan operations, cost operations and products, and pay workers

(c) Development and application of job evaluation schemes based on job descriptions

(d) Specification of plant facilities, layout and space utilisation

(e) Assessment of the most profitable alternative combinations of personnel, materials and equipment

(f) Development of procedures for planning and control of work and material usage

(g) Development of procedures for presenting information to management about work performance

6.3 The use of work study is of value for the following reasons.

- Tangible results are produced quickly.
- No large capital outlay is required.
- It is, in its basic form, simple and readily grasped in outline, by all.
- The facts it produces can be used to increase efficiency throughout the organisation.
- There is no work to which it cannot be applied.

6.4 The obvious application of work study is in production where it was first developed, but the technique is now applied in such industries as building and construction, agriculture, transport, hospitals, national and local government and many others.

6.5 **Direct observation methods** of work study involve observing jobs in practice, but **synthetic methods** are used to estimate the work study content of jobs without having to observe them. There are some occasions when observation is not possible, such as planning in advance for the manufacture of a new product. There are occasions when direct observation may be possible but inconvenient, or it may take too long and be too expensive. In these circumstances it is possible to estimate a standard time on the basis of previous experience from similar jobs.

Organisation and methods (O & M)

KEY TERM

Organisation and methods (O&M) is a term for techniques, including method study and work measurement, that are used to examine clerical, administrative and management procedures in order to make improvements.

6.6 O & M is **primarily concerned with office work** and looks in particular at areas such as the following.

- Organisation
- Office layout
- Office mechanisation
- Documentation and the design of forms

- Duties
- Staffing
- Methods of procedure

6.7 Work study and O & M are perhaps associated in your mind with establishing standard times for work, but the real aim is to decide the most efficient methods of getting work done. More efficient methods and tighter standards will improve efficiency and productivity, and so reduce costs.

Question 5

Do you think a work study or O&M programme would discover any ways in which the work methods you use could be improved so as to reduce costs?

7 OTHER ASPECTS OF COST REDUCTION 5/01

Finance costs

7.1 Finance costs might offer some scope for savings.

(a) There might be a finance cost in taking credit from suppliers, in the form of an **opportunity cost of failing to take advantage of discounts for early payment** that suppliers might be offering.

(b) Similarly, a company should give some thought to the credit terms it offers to customers. Finance tied up in working capital involves a cost. (This might be the interest charges on a bank overdraft, the cost of borrowing long-term finance, or the opportunity cost of the capital tied up.) Costs might be reduced by **reassessing policies for offering early payment discounts** to credit customers.

(c) A company might wish to reassess its sources of finance. **Is it borrowing at the lowest obtainable rates**?

(d) Savings might be achievable from **improved foreign exchange dealings**, for companies involved in buying and selling abroad.

Rationalisation

7.2 Where organisations grow, especially by means of mergers and takeovers, there is a tendency for work to be duplicated in different parts of the organisation. Two or three factories, for example, might make the same product, when it would be more economical to concentrate all production in one factory. The **elimination of unnecessary duplication and the concentration of resources** is a form of rationalisation. The end result of such rationalisation is therefore to reduce costs through greater efficiency.

Expense items

7.3 Expense items, other than materials and labour, may be a significant part of total costs, and these too should be controlled. Examples are as follows.

(a) **Capital expenditure proposals should be carefully evaluated.**

(b) Management should continually question the need for any cost item.

(c) Consultancy organisations have specialised in advising companies on how to reduce telephone bills without restricting or hampering the company's operations.

Control over spending decisions

7.4 Cost reduction might be achieved if senior managers ensure that there is proper control over spending decisions. All too often, costly spending decisions are taken by junior managers without proper consideration of the long-term cost.

7.5 Authority for different types of spending is usually given to management at various levels in the hierarchy, depending on the nature of the cost. Consider the following example.

Nature of cost	Authorised by	Based on a cost of	Ten year cost
Purchase of equipment for £200,000: ten year life	Board	£200,000	£200,000
Hire of office manager: salary £20,000	Director	£20,000	£200,000
Hire of two secretaries: wages £200 per week each	Office Manager	£200/week each	£200,000
Wage deal: 100 employees getting extra £400 pa	?	£40,000	£400,000

7.6   In the example, as the hire of two secretaries is as important as the purchase of the equipment, should an office manager be allowed to commit the company to £200,000 of cost over ten years? The hire of labour is in many ways a more permanent investment than buying equipment. Machinery can be sold, but it is much more difficult, without incurring redundancy costs, to reduce a labour force in size.

Why cost reduction exercises often fail

7.7   In their article *Market-Focused Cost Reduction* (Management Accounting, January 1998), Osborne and Ringrose give the following reasons. (The emphasis is BPP's.)

'The cost savings identified are typically unsustainable in the long term and so costs creep back into the business. There are several reasons for failure:

- a focus on **head-count reduction with little thought given to the services performed by redundant staff**, how these services support the business or how critical they are to business goals. Successful cost reduction requires a methodology to identify sustainable savings;

- **weak sponsorship**, both at senior and intermediate levels in the organisation. Without effective sponsorship, managers and staff may view the project as just another management fad that will go away if ignored for long enough;

- **lack of ownership at grass roots** level, because cuts are randomly applied without consultation. This undermines any commitment to sustain cost savings;

- **lack of performance measures** to track implementation, or reward systems linked to their delivery.'

Case example

A financial services organisation introduced recharging of service costs as a method of reducing costs. 'When managers were asked whether recharging did in fact reduce costs, they were unable to identify any significant examples of costs which had been reduced as a direct consequence of the cost information provided by the recharging system. On further probing, respondents stated that recharging did not reduce costs *per se*, but it created an atmosphere in which it was possible to reduce costs. This led to an acceptance of several rounds of redundancies which delivered the necessary cost reduction.'

(T Scrace and L McAulay, Recharging Service Costs in Financial Services: is there an Optimum Charge?, *Management Accounting*, February 1997)

8   VALUE ANALYSIS   5/01

8.1   One approach to cost reduction, which embraces many of the techniques already mentioned, is value analysis (VA).

KEY TERM

Value analysis is 'A systematic inter-disciplinary examination of factors affecting the cost of a product or service, in order to devise means of achieving the specified purpose most economically at the required standard of quality and reliability'.

(CIMA *Official Terminology*)

The **value of the product must therefore be kept the same or else improved, at a reduced cost.**

KEY TERM

Value engineering is 'An activity which helps to design products which meet customer needs at the lowest cost while assuring the required standard of quality and reliability'.

(CIMA *Official Terminology*)

8.2 Another definition, from G Scullion and A Galway (*Management Accounting*, March 1984) is as follows.

'Value analysis is a method of ensuring worth, whereby the value of each product is critically analysed, part by part, with the objective of achieving the required function with reduced cost. The design stage of a product is the most advantageous time at which to minimise costs. However, during the production period the costs will be subject to change owing to prevailing environmental conditions. These costs need to be examined and reduced using value analysis.'

8.3 The distinction between value engineering and value analysis is not clear cut but, in general, **value engineering is cost avoidance or cost prevention before production** whereas **value analysis is cost reduction during production**.

What is different about value analysis?

8.4 There are two features of value analysis that distinguish it from other approaches to cost reduction.

(a) It encourages innovation and a more radical outlook for ways of reducing costs because ideas for cost reduction are not constrained by the existing product design.

(b) It recognises the various types of value which a product or service provides, analyses this value, and then seeks ways of improving or maintaining aspects of this value but at a lower cost.

8.5 **Conventional cost reduction techniques try to achieve the lowest production costs for a specific product design whereas value analysis tries to find the least-cost method of making a product that achieves its desired function,** not the least-cost method of accomplishing a product design to a mandatory and detailed specification.

Value

8.6 Four aspects of 'value' should be considered.

KEY TERMS

- **Cost value** is the cost of producing and selling an item.

- **Exchange value** is the market value of the product or service.

- **Use value** is what the article does, the purposes it fulfils.

- **Esteem value** is the prestige the customer attaches to the product.

(a) Value analysis seeks to reduce unit costs, and so cost value is the one aspect of value to be reduced.

(b) Value analysis attempts to provide the same (or a better) use value at the lowest cost. Use value therefore involves considerations of the performance and reliability of the product or service.

(c) Value analysis attempts to maintain or enhance the esteem value of a product at the lowest cost.

Question 6

Below are three features of a product.

(a) The product can be sold for £27.50.
(b) The product is available in six colours to suit customers' tastes.
(c) The product will last for at least ten years.

The correct classifications of the features using the types of value in Paragraph 8.6 are

A   (a) exchange value; (b) esteem value; (c) use value
B   (a) esteem value; (b) use value; (c) exchange value
C   (a) cost value; (b) esteem value; (c) use value
D   (a) exchange value; (b) use value; (c) esteem value

Answer

The correct answer is A.

8.7 Value analysis involves the systematic investigation of every source of cost and technique of production with the aim of getting rid of all unnecessary costs. An unnecessary cost is an additional cost incurred without adding use, exchange or esteem value to a product.

8.8 Of course, value analysis is not quite as simple as this, and in practice there might be a conflict between reducing costs and maintaining the aesthetic value (esteem value) of a product. Where cost cutting and aesthetics are incompatible, there should be a clear direction from senior management about which is more important.

9   THE SCOPE OF VALUE ANALYSIS   5/01

9.1 Any commercial organisation should be continually seeking lower costs, better products and higher profits. These can be achieved in any of the following ways.

• Cost elimination or cost prevention
• Cost reduction
• Improving product quality and so selling greater quantities at the same price as before
• Improving product quality and so being able to increase the sales price

Value analysis can achieve all four of these objectives.

Question 7

In addition to the above, what other benefits of a VA programme can you think of?

Answer

•   Improved product performance and product reliability
•   Improved product quality

- An increased product life, in terms of both the marketable life of the product (for the company) and the usable life of each product unit (for the customer)

- Possibly, shorter delivery 'lead times' to customers because of a shorter production cycle

- The increased use of standard parts and components which contribute to lower costs for the customer

- A more economic use of scarce resources

- Encouraging employees to show innovation and creative ideas

9.2 Three areas of special importance are as follows.

Area	Method
Product design	At the design stage value analysis is called value engineering. The designer should be cost conscious and avoid unnecessary complications. Simple product design can avoid production and quality control problems, thereby resulting in lower costs.
Components and material costs	The purchasing department should beware of lapsing into habit with routine buying decisions. It has a crucial role to play in reducing costs and improving value by procuring the desired quality materials at the lowest possible price.
Production methods	These ought to be reviewed continually, on a product-by product basis, especially with changing technology.

10 CARRYING OUT A VALUE ANALYSIS   5/01

10.1 Typical considerations in value analysis

(a) **Can a cheaper substitute material be found** which is as good, if not better, than the material currently used?

(b) **Can unnecessary weight or embellishments be removed** without reducing the product's attractions or desirability?

(c) **Is it possible to use standardised components** (or to make components to a particular standard) thereby reducing the variety of units used and produced? Variety reduction through standardisation facilitates longer production runs at lower unit costs.

(d) **Is it possible to reduce the number of components,** for example could a product be assembled safely with a smaller number of screws?

10.2 The origins of value analysis were in the engineering industry, but it **can be applied to services, or aspects of office work, or to management information systems** (for example the value of information, reports and so on).

The steps in value analysis

10.3 A value analysis study should be carried out by a team of experts, preferably with varying backgrounds, which blends experience, skill and imagination.

10.4 **The steps in value analysis**

Step 1. **Selecting a product or service for study**. The product selected should be one which accounts for a high proportion of the organisation's costs, since the greatest cost savings should be obtainable from high cost areas. The choice should also take into account the stage of its 'life cycle' that it has reached. A product reaching the end of its marketable life is unlikely to offer scope for substantial savings.

Step 2. **Obtaining and recording information.** The questions to be asked include: what is the product or service supposed to do? Does it succeed? Are there alternative ways of making or providing it? What do these alternatives cost?

Step 3. **Analysing the information and evaluating the product.** Each aspect of the product or service should now be analysed. Any cost reductions must be achieved without the loss of use or esteem value. (Or at least, cost savings must exceed any loss in value suffered, and customers would then have to be compensated for the loss in use or esteem value in the form of a lower selling price.) The type of questions to be asked and answered in the analysis stage are as follows.

- Are all the parts necessary?
- Can the parts be obtained or made at a lower cost?
- Can standardised parts be used?
- Does the value provided by each feature justify its cost?

Step 4. **Considering alternatives.** From the analysis, a variety of options can be devised. This is the 'new ideas' stage of the study, and alternative options would mix ideas for eliminating unnecessary parts or features, standardising certain components or features, or introducing new methods of operation.

Step 5. **Selection of the least cost alternative.** The costs (and other aspects of value) of each alternative should be compared.

Step 6. **Recommendation.** The preferred alternative should then be recommended to the decision makers for approval.

Step 7. **Implementation and follow-up.** Once a value analysis proposal is approved and accepted, its implementation must be properly planned and co-ordinated. The VA team should review the implementation and, where appropriate, improve the new product or method in the light of practical experience.

10.5 To be successful, **value analysis programmes must have the full backing of senior management.**

Exam focus point

A May 2001 exam question asked for an explanation of how cost reduction, value analysis and ZBB could be used by a hotel group to improve the profitability of the hotels.

11 FUNCTIONAL ANALYSIS

11.1 Functional analysis is a cost management technique which has similarities with value analysis. In basic terms, it is a group activity, most commonly applied during the development of new products, which uses the functions of a product or service (such as 'to make a mark' for a pen) as the **basis for cost management**.

11.2 Functional analysis is concerned with **improving profits** by attempting to **reduce costs** and/or by **improving products** by adding new features in a cost-effective way that are so attractive to customers that profits actually increase.

KEY TERM

Functional analysis is 'An analysis of the relationships between product functions, their perceived value to the customer and their cost of provision'. (CIMA *Official Terminology*)

Basic steps

11.3 The technique involves the following nine steps, some of which are similar to those required in value analysis.

Step 1. **Choose the object of analysis (such as product, service or overhead area).** If it is not a new product, **a high volume** product with a complex design and relatively large production costs is often an ideal candidate. Other reasons for selecting a particular product might include apparently high cost, low yield rates, manufacturing problems, market demand (such as remodelling required) or a need for a more compact design. The product selected will determine the precise objective of the analysis exercise (reduce weight by 25%, reduce cost by 30% while maintaining the existing level of quality).

Step 2. **Select members for the functional analysis team.** The team will usually consist of six to eight members from a number of different departments (such as accounting, production, purchasing, engineering, design and marketing).

Step 3. **Gather information.** This will include information both from inside the organisation (detailed design, manufacturing and marketing information, for example) and from outside the organisation (such as information about new technologies).

Step 4. **Define the functions of the object.** The various functions of the product should be defined in terms of a verb and a noun. 'The major function of a propelling ball-point pen can be described as 'make a mark', but supporting functions are also required, such as 'put colour', 'guide tip' and 'prevent loss'. These, in turn, may also require their own supporting functions.' (*Contemporary Cost Management*, Tanaka, Yoshikawa, Innes and Mitchell). Functions should be classified as basic or secondary in terms of the importance of that particular function for the product.

Step 5. **Draw a functional family tree.** The functions identified in step 4 should be arranged in a logical order in a family-tree diagram. A table illustrating the relationship between the functions and the parts of the product, as well as relevant existing costs, should also be drawn up. An extract for a propelling ball point pen is shown below.

| | | Function | | |
Part number	Name of part	Verb	Noun	Cost
5	ink	put	colour	£0.03
9	clip	prevent	loss	£0.02

Step 6. **Evaluate the functions.** The relative value of each function to a total target cost from the customers' point of view has to be estimated (either using market research or by each member of the team placing values and a consensus being reached for each function). This relative value provides a target cost for each function. Those functions where the actual cost is greater than the assigned target cost should be highlighted as potential problem functions (although the absolute amount of money involved should also be taken into consideration).

Step 7. **Suggest alternatives and compare these with the target cost.** Alternatives might include the use of new materials or parts, a different method of manufacturing the product, suggestions for completely new products or new product functions, modifications to the functions of the product, the combination of different functions or even the elimination of certain functions.

Step 8. **Choose the alternatives for manufacturing.** The alternatives must be assessed and a final choice made of those to implement.

Step 9. **Review the actual results.** An audit or review of the changes implemented should be conducted promptly and the findings reported to senior management. This will prevent over-optimistic assessments of the functional analysis exercise and provide feedback so that future functional analysis can be improved.

11.4 Advantages

(a) Competitive advantage resulting from improved, cost-effective design or redesign of products

(b) Probably of most benefit during the planning and design stages of new products (because up to 90% of the costs of many products are committed by the end of the design stage)

(c) Flexible application (has been applied to services, particular overhead areas, organisational restructuring and corporate strategy) because it views objects in abstract (service potential) terms rather than in physical (parts and people) terms

(d) Information about product functions and about the views of customers is integrated into the formal reporting system

Exam focus point

Cost reduction, value analysis and functional analysis did not appear in the pilot paper.

Chapter roundup

- **Cost reduction** is a planned and positive approach to reducing expenditure.

- Cost reduction measures ought to be planned programmes to reduce costs rather than crash programmes to cut spending levels.

- Ways in which costs can be reduced include improving the efficiency of materials usage, the productivity of labour or the efficiencies of machinery or other equipment.

- **Work study** is a means of raising productivity of an operating unit by the reorganisation of work. The two main parts of work study are **method study** and **work measurement**. **O & M** is a specialist branch of work study in that it is geared to dealing with office work and its allied spheres.

- **Value analysis** is a planned, scientific approach to cost reduction which reviews the material composition of a product and production design so that modifications and improvements can be made which do not reduce the value of the product to the customer or to the user. **Value engineering** is the application of value analysis techniques to new products.

- Four aspects of value should be considered in value analysis (**cost value, exchange value, use value, esteem value**).

- **Functional analysis** is concerned with improving profits by attempting to reduce costs and/or by improving products by adding new features in a cost-effective way that are so attractive to customers that profits actually increase.

Quick quiz

1   *Choose the correct words from those highlighted.*

Cost reduction/control is about regulating the costs of operating a business and keeping costs within acceptable limits whereas **cost reduction/control** is a planned and positive approach to reducing expenditure.

2   *Fill in the blanks.*

(a)   .... is a way of raising productivity by reorganising work.

(b)   .... involves systematically recording and critically examining existing and proposed ways of doing work in order to develop and apply easier and more effective methods and reduce costs.

(c)   .... involves establishing the time for a qualified worker to carry out a specified job at a specified level of performance.

3   *Match the method to the description.*

Methods

Direct observation methods
Synthetic methods
Organisation and methods

Descriptions

(a)   Involves observing jobs in practice
(b)   Used to estimate the work study content of jobs without having to observe them
(c)   Looks at areas such as office layout and staffing

4   *Choose the correct words from those highlighted.*

Value **engineering/analysis** is cost avoidance or cost prevention before production whereas value **engineering/analysis** is cost reduction during production.

5   Match the terms to the correct definitions.

Terms

Cost value
Exchange value
Use value
Esteem value

Definitions

(a)   The prestige the customer attaches to the product
(b)   The market value of the product
(c)   What the product does
(d)   The cost of producing and selling the product

6   Fill in the action to take at each step in a value analysis.

Step 1.   ....

Step 2.   ....

Step 3.   ....

Step 4.   ....

Step 5.   ....

Step 6.   ....

Step 7.   ....

7   Fill in the blanks.

Functional analysis is an analysis of the relationships between ...., their
.... and their ....

Answers to quick quiz

1   First term should be cost control, the second term cost reduction.

2   Work study
    Method study
    Work measurement

3   Direct observation methods   (a)
    Synthetic methods   (b)
    Organisation and methods   (c)

4   First term should be value engineering, the second term value analysis.

5   Cost value   (d)
    Exchange value   (b)
    Use value   (c)
    Esteem value   (a)

6   Step 1   Select a product or service for study
    Step 2   Obtain and record information
    Step 3   Analyse the information and evaluate the product
    Step 4   Consider alternatives
    Step 5   Select the least cost alternative
    Step 6   Make a recommendation
    Step 7   Implement and follow up

7   Functional analysis is an analysis of the relationships between product functions, their
    perceived value to the customer and their cost of provision.

Now try the question below from the Exam Question Bank

Number	Level	Marks	Time
Q15	Exam standard	25	45 mins

Chapter 12

MULTIPLE PRODUCT CVP ANALYSIS

Topic list	Syllabus reference	Ability required
1 CVP analysis in a multiple product environment	(iii)	Analysis
2 Breakeven point for multiple products	(iii)	Application/analysis
3 Contribution to sales (C/S) ratio for multiple products	(iii)	Application/analysis
4 Sales/product mix decisions	(iii)	Application/analysis
5 Target profits for multiple products	(iii)	Application/analysis
6 Margin of safety for multiple products	(iii)	Application/analysis
7 Multi-product CVP charts	(iii)	Application

Introduction

You will have **already encountered CVP (or breakeven) analysis** in your MAF studies so you should not be surprised by the terminology or basic techniques that you meet in this chapter. But in case your memory needs refreshing we have included a brief reminder of the material covered in MAF in a 'Knowledge Brought Forward' box at the beginning of the chapter.

You should remember that one of the **major assumptions** underpinning CVP analysis is that it can **only be applied to one product or to a constant (fixed proportions) mix of products.** So far you will only have studied single product CVP analysis but as most organisations produce and sell a range of products we are going to look at what is known as multiple product CVP analysis. We will find out how to carry out breakeven calculations and prepare charts for multiple products.

Learning outcomes covered in this chapter

- **Calculate** and interpret the breakeven point, profit target, margin of safety and profit/volume ratio for multiple products.

- **Prepare** breakeven charts and profit/volume charts for multiple products.

- **Discuss** multiple product CVP analysis.

Syllabus content covered in this chapter

- Multi-product CVP analysis including break even, profit target, margin of safety, contribution/sales ratio, breakeven charts, contribution, profit/volume graphs.

BPP PUBLISHING

Knowledge brought forward

Cost-volume-profit (breakeven) analysis

- Contribution per unit = unit selling price – unit variable costs

- Profit = (sales volume × contribution per unit) – fixed costs

- Breakeven point = activity level at which there is neither profit nor loss

$$= \frac{\text{total fixed costs}}{\text{contribution per unit}} = \frac{\text{contribution required to breakeven}}{\text{contribution per unit}}$$

- Contribution/sales (C/S) ratio = profit/volume (P/V) ratio = (contribution/sales) × 100%

- Sales revenue at breakeven point = fixed costs ÷ C/S ratio

- Margin of safety (in units) = budgeted sales units – breakeven sales units

- Margin of safety (as %) $= \dfrac{\text{budgeted sales } - \text{ breakeven sales}}{\text{budgeted sales}} \times 100\%$

- Sales volume to achieve a target profit $= \dfrac{\text{fixed cost } + \text{ target profit}}{\text{contribution per unit}}$

- Breakeven chart

- Contribution (contribution breakeven) chart

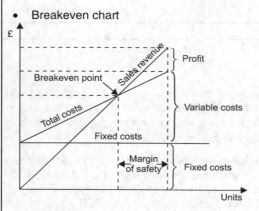

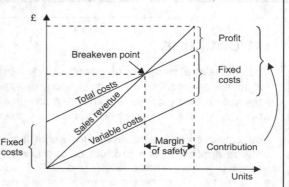

- Profit/volume (P/V) chart

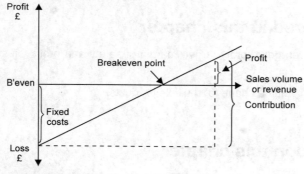

The gradient of the straight line is the contribution per unit (if the horizontal axis is measured in sales units) or the c/s ratio (if the horizontal axis is measured in sales value).

- Assumptions

  o Can only apply to one product or constant mix
  o Fixed costs same in total and unit variable costs same at all levels of output
  o Sales prices constant at all levels of activity
  o Production = sales

1 CVP ANALYSIS IN A MULTIPLE PRODUCT ENVIRONMENT

A major assumption

1.1 Organisations typically produce and sell a variety of products and services. To perform CVP analysis in a multi-product organisation, however, a **constant product sales mix must be assumed**. In other words, we have to assume that whenever x units of product A are sold, y units of product B and z units of product C are also sold.

1.2 Such an assumption allows us to **calculate** a **weighted average contribution per mix**, the weighting being on the basis of the quantities of each product in the constant mix. This means that the unit contribution of the product that makes up the largest proportion of the mix has the greatest impact on the average contribution per mix.

1.3 The only situation when the mix of products does not affect the analysis is when **all of the products have the same ratio of contribution to sales (C/S ratio)**.

2 BREAKEVEN POINT FOR MULTIPLE PRODUCTS

2.1 This calculation is exactly the same as that for single products but the single product is the standard mix. Let's look at an example.

2.2 EXAMPLE: BREAKEVEN POINT FOR MULTIPLE PRODUCTS

Suppose that P Ltd produces and sells two products. The M sells for £7 per unit and has a total variable cost of £2.94 per unit, while the N sells for £15 per unit and has a total variable cost of £4.50 per unit. The marketing department has estimated that for every five units of M sold, one unit of N will be sold. The organisation's fixed costs total £36,000.

2.3 SOLUTION

We calculate the breakeven point as follows.

Step 1. Calculate **contribution per unit**

	M	*N*
	£ per unit	£ per unit
Selling price	7.00	15.00
Variable cost	2.94	4.50
Contribution	4.06	10.50

Step 2. Calculate **contribution per mix**

= (£4.06 × 5) + (£10.50 × 1) = £30.80

Step 3. Calculate the **breakeven point** in terms of the **number of mixes**

= fixed costs/contribution per mix = £36,000/£30.80
= 1,169 mixes (rounded)

Step 4. Calculate the **breakeven point** in terms of the **number of units of the products**

= (1,169 × 5) 5,845 units of M and (1,169 × 1) 1,169 units of N (rounded)

Step 5. Calculate the **breakeven point** in terms of **revenue**

= (5,845 × £7) + (1,169 × £15)
= £40,915 of M and £17,535 of N = £58,450 in total

2.4 It is important to note that the breakeven point is not £58,450 of revenue, whatever the mix of products. The breakeven point is £58,450 provided that the sales mix remains 5:1.

Likewise the breakeven point is not at a production/sales level of (5,845 + 1,169) 7,014 units. Rather, it is when 5,845 units of M and 1,169 units of N are sold, assuming a sales mix of 5:1.

Question 1

Alpha Ltd manufactures and sells three products, the beta, the gamma and the delta. Relevant information is as follows.

	Beta £ per unit	Gamma £ per unit	Delta £ per unit
Selling price	135.00	165.00	220.00
Variable cost	73.50	58.90	146.20

Total fixed costs are £950,000.

An analysis of past trading patterns indicates that the products are sold in the ratio 3:4:5.

Required

Calculate Alpha Ltd's breakeven point in terms of units and revenue of the three products.

Answer

Step 1. Calculate **contribution per unit**

	Beta £ per unit	Gamma £ per unit	Delta £ per unit
Selling price	135.00	165.00	220.00
Variable cost	73.50	58.90	146.20
Contribution	61.50	106.10	73.80

Step 2. Calculate **contribution per mix**

= (£61.50 × 3) + (£106.10 × 4) + (£73.80 × 5)
= £977.90

Step 3. Calculate the **breakeven point** in terms of the **number of mixes**

= fixed costs/contribution per mix
= £950,000/£977.90 = 972 mixes (rounded up)

Step 4. Calculate the **breakeven point** in terms of the **number of units of the products**

= (972 × 3) 2,916 units of Beta, (972 × 4) 3,888 units of Gamma and (972 × 5) 4,860 units of Delta (rounded)

Step 5. Calculate the **breakeven point** in terms of **revenue**

= (2,916 × £135) + (3,888 × £165) + (4,860 × £220)
= £393,660 of Beta, £641,520 of Gamma and £1,069,200 of Delta = £2,104,380 in total

3 CONTRIBUTION TO SALES (C/S) RATIO FOR MULTIPLE PRODUCTS

3.1 An alternative way of **calculating the breakeven point** is to use the **average contribution to sales (C/S) ratio** for the standard mix.

3.2 As you should already know, the C/S ratio is sometimes called the **profit/volume ratio** or **P/V ratio**.

3.3 We can calculate the breakeven point of P Ltd (see Paragraph 2.2) as follows.

Step 1. Calculate **revenue per mix**
= (5 × £7) + (1 × £15) = £50

Step 2. Calculate **contribution per mix**
= £30.80 (see Paragraph 2.3)

Step 3. Calculate **average C/S ratio**
= (£30.80/£50.00) × 100% = 61.6%

Step 4. Calculate **breakeven point** (total)
= fixed costs ÷ C/S ratio
= £36,000/0.616 = £58,442 (rounded)

Step 5. Calculate **revenue ratio of mix**
= 35:15, or 7:3

Step 6. **Calculate breakeven sales**
Breakeven sales of M = £58,442 × 7/10 = £40,909 rounded
Breakeven sales of N = £58,442 × 3/10 = £17,533 rounded

Question 2

Calculate the breakeven sales revenue of product Beta, Gamma and Delta (see Question 1) using the approach shown in Paragraph 3.3.

Answer

Step 1. Calculate revenue per mix
= (3 × £135) + (4 × £165) + (5 × £220)
= £2,165

Step 2. Calculate contribution per mix
= £977.90 (from Question 1)

Step 3. Calculate average C/S ratio
= (£977.90/£2,165) × 100%
= 45.17%

Step 4. Calculate breakeven point (total)
= fixed costs ÷ C/S ratio
= £950,000/0.4517
= £2,103,166 (rounded)

Step 5. Calculate revenue ratio of mix
= 405:660:1,100, or 81:132:220

Step 6. Calculate breakeven sales

Breakeven sales of Beta = 81/433 × £2,103,166 = £393,433
Breakeven sales of Gamma = 132/433 × £2,103,166 = £641,150
Breakeven sales of Delta = 220/433 × £2,103,166 = £1,068,583

3.4 Alternatively you might be provided with the individual C/S ratios of a number of products. For example if an organisation sells two products (A and B) in the **ratio 2:5** and if the C/S ratio of A is **10%** whereas that of B is **50%**, the average C/S ratio is calculated as follows.

$$\textbf{Average C/S ratio} = \frac{(2 \times 10\%) + (5 \times 50\%)}{2 + 5} = 38.6\%$$

Question 3

TIM Ltd produces and sells two products, the MK and the KL. The company expects to sell 1 MK for every 2 KLs and have monthly sales revenue of £150,000. The MK has a C/S ratio of 20% whereas the KL has a C/S ratio of 40%. Budgeted monthly fixed costs are £30,000.

What is the budgeted breakeven sales revenue?

A   £150,000
B   £300,000
C   £90,000
D   £50,000

Answer

The correct answer is C.

$$\text{Average C/S ratio} = \frac{(20\% \times 1) + (40\% \times 2)}{3} = 33^{1}/_{3}\%$$

$$\text{Sales revenue at the breakeven point} = \frac{\text{fixed costs}}{\text{C/S ratio}} = \frac{£30,000}{0.333} = £90,000$$

3.5   The C/S ratio is a measure of how much contribution is earned from each £1 of sales of the standard mix. The **C/S ratio of 33$^{1}/_{3}$%** in the question above means that for every £1 of sales of the standard mix of products, a contribution of 33.33p is earned. To **earn a total contribution of, say, £20,000, sales revenue from the standard mix** must therefore be

$$\frac{£1}{33.33p} \times £20,000 = £60,006$$

Question 4

Refer back to the information in Paragraph 3.4. Suppose the organisation in question has fixed costs of £100,000, and wishes to earn total contribution of £200,000. What level of revenue must be achieved?

A   £459,067
B   £518,135
C   £618,135
D   £777,202

Answer

The correct answer is B.

$$\text{Sales revenue must be } \frac{£1}{38.6p} \times £200,000 = £518,135$$

Points to bear in mind

3.6   **Any change in the proportions of products in the mix will change the contribution per mix and the average C/S ratio and hence the breakeven point.**

(a)   If the mix shifts towards products with lower contribution margins, the breakeven point (in units) will increase and profits will fall unless there is a corresponding increase in total revenue.

(b)   A shift towards products with higher contribution margins without a corresponding decrease in revenues will cause an increase in profits and a lower breakeven point.

(c)   If sales are at the specified level but not in the specified mix, there will be either a profit or a loss depending on whether the mix shifts towards products with higher or lower contribution margins.

4   SALES/PRODUCT MIX DECISIONS

4.1   One use of the methodology we have been looking at is to **determine the most profitable sales mix option** of a number open to management.

4.2   EXAMPLE: SALES MIX DECISIONS

JM Ltd makes and sells two products, the J and the M. The budgeted selling price of the J is £60 and that of the M, £72. Variable costs associated with producing and selling the J are £30 and, with the M, £60. Annual fixed production and selling costs of JM Ltd are £3,369,600.

JM Ltd has two production/sales options. The J and the M can be sold either in the ratio two Js to three Ms or in the ratio one J to two Ms.

4.3   We can decide on the optimal mix by looking at breakeven points. We need to begin by determining contribution per unit.

	J £ per unit	*M* £ per unit
Selling price	60	72
Variable cost	30	60
Contribution	30	12

Mix 1

Contribution per 5 units sold = (£30 × 2) + (£12 × 3) = £96

Breakeven point = $\dfrac{£3,369,600}{£96}$ = 35,100 sets of five units

	J		*M*	
Breakeven point:				
in units	(35,100 × 2)	70,200	(35,100 × 3)	105,300
in £	(70,200 × £60)	£4,212,000	(105,300 × £72)	£7,581,600

'Total' breakeven point = £11,793,600

Mix 2

Contribution per 3 units sold = (£30 × 1) + (£12 × 2) = £54

Breakeven point = $\dfrac{£3,369,600}{£54}$ = 62,400 sets of three units.

	J		*M*	
Breakeven point:				
in units	(62,400 × 1)	62,400	(62,400 × 2)	124,800
in £	(62,400 × £60)	£3,744,000	(124,800 × £72)	£8,985,600

'Total' breakeven point = £12,729,600

4.4   Ignoring commercial considerations, mix 1 is preferable to mix 2. This is because it results in a lower level of sales to break even (because of the higher average contribution per unit sold). The average contribution for mix 1 is £19.20 (£96 ÷ 5). In mix 2 it is £18 (£54 ÷ 3). Mix 1 contains a higher proportion (40% as opposed to 33^1/₃%) of the more profitable product.

4.5   The following question looks at the **effect on the overall C/S ratio of changing a product/sales mix.**

4.6 QUESTION: CHANGING THE PRODUCT MIX

A Ltd sells three products - Exe, Why and Zed - in equal quantities and at the same selling price per unit. The C/S ratio for the Exe is 50%, that of the Why is 60% and the total C/S ratio is 55%. Suppose the product mix is changed to Exe 20%, Why 50% and Zed 30%.

Required

Calculate the revised total contribution/total sales ratio.

4.7 SOLUTION

Original proportions

	Exe	Why	Zed	Total
C/S ratio	0.5	0.6	0.549 (W2)	
Market share	× 1/3	× 1/3	× 1/3	
	0.167	0.200	0.183 (W1)	0.55

Workings

1   The total C/S ratio is the sum of the weighted C/S ratios and so this figure is calculated as $0.55 - 0.167 - 0.2 = 0.183$

2   This figure is then calculated as $0.183 \div {}^1/_3 = 0.549$

Revised proportions

	Exe	Why	Zed	Total
C/S ratio (as above)	0.5	0.6	0.549	
Market share	× 0.2	× 0.5	× 0.3	
	0.1	0.3	0.1647	0.5647

The total C/S ratio will increase because of the inclusion in the mix of proportionately more of Why, which has the highest C/S ratio.

Question 5

L Ltd currently sells three products U, C and Y at the same selling price per unit.

Current product mix

U – 25%   C – 35%   Y – 40%

Current P/V ratio

Total – 43.5%   C – 45%   Y – 35%

L Ltd decides to change the product mix.

Revised product mix

U – 30%   C – 40%   Y – 30%

What is the revised total contribution/total sales ratio?

A   45%
B   43.5%
C   55%
D   33¹/₃%

Answer

The correct answer is A.

	U	C	Y	Total
P/V ratio	0.55*	0.45	0.35	
Market share	× 0.25	× 0.35	× 0.40	
	0.1375	0.1575	0.140	0.435

* 0.1375/0.25

With revised proportions:

	U	C	Y	Total
P/V ratio	0.55	0.45	0.35	
Market share	× 0.30	× 0.40	× 0.30	
	0.165	0.18	0.105	0.45

5 TARGET PROFITS FOR MULTIPLE PRODUCTS

5.1 At **breakeven point**, sales revenue (S) is equal to variable costs plus fixed costs (V+F), and there is no profit:

S = V+F

Suppose an organisation wishes to achieve a certain level of profit (P) during a period. To achieve this profit, sales must cover all costs and leave the required profit:

S = V + F + P

∴ S – V = F + P

So total contribution required = F + P

5.2 Once we know the total contribution required we can calculate the sales revenue of each product needed to achieve a target profit. The method is similar to the method used to calculate the breakeven point.

5.3 EXAMPLE: TARGET PROFITS FOR MULTIPLE PRODUCTS

A company makes and sells three products, F, G and H. The products are sold in the proportions F:G:H = 2:1:3. The company's fixed costs are £80,000 per month and details of the products are as follows.

Product	Selling price £ per unit	Variable cost £ per unit
F	22	16
G	15	12
H	19	13

The company wishes to earn a profit of £52,000 next month. Calculate the required sales value of each product in order to achieve this target profit.

5.4 SOLUTION

Step 1. Calculate **contribution per unit**

	F £ per unit	G £ per unit	H £ per unit
Selling price	22	15	19
Variable cost	16	12	13
Contribution	6	3	6

Step 2. Calculate **contribution per mix**

= (£6 × 2) + (£3 × 1) + (£6 × 3) = £33

Step 3. Calculate the **required number of mixes**

= fixed costs + required profit/contribution per mix

= (£80,000 + £52,000)/£33

= 4,000 mixes

Step 4. Calculate the **required sales** in terms of the **number of units of the products** and **sales revenue of each product**

Product		Units	Selling price £ per unit	Sales revenue required £
F	4,000 × 2	8,000	22	176,000
G	4,000 × 1	4,000	15	60,000
H	4,000 × 3	12,000	19	228,000
Total				464,000

The sales revenue of £464,000 will generate a profit of £52,000 if the products are sold in the mix 2:1:3.

5.5 Alternatively the C/S ratio could be used to determine the required sales revenue for a profit of £52,000. The method is again similar to that demonstrated earlier when calculating the breakeven point.

5.6 EXAMPLE: USING THE C/S RATIO TO DETERMINE THE REQUIRED SALES

We'll use the data from Paragraph 5.3.

Step 1. **Calculate revenue per mix**
= $(2 \times £22) + (1 \times £15) + (3 \times £19)$
= £116

Step 2. **Calculate contribution per mix**
= £33 (from Paragraph 5.4)

Step 3. **Calculate average C/S ratio**
= $(£33/£116) \times 100\%$
= 28.45%

Step 4. **Calculate required total revenue**
= required contribution ÷ C/S ratio
= $(£80,000 + £52,000) \div 0.2845$
= £463,972

Step 5. **Calculate revenue ratio of mix**
= $(2 \times £22) : (1 \times £15) : (3 \times £19)$
= 44:15:57

Step 6. **Calculate required sales**

Required sales of F	= $44/116 \times £463,972$	= £175,989
Required sales of G	= $15/116 \times £463,972$	= £59,996
Required sales of H	= $57/116 \times £463,972$	= £227,986

Which, allowing for roundings, is the same answer as calculated in Paragraph 5.4.

6 MARGIN OF SAFETY FOR MULTIPLE PRODUCTS

6.1 It should not surprise you to learn that the calculation of the margin of safety for multiple products is exactly the same as for single products, but the single product is the standard mix. The easiest way to see how its done is to look at an example.

6.2 EXAMPLE: MARGIN OF SAFETY FOR MULTIPLE PRODUCTS

J Ltd produces and sells two products. The W sells for £8 per unit and has a total variable cost of £3.80 per unit, while the R sells for £14 per unit and has a total variable cost of £4.20. For every five units of W sold, six units of R are sold. J Ltd's fixed costs are £43,890 per period.

Budgeted sales revenue for next period is £74,400, in the standard mix.

6.3 SOLUTION

To calculate the margin of safety we must first determine the **breakeven point.**

Step 1. Calculate **contribution per unit**

	W	R
	£ per unit	£ per unit
Selling price	8.00	14.00
Variable cost	3.80	4.20
Contribution	4.20	9.80

Step 2. Calculate **contribution per mix**

= (£4.20 × 5) + (£9.80 × 6) = £79.80

Step 3. Calculate the **breakeven point** in terms of the **number of mixes**

= fixed costs/contribution per mix = £43,890/£79.80
= 550 mixes

Step 4. Calculate the **breakeven point** in terms of the **number of units of the products**

= (550 × 5) 2,750 units of W and (550 × 6) 3,300 units of R

Step 5. Calculate the **breakeven point** in terms of **revenue**

= (2,750 × £8) + (3,300 × £14)
= £22,000 of W and £46,200 of R = £68,200 in total

Step 6. Calculate the **margin of safety**

= budgeted sales – breakeven sales
= £74,400 – £68,200
= £6,200 sales in total, in the standard mix

Or, as a percentage

= (£74,400 – £68,200)/£74,400 × 100%
= 8.3% of budgeted sales

7 MULTI-PRODUCT CVP CHARTS

Breakeven charts

7.1 A very serious limitation of breakeven charts is that they can show the costs, revenues, profits and margins of safety for a single product only, or at best for a **single 'sales mix' of products.**

7.2 For example suppose that Farmyard Ltd sells three products, X, Y and Z which have variable unit costs of £3, £4 and £5 respectively. The sales price of X is £8, the price of Y is £6 and the price of Z is £6. Fixed costs per annum are £10,000.

7.3 A breakeven chart cannot be drawn, because we do not know the proportions of X, Y and Z in the sales mix.

> **ATTENTION!**
>
> If you are not sure about this point, you should try to draw a breakeven chart with the information given. It should not be possible.

7.4 If, however, we now assume that budgeted sales are 2,000 units of X, 4,000 units of Y and 3,000 units of Z, a breakeven chart can be drawn. The chart would make the assumption that output and sales of X, Y and Z are in the proportions 2,000 : 4,000: 3,000 at all levels of activity, in other words that the sales mix is 'fixed' in these proportions.

7.5 We begin by carrying out some calculations.

Budgeted costs		*Costs* £		*Revenue* £
Variable costs of X	(2,000 × £3)	6,000	X (2,000 × £8)	16,000
Variable costs of Y	(4,000 × £4)	16,000	Y (4,000 × £6)	24,000
Variable costs of Z	(3,000 × £5)	15,000	Z (3,000 × £6)	18,000
Total variable costs		37,000	Budgeted revenue	58,000
Fixed costs		10,000		
Total budgeted costs		47,000		

7.6 The **breakeven chart** can now be drawn.

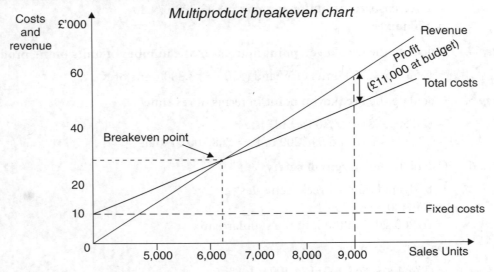

7.7 The **breakeven point** is approximately £27,500 of sales revenue. This may either be **read from the chart or computed mathematically**.

(a) The budgeted C/S ratio for all three products together is contribution/sales = £(58,000 – 37,000)/£58,000 = 36.21%.

(b) The required contribution to break even is £10,000, the amount of fixed costs. The breakeven point is £10,000/36.21% = £27,500 (approx) in sales revenue.

P/V charts

7.8 The same information could be shown on a **P/V chart**, as follows.

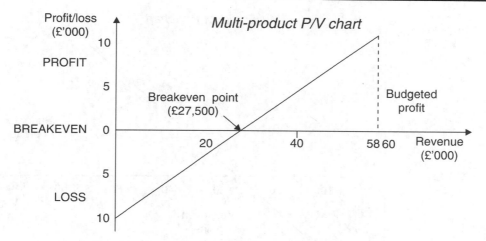

Multi-product P/V chart

7.9 An **addition** to the chart would **show further information about the contribution earned by each product individually,** so that their performance and profitability can be compared.

	Contribution £	Sales £	C/S ratio %
Product X	10,000	16,000	62.50
Product Y	8,000	24,000	33.33
Product Z	3,000	18,000	16.67
Total	21,000	58,000	36.21

7.10 By convention, the **products are shown individually** on a P/V chart from **left to right,** in **order of the size of their C/S ratio.** In this example, product X will be plotted first, then product Y and finally product Z. A **dotted line** is used to show the **cumulative profit/loss and the cumulative sales** as each product's sales and contribution in turn are added to the sales mix.

Product	Cumulative sales £		Cumulative profit £
X	16,000	(£10,000 – £10,000)	-
X and Y	40,000		8,000
X, Y and Z	58,000		11,000

7.11 You will see on the graph which follows that these three pairs of data are used to plot the dotted line, to indicate the contribution from each product. The **solid line** which joins the two ends of this dotted line **indicates the average profit** which will be earned from sales of the three products in this mix.

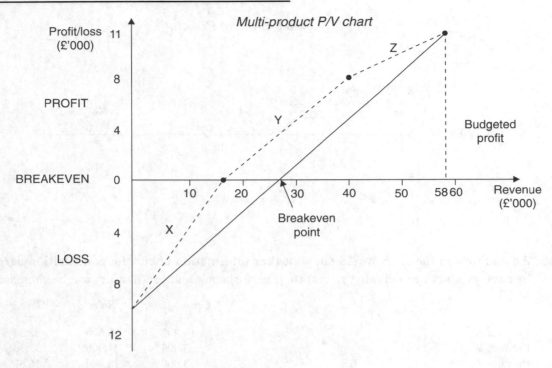

Multi-product P/V chart

7.12 The diagram **highlights** the following points.

(a) Since X is the most profitable in terms of C/S ratio, it might be worth considering an increase in the sales of X, even if there is a consequent fall in the sales of Z.

(b) Alternatively, the pricing structure of the products should be reviewed and a decision made as to whether the price of product Z should be raised so as to increase its C/S ratio (although an increase is likely to result in some fall in sales volume).

7.13 The **multi-product P/V chart** therefore helps to **identify** the following.

(a) The overall company breakeven point.

(b) Which products should be expanded in output and which, if any, should be discontinued.

(c) What effect changes in selling price and sales volume will have on the company's breakeven point and profit.

Question 6

A company sells three products, X, Y and Z. Cost and sales data for one period are as follows.

	X	Y	Z
Sales volume	2,000 units	2,000 units	5,000 units
Sales price per unit	£3	£4	£2
Variable cost per unit	£2.25	£3.50	£1.25
Total fixed costs	£3,250		

Required

Construct a multi-product P/V chart based on the above information.

Answer

	X	Y	Z	Total
				£
Contribution per unit	£0.75	£0.50	£0.75	
Budgeted contribution (total)	£1,500	£1,000	£3,750	6,250
Fixed costs				3,250
Budgeted profit				3,000

Product	Cumulative sales £		Cumulative profit £
Z	10,000	(£3,750 – £3,250)	500
Z and X	16,000		2,000
Z, X and Y	24,000		3,000

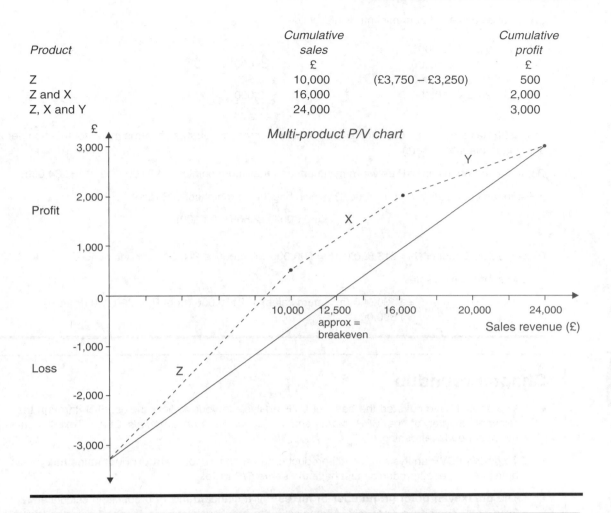

Multi-product P/V chart

Exam focus point

CVP analysis calculations are particularly suitable for multiple choice questions. The question below is similar to an MCQ which appeared in the May 2001 exam.

Question 7

Sutton Ltd produces four products. Relevant data is shown below for period 2.

	Product M	Product A	Product R	Product P
C/S ratio	5%	10%	15%	20%
Maximum sales value	£200,000	£120,000	£200,000	£180,000
Minimum sales value	£50,000	£50,000	£20,000	£10,000

The fixed costs for period 2 are budgeted at £60,000.

Required

Calculate the lowest breakeven sales value per period, subject to meeting the minimum sales value constraints.

Answer

Breakeven point occurs when contribution = fixed costs

∴ Minimum breakeven point occurs when contribution is £60,000.

  BPP PUBLISHING

Contribution achieved from minimum sales value

		£
M	5% × £50,000	2,500
A	10% × £50,000	5,000
R	15% × £20,000	3,000
P	20% × £10,000	2,000
		12,500

Product P has the highest C/S ratio and so should be produced first (as it earns more contribution per £ of revenue than the others).

Contribution from sales of P between minimum and maximum points = £170,000 × 20% = £34,000

∴ Required contribution from Product R (which has the next highest C/S ratio)

$$= £(60,000 - 12,500 - 34,000)$$
$$= £13,500$$

Revenue from Product R of £13,500/0.15 = £90,000 will produce £13,500 of contribution.

∴ Lowest breakeven sales

$$= £130,000 \text{ (minimum sales)} + £170,000 \text{ (from P)} + £90,000 \text{ (from R)}$$
$$= £390,000$$

Chapter roundup

- You should have covered the basis of CVP analysis in your earlier studies. Flick through the relevant chapter of the BPP *Management Accounting Fundamentals* Study Text if your memory needs refreshing.

- To perform CVP analysis in a multi-product organisation, a **constant product sales mix** must be assumed, or all products must have the **same C/S ratio.**

- The **breakeven point (in number of mixes)** for a standard mix of products is calculated as fixed costs/contribution per mix. Alternatively the breakeven point in terms of sales revenue can be calculated as fixed costs/average C/S ratio.

- The number of mixes of products required to be sold to achieve a **target profit** is calculated as (fixed costs + required profit)/contribution per mix.

- The **margin of safety** for a multi-product organisation is equal to the budgeted sales in the standard mix less the breakeven sales in the standard mix. It may be expressed as a percentage of the budgeted sales.

- **Breakeven charts** for multiple products can be drawn if a constant product sales mix is assumed. The **PV chart** can show further information about each product individually.

Quick quiz

1   *Fill in the blanks.*

$$\text{Breakeven point} = \frac{}{\text{Contribution per unit}} = \frac{}{\text{Contribution per unit}}$$

2   C/S ratio = P/V ratio × 100. *True or false?*

3   *Fill in the blanks.*

$$\text{Margin of safety (as \%)} = \left(\frac{\text{.................... sales} - \text{.................... sales}}{\text{.................... sales}} \right) \times 100\%$$

4   *Mark the following on the breakeven chart below.*

- Profit
- Sales revenue
- Total costs
- Margin of safety

- Variable costs
- Fixed costs
- Breakeven point

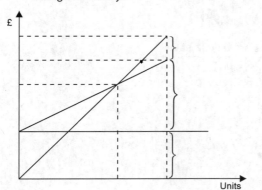

5   *Mark the following on the P/V chart below.*

- Breakeven point
- Fixed costs

- Contribution
- Profit

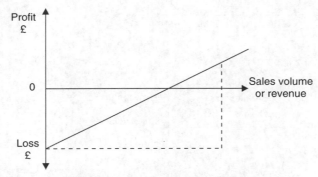

6   Which of the following is not a major assumption of CVP analysis?

A   It can only apply to one product or a constant mix.
B   Fixed costs are the same in total and unit variable costs are the same at all levels of output.
C   Sales prices vary in line with levels of activity.
D   Production level is equal to sales level.

7   *Choose the appropriate words from those highlighted and fill in the blanks.*

When showing multiple products individually on a P/V chart, the products are shown from **left to right/right to left**, in order of **increasing/decreasing** size of C/S ratio. The line joining the two ends of the dotted line (which shows ....) indicates ....

BPP
PUBLISHING

Answers to quick quiz

1   Breakeven point = $\dfrac{\text{Total fixed costs}}{\text{Contribution per unit}}$ = $\dfrac{\text{Contribution required to breakeven}}{\text{Contribution per unit}}$

2   False. The C/S ratio is another name for the P/V ratio.

3   Margin of safety (as %) = $\left(\dfrac{\text{Budgeted sales} - \text{breakeven sales}}{\text{Budgeted sales}} \right)$ x 100%

4

5

6   C. Sales prices *are constant* at all levels of activity.

7   When showing multiple products individually on a P/V chart, the products are shown from left to right, in order of decreasing size of C/S ratio. The line joining the two ends of the dotted line (which shows the cumulative profit/loss and the cumulative sales) indicates the average profit which will be earned from sales of the products in the mix.

Now try the question below from the Exam Question Bank

Number	Level	Marks	Time
Q16	Exam standard	25	45 mins

Chapter 13

LIMITING FACTOR ANALYSIS

Topic list	Syllabus reference	Ability required
1 Limiting factors	(iii)	Application/analysis
2 Limiting factor analysis and restricted freedom of action	(iii)	Application/analysis
3 Make or buy decisions and scarce resources	(iii)	Application/analysis
4 Limiting factors and shadow prices	(iii)	Application/analysis
5 Using limiting factor analysis	(iii)	Application/analysis

Introduction

You have **already encountered limiting factor analysis** in your earlier studies and so we have included a 'Knowledge Brought Forward' box at the beginning of this chapter so that you can remind yourself of the key concepts and basic techniques involved in the approach to allocating resources.

You need to build on the knowledge you acquired at the Foundation level, however, and deal with situations in which organisations have **'restricted freedom of action'**. For example, the profit-maximising production/sales levels may be restricted by orders that the organisation has already taken on or a need to maintain market share.

We will also be looking at the concept of the **shadow price** of a scarce resource and at the issues to bear in mind when using limiting factor analysis.

As you will already be aware, limiting factor analysis can only be used if there is one limiting factor. If there are two or more limiting factors, a technique known as linear programming must be applied. This is covered in Chapters 14 and 15.

Learning outcomes covered in this chapter

- **Calculate** and **interpret** the profit-maximising sales mix for a company with a single resource constraint and limited freedom of action

Syllabus content covered in this chapter

- Single limiting factor analysis where a company has restricted freedom of action

1   LIMITING FACTORS

5/01

KEY TERM

A **limiting factor** or **key factor** is 'Anything which limits the activity of an entity. An entity seeks to optimise the benefit it obtains from the limiting factor'.

(CIMA *Official Terminology*)

Knowledge brought forward

Limiting factor analysis

- An organisation might be faced with just one limiting factor (other than maximum sales demand) but there might also be several scarce resources, with two or more of them putting an effective limit on the level of activity that can be achieved.

- Examples of limiting factors are as follows.

   o   Sales. There may be a limit to sales demand.

   o   Labour. The limit may be either in terms of total quantity or of particular skills.

   o   Materials. There may be insufficient available materials to produce enough units to satisfy sales demand.

   o   Manufacturing capacity. There may not be sufficient machine capacity for the production required to meet sales demand.

- It is assumed in limiting factor analysis that management would select a product mix or service mix that would maximise profit and that profit is maximised when contribution is maximised (given no change in fixed cost expenditure incurred). In other words, marginal costing ideas are applied.

   o   Contribution will be maximised by earning the biggest possible contribution per unit of limiting factor. For example if grade A labour is the limiting factor, contribution will be maximised by earning the biggest contribution per hour of grade A labour worked.

   o   The limiting factor decision therefore involves the determination of the contribution earned per unit of limiting factor by each different product.

   o   If the sales demand is limited, the profit-maximising decision will be to produce the top-ranked product(s) up to the sales demand limit.

- In limiting factor decisions, we generally assume that fixed costs are the same whatever product or service mix is selected, so that the only relevant costs are variable costs.

- When there is just one limiting factor, the technique for establishing the contribution-maximising product mix or service mix is to rank the products or services in order of contribution-earning ability per unit of limiting factor.

1.1   EXAMPLE: LIMITING FACTOR DECISION

Sausage Ltd makes two products, the Mash and the Sauce. Unit variable costs are as follows.

	Mash	Sauce
	£	£
Direct materials	1	3
Direct labour (£3 per hour)	6	3
Variable overhead	1	1
	8	7

The sales price per unit is £14 per Mash and £11 per Sauce. During July the available direct labour is limited to 8,000 hours. Sales demand in July is expected to be as follows.

Mash	3,000 units
Sauce	5,000 units

Required

Determine the production budget that will maximise profit, assuming that fixed costs per month are £20,000 and that there are no opening stock of finished goods or work in progress.

1.2 SOLUTION

Step 1. Confirm that the limiting factor is something other than sales demand.

	Mash	*Sauces*	*Total*
Labour hours per unit	2 hrs	1 hr	
Sales demand	3,000 units	5,000 units	
Labour hours needed	6,000 hrs	5,000 hrs	11,000 hrs
Labour hours available			8,000 hrs
Shortfall			3,000 hrs

Labour is the limiting factor on production.

Step 2. Identify the contribution earned by each product per unit of scarce resource, that is, per labour hour worked.

	Mash	*Sauce*
	£	£
Sales price	14	11
Variable cost	8	7
Unit contribution	6	4
Labour hours per unit	2 hrs	1 hr
Contribution per labour hour (= per unit of limiting factor)	£3	£4

Although Mashes have a higher unit contribution than Sauces, two Sauces can be made in the time it takes to make one Mash. Because labour is in short supply it is more profitable to make Sauces than Mashes.

Step 3. Determine the budgeted production and sales. Sufficient Sauces will be made to meet the full sales demand, and the remaining labour hours available will then be used to make Mashes.

(a)

Product	*Demand*	*Hours required*	*Hours available*	*Priority for manufacture*
Sauces	5,000	5,000	5,000	1st
Mashes	3,000	6,000	3,000 (bal)	2nd
		11,000	8,000	

(b)

Product	*Units*	*Hours needed*	*Contribution per unit*	*Total*
			£	
Sauces	5,000	5,000	4	20,000
Mashes (balance)	1,500	3,000	6	9,000
		8,000		29,000
Less fixed costs				20,000
Profit				9,000

Conclusion

(a) Unit contribution is *not* the correct way to decide priorities.

(b) Labour hours are the scarce resource, therefore **contribution per labour hour** is the correct way to decide priorities.

(c) The Sauce earns £4 contribution per labour hour, and the Mash earns £3 contribution per labour hour. Sauces therefore make more profitable use of the scarce resource, and should be manufactured first.

Question 1

Twickers Ltd makes two products, widgets and splodgets, for which there is unlimited demand at the budgeted selling prices. A widget takes three hours to make, and has a variable cost of £18 and a selling price of £30. A splodget takes two hours to make, and has a variable cost of £10 and a selling price of £20. Both products use the same type of labour, which is in short supply.

Required

Determine the product which should be made to maximise profits, and describe the other considerations which might alter your decision.

Answer

We must **rank** the products in order of **contribution earning capability per labour hour**.

	Widgets per unit	Splodgets per unit
	£	£
Sales price	30	20
Variable costs	18	10
Contribution	12	10
Hours per unit	3	2
Contribution per labour hour	£4	£5

Although widgets have the higher unit contribution, splodgets are more profitable because they make a greater contribution per labour hour. Three splodgets (worth 3 x £10 = £30) can be made in the same time as two widgets (worth only 2 x £12 = £24).

A profit-maximising decision would therefore be to produce splodgets only, given the assumptions made. It is important to remember, however, that **other considerations**, so far excluded from the problem, might alter the decision.

(a) Can the selling price of either product be raised, thereby increasing unit contribution, and the contribution per labour hour, and also reducing demand? Since demand is apparently unlimited, it would be reasonable to suspect that both products are underpriced.

(b) Would a decision to make and sell only splodgets have a harmful effect on customer loyalty and demand? To what extent are sales of each product interdependent? For example, a manufacturer of knives and forks could not expect to cease production of knives without affecting demand for forks.

(c) Would a decision to cease production of widgets have no effect on fixed costs? The assumption that fixed costs are unaffected by limiting factor decisions is not always valid, and closure of either the widgets or the splodgets production line might result in fixed cost savings. These savings would need to be considered when making the product mix decision.

(d) Will the decision affect the long-term plans of the company as well as the short term? If widgets are not produced, it is likely that competitors will take over the markets vacated by Twickers Ltd. Labour skilled in the manufacture of widgets will be lost, and a decision at a later date to re-open manufacture of widgets might not be possible.

Question 2

The following details relate to three products made by DSF Ltd.

	V	A	L
	£ per unit	£ per unit	£ per unit
Selling price	120	170	176
Direct materials	30	40	60
Direct labour	20	30	20
Variable overhead	10	16	20
Fixed overhead	20	32	40
	80	118	140
Profit	40	52	36

All three products use the same direct labour and direct materials, but in different quantities.

In a period when the labour used on these products is in short supply, the most and least profitable use of the labour is

	Most profitable	Least profitable
A	L	V
B	L	A
C	V	A
D	A	L

Answer

The correct answer is B.

	V	A	L
	£	£	£
Selling price per unit	120	170	176
Variable cost per unit	60	86	100
Contribution per unit	60	84	76
Labour cost per unit	£20	£30	£20
Contribution per £ of labour	£3	£2.80	£3.80
Ranking	2	3	1

Two potentially limiting factors

1.3 You may be asked to deal with situations where two limiting factors (and also demand) are **potentially** limiting. The approach in these situations is to find out which factor (if any) prevents the business from fulfilling maximum demand.

1.4 EXAMPLE: TWO POTENTIALLY LIMITING FACTORS

Lucky Ltd manufactures and sells three products, X, Y and Z, for which budgeted sales demand, unit selling prices and unit variable costs are as follows.

		X		Y		Z	
Budgeted sales demand		550 units		500 units		400 units	
		£	£	£	£	£	£
Unit sales price			16		18		14
Variable costs:	materials	8		6		2	
	labour	4		6		9	
			12		12		11
Unit contribution			4		6		3

The company has existing stocks of 250 units of X and 200 units of Z, which it is quite willing to use up to meet sales demand.

All three products use the same direct materials and the same type of direct labour. In the next year, the available supply of materials will be restricted to £4,800 (at cost) and the available supply of labour to £6,600 (at cost).

Required

Determine what product mix and sales mix would maximise the company's profits in the next year.

1.5 SOLUTION

There **appear to be two scarce resources**, direct materials and direct labour. This is not certain, however, and because there is a limited sales demand as well, either of the following might apply.

- There is **no limiting factor at all**, except sales demand.

- There is **only one scarce resource** that prevents the full potential sales demand being achieved.

Step 1. **Establish which of the resources, if any, is scarce.**

	X Units	Y Units	Z Units
Budgeted sales	550	500	400
Stock in hand	250	0	200
Minimum production to meet demand	300	500	200

	Minimum production to meet sales demand Units	Required materials at cost £	Required labour at cost £
X	300	2,400	1,200
Y	500	3,000	3,000
Z	200	400	1,800
Total required		5,800	6,000
Total available		4,800	6,600
(Shortfall)/Surplus		(1,000)	600

Materials are a limiting factor, but labour is not.

Step 2. **Rank X, Y and Z in order of contribution earned per £1 of direct materials consumed.**

	X £	Y £	Z £
Unit contribution	4	6	3
Cost of materials	8	6	2
Contribution per £1 materials	£0.50	£1.00	£1.50
Ranking	3rd	2nd	1st

Step 3. **Determine a production plan.** Z should be manufactured up to the limit where units produced plus units in stock will meet sales demand, then Y second and X third, until all the available materials are used up.

Ranking	Product	Sales demand less units in stock Units	Production quantity Units		Materials cost £
1st	Z	200	200	(× £2)	400
2nd	Y	500	500	(× £6)	3,000
3rd	X	300	175	(× £8)	*1,400
			Total available		4,800

* Balancing amount using up total available.

Step 4. **Draw up a budget.** The profit-maximising budget is as follows.

	X Units	Y Units	Z Units
Opening stock	250	0	200
Add production	175	500	200
Sales	425	500	400

	X £	Y £	Z £	Total £
Revenue	6,800	9,000	5,600	21,400
Variable costs	5,100	6,000	4,400	15,500
Contribution	1,700	3,000	1,200	5,900

2 LIMITING FACTOR ANALYSIS AND RESTRICTED FREEDOM OF ACTION

2.1 In certain circumstances an organisation faced with a limiting factor on production and sales **might not be able to produce the profit-maximising product mix** because the mix and/or volume of products that can be produced and sold is also restricted by a factor other than a scarce resource.

(a) The organisation might have **contracted to supply a certain number of products** to a customer.

(b) The organisation might have to produce and sell a minimum quantity of one or more of its products to **provide a complete product range and/or to maintain customer goodwill.**

(c) The organisation might need to **maintain a certain market share** of one or more of its products.

2.2 In each of these cases, the organisation might have to **produce more of a particular product or products than the level established by ranking** according to contribution per unit of limiting factor.

2.3 The basic approach to dealing with such situations is to **rank the products in the normal way** but the **optimum production plan must take into account the minimum production requirements. The remaining resource must then be allocated according to the ranking.**

2.4 Work carefully through the following example which illustrates this approach.

2.5 EXAMPLE: RESTRICTED FREEDOM OF ACTION

Harvey Ltd is currently preparing its budget for the year ending 30 September 20X2. The company manufactures and sells three products, Beta, Delta and Gamma.

The unit selling price and cost structure of each product is budgeted as follows.

	Beta	Delta	Gamma
	£	£	£
Selling price	100	124	32
Variable costs:			
Labour	24	48	6
Materials	26	7	8
Overhead	10	5	6
	60	60	20
Contribution per unit	40	64	12

Direct labour rate is budgeted at £6 per hour, and fixed costs at £1,300,000 per annum. The company has a maximum production capacity of 228,000 direct labour hours.

A meeting of the board of directors has been convened to discuss the budget and to resolve the problem as to the quantity of each product which should be made and sold. The sales director presented the results of a recent market survey which reveals that market demand for the company's products will be as follows.

Product	Units
Beta	24,000
Delta	12,000
Gamma	60,000

The production director proposes that since Gamma only contributes £12 per unit, the product should no longer be produced, and the surplus capacity transferred to produce additional quantities of Beta and Delta. The sales director does not agree with the proposal. Gamma is considered necessary to complement the product range and to maintain customer goodwill. If Gamma is not offered, the sales director believes that sales of Beta and Delta will be seriously affected. After further discussion the board decided that a minimum of 10,000 units of each product should be produced. The remaining production capacity would then be allocated so as to achieve the maximum profit possible.

Required

Prepare a budget statement which clearly shows the maximum profit which could be achieved in the year ending 30 September 20X2.

2.6 SOLUTION

Step 1. **Ascertain whether labour hours are a scarce resource.**

	Units demanded	*Labour hours per unit*	*Total labour hours*
Beta	24,000	4 (£24/£6)	96,000
Delta	12,000	8 (£48/£6)	96,000
Gamma	60,000	1 (£6/£6)	60,000
			252,000

Step 2. **Rank the products.**

Since only 228,000 hours are available we need to establish which product earns the greatest contribution per labour hour.

	Beta	*Delta*	*Gamma*
Contribution	40	64	12
Labour hours	4	8	1
Contribution per labour hour	£10	£8	£12
Ranking	2nd	3rd	1st

Step 3. **Determine a production plan.**

The optimum production plan must take into account the requirement that 10,000 units of each product are produced, and then allocate the remaining hours according to the above ranking.

			Hours
Beta	10,000 units × 4 hours		40,000
Delta	10,000 units × 8 hours		80,000
Gamma	10,000 units × 1 hour		10,000
			130,000
Gamma	50,000 units × 1 hour (full demand)		50,000
Beta	12,000 units × 4 hours (balance)		48,000
			228,000

Step 4. **Draw up a budget.**

BUDGET STATEMENT

Contribution	£
Beta (22,000 units × £40)	880,000
Delta (10,000 units × £64)	640,000
Gamma (60,000 units × £12)	720,000
	2,240,000
Fixed costs	1,300,000
Profit	940,000

Question 3

Jam Ltd makes two products, the K and the L. The K sells for £50 per unit, the L for £70 per unit. The variable cost per unit of the K is £35, that of the L £40. Each unit of K uses 2 kgs of raw material. Each unit of L uses 3 kgs of material.

In the forthcoming period the availability of raw material is limited to 2,000 kgs. Jam Ltd is contracted to supply 500 units of K. Maximum demand for the L is 250 units. Demand for the K is unlimited.

What is the profit-maximising product mix?

	K	L
A	250 units	625 units
B	1,250 units	750 units
C	625 units	250 units
D	750 units	1,250 units

Answer

The correct answer is C.

	K	L
Contribution per unit	£15	£30
Contribution per unit of limiting factor	£15/2 = £7.50	£30/3 = £10
Ranking	2	1

Production plan	*Raw material used*
	kg
Contracted supply of K (500 x 2 kg)	1,000
Meet demand for L (250 x 3 kg)	750
Remainder of resource for K (125 x 2 kg)	250
	2,000

3 MAKE OR BUY DECISIONS AND SCARCE RESOURCES

3.1 A company might **want to do more things than it has the resources for,** and so its alternatives would be as follows.

(a) Make the best use of the available resources and ignore the opportunities to buy help from outside

(b) Combine internal resources with buying externally so as to do more and increase profitability

3.2 Buying help from outside is justifiable if it adds to profits. A further decision is then required on how to split the work between internal and external effort. What parts of the work should be given to suppliers or sub-contractors so as to maximise profitability?

3.3 In a situation where a company must **sub-contract work to make up a shortfall in its own in-house capabilities,** its **total costs will be minimised** if those **units bought have the lowest extra variable cost of buying per unit of scarce resource saved.**

This basic principle can be illustrated with a simple example.

3.4 EXAMPLE: MAKE OR BUY DECISION WITH SCARCE RESOURCES

Seaman Ltd manufactures three components, S, A and T using the same machines for each. The budget for the next year calls for the production and assembly of 4,000 of each component. The variable production cost per unit of the final product is as follows.

	Machine hours	Variable cost
		£
1 unit of S	3	20
1 unit of A	2	36
1 unit of T	4	24
Assembly		20
		100

Only 24,000 hours of machine time will be available during the year, and a sub-contractor has quoted the following unit prices for supplying components: S £29; A £40; T £34.

Required

Advise Seaman Ltd.

3.5   SOLUTION

The company's budget calls for 36,000 hours of machine time, if all the components are to be produced in-house. Only 24,000 hours are available, and so there is a shortfall of 12,000 hours of machine time, which is therefore a limiting factor. The shortage can be overcome by subcontracting the equivalent of 12,000 machine hours' output to the subcontractor.

The assembly costs are not relevant costs because they are unaffected by the decision.

The decision rule is to **minimise the extra variable costs of sub-contracting per unit of scarce resource saved** (that is, per machine hour saved).

	S	A	T
	£	£	£
Variable cost of making	20	36	24
Variable cost of buying	29	40	34
Extra variable cost of buying	9	4	10
Machine hours saved by buying	3 hrs	2 hrs	4 hrs
Extra variable cost of buying per hour saved	£3	£2	£2.50

This analysis shows that it is **cheaper to buy A than to buy T** and it is **most expensive to buy S**. The **priority for making** the components in-house will be in the **reverse order**: S, then T, then A. There are enough machine hours to make all 4,000 units of S (12,000 hours) and to produce 3,000 units of T (another 12,000 hours). 12,000 hours' production of T and A must be sub-contracted.

The cost-minimising and so profit-maximising make and buy schedule is as follows.

	Component	Machine hours used/saved	Number of units	Unit variable cost	Total variable cost
				£	£
Make:	S	12,000	4,000	20	80,000
	T	12,000	3,000	24	72,000
		24,000			152,000
Buy:	T	4,000	1,000	34	34,000
	A	8,000	4,000	40	160,000
		12,000			
Total variable cost of components, excluding assembly costs					346,000

Question 4

TW Ltd manufactures two products, the D and the E, using the same material for each. Annual demand for the D is 9,000 units, while demand for the E is 12,000 units.

The variable production cost per unit of the D is £10, that of the E £15. The D requires 3.5 kgs of raw material per unit, the E requires 8 kgs of raw material per unit.

Supply of raw material will be limited to 87,500 kgs during the year.

A sub contractor has quoted prices of £17 per unit for the D and £25 per unit for the E to supply the product.

How many of each product should TW Ltd manufacture in order to maximise profits?

A   9,000 units of D, no units of E
B   9,625 units of E, 3,000 units of D
C   7,000 units of D, 9,000 units of E
D   9,000 units of D, 7,000 units of E

Answer

The correct answer is D.

	D	*E*
	£ per unit	£ per unit
Variable cost of making	10	15
Variable cost of buying	17	25
Extra variable cost of buying	7	10
Raw material saved by buying	3.5 kgs	8 kgs
Extra variable cost of buying per kg saved	£2	£1.25
Priority for internal manufacture	1	2

Production plan			*Material used*
			kgs
∴ Make	D	(9,000 × 3.5 kgs)	31,500
	E	(7,000 × 8 kgs)	56,000
			87,500

The remaining 5,000 units of E should be purchased from the contractor.

Exam focus point

Question 6 of the pilot paper tests your ability to deal with fixed and variable costs (a skill you should have developed in your earlier studies) and to maximise the benefit from the use of available resources.

4   LIMITING FACTORS AND SHADOW PRICES

4.1   Whenever there are limiting factors, there will be **opportunity costs**. These are the **benefits forgone by using a limiting factor in one way instead of in the next most profitable way.**

KEY TERM

Opportunity cost is 'The value of the benefit sacrificed when one course of action is chosen, in preference to an alternative. The opportunity cost is represented by the forgone potential benefit from the best rejected course of action'.

(CIMA *Official Terminology*)

4.2   For example, suppose that a company manufactures two items X and Y, which earn a contribution of £24 and £18 per unit respectively. Product X requires 4 machine hours per unit, and product Y 2 hours. Only 5,000 machine hours are available, and potential sales demand is for 1,000 units each of X and Y.

4.3 Machine hours would be a limiting factor, and with X earning £6 per hour and Y earning £9 per hour, the profit-maximising decision would be as follows.

	Units	Hours	Contribution £
Y	1,000	2,000	18,000
X (balance)	750	3,000	18,000
		5,000	36,000

Priority is given to Y because the **opportunity cost** of making Y instead of more units of X is £6 per hour (X's contribution per machine hour), and since Y earns £9 per hour, the incremental benefit of making Y instead of X would be £3 per hour.

4.4 If extra machine hours could be made available, more units of X (up to 1,000) would be made, and an extra contribution of £6 per hour could be earned. Similarly, if fewer machine hours were available, the decision would be to make fewer units of X and to keep production of Y at 1,000 units, and so the loss of machine hours would cost the company £6 per hour in lost contribution. This £6 per hour, the **marginal contribution-earning potential of the limiting factor at the profit-maximising output level**, is referred to as the **shadow price** (or **dual price**) of the limiting factor.

KEY TERM

A **shadow price** is 'An increase in value which would be created by having available one additional unit of a limiting resource at the original cost'. (CIMA *Official Terminology*)

Note that the shadow price only applies while the extra unit of resource can be obtained at its normal variable cost. The shadow price also indicates the amount by which contribution could fall if an organisation is deprived of one unit of the resource.

4.5 The shadow price of a resource is its **internal opportunity cost.** This is the marginal contribution towards fixed costs and profit that can be earned for each unit of the limiting factor that is available. A knowledge of the shadow price of a resource will help managers to decide how much it is worth paying to acquire another unit of the resource.

5 USING LIMITING FACTOR ANALYSIS

5.1 Limiting factor analysis provides us with a profit-maximising product mix, within the assumptions made. It is important to remember, however, that other considerations, so far not considered in our examples, might entirely alter the decision reached.

Qualitative factors

5.2 When a decision is being made, qualitative factors should also be borne in mind.

Factor	Examples
Demand	Will the decision reached (perhaps to make and sell just one product rather than two) have a harmful effect on customer loyalty and sales demand? For example, a manufacturer of knives and forks could not expect to cease production of knives without affecting sales demand for the forks.
Long-term effects	Is the decision going to affect the long-term as well as the short-term plans of the organisation? If a particular product is not produced, or produced at a level below sales demand, is it likely that competitors will take over vacated markets? Labour skilled in the manufacture of the product may be lost and a decision to reopen or expand production of the product in the future may not be possible.
Labour	If labour is a limiting factor, is it because the skills required are difficult to obtain, perhaps because the organisation is using very old-fashioned production methods, or is the organisation a high-tech newcomer in a low-tech area? Or perhaps the conditions of work are so unappealing the people simply do not want to work for the organisation.
Other limiting factors	The same sort of questions should be asked whatever the limiting factor. If machine hours are in short supply is this because more machines are needed, or newer, more reliable and efficient machines? If materials are in short supply, what are competitors doing? Have they found an equivalent or better substitute? Is it time to redesign the product?

Assumptions in limiting factor analysis

5.3 In the examples covered in the chapter, certain assumptions were made. If any of the assumptions are not valid, then the profit-maximising decision might be different. These assumptions are as follows.

(a) **Fixed costs will be the same** regardless of the decision that is taken, and so the profit-maximising and contribution-maximising output level will be the same.

This will not necessarily be true, since some fixed costs might be directly attributable to a product or service. A decision to reduce or cease altogether activity on a product or service might therefore result in some fixed cost savings, which would have to be taken into account.

(b) **The unit variable cost is constant,** regardless of the output quantity of a product or service. This implies the following.

(i) The price of resources will be unchanged regardless of quantity; for example, there will be no bulk purchase discount of raw materials.

(ii) Efficiency and productivity levels will be unchanged; regardless of output quantity the direct labour productivity, the machine time per unit, and the materials consumption per unit will remain the same.

(c) **The estimates of sales demand** for each product, and the **resources required** to make each product, **are known with certainty.**

In the example in Paragraph 1.4, there were estimates of the maximum sales demand for each of three products, and these estimates were used to establish the profit-maximising product mix. Suppose the estimates were wrong? The product mix finally chosen would then either mean that some sales demand of the most profitable item would be unsatisfied, or that production would exceed sales demand, leaving some stock unsold. Clearly, once a profit-maximising output decision is reached, management will have to keep their decision under continual review, and adjust their decision as appropriate in the light of actual results.

(d) **Units of output are divisible,** and a profit-maximising solution might include fractions of units as the optimum output level.

Where fractional answers are not realistic, some rounding of the figures will be necessary.

Chapter roundup

- A scarce resource is a resource of which there is a limited supply.

- Once a scarce resource affects the ability of an organisation to earn profits, a scarce resource becomes known as a limiting factor.

- If resources are limiting factors, contribution will be maximised by earning the biggest possible contribution per unit of limiting factor.

- Where there is just one limiting factor, the technique for establishing the contribution-maximising product or service mix is to rank the products or services in order of contribution-earning ability per unit of limiting factor.

- Where there is a maximum potential sales demand for an organisation's products or services, they should still be ranked in order of contribution-earning ability per unit of the limiting factor. The contribution-maximising decision, however, will be to produce the top-ranked products (or to provide the top-ranked services) up to the sales demand limit.

- If an organisation has to produce more of a particular product or products than the level established by ranking according to contribution per unit of limiting factor, the products should be ranked in the normal way but the optimum production plan must first take into account the minimum production requirements. The remaining resource must then be allocated according to the ranking.

- In a situation where an organisation must subcontract work to make up a shortfall in its own in-house capabilities, its total costs will be minimised if the units bought have the lowest extra variable cost of buying per unit of scarce resource saved by buying.

- The shadow price or dual price of a limiting factor is the increase in value which would be created by having one additional unit of the limiting factor at the original cost.

- Qualitative factors, such as effect on customer goodwill, ability to restart production and reasons for a resource being a limiting factor, should also be borne in mind in product mix decisions.

- Various assumptions are made in limiting factor analysis.

  ° Fixed costs remain the same regardless of the decision taken
  ° Unit variable cost is constant regardless of the decision taken
  ° Estimates of sales demand and resources required are known with certainty
  ° Units of output are divisible

- If you suspect the existence of a limiting factor, calculate the amount of the scarce resource needed to meet potential sales demand, calculate the amount of the scarce resource available and then compare the two figures.

Quick quiz

1   *Choose the correct word from those highlighted.*

    When there is just one limiting factor, the product with the **biggest/smallest** contribution earning ability per unit of limiting factor should be produced first.

2   Which of the following is not an example of a limiting factor?

    A   Sales demand
    B   Materials
    C   Machine time
    D   Profit

3   Marginal costing ideas are applied in limiting factor analysis. *True or false?*

4   *Put the following in the correct order of approach to adopt when dealing with limiting factor analysis and limited freedom of action.*

    (a)   Allocate resource according to ranking
    (b)   Rank the products

(c)   Take into account minimum production requirements

5   *Choose the correct words from those highlighted.*

If an organisation has to subcontract work to make up a shortfall in its own in-house capabilities, its total costs will be minimised if those units bought have the **highest/lowest** extra **variable cost/resource requirement** of buying per **unit of scarce resource/£** saved.

6   *Fill in the blanks.*

The shadow price of a scarce resource indicates the amount by which contribution would .... if an organisation were deprived of one unit of the resource. The shadow price only applies while the extra unit of resource can be obtained at its .... cost.

7   *Use the words listed below to fill in the blanks in the following statements about the assumptions in limiting factor analysis.*

Missing words: units of output; sales demand and resources required per unit; unit variable cost; fixed costs.

(a)   .... will be the same regardless of the decision taken.

(b)   The .... is constant, regardless of the output quantity.

(c)   The estimates of .... are known with certainty.

(d)   .... are divisible.

Answers to quick quiz

1   Biggest

2   D

3   True

4   (b), (c), (a)

5   Lowest
Variable cost
Unit of scarce resource

6   Fall
Normal variable

7   (a)   Fixed costs
(b)   Unit variable cost
(c)   Sales demand and resources required per unit
(d)   Units of output

Now try the question below from the Exam Question Bank

Number	Level	Marks	Time
Q17	Exam standard	25	45 mins

Chapter 14

LINEAR PROGRAMMING: THE GRAPHICAL METHOD

Topic list	Syllabus reference	Ability required
1　The graphical method	(iii)	Application
2　The graphical method using simultaneous equations	(iii)	Application
3　Minimisation problems	(iii)	Application
4　Sensitivity analysis	(iii)	Application

Introduction

In the previous chapter we saw how to determine the profit-maximising allocation of resources when an organisation is faced with one resource constraint and limited freedom of action. When there is **more than one resource constraint** it is no longer possible to use the simple technique of ranking items according to their contribution per unit of limiting factor in order to determine the profit-maximising allocation of resources. Instead, the technique of **linear programming** can be used. This technique can be applied to problems with the following features.

- There is a **single objective**, which is to **maximise** or **minimise the value of a certain function**. The objective in commercial decision making is usually to **maximise contribution** and **thus maximise profit.**

- There are **several constraints**, typically scarce resources, that limit the value of the objective function.

There are two linear programming techniques.

- The **graphical method** is used for problems involving **two products.**

- The **simplex method** is used if the problem involves **more than two products.**

We will be looking at the graphical method in this chapter, the simplex method in the next.

Learning outcomes covered in this chapter

- **Solve** a two-plus constraint/limitation problem for two products using the graphical method and interpret the results

Syllabus content covered in this chapter

- Linear programming

BPP PUBLISHING

1 THE GRAPHICAL METHOD

Formulating the problem

1.1 Let us suppose that W Ltd manufactures two products, A and B. Both products pass through two production departments, mixing and shaping. The company's objective is to maximise contribution to fixed costs.

1.2 Product A is sold for £1.50 whereas product B is priced at £2.00. There is unlimited demand for product A but demand for B is limited to 13,000 units per annum. The machine hours available in each department are restricted to 2,400 per annum.

1.3 Other relevant data are as follows.

Machine hours required

	Mixing Hrs	*Shaping* Hrs
Product A	0.06	0.04
Product B	0.08	0.12

Variable cost per unit

	£
Product A	1.30
Product B	1.70

1.4 Before we work through the steps involved in solving this constraints problem using the graphical approach to linear programming, it is worth reading the CIMA *Official Terminology* definition of linear programming to get a glimpse of what we will be doing.

KEY TERM

Linear programming is 'The use of a series of linear equations to construct a mathematical model. The objective is to obtain an optimal solution to a complex operational problem, which may involve the production of a number of products in an environment in which there are many constraints'. (CIMA *Official Terminology*)

Question 1

What are the constraints in the situation facing W Ltd?

(i) Machine hours in each department
(ii) Labour hours in each department
(iii) Sales demand for product B
(iv) Selling price of product A

A (i) and (iii)
B (i) only
C (ii) and (iv)
D (i), (ii) and (iii)

Answer

The correct answer is A.

1.5   Let's start solving W Ltd's problem.

Step 1.   **Define variables**

What are the **quantities that W Ltd can vary?** Obviously not the number of machine hours or the demand for product B. The only things which it can vary are the **number of units of each type of product produced.** It is those numbers which the company has to determine in such a way as to obtain the maximum possible profit. Our **variables** (which are usually products being produced) will therefore be as follows.

Let x = number of units of product A produced.
Let y = number of units of product B produced.

Step 2.   **Establish objective function**

KEY TERM

The **objective function** is a quantified statement of the aim of the resource allocation decision.

We now need to introduce the question of contribution or profit. We know that the **contribution on each type of product** is as follows.

		£ per unit
Product A	£(1.50 – 1.30) =	0.20
Product B	£(2.00 – 1.70) =	0.30

The **objective of the company is to maximise contribution** and so the **objective function to be maximised** is as follows.

Contribution (C) = 0.2x + 0.3y

Step 3.   **Establish constraints**

The **value of the objective function** (the maximum contribution achievable from producing products A and B) is **limited by the constraints** facing W Ltd, however. To incorporate this into the problem we need to **translate the constraints into inequalities involving the variables** defined in Step 1. An inequality is an equation taking the form 'greater than or equal to' or 'less than or equal to'.

(a)   Consider the **mixing department machine hours** constraint.

   (i)   **Each unit of product A** requires 0.06 hours of machine time. Producing five units therefore requires 5×0.06 hours of machine time and, more generally, **producing x units will require 0.06x hours.**

   (ii)   Likewise producing **y units of product B will require 0.08y hours.**

   (iii) The total machine hours needed in the mixing department to make x units of product A and y units of product B is 0.06x + 0.08y.

   (iv)   We know that this **cannot be greater than 2,400 hours** and so we arrive at the following inequality.

   $$0.06x + 0.08y \leq 2,400$$

Question 2

How can the constraint facing the shaping department be written as an inequality?

A $0.4x + 0.012y \geq 2{,}400$
B $0.04x + 0.12y \leq 2{,}400$
C $0.4x + 0.012y \leq 2{,}400$
D $0.04x + 0.12y \geq 2{,}400$

Answer

The correct answer is B.

(b)   The final inequality is easier to obtain. The **number of units of product B produced and sold is y** but this has to be **less than or equal to 13,000.** Our inequality is therefore as follows.

$$y \leq 13{,}000$$

(c)   We also need to add **non-negativity constraints** ($x \geq 0$, $y \geq 0$) since negative numbers of products cannot be produced. (Linear programming is simply a mathematical tool and so there is nothing in this method which guarantees that the answer will 'make sense'. An unprofitable product may produce an answer which is negative. This is mathematically correct but nonsense in operational terms. Always remember to include the non-negativity constraints. The examiner will not appreciate 'impossible' solutions.)

1.6   The **problem** has now been **reduced** to the following **four inequalities** and **one equation.**

Maximise contribution (C) $= 0.2x + 0.3y$, subject to the following constraints:

$$
\begin{aligned}
0.06x + 0.08y &\leq 2{,}400 \\
0.04x + 0.12y &\leq 2{,}400 \\
0 \leq y &\leq 13{,}000 \\
0 &\leq x
\end{aligned}
$$

Question 3

A company makes two products, X and Y. Product X has a contribution of £124 per unit and product Y £80 per unit. Both products pass through two departments for processing and the times in minutes per unit are as follows.

	Product X	Product Y
Department 1	150	90
Department 2	100	120

Currently there is a maximum of 225 hours per week available in department 1 and 200 hours in department 2. The company can sell all it can produce of X but EU quotas restrict the sale of Y to a maximum of 75 units per week. The company, which wishes to maximise contribution, currently makes and sells 30 units of X and 75 units of Y per week.

Required

Formulate a linear programming model of this problem.

Answer

Define variables

Let x, y be the number of units of products X and Y produced per week.

Establish objective function

The objective function is to maximise weekly contribution, given by C = 124x + 80y, subject to the constraints below.

Establish constraints

Department 1	150x + 90y	≤	225 x 60 minutes
Department 2	100x + 120y	≤	200 x 60 minutes
EU quota	y	≤	75
Non-negativity	x, y	≥	0

These constraints can be simplified to:

Department 1	15x + 9y	≤	1,350
Department 2	10x + 12y	≤	1,200
EU quota	y	≤	75
Non-negativity	x, y	≥	0

Graphing the problem

1.7 A **graphical solution** is **only possible** when there are **two variables** in the problem. One variable is represented by the **x axis** of the graph and one by the **y axis**. Since non-negative values are not usually allowed, the graph shows **only zero and positive values of x and y**.

Graphing equations and constraints

1.8 A **linear equation with one or two variables** is shown as a **straight line on a graph**. Thus y = 6 would be shown as follows.

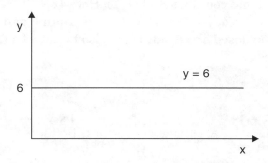

If the problem included a **constraint that y could not exceed 6**, the **inequality y ≤ 6** would be represented by the **shaded area of the graph below**.

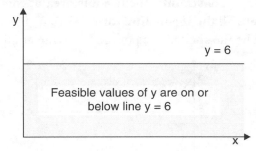

1.9 The equation 4x + 3y = 24 is also a straight line on a graph. To **draw any straight line**, we **need only to plot two points and join them up**. The easiest points to plot are the following.

- x = 0 (in this example, if x = 0, 3y = 24, y = 8)
- y = 0 (in this example, if y = 0, 4x = 24, x = 6)

By plotting the points, (0, 8) and (6, 0) on a graph, and joining them up, we have the line for 4x + 3y = 24.

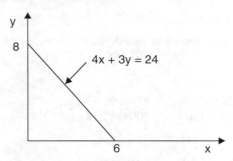

Any combination of values for x and y on the line satisfies the equation. Thus at a point where x = 3 and y = 4, 4x + 3y = 24. Similarly, at a point where x = 4.5 and y = 2, 4x + 3y = 24.

1.10 If we had a **constraint 4x + 3y ≤ 24, any combined value of x and y within the shaded area below (on or below the line) would satisfy the constraint.**

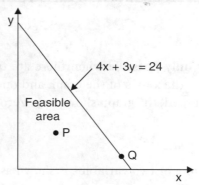

Consider point P which has coordinates of (2, 2). Here 4x + 3y = 14, which is less than 24; and at point Q where x = 5½, y = 2/3, 4x + 3y = 24. **Both P and Q lie within the feasible area. A feasible area enclosed on all sides may also be called a feasible polygon.**

KEY TERM

A **feasible area** (or **feasible region**) is an area on a graph whose boundaries delineate the limits of what is achievable. A feasible area enclosed on all sides may also be called a **feasible polygon**.

1.11 When there are **several constraints**, the **feasible area** of combinations of values of x and y must be an area **where all the inequalities are satisfied.** Thus, if **y ≤ 6 and 4x + 3y ≤ 24** the **feasible area** would be the **shaded area** in the following graph.

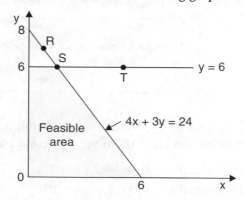

(a) Point R (x = 0.75, y = 7) is not in the feasible area because although it satisfies the inequality 4x + 3y ≤ 24, it does not satisfy y ≤ 6.

(b) Point T (x = 5, y = 6) is not in the feasible area, because although it satisfies the inequality y ≤ 6, it does not satisfy 4x + 3y ≤ 24.

(c) Point S (x = 1.5, y = 6) satisfies both inequalities and lies just on the boundary of the feasible area since y = 6 exactly, and 4x + 3y = 24. Point S is thus at the intersection of the two lines.

1.12 Similarly, if y ≥ 6 and 4x + 3y ≥ 24 but x is ≤ 6, the feasible area would be the shaded area in the graph below.

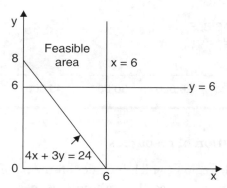

1.13 EXAMPLE: FEASIBLE VALUES

Draw the feasibility polygon for the following inequalities.

2x + 3y ≤ 12
y ≥ 2x
x ≥ 0, y ≥ 0

1.14 SOLUTION

The new problem here is the inequality y ≥ 2x. The equation y = 2x is a straight line, and you need to plot two points to draw it, such as (0, 0) and (2, 4).

Since y ≥ 2x, feasible combinations of x and y lie above this line (for example if x = 2, y must be 4 or more).

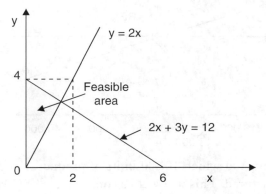

Question 4

Draw the feasible region which arises from the constraints facing W Ltd.

Answer

If 0.06x + 0.08y = 2,400, then if x = 0, y = 30,000 and if y = 0, x = 40,000.
If 0.04x + 0.12y = 2,400, then if x = 0, y = 20,000 and if y = 0, x = 60,000.

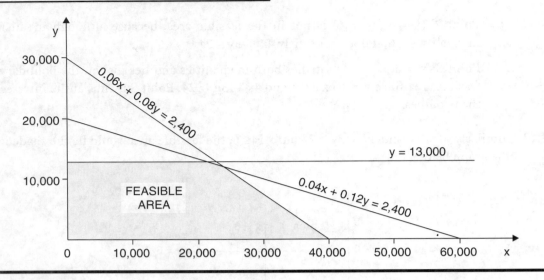

Finding the optimum allocation of resources

1.15 Having found the feasible region (which includes all the possible solutions to the problem) we need to **find which of these possible solutions is 'best'** in the sense that it yields the maximum possible contribution.

1.16 Look at the feasible region of the problem faced by W Ltd (see the solution to Question 4). Even in such a simple problem as this, there are a **great many possible solution points within the feasible area.** Even to write them all down would be a time-consuming process and also an unnecessary one, as we shall see.

1.17 Here is the graph of W Ltd's problem.

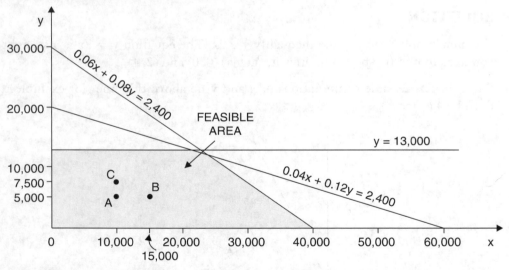

(a) Consider point A at which 10,000 units of product A and 5,000 units of product B are being manufactured. This will yield a contribution of (10,000 × £0.20) + (5,000 × £0.30) = £3,500.

(b) We would clearly get more contribution at point B, where the same number of units of product B are being produced but where the number of units of product A has increased by 5,000.

(c) We would also get more contribution at point C where the number of units of product A is the same but 2,500 more units of product B are being produced.

This argument suggests that the **'best' solution** is going to be at a **point on the edge of the feasible area** rather than in the middle of it.

1.18 This still leaves us with quite a few points to look at but there is a way in which we can **narrow down still further the likely points at which the best solution will be found.** Suppose that W Ltd wishes to earn contribution of £3,000. The company could sell the following combinations of the two products.

- 15,000 units of A, no B.
- No A, 10,000 units of B.
- A suitable mix of the two, such as 7,500 A and 5,000 B.

1.19 The **possible combinations required to earn contribution of £3,000** could be **shown by the straight line 0.2x + 0.3y = 3,000.**

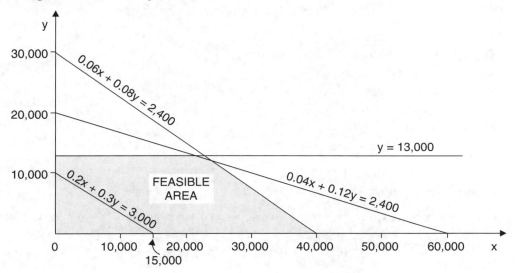

1.20 Likewise for profits of £6,000 and £1,500, lines of 0.2x + 0.3y = 6,000 and 0.2x + 0.3y = 1,500 could be drawn **showing the combination of the two products** which would **achieve contribution of £6,000 or £1,500.**

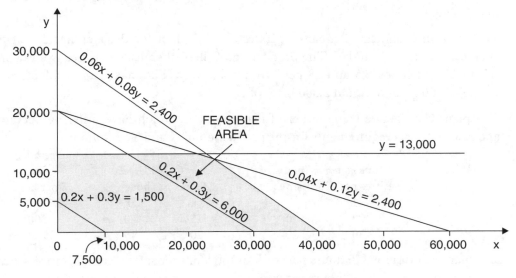

1.21 The **contribution lines are all parallel.** (They are called **iso-contribution lines,** 'iso' meaning equal.) A similar line drawn for any other total contribution would also be parallel to the three lines shown here. **Bigger contribution is shown by lines further from the origin** (0.2x + 0.3y = 6,000), smaller contribution by lines closer to the origin (0.2x + 3y = 1,500). As W Ltd tries to increase possible contribution, we need to 'slide' any contribution line outwards from the origin, while always keeping it parallel to the other contribution lines.

1.22 As we do this there will come a point at which, if we were to **move the contribution line out any further, it would cease to lie in the feasible region**. Greater contribution could not be achieved, because of the constraints. In our example concerning W Ltd this will happen, as you should test for yourself, where the contribution line just passes through the intersection of 0.06x + 0.08y = 2,400 and 0.04x + 0.12y = 2,400 (at coordinates (24,000, 12,000)). The point (24,000, 12,000) will therefore give us the optimal allocation of resources (to produce 24,000 units of A and 12,000 units of B).

SUMMARY

We can usefully summarise the graphical approach to linear programming as follows.

Step 1. Define variables.

Step 2. Establish objective function.

Step 3. Establish constraints.

Step 4. Graph the problem.

Step 5. Define feasible area.

Step 6. Determine optimal solution.

Exam focus point

The graphical approach to linear programming is the subject of one of the (optional) questions in Section D of the Pilot paper. The question is extremely straightforward and provides plenty of easy mark-earning opportunities.

1.23 EXAMPLE: THE GRAPHICAL SOLUTION WITH A TWIST

This example shows that it is not always necessarily easy to identify the decision variables in a problem.

The Dervish Chemical Company operates a small plant for the manufacture of two joint chemical products X and Y. The production of these chemicals requires two raw materials, A and B, which cost £5 and £8 per litre respectively. The maximum available supply per week is 2,700 litres of A and 2,000 litres of B.

The plant can operate using either of two processes, which have differing operating costs and raw materials requirements for the production of X and Y, as follows.

Process	Raw materials consumed Litres per processing hour		Output Litres per hour		Operating cost £ per hour
	A	B	X	Y	
1	20	10	15	20	500
2	30	20	20	10	230

The plant can run for 120 hours per week in total, but for safety reasons, process 2 cannot be operated for more than 80 hours per week.

X sells for £18 per litre, Y for £24 per litre.

Required

Formulate a linear programming model, and then solve it, to determine how the plant should be operated each week.

1.24 SOLUTION

Step 1. **Define variables**

You might decide that there are two decision variables in the problem, the quantity of X and the quantity of Y to make each week. If so, begin by letting these be x and y respectively.

You might also readily recognise that the aim should be to maximise the total weekly contribution, and so the objective function should be expressed in terms of maximising the total contribution from X and Y.

The contribution per litre from X and Y cannot be calculated because the operating costs are expressed in terms of processing hours.

		Process 1		*Process 2*	
		£ per hour	£ per hour	£ per hour	£ per hour
Costs:					
Material A			100		150
Material B			80		160
Operating cost			500		230
			680		540
Revenue:					
X	$(15 \times £18)$	270		360	
Y	$(20 \times £24)$	480		240	
			750		600
Contribution			70		60

The **decision variables** should be **processing hours in each process**, rather than litres of X and Y. If we let the processing hours per week for process 1 be P_1 and the processing hours per week for process 2 be P_2 we can now formulate an objective function, and constraints, as follows.

Step 2. **Establish objective function**

Maximise $70P_1 + 60P_2$ (total contribution) subject to the constraints below

Step 3. **Establish constraints**

$$20P_1 + 30P_2 \leq 2,700 \quad \text{(material A supply)}$$
$$10P_1 + 20P_2 \leq 2,000 \quad \text{(material B supply)}$$
$$P_2 \leq 80 \quad \text{(maximum time for } P_2)$$
$$P_1 + P_2 \leq 120 \quad \text{(total maximum time)}$$
$$P_1, P_2 \geq 0$$

Step 4. **Graph the problem**

The graphical solution looks like this.

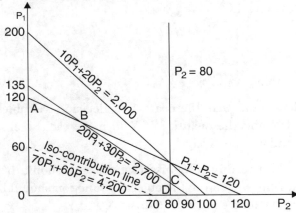

Step 5. **Define feasible area**

The material B constraint is not critical, and the feasible area for a solution is shown as ABCDO on the graph.

Step 6. **Define variables**

Determine optimal solution

The optimal solution, determined using the iso-contribution line $70P1 + 60P2 = 4,200$, is at point A, where $P1 = 120$ and $P2 = 0$.

Production would be (120×15) 1,800 litres of X and (120×20) 2,400 litres of Y.

Total contribution would be $(120 \times £70) = £8,400$ per week.

Question 5

On 20 days of every month Greece Ltd makes two products, the Crete and the Corfu. Production is carried out in three departments - tanning, plunging and watering. Relevant information is as follows.

	Crete	Corfu
Profit per unit	£100	£50
Minutes in tanning department per unit	10	12
Minutes in plunging department per unit	15	10
Minutes in watering department per unit	6	15
Maximum daily sales (due to government quota restrictions)	175	200

	Tanning	Plunging	Watering
Number of employees	7	10	5
Hours at work per day per employee	7	6	10
Number of idle hours per day per employee	0.5	1	0.25

Due to union restrictions, employees cannot be at work for longer than the hours detailed above.

Required

Use the graphical method of linear programming to determine the optimum monthly production of Cretes and Corfus and the monthly profit if Greece Ltd's objective is to maximise profit.

Answer

Calculate the number of productive hours worked in each department each month

Number of employees x number of productive hours worked each day x number of days each month.

Tanning	=	7 x (7 – 0.5) x 20 = 910 hours
Plunging	=	10 x (6 – 1) x 20 = 1,000 hours
Watering	=	5 x (10 – 0.25) x 20 = 975 hours

Step 1. **Define variables**

Let the number of Cretes produced each month = x and the number of Corfus produced each month = y.

Step 2. **Establish objective function**

The profit is £100 per Crete and £50 per Corfu. The objective function is therefore maximise P = 100x + 50y subject to the constraints below.

Step 3. **Establish constraints**

Tanning	x/6 + y/5 ≤ 910
Plunging	x/4 + y/6 ≤ 1,000
Watering	x/10 + y/4 ≤ 975
Monthly sales units	x ≤ 3,500, y ≤ 4,000
Non negativity	x ≥ 0, y ≥ 0

Step 4. **Graph the problem**

The problem can be solved using the following graph which includes a sample contribution line 100x + 50y = 150,000.

Number of Corfu produced

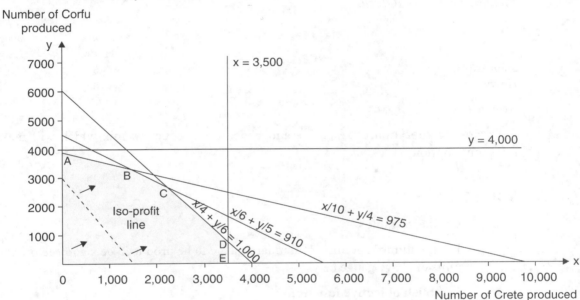

Step 5. **Define the feasible area**

The feasible region for a solution is OABCDE.

Step 6. **Determine the optimal solution**

Moving the sample profit line across the feasible region it can be seen that the optimum solution is at point D where the line x = 3,500 and x/4 + x/6 = 1,000 meet. The coordinates of point D are (3,500, 750).

The optimal solution is therefore to produce 3,500 Cretes and 750 Corfus per month, resulting in a profit of £[(3,500 x 100) + (750 x 50)] = £387,500 per month.

---

2 THE GRAPHICAL METHOD USING SIMULTANEOUS EQUATIONS

2.1 Instead of a 'sliding the contribution line out' approach, **simultaneous equations** can be used to determine the optimal allocation of resources, as shown in the following example.

2.2 EXAMPLE: USING SIMULTANEOUS EQUATIONS

A company manufactures plastic-covered steel fencing in two qualities: standard and heavy gauge. Both products pass through the same processes involving steel forming and plastic bonding.

The standard gauge sells at £15 a roll and the heavy gauge at £20 a roll. There is an unlimited market for the standard gauge but outlets for the heavy gauge are limited to 13,000 rolls a year. The factory operations of each process are limited to 2,400 hours a year. Other relevant data is given below.

Variable costs per roll

	Direct material	*Direct wages*	*Direct expense*
	£	£	£
Standard	5	7	1
Heavy	7	8	2

Processing hours per 100 rolls

	Steel forming Hours	*Plastic bonding* Hours
Standard	6	4
Heavy	8	12

Required

Calculate the allocation of resources and hence the production mix which will maximise total contribution.

2.3 SOLUTION

Step 1. **Define variables**

Let the number of units of standard gauge to be produced be x and the number of units of heavy gauge be y.

Step 2. **Establish objective function**

Standard gauge produces a contribution of £2 per unit (£15 – £(5 + 7 + 1)) and heavy gauge a contribution of £3 (£20 – £(7 + 8 + 2)).

Therefore the objective is to maximise contribution (C) = 2x + 3y subject to the constraints below.

Step 3. **Establish constraints**

The constraints are as follows.

$$0.06x + 0.08y \leq 2,400 \qquad \text{(steel forming hours)}$$
$$0.04x + 0.12y \leq 2,400 \qquad \text{(plastic bonding hours)}$$
$$y \leq 13,000 \qquad \text{(demand for heavy gauge)}$$
$$x, y \geq 0 \qquad \text{(non-negativity)}$$

Step 4. **Graph problem**

The graph of the problem can now be drawn.

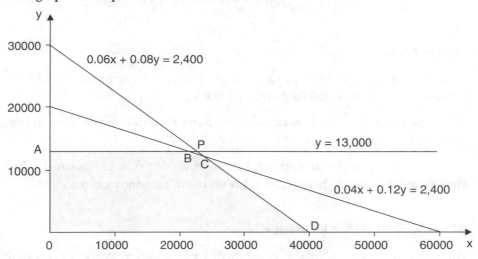

Step 5. **Define feasible area**

The combinations of x and y that satisfy all three constraints are represented by the area OABCD.

Step 6. **Determine optimal solution**

Which combination will maximise contribution? Obviously, the more units of x and y, the bigger the contribution will be, and the optimal solution will be at point B, C or D. It will not be at A, since at A, y = 13,000 and x = 0, whereas at B, y = 13,000 (the same) and x is greater than zero.

Using simultaneous equations to calculate the value of x and y at each of points B, C and D, and then working out total contribution at each point from this, we can establish the contribution-maximising product mix.

Point B

$$
\begin{aligned}
y &= 13{,}000 & (1) \\
0.04x + 0.12y &= 2{,}400 & (2) \\
0.12y &= 1{,}560 & (3)\,((1) \times 0.12) \\
0.04x &= 840 & (4)\,((2) - (3)) \\
x &= 21{,}000 & (5)
\end{aligned}
$$

Total contribution = $(21{,}000 \times £2) + (13{,}000 \times £3) = £81{,}000$.

Point C

$$
\begin{aligned}
0.06x + 0.08y &= 2{,}400 & (1) \\
0.04x + 0.12y &= 2{,}400 & (2) \\
0.12x + 0.16y &= 4{,}800 & (3)\,((1) \times 2) \\
0.12x + 0.36y &= 7{,}200 & (4)\,((2) \times 3) \\
0.2y &= 2{,}400 & (5)\,((4) - (3)) \\
y &= 12{,}000 & (6) \\
0.06x + 960 &= 2{,}400 & (7)\,(\text{substitute in }(1)) \\
x &= 24{,}000 & (8)
\end{aligned}
$$

Total contribution = $(24{,}000 \times £2) + (12{,}000 \times £3) = £84{,}000$.

Point D

Total contribution = $40{,}000 \times £2 = £80{,}000$.

Comparing B, C and D, we can see that contribution is maximised at C, by making 24,000 rolls of standard gauge and 12,000 rolls of heavy gauge, to earn a contribution of £84,000.

Slack and surplus

2.4 If, at the optimal solution, the resource used equals the resource available there is **no spare capacity** of a resource and so there is **no slack.**

If a resource which has a **maximum availability** is **not binding** at the optimal solution, there will be **slack**.

If a minimum quantity of a resource must be used and, at the optimal solution, **more than that quantity is used**, there is a **surplus** on the minimum requirement.

3 MINIMISATION PROBLEMS

3.1 Although decision problems concerned with resource constraints usually involve the maximisation of contribution, there may be a **requirement to minimise costs.** The approach is similar to the one we have been looking at, with the exception that instead of finding a contribution line touching the feasible polygon at a tangent as far away from the origin as possible, we **look for a total cost line touching the feasible polygon at a tangent as close to the origin as possible.**

3.2 EXAMPLE: MINIMISING COSTS

Bilton Sandys Ltd has undertaken a contract to supply a customer with at least 260 units in total of two products, X and Y, during the next month. At least 50% of the total output must be units of X. The products are each made by two grades of labour, as follows.

	X Hrs	Y Hrs
Grade A labour	4	6
Grade B labour	4	2

Although additional labour can be made available at short notice, the company wishes to make use of 1,200 hours of grade A labour and 800 hours of grade B labour which have already been assigned to working on the contract next month. The total variable cost per unit is £120 for X and £100 for Y.

Bilton Sandys Ltd wishes to minimise expenditure on the contract next month.

Required

Calculate the number of units of X and Y that should be supplied in order to meet the terms of the contract.

3.3 SOLUTION

Step 1. **Define variables**

Let the number of units of X supplied be x, and the number of units of Y supplied be y.

Step 2. **Define objective function**

Minimise $120x + 100y$ (costs) subject to the constraints below.

Step 3. **Establish constraints**

$$x + y \geq 260 \qquad \text{(supply total)}$$
$$x \geq 0.5 (x + y) \qquad \text{(proportion of x in total)}$$
$$4x + 6y \geq 1,200 \qquad \text{(grade A labour)}$$
$$4x + 2y \geq 800 \qquad \text{(grade B labour)}$$
$$x, y \geq 0$$

The constraint $x \geq 0.5 (x + y)$ needs simplifying further.

If $\qquad x \geq 0.5 (x + y)$
then $\qquad 2x \geq x + y$
and $\qquad x \geq y$

Steps 4 and 5. **Graph the problem and define the feasible area**

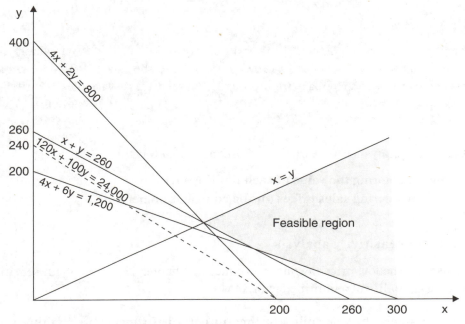

Step 6. **Determine the optimal solution**

The cost line $120x + 100y = 24,000$ has been drawn to show the slope of every cost line $120x + 100y$. Costs are minimised where a cost line touches the feasible region at a tangent, as close as possible to the origin of the graph. This occurs where the constraints line $4x + 2y = 800$ crosses the line $x + y = 260$. At this point

$$x + y = 260 \qquad \text{.......} (1)$$
$$4x + 2y = 800 \qquad \text{.......} (2)$$

Divide (2) by 2 $\qquad 2x + y = 400 \qquad \text{.......} (3)$
Subtract (1) from (3) $\qquad x = 140$
Substitute in (1) $\qquad y = 120$

Costs will be minimised by supplying the following output.

	Unit cost	Total cost
	£	£
140 units of X	120	16,800
120 units of Y	100	12,000
		28,800

The proportion of units of X in the total would exceed 50%, and demand for grade A labour would exceed the 1,200 hours minimum.

4 SENSITIVITY ANALYSIS

4.1 Once a graphical linear programming solution has been found, it should be possible to provide further information by interpreting the graph more fully to see what would happen if certain values in the scenario were to change.

- What if the contribution from product A was £1 lower than expected?

- What if the sales price of product B was raised by £2?

- What would happen if we had less or more of a limiting factor, such as materials or labour?

4.2 We will use our example about W Ltd (see Section 1) to carry out such sensitivity analysis.

> **KEY TERM**
>
> **Sensitivity analysis** is 'A modelling and risk assessment procedure in which changes are made to significant variables in order to determine the effect of these changes on the planned outcome. Particular attention is thereafter paid to variables identified as being of special significance'. (CIMA *Official Terminology*)

4.3 **Sensitivity analysis** can be carried out in one of two ways.

- By **considering the value of each limiting factor**
- By **considering sales prices (or the contribution per unit)**

Limiting factor sensitivity analysis

4.4 We use the shadow price (a concept we met in Chapter 13) to carry out sensitivity analysis on the availability of a limiting factor.

4.5 In our example the availability of time in both departments are limiting factors because both are used up fully in the planned product mix. Let us therefore calculate the effect if W Ltd were **deprived of one hour of shaping department machine time** so that only 2,399 hours were available.

4.6 The **new optimal product mix would still be at the intersection of the two constraint lines** $0.06x + 0.08y = 2,400$ and $0.04x + 0.12y = 2,399$.

Solution by simultaneous equations gives $x = 24,020$ and $y = 11,985$.

(You should solve the problem yourself if you are doubtful about the derivation of the solution.)

Product	Units	Contribution per unit £	Total contribution £
A	24,020	0.20	4,804.0
B	11,985	0.30	3,595.5
			8,399.5

Contribution in original problem $((24,000 \times £0.20) + (12,000 \times £0.30))$		8,400.0
Reduction in contribution from loss of one hour of shaping time		0.5

The **shadow price of an hour of machining time in the shaping department is therefore £0.50.**

Question 6

What is the shadow price of one hour of machine time in the mixing department?

A   £3
B   £7
C   £10.50
D   £1,193

Answer

The correct answer is A.

New optimal solution at the intersection of 0.06x + 0.08y = 2,399 and 0.04x + 0.12y = 2,400

Solution by simultaneous equations gives x = 23,970, y = 12,010

Product	Units	Contribution per unit £	Total contribution £
A	23,970	0.20	4,794
B	12,010	0.30	3,603
			8,397
Contribution in original problem			8,400
Reduction in contribution			3

∴ Shadow price of one hour of machine time in the mixing department is £3.

4.7   The **shadow price** of a limiting factor also shows by **how much contribution would increase if an additional unit of the resource were made available.** The dual price of an hour of machine time in the shaping department would again be calculated as £0.50.

4.8   Note, however, that this **increase in contribution** of £0.50 per extra machine hour in the shaping department is calculated on the **assumption that the extra machine hour would cost W Ltd the normal variable cost.**

4.9   We can now make the following points.

(a)   The management of W Ltd should be prepared to **pay up to £0.50 extra per hour** (ie £0.50 over and above the normal price) of shaping department machine time to obtain more machine hours.

(b)   This **value** of machine time **only applies as long as shaping machine time is a limiting factor.** If more and more machine hours become available, there will eventually be so much machine time that it is no longer a limiting factor.

4.10   We can calculate **how many hours will be available before machine time in the shaping department ceases to be limiting factor.**

Look back at the graph in Paragraph 1.17. As more hours become available the constraint line moves out away from the origin. It ceases to be a limiting factor when it passes through the intersection of the sales constraint and the mixing department machine time constraint which is at the point (22,667, 13,000).

So, if x = 22,667 and y = 13,000, our new constraint would be 0.04x + 0.12y = H (hours) where H = (0.04 × 22,667) + (0.12 × 13,000) = 2,466.68 hours.

4.11   The shadow price of shaping department machine time is therefore £0.50 but only up to a maximum supply of 2,466.68 hours (that is 66.68 hours more than the original 2,400 hours). Extra availability of machine time above 2,466.68 hours would not have any use, and the two limiting factors would become sales demand for product B and machine time in the mixing department.

Sales price sensitivity analysis

4.12 The optimal solution in our W Ltd example was to make 24,000 units of product A and 12,000 units of product B. Would this solution change if the **unit sales price of A increased by 10p?**

4.13 The **contribution would increase** to 0.3x + 0.3y (in place of 0.2x + 0.3y). The **iso-contribution lines would now have a steeper slope** than previously, parallel (for example) to 0.3x + 0.3y = 3,000.

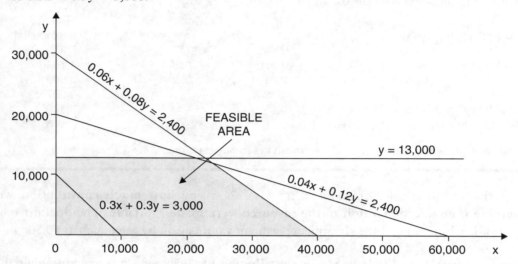

4.14 If you were to place a ruler along the iso-contribution line and move it away from the origin as usual, you would find its **last point within the feasible region** was the point (40,000, 0).

4.15 Therefore if the sales price of A is raised by 10p, W Ltd's contribution-maximising product mix would be to produce 40,000 units of A and none of B.

4.16 EXAMPLE: SENSITIVITY ANALYSIS

Constrained Ltd makes two products, X and Y, which each earn a contribution of £8 per unit. The resources required to make one unit of each product are as follows.

	Labour hours	*Machine hours*
Product X	4	3
Product Y	3	5

Total weekly capacity is 1,200 labour hours and 1,725 machine hours. There is a standing weekly order for 100 units of X which must be met. In addition, for technical reasons, it is necessary to produce at least twice as many units of Y as units of X.

Required

(a) Determine the contribution-maximising production plan each week.

(b) Calculate the shadow price of the following.

    (i)   Machine hours

    (ii)   Labour hours

    (iii) The minimum weekly demand for X of 100 units

4.17 SOLUTION: PRODUCTION PLAN

The linear programming problem may be formulated as follows.

Step 1. **Define variables**

Let x = number of units of X produced and y = number of units of Y produced.

Step 2. **Establish objective function**

Maximise contribution (c) = 8x + 8y subject to the constraints below.

Step 3. **Establish constraints**

$$4x + 3y \leq 1,200 \qquad \text{(labour hours)}$$
$$3x + 5y \leq 1,725 \qquad \text{(machine hours)}$$
$$x \geq 100 \qquad \text{(minimum demand)}$$
$$y \geq 2x \qquad \text{(technical constraint)}$$
$$y \geq 0 \qquad \text{(non-negativity)}$$

Step 4. **Graph the problem**

The graph of this problem would be drawn as follows, using 8x + 8y = 2,400 as an iso-contribution line.

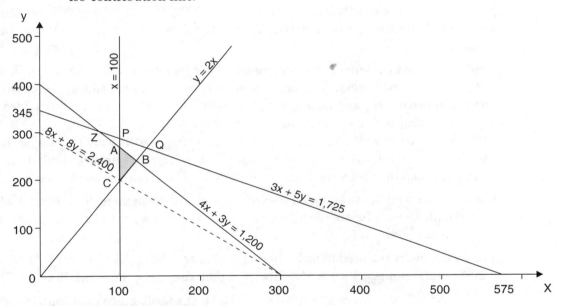

Step 5. **Establish feasible polygon**

The feasible polygon is ABC. Using the slope of the iso-contribution line, we can measure that the contribution-maximising point is point A.

Step 6. **Determine optimal solution**

At point A, the effective constraints are x = 100 and 4x + 3y = 1,200.

$$\therefore \text{ If } x = 100, (4 \times 100) + 3y = 1,200$$
$$\therefore 3y = 1,200 - 400$$
$$y = 266^2/_3$$

It is important to be aware that in linear programming, the optimal solution is likely to give values to the decision variables which are in fractions of a unit. In this example, contribution will be maximised by making 2662/3 units of Y.

BPP PUBLISHING

	Contribution
	£
Make 100 units of X	800.00
266²/₃ units of Y	2,133.33
Total weekly contribution	2,933.33

4.18 SOLUTION

(a) **Machine hours** are not fully utilised in the optimal solution. 100 units of X and $266^2/_3$ units of Y need $(300 + 1,333.33) = 1,633.33$ machine hours, leaving 91.67 **machine hours unused**. Machine hours, not being an effective constraint in the optimal solution, have a **shadow price of £0**. Obtaining one extra machine hour would add nothing to the contribution.

(b) The shadow price of **labour hours** would be obtained by calculating the total weekly contribution if the labour hours constraint were 1,201 hours. It should be possible to see fairly easily that the **new optimal solution** would be where x = 100 and 4x + 3y = 1,201. Therefore x = 100, y = 267 and total weekly contribution would be $(100 + 267) \times £8 = £2,936$.

Since contribution with 1,200 labour hours as the constraint was £2,933.33, the shadow price of labour hours is $£(2,936 - 2,933.33) = £2.67$ per hour. This is the amount by which total contribution would rise if one extra labour hour per week were made available.

Note that there is a limitation to the number of extra labour hours that could be used to earn extra contribution. As more and more labour hours are added, the constraint line will move further and further away from the origin. For example if we added 800 labour hours capacity each week, the constraint $4x + 3y \leq (1,200 + 800)$ (ie $4x + 3y \leq 2,000$) would be so much further away from the origin that it would no longer be an effective constraint. Machine hours would now help to impose limitations on production, and the profit-maximising output would be at point P on the graph.

Labour hours could only be added to earn more contribution up to point P, after which they would cease to be an effective constraint. At point P, x = 100 and 3x + 5y = 1,725. Therefore y = 285.

The labour hours required to make 100 units of X and 285 units of Y are $(4 \times 100) + (3 \times 285) = 1,255$ hours, which is 55 hours more than the initial constraint limit.

Total contribution at point P = $(100 + 285) \times £8 = £3,080$. Since total contribution at point A, where labour hours were limited to 1,200 hours, was £2,933.33, the extra contribution from the 55 extra labour hours would be $£(3,080 - 2,933.33)/55 = £2.67$ per hour (as calculated previously).

Thus, the shadow price of labour hours is £2.67 per hour, for a maximum of 55 extra hours per week, after which additional labour hours would add nothing to the weekly contribution.

(c) The shadow price of the **minimum weekly demand for X** may be obtained by calculating the weekly contribution if the minimum demand is reduced by one unit to 99, so that $x \geq 99$, given no change in the other original constraints in the problem.

The new optimal solution would occur where x = 99 and 4x + 3y = 1,200. Therefore y = 268.

Total contribution per week when x = 99 and y = 268 is $(99 + 268) \times £8 = £2,936$. Since the contribution when $x \geq 100$ was £2,933.33, the **shadow price** of the minimum demand for X is $£(2,936 - 2,933.33) = £2.67$ **per unit**. In other words, by reducing the minimum demand for X, the weekly contribution can be raised by £2.67 for each unit by which the minimum demand is reduced below 100 per week.

As with the constraint on labour hours, this shadow price is **only applicable up to a certain amount.** If you refer back to the graph of the problem, you should be able to see that if the minimum constraint on X is reduced beyond point Z, it will cease to be an effective constraint in the optimal solution, because at point Z the machine hours limitation will begin to apply.

Question 7

By how many units per week can the minimum demand be reduced before the shadow price of £2.67 per unit referred to above ceases to apply?

A   300 units
B   100 units
C   75 units
D   25 units

Answer

The correct answer is D.

At point Z:	$4x + 3y = 1,200$	.... (1)
	$3x + 5y = 1,725$	.... (2)
Multiply (1) by 3	$12x + 9y = 3,600$	.... (3)
Multiply (2) by 4	$12x + 20y = 6,900$	.... (4)
Subtract (3) from (4)	$11y = 3,300$	
	$y = 300$	
Substituting in (1)	$4x + 900 = 1,200$	
	$4x = 300$	
	$x = 75$	

The shadow price of the minimum demand for X is £2.67 per unit demanded, but only up to a total reduction in the minimum demand of $(100 - 75) = 25$ units per week.

Chapter roundup

- The technique of **linear programming** must be used for problems with **more than** one resource constraint.

- The linear programming technique can be applied to problems with the following features.

  ° There is a **single objective**, which is to maximise or minimise the value of a certain function. The objective in commercial decision making is usually to maximise contribution and thus maximise profit.

  ° There are **several constraints**, typically scarce resources, that limit the value of the objective function.

- The **graphical method** of linear programming is used for problems involving two products.

- The steps in the graphical method are as follows.

  ° Define variables
  ° Establish objective function
  ° Establish constraints
  ° Draw a graph of the constraints
  ° Establish the feasible region
  ° Determine the optimal product mix

- The **shadow price** of a resource which is a limiting factor on production is the amount by which total contribution would fall if the company were deprived of one unit of the resource. The shadow price also indicates the amount by which total contribution would rise if the company were able to obtain one extra unit of the resource, **provided that** the resource remains an effective constraint on production and **provided also that** the extra unit of resource can be obtained at its normal variable cost.

Quick quiz

1   *Fill in the blanks in the statements below with one of the following terms.*

   Objective function; decision variable; constraint; inequality; non-negativity constraints.

   (a)   .... should be included when formulating linear programming solutions to ensure that the answer makes sense in operational terms.

   (b)   A .... is an equation taking the form 'greater than or equal to' or 'less than or equal to'.

   (c)   A .... is a quantified statement of the aim of a resource allocation decision.

2   *Choose the correct words from those highlighted.*

   A feasible **polygon/area** enclosed on all sides is known as a feasible **polygon/area.**

3   *Put the following steps in the graphical approach to linear programming in the correct order.*

   Draw a graph of the constraints
   Define variables
   Establish the feasible region
   Establish constraints
   Establish objective function
   Determine optimal product mix

4   *Choose the correct words from those highlighted.*

   When dealing with a problem in which there is a requirement to minimise costs, we look for a total cost line touching the feasible area at a tangent **as close to/as far from** the origin as possible.

5   The shadow price of a scarce resource is not the same as its dual price. *True or false?*

Answers to quick quiz

1   (a)   Non-negativity constraints
    (b)   Inequality
    (c)   Objective function

2   Polygon

    Area

3   Define variables
    Establish objective function
    Establish constraints
    Draw a graph of the constraints
    Establish the feasible region
    Determine optimal product mix

4   As close to

5   False

Now try the question below from the Exam Question Bank

Number	Level	Marks	Time
Q18	Exam standard	25	45 mins

Chapter 15

LINEAR PROGRAMMING: THE SIMPLEX METHOD

Chapter topic	Syllabus reference	Ability required
1 The principles of the Simplex method	(iii)	Application
2 Sensitivity analysis	(iii)	Application
3 Using linear programming	(iii)	Analysis

Introduction

The linear programming problems that we looked at in Chapter 14 included only two decision variables. In practice, few problems will be this simple. In this chapter we will therefore be considering a method of solving linear programming problems with **two or more decision variables** – the **Simplex method.**

Learning outcomes covered in this chapter

- **Prepare** formulae for a two-plus constraint/limitation problem for two-plus products using the Simplex method and interpret the results.

- **Discuss** the linear programming model.

Syllabus content covered in this chapter

- Linear programming

1   THE PRINCIPLES OF THE SIMPLEX METHOD

KEY TERM

The **Simplex method** is a method of solving linear programming problems with two or more decision variables.

General points about the Simplex method

1.1   Before introducing an illustrative example to explain the technique, it may be helpful to make a few introductory points. Don't worry if you get confused, working through the example will make things clearer.

(a) The Simplex method involves **testing one feasible solution after another**, in a **succession of tables or tableaux, until the optimal solution is found**. It can be used for problems with **any number of decision variables, from two upwards**.

(b) In addition to the decision variables, the method introduces additional variables, known as **slack variables** or **surplus variables**. There will be **one slack (or surplus) variable for each constraint** in the problem (**excluding non-negativity constraints**).

For example, if a linear programming problem has three decision variables and four constraints, there will be four slack or surplus variables in the problem. With the three decision variables, there will therefore be a total of seven variables and four constraints in the problem.

(c) The technique is a **repetitive, step-by-step process**, with each step having the following **purposes**.

   (i) To **establish a feasible solution** (in other words, a feasible combination of decision variable values and slack variable values) and the **value of the objective function** for that solution.

   (ii) To **establish** whether that particular **solution** is one that **optimises** the value of the objective function.

(d) Each feasible solution is tested by drawing up a **matrix** or **tableau** with the following rows and columns.

   - **One row per constraint, plus a solution row**

   - **One column per decision variable and per slack variable, plus a solution column**

(e) **Every variable**, whether a decision variable, slack variable or surplus variable, **must be ≥ 0 in any feasible solution**.

(f) A feature of the Simplex method is that if there are **n constraints**, there will be **n variables with a value greater than 0 in any feasible solution**. Thus, if there are seven variables in a problem, and four constraints, there will be four variables with a positive value in the solution, and three variables with a value equal to 0.

Keep these points in mind as we work through an example.

Exam focus point

Note that you do not need to be able to test solutions in the exam. You simply need to be able to prepare the appropriate formulae and interpret the final (optimal solution) tableau.

1.2 EXAMPLE: THE SIMPLEX METHOD

Shore Ltd produces and sells two products, X and Y. Relevant information is as follows.

	Materials units	*Labour* hours	*Machine time* hours	*Contribution per unit* £
X, per unit	5	1	3	20
Y, per unit	2	3	2	16
Total available, each week	3,000	1,750	2,100	

Required

Use the Simplex method to determine the profit-maximising product mix.

1.3 SOLUTION: FORMULATE THE PROBLEM

We have just two decision variables in this problem, but we can still use the Simplex method to solve it.

Define variables

Let x be the number of units of X that should be produced and sold.
Let y be the number of units of Y that should be produced and sold.

Establish objective function

Maximum contribution (C) = 20x + 16y subject to the constraints below.

Establish constraints

The constraints are as follows.

Materials	$5x + 2y \leq 3{,}000$
Labour	$x + 3y \leq 1{,}750$
Machine time	$3x + 2y \leq 2{,}100$
Non-negativity	$x \geq 0, y \geq 0$

Introduce slack variables

Begin by **turning each constraint** (ignoring the non-negativity constraints now) **into an equation.** This is done by **introducing slack variables.**

KEY TERM

A **slack variable** represents the amount of a constraining resource or item that is unused.

Let	a	be the quantity of unused materials
	b	be the number of unused labour hours
	c	be the number of unused machine hours

Question 1

A problem to be solved using linear programming has three decision variables, six constraints (including two non-negativity constraints) and one objective function. How many slack variables will be required if the Simplex method is used?

A   3
B   4
C   5
D   6

Answer

The correct answer is B.

A slack variable is required for each constraint (ignoring non-negativity constraints). There are 6 − 2 = 4 such constraints.

We can now express the original constraints as equations.

$$5x + 2y + a = 3{,}000$$
$$x + 3y + b = 1{,}750$$
$$3x + 2y + c = 2{,}100$$

The **slack variables** a, b and c will be **equal to 0 in the final solution only if the combined production of X and Y uses up all the available materials, labour hours and machine hours.**

Values of variables - non-negative or zero?

In this example, there are **five variables** (x, y, a, b and c) and **three equations**, and so in any **feasible solution** that is tested, **three variables** will have a **non-negative value** (since there are three equations) which means that **two variables** will have a value of **zero.**

Question 2

A problem to be solved using linear programming has seven variables and four equations based on the original constraints. How many variables will have a value of zero in any feasible solution determined using the Simplex method?

A   7
B   5
C   4
D   3

Answer

The correct answer is D.

Four variables will have a non-negative value (since these are four equations), which means that $7 - 4 = 3$ variables will have a value of zero.

Express objective function as an equation

It is usual to express the objective function as an equation with the **right hand side equal to zero.** In order to keep the problem consistent, the **slack (or surplus) variables are inserted into the objective function equation,** but as the quantities they represent should have no effect on the objective function they are given **zero coefficients.** In our example, the objective function will be expressed as follows.

Maximise contribution (C) given by $C - 20x - 16y + 0a + 0b + 0c = 0$.

1.4   SOLUTION: DRAW UP INITIAL TABLEAU AND TEST INITIAL FEASIBLE SOLUTION

ATTENTION!

You will not be required to do this in the exam but seeing how the initial tableau is drawn up will give you additional insight into the technique.

We begin by testing a solution that **all the decision variables have a zero value,** and **all the slack variables have a non-negative value.**

Obviously, this is **not going to be the optimal solution,** but it gives us a starting point from which we can develop other feasible solutions.

Simplex tableaux can be **drawn in several different ways,** and if you are asked to interpret a given tableau in an examination question, you may need to adapt your understanding of the tableau format in this Study Text to the format in the question. The following points apply to all tableau, however.

(a) There should be a **column for each variable** and also a **solution column.**

(b) It helps to add a **further column on the left,** to **indicate the variable which is in the solution to which the corresponding value in the solution column relates.**

(c) There is a **row for each equation** in the problem, and a **solution row.**

Here is the initial matrix for our problem. Information on how it has been derived is given below.

Variables in solution	x	y	a	b	c	Solution
a	5	2	1	0	0	3,000
b	1	3	0	1	0	1,750
c	3	2	0	0	1	2,100
Solution	−20	−16	0	0	0	0

(a) The **figures in each** row correspond with the **coefficients of the variables in each of the initial constraints.** The bottom row or **solution row** holds the **coefficients of the objective function.** For example the materials constraint $5x + 2y + a = 3,000$ gives us the first row, 5 (number of x's), 2 (number of y's), 1 (number of a's), then zeros in the b and c columns (since these do not feature in the constraint equation) and finally 3,000 in the solution column.

(b) The **variables in the solution are a, b and c** (the unused resources).

   (i) The **value of each variable is shown in the solution column.** We are testing a solution that all decision variables have a zero value, so there is no production and hence no resources are used. The total resource available is therefore unused.

   (ii) The **column values** for each variable in the solution are as follows.

   - **1 in the variable's own solution row**
   - **0 in every other row, including the solution row.**

(c) The **contribution per unit obtainable from x and y** is given in the **solution row.** These are the **dual prices** or **shadow prices** of the products X and Y. The minus signs are of no particular significance, except that in the solution given here they have the following meanings.

   (i) A **minus shadow price** indicates that the **value of the objective function can be increased by the amount of the shadow price per unit** of the variable that is introduced into the solution, given no change in the current objective function or existing constraints.

   (ii) A **positive shadow price** indicates the amount by which the **value of the objective function would be decreased** per unit of the variable introduced into the solution, given no change in the current objective function or the existing constraints.

1.5 SOLUTION: INTERPRET THE TABLEAU AND TEST FOR IMPROVEMENT

We can see that the **solution is testing a = 3,000, b = 1,750 and c = 2,100, contribution = 0.** The co-efficients for the variables not in this solution, x and y, are the dual prices or **shadow prices** of these variables, given the solution being tested. A **negative value** to a dual price means that the **objective function can be increased;** therefore the **solution in the tableau is not the optimal solution.**

The **shadow prices** in the initial solution (tableau) **indicate** the following.

(a) The profit would be increased by £20 for every extra unit of x produced (because the shadow price of x is £20 per unit).

(b) Similarly, the profit would be increased by £16 for every extra unit of y produced (because its shadow price is £16 per unit).

Since the **solution is not optimal,** the **contribution may be improved by introducing either x or y into the solution.**

1.6 SOLUTION: THE NEXT STEP

The next step is to **test another feasible solution.** We do this by **introducing one variable into the solution, in the place of one variable that is now removed.** In our example, we **introduce x or y in place of a, b or c.**

The Simplex technique continues in this way, producing a feasible solution in each successive tableau, until the optimal solution is reached.

1.7 SOLUTION: INTERPRET THE FINAL TABLEAU

After a number of iterations, the following tableau is produced.

Variables in solution	x	y	a	b	c	Solution column
x	1	0	0	-0.2857	0.4286	400
a	0	0	1	0.5714	-1.8571	100
y	0	1	0	0.4286	-0.1429	450
Solution row	0	0	0	1.1428	6.2858	15,200

This can be interpreted as follows.

(a) The solution in the fourth tableau is the **optimal** one, because the **shadow prices on the bottom row are all positive.**

(b) The optimal solution is to **make and sell 400 units of X** and **450 units of Y, to earn a contribution of £15,200.**

(c) The solution will leave **100 units of material unused,** but will use up all available labour and machine time.

(d) The **shadow price of labour time (b) is £1.1428 per hour,** which **indicates the amount by which contribution could be increased if more labour time could be made available at its normal variable cost.**

(e) The **shadow price of machine time (c) is £6.2858 per hour,** which **indicates the amount by which contribution could be increased if more machine time could be made available, at its normal variable cost.**

(f) The **shadow price of materials is nil,** because there are 100 units of **unused** materials in the solution.

Question 3

TDS Ltd manufactures two products, X and Y, which earn a contribution of £8 and £14 per unit respectively. At current selling prices, there is no limit to sales demand for Y, but maximum demand for X would be 1,200 units. The company aims to maximise its annual profits, and fixed costs are £15,000 per annum.

In the year to 30 June 20X2, the company expects to have a limited availability of resources and estimates of availability are as follows.

Skilled labour   maximum 9,000 hours
Machine time   maximum 4,000 hours
Material M   maximum 1,000 tonnes

The usage of these resources per unit of product are as follows.

	X	Y
Skilled labour time	3 hours	4 hours
Machine time	1 hour	2 hours
Material M	½ tonne	¼ tonne

Required

(a) Formulate the problem using the Simplex method of linear programming.

(b) Determine how many variables will have a positive value and how many a value of zero in any feasible solution.

Answer

(a) The linear programming problem would be formulated as follows.

Define variables

Let x and y be the number of units made and sold of product X and product Y respectively.

Establish objective function

Maximise contribution (C) = 8x + 14y subject to the constraints below.

Establish constraints

3x + 4y	≤	9,000	(skilled labour)*
x + 2y	≤	4,000	(machine time)
0.5x + 0.25y	≤	1,000	(material M)
x	≤	1,200	(demand for X)
x, y	≥	0	

* This constraint is that skilled labour hours cannot exceed 9,000 hours, and since a unit of X needs 3 hours and a unit of Y needs 4 hours, 3x + 4y cannot exceed 9,000. The other constraints are formulated in a similar way.

Introduce slack variables

Introduce a **slack variable** into each constraint, to turn the inequality into an equation.

Let	a	=	the number of unused skilled labour hours
	b	=	the number of unused machine hours
	c	=	the number of unused tonnes of material M
	d	=	the amount by which demand for X falls short of 1,200 units

Then

3x + 4y + a	=	9,000 (labour hours)
x + 2y + b	=	4,000 (machine hours)
0.5x + 0.25y + c	=	1,000 (tonnes of M)
x + d	=	1,200 (demand for X)

and maximise contribution (C) given by C − 8x − 14y + 0a + 0b + 0c + 0d = 0

(b) There are six variables (x, y, a, b, c, d) and four equations. In any feasible solution four variables will have a non-negative value (as there are four equations), while two variables will have a value of zero.

Question 4

The final tableau to the problem in Question 3 is shown below.

Interpret the tableau

Variables in the solution	x	y	a	b	c	d	Solution column
x	1	0	0	-2	0	0	1,000
y	0	1	-0.5	1.5	0	0	1,500
c	0	0	-0.375	0.625	1	0	125
d	0	0	-1	2	0	1	200
Solution row	0	0	1	5	0	0	29,000

Answer

There is a column in the tableau for every variable, including the slack variables, but the important parts of the tableau are the 'variables in the solution' column, the solution row, and the solution column. These tell us a number of things.

Identifying the variables in the solution

The variables in the solution are x, y, c and d. It follows that a and b have zero values. To be the variable in the solution on a particular row of the table, a value of 1 must appear in the **column** for that variable, with zero values in every other row of that column. For example, x is the variable in the solution for the row which has 1 in the x column. There are zeros in every other row in the x column.

The value of the variables

The solution **column** gives the value of each variable.

x	1,000	(units made of X)
y	1,500	(units made of Y)
c	125	(unused material M)
d	200	(amount below the 1,200 maximum of demand for X)

This means that contribution will be maximised by making and selling 1,000 units of X and 1,500 units of Y. This will leave 125 unused tonnes of material M, and production and sales of X will be 200 units below the limit of sales demand. Since a and b are both zero, there is no unused labour and machine time; in other words, all the available labour and machine hours will be fully utilised.

The total contribution

The value of the objective function - here, the total contribution - is in both the solution row and the solution column. Here it is £29,000.

Shadow prices

The solution **row** gives the **shadow prices** of each variable.

Here, the shadow prices are as follows.

a	£1 per labour hour
b	£5 per machine hour

This means that if more labour hours could be made available **at their normal variable cost per hour**, total contribution could be increased by £1 per extra labour hour. Similarly, if more machine time could be made available, **at its normal variable cost**, total contribution could be increased by £5 per extra machine hour.

Question 5

Here is the final tableau of a problem involving the production of products X and Y solved using the Simplex method of linear programming.

Variables in solution	x	y	a	b	c	d	e	Solution column
x	1	0	-2.0	0	3.0	0	0	550
y	0	1	-0.8	0	0.5	0	0	720
b	0	0	1.5	1	1.0	0	0	95
d	0	0	0.7	0	-1.1	1	0	50
e	0	0	2.0	0	1.8	0	1	104
Solution row	0	0	7.0	0	4.0	0	0	14,110

What are the variables in the solution?

A   x, y, b, d, e
B   x, y, a, b, c, d, e
C   x, y
D   None of the above

Answer

The correct answer is A.

To be a variable in the solution, a value of 1 must appear in the column for the variable, with zero values in every other row.

Question 6

Refer to the tableau in Question 5. What is the profit-maximising product mix?

A   Make 95 units of B, 50 units of D and 104 units of E
B   Make 550 units of X and 720 units of Y
C   Make 4 units of C and 7 units of A
D   None of the above

Answer

The correct answer is B.

Question 7

Refer to the tableau in Question 5. Suppose that variables a to e refer to the unused quantity of resources A to E.

How much of resource A will be unused?

A   8 units
B   7 units
C   2 units
D   0 units

Answer

The correct answer is D.

A has a zero value in the solution column and so resource A is fully used.

Question 8

Refer to the tableau in Question 5. What is the shadow price of resource C?

A   £14,110
B   £4
C   £3
D   £0.50

Answer

The correct answer is B.

The solution row gives the shadow price of each variable.

2   SENSITIVITY ANALYSIS

2.1   You might be asked to carry out some **sensitivity analysis** on a simplex tableau giving the optimal solution to a linear programming problem. This could involve the following.

(a)   Testing **how the optimal solution** would change if there were either **more or less of a scarce resource.**

(b)   Testing whether it would be **worthwhile obtaining more of a scarce resource by paying a premium** for the additional resources, for example by paying an overtime premium for extra labour hours, or by paying a supplier a higher price for extra raw materials.

The effect of having more or less of a scarce resource

2.2   The optimal solution to a linear programming problem is based on the assumption that the constraints are known with certainty, and fixed in quantity. Sensitivity analysis enables us to test how the solution would alter if the quantity of a scarce resource (the size of a constraint) were to change.

2.3   EXAMPLE: THE EFFECT OF HAVING MORE OR LESS OF A SCARCE RESOURCE

Return to our previous example, and the optimal solution in Paragraph 1.7, in which both labour hours and machine hours are fully used. How would the solution change if more labour hours (variable b) were available?

2.4   SOLUTION

The simplex tableau, and in particular the **figures in the b column,** provide the following information for each extra labour hour that is available.

*   The **contribution** would **increase by £1.1428**
*   The value of **x** would **fall by 0.2857 units**
*   The value of **a** (unused materials) would **increase by 0.5714 units**
*   The value of **y** would **increase by 0.4286 units**

In other words, we would be able to make 0.4286 units of Y extra, to earn contribution of ($\times$ £16) £6.8576, but we would make 0.2857 units less of X and so lose contribution of ($\times$ £20) £5.714, leaving a net increase in contribution of £(6.8576 – 5.714) = £1.1436. Allowing for rounding errors of £0.0008, this is the figure already given above for the increase in contribution.

Since x = 400 in the optimal tableau, and extra labour hours would lead to a reduction of 0.2857 units of x, there is a **limit to the number of extra labour hours that would earn an extra £1.1428**. This limit is calculated as 400/0.2857 = 1,400 extra labour hours.

In other words, the **shadow price** of £1.1428 per hour for labour is **only valid for about 1,400 extra labour hours** on top of the given constraint in the initial problem, which was 1,750 hours, (that is up to a **total limit of 3,150 hours**).

If there were **fewer labour hours available**, the same sort of analysis would apply, but in reverse.

- The contribution would fall by £1.1428 per hour unavailable
- The value of x would increase by 0.2857 units
- The value of a would fall by 0.5714 units
- The value of y would fall by 0.4286 units

2.5 EXAMPLE: OBTAINING EXTRA RESOURCES AT A PREMIUM ON COST

Suppose we are given the following additional information about our example.

(a) The normal variable cost of labour hours (variable b) is £4 per hour, but extra labour hours could be worked in overtime, when the rate of pay would be time-and-a-half.

(b) The normal variable cost of machine time is £1.50 per hour, but some extra machine time could be made available by renting another machine for 40 hours per week, at a rental cost of £160. Variable running costs of this machine would be £1.50 per hour.

Would it be worth obtaining the extra resources?

2.6 SOLUTION

We know that the shadow price of labour hours is £1.1428 and of machine hours is £6.2858. We can therefore deduce the following.

(a) **Paying an overtime premium** of £2 per hour for labour **would not be worthwhile**, because the extra contribution of £1.1428 per hour would be more than offset by the cost of the premium, leaving the company worse off by £0.8572 per hour worked in overtime.

(b) **Renting the extra machine would be worthwhile**, but only by £91.43 (which is perhaps too small an amount to bother with).

	£
Extra contribution from 40 hours of machine time (× £6.2858)	251.43
Rental cost	160.00
Net increase in profit	91.43

Note that the variable running costs do not enter into this calculation since they are identical to the normal variable costs of machine time. We are **concerned here only with the additional costs**.

Question 9

A company manufactures three products, tanks, trays and tubs, each of which passes through three processes, X, Y and Z.

Process	Process hours per unit			Total process hours available
	Tanks	Trays	Tubs	
X	5	2	4	12,000
Y	4	5	6	24,000
Z	3	5	4	18,000

The contribution to profit of each product are £2 for each tank, £3 per tray and £4 per tub.

Required

(a) Formulate these data into a Simplex linear programming model using the following notation.

Let a be the number of units of tanks produced
      b be the number of units of trays produced
      c be the number of units of tubs produced

(b) The final Simplex tableau looks like this.

Variables in solution	a	b	c	x	y	z	Solution column
c	1.583	0	1	0.417	0	-0.167	2,000
y	-2.167	0	0	-0.833	1	-0.667	2,000
b	-0.667	1	0	-0.333	0	0.333	2,000
Solution row	2.333	0	0	0.667	0	0.333	14,000

(i) Determine how many of each product should be produced and the maximum contribution. Calculate how much slack time, if any, is available in the processes.

(ii) Explain how your solution would vary if an extra 3,000 hours of process X time could be made available.

(iii) Describe what would happen to the production schedule and budgeted contribution if an order were received for 300 units of tanks which the company felt that it had to accept, because of the importance of the customer. **Ignore** the increase of process X time in part (ii) above.

Answer

(a) **Define variables**

a, b, c defined in question.

Slack variables

Let x = quantity of unused process X hours
      y = quantity of unused process Y hours
      z = quantity of unused process Z hours

Establish objective function

Maximise contribution (C) given by C – 2a – 3b – 4c + 0x + 0y + 0z subject to the constraints below.

Establish constraints

5a + 2b + 4c + x = 12,000 (process X hours)
4a + 5b + 6c + y = 24,000 (process Y hours)
3a + 5b + 4c + z = 18,000 (process Z hours)

(b) (i) **Contribution is maximised at £14,000** by making **2,000 units of tubs** and **2,000 units of trays. No tanks** would be made.

There will be **2,000 slack hours in process Y.** Process X and process Z hours will be fully utilised.

(ii) The shadow price of process X time is £0.667 per hour, and for every extra hour of process X time that can be made available (at its normal variable cost), the production quantities could be altered in such a way that the following would happen.

- **Contribution would go up by £0.667 per extra process X** hour used.
- c (the quantity of tubs) would **go up by 0.417 units.**
- b (the quantity of trays) would **go down by 0.333 units**.
- **y** (unused process Y time) would **fall by 0.833 hours.**

This is **only true up to the point** where so many extra process X hours have been made available that either b or y reaches 0 in value. This will be at the following points.

- For y, after $\dfrac{2,000}{0.833}$ = 2,400 extra process X hours

- For b, after $\dfrac{2,000}{0.333}$ = 6,000 extra process X hours

2,400 is the lowest of these two limits.

The shadow price is therefore **valid only for up to 2,400 extra process X hours,** so that the full 3,000 available would not be required.

The **new optimal solution** would therefore be to make and sell the following.

c   2,000 + (2,400 × 0.417) = 3,000 units
b   2,000 − (2,400 × 0.333) = 1,200 units

These would require a total of 14,400 hours in process X, 24,000 hours in process Y and 18,000 hours in process Z.

Contribution would be as follows.

		£
Tubs	3,000 × £4	12,000
Trays	1,200 × £3	3,600
		15,600
Contribution in initial solution		14,000
Increase in contribution (2,400 × £0.667)		1,600

(iii)   Going back to the original solution, if an order is received for 300 units of tanks, the production schedule would be re-arranged so that **for each unit of tank made the following would happen.**

- **Contribution would fall** by £2.333.
- 1.583 **units less of tubs** (variable c) would be made.
- 0.667 **units more of trays** (variable b) would be made.
- **Unused process Y time would increase** by 2.167 hours.

The new production and contribution budget would be as follows.

Product		Units	Process X time Hours	Process Y time Hours	Process Z time Hours	Contribution £
Tanks	(a)	300	1,500	1,200	900	600
Trays	(b)	2,200*	4,400	11,000	11,000	6,600
Tubs	(c)	1,525**	6,100	9,150	6,100	6,100
			12,000	21,350	18,000	13,300

*   2,000 + (300 × 0.667)
**   2,000 − (300 × 1.583)

The contribution is £700 lower than in the original optimal solution (which represents 300 tanks × £2.333).

Unused process Y time is 2,650 hours, which is 650 more than in the original solution (which represents 300 × 2.167)

Using computer packages

2.7   Nowadays, modern spreadsheet packages can be used to solve linear programming problems.

2.8   Suppose an organisation produces three products, X and Y and Z, subject to four constraints (1, 2, 3, 4).

- **Constraints 1 and 2** are **'less than or equal to' resource constraints**.

- **Constraint 3** provides **a limit on the number of X** that be produced.

- **Constraint 4** is a **'greater than or equal to' constraint** and provides for a **minimum number of Z** to be produced (400).

The organisation wishes to maximise contribution.

2.9   Typical output from a spreadsheet package for such a problem is shown below.

Objective function (c)		137,500
Variable	*Value*	*Relative loss*
x	475.000	0.000
y	0.000	105.000
z	510.000	0.000
Constraint	*Slack/surplus*	*Worth*
1	17.000	0.000
2	0.000	290.000
3	0.000	1,150.000
4	210.000	0.000

Interpretation

2.10   (a)   Total optimal **contribution (c)** will be £137,500.

(b)   The **variable** and **value columns** mean that x = 475, y = 0 and z = 510.

To maximise contribution, 475 units of X and 510 units of Z should therefore be produced. No units of Y should be produced.

(c)   The **constraint** and **slack/surplus** columns provide information about the slack values of 'less than or equal to' constraints and the surplus values for any 'greater than or equal to' constraints.

(i)   **Constraint 1** is a 'less than or equal to' resource constraint. The slack is 17 and so 17 units of resource 1 will be unused in the optimal solution.

(ii)   **Constraint 2** is a 'less than or equal to' resource constraint. The slack is zero, indicating that all available resource 2 will be used in the optimal solution.

(iii)   **Constraint 3** provides a limit on x. The slack is zero, showing that the limit has been met.

(iv)   **Constraint 4** provides for a minimum z. The surplus is 210, meaning 400 + 210 = 610 units of Z are made.

(d) **Worth**. This column shows the positive shadow price of resources (the amount that contribution (or, in general terms, c) alters if the availability of the resource is changed by one unit).

    (i) Contribution would increase by £290 if one extra unit of resource 2 were made available.

    (ii) Contribution would increase by £1,150 if the limit on the minimum number of Z to be produced altered by 1.

    (iii) Resource 1 has a worth of 0 because 17 units of the resource are unused in the optimal solution.

ATTENTION!

In general, any constraint with a slack of zero has a positive worth figure, while any constraint with a positive slack figure will have a worth of zero.

(e) **Relative loss.** This indicates that if one unit of Y were produced, total contribution (or generally c) would fall by £105. A relative loss of £105 would therefore be made for every unit of Y made. Units of Y should only be made if unit contribution of Y increases by £105.

X and Z have relative losses of zero, indicating that they should be made.

ATTENTION!

In general, only those decision variables with a relative loss of zero will have a positive value in the optimal solution.

---

3 USING LINEAR PROGRAMMING

3.1 The further considerations, qualitative factors and assumptions in limiting factor analysis that we looked at in Chapter 13 apply equally to linear programming.

Question 10

List four qualitative factors to consider and four assumptions of a limiting factor analysis.

Answer

Look back at Chapter 13.

Further assumptions

3.2 In addition, there are **further assumptions** if we are dealing with product mix decisions involving several limiting factors.

(a) The **total amount available of each scarce resource is known with accuracy.**

(b) There is **no interdependence between the demand** for the different products or services, so that there is a completely free choice in the product or service mix without having to consider the consequences for demand or selling prices per unit.

3.3   In spite of these assumptions, linear programming is a useful technique in practice. Some statistical studies have been carried out suggesting that linear cost functions do apply over fairly wide ranges of output, and so the assumptions underlying linear programming may be valid.

Uses of linear programming

3.4   (a)   **Budgeting**. If scarce resources are ignored when a budget is prepared, the budget is unattainable and is of little use for planning and control. When there is more than one scarce resource, linear programming can be used to identify the most profitable use of resources.

(b)   **Calculation of relevant costs**. The calculation of relevant costs is essential for decision making. The **relevant cost** of a **scarce resource** is calculated as **acquisition cost of the resource plus opportunity cost**. When **more than one scarce** resource exists, the **opportunity cost** (or **shadow price**) should be established using linear programming techniques.

(c)   **Selling different products.** Suppose that an organisation faced with resource constraints manufactures products X and Y and linear programming has been used to determine the shadow prices of the scarce resources. If the organisation now wishes to manufacture and sell a modified version of product X (Z), requiring inputs of the scarce resources, the relevant costs of these scarce resources can be determined (see above) to ascertain whether the production of X and Y should be restricted in order to produce Z.

(d)   **Maximum payment for additional scarce resources**. This use of shadow prices has been covered in both this chapter and Chapter 13.

(e)   **Control.** Opportunity costs are also important for cost control: standard costing can be improved by incorporating opportunity costs into variance calculations. For example, adverse material usage variances can be an indication of material wastage. Such variances should be valued at the standard cost of the material plus the opportunity cost of the loss of one scarce unit of material. Such an approach highlights the true cost of the inefficient use of scarce resources and encourages managers of responsibility centres to pay special attention to the control of scarce factors of production. For organisations using an optimised production technology (OPT) strategy (see Chapter 9), this approach is particularly useful because variances arising from bottleneck operations will be reported in terms of opportunity cost rather than purchase cost.

(f)   **Capital budgeting**. Linear programming can be used to determine the combination of investment proposals that should be selected if investment funds are restricted in more than one period.

Practical difficulties with using linear programming

3.5   Difficulties with applying the linear programming technique in practice include the following.

(a)   It may be **difficult to identify** which **resources** are likely to be **in short supply** and **what the amount of their availability will be.**

With linear programming, the profit-maximising product mix and the shadow price of each limiting factor depend on the total estimated availability of each scarce resource. So it is not sufficient to know that labour hours and machine hours will be in short supply, it is also necessary to guess how many labour hours and machine hours will be available. Estimates of future availability will inevitably be prone to **inaccuracy** and any such inaccuracies will invalidate the profit-maximising product mix derived from the use of linear programming.

(b) Management may **not make product mix decisions which are profit-maximising**. They may be more concerned to develop a production/sales plan which has the following features.

- Realistic
- Acceptable to the individual managers throughout the organisation
- Acceptable to the rest of the workforce
- Promises a 'satisfactory' profit and accounting return

In other words, management might look for a **satisfactory product mix** which achieves a satisfactory return, sales turnover and market share whilst at the same time plans operations and targets of achievement which employees can accept as realistic, not too demanding and unreasonable, and not too threatening to their job security.

If a 'satisfactory' output decision is adopted, the product mix or service mix **recommended by the linear programming** (profit-maximising) technique will inevitably be **'watered down', amended or ignored**.

(c) The **assumption of linearity may be totally invalid except over smaller ranges**. For example, in a profit maximisation problem, it may well be found that there are substantial changes in unit variable costs arising from increasing or decreasing returns to scale.

(d) The linear programming model is essentially **static** and is therefore not really suitable for analysing in detail the effects of changes in the various parameters, for example over time.

(e) In some circumstances, a practical solution derived from a linear programming model may be of **limited use** as, for example, where the variables may only take on **integer values**. A solution must then be found by a combination of rounding up and trial and error.

(f) The **shadow price** of a scarce resource **only applies up to a certain limit**.

Chapter roundup

- The **Simplex method** of linear programming should be used when there are two or more decision variables.

- The formulation of the problem is similar to that required when the graphical method is used but **slack variables** must be incorporated into the constraints and the objective function.

- A slack variable represents the amount of a constraining resource or item that is unused.

- In any feasible solution, if a problem involves x constraints and y variables (decision plus slack), x variables will have a positive value and (y–x) variables will have a value of zero.

- Feasible solutions to a problem are shown in a **tableau**.

- If the shadow prices on the bottom (solution) row of a tableau are all positive, the tableau shows the optimal solution.

  - ° The solution column shows the optimal production levels and the units of unused resource.

  - ° The figure at the bottom of the solution column/right-hand side of the solution row shows the value of the objective function.

  - ° The figures in the solution row indicate the shadow prices of resources.

- **Sensitivity analysis** can be applied to the final tableau to determine the effect of having more or less of a scarce resource (indicated by figures in the column for the resource's slack variable) and to test whether or not it would be worthwhile to obtain more of a scarce resource by paying a premium for additional supplies (only if the shadow price is greater than the additional cost).

- **Spreadsheet packages** can be used to solve linear programming problems.

- There are a number of assumptions and practical difficulties in the use of linear programming.

Quick quiz

1   *Choose the correct words from those highlighted.*

   The Simplex method can be used for problems with **one / two / three / more than three / any number of** decision variables.

2   *Fill in the blanks.*

   If a linear programming problem has four decision variables and five constraints (excluding non-negativity constraints), there will be .... slack variables and a total of .... variables. Each feasible solution matrix will have .... rows and .... columns. There will be .... variables with a value greater than 0 in any feasible solution.

3   A slack variable represents the amount of constraining resource that is used. *True or false?*

4   What is the general form of an objective function to maximise contribution (C) for a problem with two decision variables (x and y, with coefficients m and n) and four slack variables (a to d)?

   A $C + nx + my + a + b + c + d = 0$
   B $C - nx - my + 0a + 0b + 0c + 0d = 0$
   C $C - nx - my + a + b + c + d = 0$
   D $C + nx + my - 0a - 0b - 0c - 0d = 0$

5   *Choose the correct words from those highlighted.*

   If, in a Simplex tableau, shadow prices have a negative value, the objective function can be **increased/decreased** and the tableau **shows the optimal solution/does not show the optimal solution.**

6   In an optimal Simplex tableau, the figure in the row for decision variable x (product X) and column for slack variable a (resource A) is –1.35. What does this indicate?

A   For each extra unit of X produced, the usage of resource A would fall by 1.35 units
B   For each extra unit of X produced, the usage of resource A would rise by 1.35 units
C   For each extra unit of resource A available, the number of units of X would rise by 1.35 units
D   For each extra unit of resource A available, the number of units of X would fall by 1.35 units

7   If a resource constraint has a worth of 356.92 in a spreadsheet package solution to a linear programming problem, what does this indicate?

A   Contribution will fall by £356.92 if one less unit of the resource is available.
B   Only 356.92 units of the resource are available.
C   356.92 units of the resource are included in the optimal solution.
D   A resource cannot have a worth.

Answers to quick quiz

1   Any number of

2   Five slack variables
     Total of nine variables
     Six rows
     Ten columns
     Five variables with a value greater than 0

3   False. It represents the amount unused.

4   B

5   increased
     does not show the optimal solution

6   D

7   A

Now try the question below from the Exam Question Bank

Number	Level	Marks	Time
Q19	Exam standard	25	45 mins

Appendix: Mathematical tables

LOGARITHMS

	0	1	2	3	4	5	6	7	8	9	1	2	3	4	5	6	7	8	9
10	0000	0043	0086	0128	0170						4	9	13	17	21	26	30	34	38
						0212	0253	0294	0334	0374	4	8	12	16	20	24	28	32	37
11	0414	0453	0492	0531	0569						4	8	12	15	19	23	27	31	35
						0607	0645	0682	0719	0755	4	7	11	15	19	22	26	30	33
12	0792	0828	0864	0899	0934	0969					3	7	11	14	18	21	25	28	32
							1004	1038	1072	1106	3	7	10	14	17	20	24	27	31
13	1139	1173	1206	1239	1271						3	7	10	13	16	20	23	26	30
						1303	1335	1367	1399	1430	3	7	10	12	16	19	22	25	29
14	1461	1492	1523	1553							3	6	9	12	15	18	21	24	28
					1584	1614	1644	1673	1703	1732	3	6	9	12	15	17	20	23	26
15	1761	1790	1818	1847	1875	1903					3	6	9	11	14	17	20	23	26
							1931	1959	1987	2014	3	5	8	11	14	16	19	22	25
16	2041	2068	2095	2122	2148						3	5	8	11	14	16	19	22	24
						2175	2201	2227	2253	2279	3	5	8	10	13	15	18	21	23
17	2304	2330	2355	2380	2405	2430					3	5	8	10	13	15	18	20	23
							2455	2480	2504	2529	2	5	7	10	12	15	17	19	22
18	2553	2577	2601	2625	2648						2	5	7	9	12	14	16	19	21
						2672	2695	2718	2742	2765	2	5	7	9	11	14	16	18	21
19	2788	2810	2833	2856	2878						2	4	7	9	11	13	16	18	20
						2900	2923	2945	2967	2989	2	4	6	8	11	13	15	17	19
20	3010	3032	3054	3075	3096	3118	3139	3160	3181	3201	2	4	6	8	11	13	15	17	19
21	3222	3243	3263	3284	3304	3324	3345	3365	3385	3404	2	4	6	8	10	12	14	16	18
22	3424	3444	3464	3483	3502	3522	3541	3560	3579	3598	2	4	6	8	10	12	14	15	17
23	3617	3636	3655	3674	3692	3711	3729	3747	3766	3784	2	4	6	7	9	11	13	15	17
24	3802	3820	3838	3856	3874	3892	3909	3927	3945	3962	2	4	5	7	9	11	12	14	16
25	3979	3997	4014	4031	4048	4065	4082	4099	4116	4133	2	3	5	7	9	10	12	14	15
26	4150	4166	4183	4200	4216	4232	4249	4265	4281	4298	2	3	5	7	8	10	11	13	15
27	4314	4330	4346	4362	4378	4393	4409	4425	4440	4456	2	3	5	6	8	9	11	13	14
28	4472	4487	4502	4518	4533	4548	4564	4579	4594	4609	2	3	5	6	8	9	11	12	14
29	4624	4639	4654	4669	4683	4698	4713	4728	4742	4757	1	3	4	6	7	9	10	12	13
30	4771	4786	4800	4814	4829	4843	4857	4871	4886	4900	1	3	4	6	7	9	10	11	13
31	4914	4928	4942	4955	4969	4983	4997	5011	5024	5038	1	3	4	6	7	8	10	11	12
32	5051	5065	5079	5092	5105	5119	5132	5145	5159	5172	1	3	4	5	7	8	9	11	12
33	5185	5198	5211	5224	5237	5250	5263	5276	5289	5302	1	3	4	5	6	8	9	10	12
34	5315	5328	5340	5353	5366	5378	5391	5403	5416	5428	1	3	4	5	6	8	9	10	11
35	5441	5453	5465	5478	5490	5502	5514	5527	5539	5551	1	2	4	5	6	7	9	10	11
36	5563	5575	5587	5599	5611	5623	5635	5647	5658	5670	1	2	4	5	6	7	8	10	11
37	5682	5694	5705	5717	5729	5740	5752	5763	5775	5786	1	2	3	5	6	7	8	9	10
38	5798	5809	5821	5832	5843	5855	5866	5877	5888	5899	1	2	3	5	6	7	8	9	10
39	5911	5922	5933	5944	5955	5966	5977	5988	5999	6010	1	2	3	4	5	7	8	9	10
40	6021	6031	6042	6053	6064	6075	6085	6096	6107	6117	1	2	3	4	5	6	8	9	10
41	6128	6138	6149	6160	6170	6180	6191	6201	6212	6222	1	2	3	4	5	6	7	8	9
42	6232	6243	6253	6263	6274	6284	6294	6304	6314	6325	1	2	3	4	5	6	7	8	9
43	6335	6345	6355	6365	6375	6385	6395	6405	6415	6425	1	2	3	4	5	6	7	8	9
44	6435	6444	6454	6464	6474	6484	6493	6503	6513	6522	1	2	3	4	5	6	7	8	9
45	6532	6542	6551	6561	6571	6580	6590	6599	6609	6618	1	2	3	4	5	6	7	8	9
46	6628	6637	6646	6656	6665	6675	6684	6693	6702	6712	1	2	3	4	5	6	7	7	8
47	6721	6730	6739	6749	6758	6767	6776	6785	6794	6803	1	2	3	4	5	5	6	7	8
48	6812	6821	6830	6839	6848	6857	6866	6875	6884	6893	1	2	3	4	4	5	6	7	8
49	6902	6911	6920	6928	6937	6946	6955	6964	6972	6981	1	2	3	4	4	5	6	7	8

BPP PUBLISHING

	0	1	2	3	4	5	6	7	8	9	1	2	3	4	5	6	7	8	9
50	6990	6998	7007	7016	7024	7033	7042	7050	7059	7067	1	2	3	3	4	5	6	7	8
51	7076	7084	7093	7101	7110	7118	7126	7135	7143	7152	1	2	3	3	4	5	6	7	8
52	7160	7168	7177	7185	7193	7202	7210	7218	7226	7235	1	2	2	3	4	5	6	7	7
53	7243	7251	7259	7267	7275	7284	7292	7300	7308	7316	1	2	2	3	4	5	6	6	7
54	7324	7332	7340	7348	7356	7364	7372	7380	7388	7396	1	2	2	3	4	5	6	6	7
55	7404	7412	7419	7427	7435	7443	7451	7459	7466	7474	1	2	2	3	4	5	5	6	7
56	7482	7490	7497	7505	7513	7520	7528	7536	7543	7551	1	2	2	3	4	5	5	6	7
57	7559	7566	7574	7582	7589	7597	7604	7612	7619	7627	1	2	2	3	4	5	5	6	7
58	7634	7642	7649	7657	7664	7672	7679	7686	7694	7701	1	1	2	3	4	4	5	6	7
59	7709	7716	7723	7731	7738	7745	7752	7760	7767	7774	1	1	2	3	4	4	5	6	7
60	7782	7789	7796	7803	7810	7818	7825	7832	7839	7846	1	1	2	3	4	4	5	6	6
61	7853	7860	7868	7875	7882	7889	7896	7903	7910	7917	1	1	2	3	4	4	5	6	6
62	7924	7931	7938	7945	7952	7959	7966	7973	7980	7987	1	1	2	3	3	4	5	6	6
63	7993	8000	8007	8014	8021	8028	8035	8041	8048	8055	1	1	2	3	3	4	5	5	6
64	8062	8069	8075	8082	8089	8096	8102	8109	8116	8122	1	1	2	3	3	4	5	5	6
65	8129	8136	8142	8149	8156	8162	8169	8176	8182	8189	1	1	2	3	3	4	5	5	6
66	8195	8202	8209	8215	8222	8228	8235	8241	8248	8254	1	1	2	3	3	4	5	5	6
67	8261	8267	8274	8280	8287	8293	8299	8306	8312	8319	1	1	2	3	3	4	5	5	6
68	8325	8331	8338	8344	8351	8357	8363	8370	8376	8382	1	1	2	3	3	4	4	5	6
69	8388	8395	8401	8407	8414	8420	8426	8432	8439	8445	1	1	2	2	3	4	4	5	6
70	8451	8457	8463	8470	8476	8482	8488	8494	8500	8506	1	1	2	2	3	4	4	5	6
71	8513	8519	8525	8531	8537	8543	8549	8555	8561	8567	1	1	2	2	3	4	4	5	5
72	8573	8579	8585	8591	8597	8603	8609	8615	8621	8627	1	1	2	2	3	4	4	5	5
73	8633	8639	8645	8651	8657	8663	8669	8675	8681	8686	1	1	2	2	3	4	4	5	5
74	8692	8698	8704	8710	8716	8722	8727	8733	8739	8745	1	1	2	2	3	4	4	5	5
75	8751	8756	8762	8768	8774	8779	8785	8791	8797	8802	1	1	2	2	3	3	4	5	5
76	8808	8814	8820	8825	8831	8837	8842	8848	8854	8859	1	1	2	2	3	3	4	5	5
77	8865	8871	8876	8882	8887	8893	8899	8904	8910	8915	1	1	2	2	3	3	4	4	5
78	8921	8927	8932	8938	8943	8949	8954	8960	8965	8971	1	1	2	2	3	3	4	4	5
79	8976	8982	8987	8993	8998	9004	9009	9015	9020	9025	1	1	2	2	3	3	4	4	5
80	9031	9036	9042	9047	9053	9058	9063	9069	9074	9079	1	1	2	2	3	3	4	4	5
81	9085	9090	9096	9101	9106	9112	9117	9122	9128	9133	1	1	2	2	3	3	4	4	5
82	9138	9143	9149	9154	9159	9165	9170	9175	9180	9186	1	1	2	2	3	3	4	4	5
83	9191	9196	9201	9206	9212	9217	9222	9227	9232	9238	1	1	2	2	3	3	4	4	5
84	9243	9248	9253	9258	9263	9269	9274	9279	9284	9289	1	1	2	2	3	3	4	4	5
85	9294	9299	9304	9309	9315	9320	9325	9330	9335	9340	1	1	2	2	3	3	4	4	5
86	9345	9350	9355	9360	9365	9370	9375	9380	9385	9390	1	1	2	2	3	3	4	4	5
87	9395	9400	9405	9410	9415	9420	9425	9430	9435	9440	0	1	1	2	2	3	3	4	4
88	9445	9450	9455	9460	9465	9469	9474	9479	9484	9489	0	1	1	2	2	3	3	4	4
89	9494	9499	9504	9509	9513	9518	9523	9528	9533	9538	0	1	1	2	2	3	3	4	4
90	9542	9547	9552	9557	9562	9566	9571	9576	9581	9586	0	1	1	2	2	3	3	4	4
91	9590	9595	9600	9605	9609	9614	9619	9624	9628	9633	0	1	1	2	2	3	3	4	4
92	9638	9643	9647	9652	9657	9661	9666	9671	9675	9680	0	1	1	2	2	3	3	4	4
93	9685	9689	9694	9699	9703	9708	9713	9717	9722	9727	0	1	1	2	2	3	3	4	4
94	9731	9736	9741	9745	9750	9754	9759	9763	9768	9773	0	1	1	2	2	3	3	4	4
95	9777	9782	9786	9791	9795	9800	9805	9809	9814	9818	0	1	1	2	2	3	3	4	4
96	9823	9827	9832	9836	9841	9845	9850	9854	9859	9863	0	1	1	2	2	3	3	4	4
97	9868	9872	9877	9881	9886	9890	9894	9899	9903	9908	0	1	1	2	2	3	3	4	4
98	9912	9917	9921	9926	9930	9934	9939	9943	9948	9952	0	1	1	2	2	3	3	4	4
99	9956	9961	9965	9969	9974	9978	9983	9987	9991	9996	0	1	1	2	2	3	3	3	4

Time series

Additive model: Series = Trend + Seasonal + Random

Multiplicative model: Series = Trend * Seasonal * Random

Regression analysis

The linear regression equation of Y on X is given by:

$$Y = a + bX \text{ or } Y - \overline{Y} = b(X - \overline{X})$$

where

$$b = \frac{\text{Covariance (XY)}}{\text{Variance (X)}} = \frac{n\sum XY - (\sum X)(\sum Y)}{n\sum X^2 - (\sum X)^2}$$

and $a = \overline{Y} - b\overline{X}$,

or solve $\sum Y = na + b\sum X$

$\sum XY = a\sum X + b\sum X^2$

Exponential $Y = ab^x$

Geometric $Y = aX^b$

Learning curve

$$Y_x = aX^b$$

where Y_x is the cumulative average time per unit to produce X units; 'a' is the time required to produce the first unit of output; X is the cumulative number of units; and 'b' is the index of learning. The exponent 'b' is defined as the log of the learning curve improvement rate divided by log 2.

BPP
PUBLISHING

Exam question bank

1 STANDARD COSTS   *15 mins*

(a) Briefly explain the term 'standard cost'.

(b) Outline the benefits which a company may obtain from a standard costing system.

(c) Discuss the problems which may arise in the development and operation of a standard costing system.

2 BACKE AND SMASH LTD   *50 mins*

Backe and Smash Ltd manufactures a brand of tennis racket, the Winsome, and a brand of squash racket, the Boastful. The budget for October was as follows.

		Winsome	*Boastful*
Production (units)		4,000	1,500
Direct materials:	wood (£0.30 per metre)	7 metres	5 metres
	gut (£1.50 per metre)	6 metres	4 metres
Other materials		£0.20	£0.15
Direct labour (£3 per hour)		30 mins	20 mins

Overheads

	£
Variable:	
power	1,500
maintenance	7,500
	9,000
Fixed:	
supervision	8,000
heating and lighting	1,200
rent	4,800
depreciation	7,000
	21,000

Variable overheads are assumed to vary with standard hours produced.

Actual results for October were as follows.

Production:	Winsome	3,700 units
	Boastful	1,890 units

Direct materials, bought and used:			£
	wood	37,100 metres	11,000
	gut	29,200 metres	44,100
	other materials		1,000
Direct labour		2,200 hours	6,850
Power			1,800
Maintenance			6,900
Supervision			7,940
Heating and lighting			1,320
Rent			4,800
Depreciation			7,000
			92,710

REQUIREMENT:

Calculate the cost variances and incorporate them into an operating statement for October, reconciling the standard and actual cost of production for the month. Assume that a standard absorption costing system is in operation.

3   **HOPSCOTCH LTD**   *45 mins*

Hopscotch Ltd manufactures a special floor tile which measures ½m × ¼m × 0.01m. The tiles are manufactured in a process which requires the following standard mix.

Material	Quantity	Price	Amount
	kg	£	£
A	40	1.50	60
B	30	1.20	36
C	10	1.40	14
D	20	0.50	10
			120

Each mix should produce 100 square metres of floor tiles of 0.01m thickness. During April, the actual output was 46,400 tiles from the following input.

Material	Quantity	Price	Amount
	kg	£	£
A	2,200	1.60	3,520
B	2,000	1.10	2,200
C	500	1.50	750
D	1,400	0.50	700
			7,170

REQUIREMENT:

Calculate the following variances for the month of April.

(a)   Cost variance for each material
(b)   Price variance for each material
(c)   Mix variance for each material
(d)   Yield variance for total materials

4   **WIMBRUSH LTD**   *45 mins*

The management of Wimbrush Ltd feel that standard costing and variance analysis have little to offer in the reporting of some of the activities of their firm.

'Although we produce a range of fairly standardised products' states the accountant of Wimbrush Ltd, 'prices of many of our raw materials are apt to change suddenly and comparison of actual prices with predetermined, and often unrealistic, standard prices is of little use.

For example, consider the experience over the last accounting period of two of our products, Widgets and Splodgets. To produce a Widget we use 5 kg of X and our plans were based on a cost of X of £3 per kg. Due to market movements the actual price changed and if we had purchased efficiently the cost would have been £4.50 per kg.

Production of Widgets was 2,000 units and usage of X amounted to 10,800 kg at a total cost of £51,840.

A Splodget uses raw material Z but again the price of this can change rapidly. It was thought that Z would cost £30 per tonne but in fact we only paid £25 per tonne and if we had purchased correctly the cost would have been less as it was freely available at only £23 per tonne. It usually takes 1.5 tonnes of Z to produce 1 Splodget but our production of 500 Splodgets used only 700 tonnes of Z.

So you can see that with our particular circumstances the traditional approach to variance analysis is of little use and we don't use it for materials although we do use it for reporting on labour and variable overhead costs.'

REQUIREMENTS:

(a)   Analyse the material variances for both Widgets and Splodgets, utilising the following.

    (i)   Traditional variance analysis

    (ii)   An approach which distinguishes between planning and operational variances   **12 Marks**

(b)   Write brief notes which do the following.

    (i)   Explain the approach to variance analysis which distinguishes between planning and operational variances.

    (ii)   Indicate the extent to which this approach is useful for firms in general and for Wimbrush Ltd in particular.

    (iii) Highlight the main difficulty in the application of this approach.   **13 Marks**

Total Marks = 25

---

5   M LTD (PILOT PAPER)   *54 mins*

M Ltd operates a standard absorption costing system in respect of its only product. The standard cost card of this product for the budget year ending 31 December 2000 is as follows.

	£	£
Selling price		120.00
Direct material A (5 kgs)	12.50	
Direct material B (10 kgs)	40.00	
Direct wages (3 hours)	18.00	
Variable overhead (3 hours)	9.00	
Fixed overhead* (3 hours)	15.00	
		94.50
Profit/unit		25.50

*Fixed overhead is absorbed on the basis of direct labour hours. Budgeted fixed overhead costs are £180,000 for the year. cost and activity levels are budgeted to be constant each month.

During January 2000, when budgeted sales and production were 1,000 units, the following actual results were achieved.

	£
Sales (900 units)	118,800
Production costs (1,050 units)	
Direct material A (5,670 kg)	14,742
Direct material B (10,460 kg)	38,179
Direct wages (3,215 hours)	19,933
Variable overhead	10,288
Fixed overhead	15,432

With the benefit of hindsight you now know that direct labour received a pay increase of 3 per cent which was not allowed for in the standard cost. The original standard is to be used for stock valuation.

You have also confirmed with the production manager that the nature of the production method is such that direct materials A and B are mixed together to produce the final product.

All materials were purchased and used during January.

REQUIREMENTS:

(a)   Prepare for the production manager a statement that reconciles the budgeted and actual profits for January 2000 using the following variances.

    (i)   sales volume profit;

    (ii)   sales price;

    (iii)   direct material price;

    (iv)   direct material mix;

    (v)   direct material yield;

    (vi)   direct labour rate, analysed between planning and operating effects;

    (vii) direct labour efficiency;

    (viii) variable production overhead expenditure;

    (ix)   variable production overhead efficiency;

    (x)   fixed production overhead expenditure;

    (xi)   fixed production overhead capacity;

(xii)   fixed production overhead efficiency.

Variances should be calculated so as to provide useful information to the production manager.

22 Marks

(b)   A further analysis of the actual fixed production overhead cost of £15,432 has shown that £3,143 was spent in the production department. The remainder of the cost is made up by charges from service departments within M Ltd for computer, maintenance and other servicing costs. These charges are levied on the basis of actual costs, plus 20 per cent.

Explain why the transfer-pricing system being used by M Ltd may be considered inappropriate, and recommend an alternative system of charging for internal services.   **8 Marks**

Total Marks = 30

6   **BENCHMARKING**   *45 mins*

Relevant information with regard to the operation of the sales order department of Cognet plc is as follows.

- A team of staff deals with existing customers in respect of problems with orders or with prospective customers enquiring about potential orders.

- The processing of orders requires communication with the production and despatch functions of the company.

- The nature of the business is such that there is some despatching of part orders to customers which helps reduce stock holding costs and helps customers in their work flow management.

- Sales literature is sent out to existing and prospective customers by means of a monthly mailshot.

The activity matrix below shows the budget for the sales order department.

Activity cost matrix - sales order department

Cost element	Total cost £'000	Customer negotiations £'000	Processing of orders Home £'000	Processing of orders Export £'000	Implementing despatches £'000	Sales literature £'000	General admin £'000
Salaries	500	80	160	100	90	20	50
Stores/supplies	90		16	6	8	60	
IT	70	10	30	20	10		
Sundry costs	80	8	10	6	20	10	26
Total	740	98	216	132	128	90	76
Volume of activity		2,000 customers	3,000 negotiations	5,000 orders	1,200 orders	11,500 despatches	

Cognet plc has decided to acquire additional computer software with internet links in order to improve the effectiveness of the sales order department. The cost to the company of this initiative is estimated at £230,000 pa.

If the proposed changes are implemented, there will be cost and volume changes to activities in the sales order department and it is estimated that the following activity cost matrix will result.

Activity cost matrix - sales order department after the proposed changes

Cost element	Total cost £'000	Customer negotiations £'000	Processing of orders Home £'000	Processing of orders Export £'000	Implementing despatches £'000	Sales literature £'000	General admin £'000
Salaries	450	72	144	90	81	18	45
Stores/supplies	54	-	16	6	8	24	-
IT	300	40	120	80	40	20	-
Sundry costs	106	16	11	10	33	10	26
Total	910	128	291	186	162	72	71
Volume of activity		2,600 customers	6,000 negotiations	5,500 orders	2,000 orders	18,750 despatches	

Recent industry average statistics for sales order department activities in businesses of similar size, customer mix and product mix are as follows.

Cost per customer per year	£300
Cost per home order processed	£50
Cost per export order processed	£60
Cost per despatch	£8
Sales literature cost per customer	£35
Average number of orders per customer per year	4.1
Average number of despatches per order	3.3

REQUIREMENT:

Prepare an analysis (both discursive and quantitative/monetary as appropriate) which examines the implications of the IT initiative. The analysis should include a benchmarking exercise on the effectiveness of the sales order department against both its current position and the industry standards provided. You should incorporate comment on additional information likely to improve the relevance of the exercise.

Total Marks = 25

7 **HYMAN OLD ERSKINE FLINT LTD** *54 mins*

(a) In a few sentences, explain the functions of a cash budget and indicate its importance in budgeting and budgetary control. **5 Marks**

(b) From the information given below you are required to prepare a cash budget for Hyman Old Erskine Flint Ltd for the months October to December 20X8.

(i)

	July £'000	Aug £'000	Sept £'000	Oct £'000	Nov £'000	Dec £'000
Sales	40	60	100	120	160	200
Direct cost of production and sales						
Materials	30	35	40	40	35	20
Labour	15	18	20	28	18	16
Overheads						
Production	16	19	22	24	18	12
Sales	6	6	12	14	15	18
Administration	8	10	10	12	8	10

(ii) Suppliers of direct materials allow on average two months' credit.

(iii) Wages outstanding for direct labour at the end of each month average one week's pay (one quarter of a month).

(iv) Production overheads include depreciation of £4,000 per month. Of the remaining costs half are paid in the month they are incurred, and half in the following month.

(v) 5% of sales overhead includes a sales commission, payable one month in arrears.

(vi) Delay in the payment of other sales and administration overhead averages one half of a month.

(vii) A new machine costing £18,000 will be installed from the beginning of November. 20% of the cost is payable at the commencement of installation work, and the balance is payable on completion (early January 20X9).

(viii) A dividend of £30,000 is payable in October 20X8.

(ix) A mortgage on a company property will raise £40,000 in November, and repayments of £2,000 per month will begin in December.

(x) The cash balance on 1 October 20X8 is expected to be £5,000.

(xi) There has been a problem with debt collection in the past, since most sales are on credit. To encourage early payment, a discount scheme was introduced on 1 July and a cash discount of 2% is offered on all cash sales and for debtors who pay within one week of sale.

(xii) 10% of sales are expected to be cash sales.

(xiii) Of credit sales, 25% are expected to take the discount. You may assume that all debtors who take the discount pay in the month of sale (although more strictly, about one quarter, who buy goods in the final week of the month, are likely to pay in the first week of the month following sale).

BPP
PUBLISHING

(xiv) Of the remainder of credit sales, half will pay in the month of sale and half in the month following sale. There are no bad debts.

25 Marks

Total Marks = 30

8   TERRY HENDSETTER

25 mins

Terry Hendsetter is the manager in your company with responsibility for monitoring sales of product XN30. He is convinced that the levels of sales is on a rising trend, but that it is seasonal, with more sales at some times of the year than at others. He has gathered the following data about sales in recent years. Trend values are shown in brackets.

Sales (thousands of units of product XN30)

Year	Spring	Summer	Autumn	Winter
20X3			250	340
20X4	186 (281)	343 (285)	263 (289)	357 (293)
20X5	203 (297)	358 (302)	278 (305)	380 (307)
20X6	207 (311)	371 (313)	290 (317)	391 (320)
20X7	222	383		

REQUIREMENTS:

(a) Show the actual sales level and the trend line on a historigram.
(b) Establish seasonal deviations from the trend.
(c) Estimate what the level of sales might be in the autumn and winter of 20X7.

9   PRESENTATION

45 mins

The following statement has been produced for presentation to the general manager of Department X.

	Month ended 31 October 20X0		
	Original budget £	Actual result £	Variance £
Sales	600,000	550,000	(50,000)
Direct materials	150,000	130,000	20,000
Direct labour	200,000	189,000	11,000
Production overhead			
Variable with direct labour	50,000	46,000	4,000
Fixed	25,000	29,000	(4,000)
Variable selling overhead	75,000	72,000	3,000
Fixed selling overhead	50,000	46,000	4,000
Total costs	550,000	512,000	38,000
Profit	50,000	38,000	(12,000)
Direct labour hours	50,000	47,500	
Sales and production units	5,000	4,500	

Note. There are no opening and closing stocks.

The general manager says that this type of statement does not provide much relevant information for him. He also thought that the profit for the month would be well up to budget and was surprised to see a large adverse profit variance.

REQUIREMENTS:

(a) Re-draft the above statement in a form which would be more relevant for the general manager.

7 Marks

(b) Calculate all sales, material, labour and overhead variances and reconcile to the statement produced in (a).

10 Marks

(c) Produce a short report explaining the principles upon which your re-drafted statement is based and what information it provides.

8 Marks

Total Marks = 25

10   BUDGETS AND PEOPLE   *45 mins*

In his study of *The Impact of Budgets on People* Argyris reported inter alia the following comment by a financial controller on the practice of participation in the setting of budgets in his company.

'We bring in the supervisors of budget areas, we tell them that we want their frank opinion but most of them just sit there and nod their heads. We know they're not coming out with exactly how they feel. I guess budgets scare them.'

REQUIREMENT:

Suggest reasons why managers may be reluctant to participate fully in setting budgets, and suggest also unwanted side effects which may arise from the imposition of budgets by senior management.

Total Marks = 25

11   MPL LTD (PILOT PAPER)   *45 mins*

MPL Ltd is a company specialising in providing consultancy services to the catering industry. MPL Ltd prepared its operating statement for period 5 of the year ending 31 August 2000. This was as follows.

	Budget	*Actual*	*Variance*
Chargeable consultancy hours	2,400	2,500	100
	£	£	£
Administration staff salaries – fixed	15,000	15,750	750
Consultants' salaries – fixed	80,000	84,000	4,000
Casual wages – variable	960	600	360
Motor and travel costs – fixed	4,400	4,400	-
Telephone – fixed	600	800	200
Telephone – variable	2,000	2,150	150
Printing, postage & stationery – variable	2,640	2,590	50
Premises and equipment costs – fixed	3,200	3,580	380
Total costs	110,400	116,480	6,080
Fees charged	180,000	200,000	20,000
Profit	69,600	83,520	13,920

While the directors are pleased that the actual profit exceeded their budget expectations they are interested to now how this has been achieved. After the budgets had been issued to them, the consultants expressed concern at the apparent simplicity of assuming that costs could be classified as being either fixed or varying in direct proportion to chargeable consultancy hours.

REQUIREMENTS:

(a)   As the newly appointed management accountant, prepare a report addressed to the board of directors of MPL Ltd which:

    (i)   explains the present approach to budgeting adopted in MPL Ltd and discusses the advantages and disadvantages of involving consultants in the preparation of future budgets;   **10 Marks**

    (ii)   critically discusses the format of the operating statement for period 5;   **5 Marks**

(b)   Explain how a spreadsheet could be set up so that a flexed budget and variance calculations could be rapidly produced by inserting only the actual data, assuming that variable costs are thought to vary in line with chargeable consultancy hours.   **10 Marks**

Total Marks = 25

12   TRANSFER PRICING   *20 mins*

Consider the advantages and disadvantages of the following.

(a)   Market price based transfer prices.
(b)   Cost based transfer prices.

Outline the main variants that exist under each heading.

13   JUST-IN-TIME (PILOT PAPER)   *45 mins*

Many organisations believe that a key element of just-in-time (JIT) systems is JIT production.

REQUIREMENTS:

(a)   Discuss five main features of a JIT production system.   **20 Marks**
(b)   State the financial benefits of JIT.   **5 Marks**

                                                            Total Marks = 25

14   BART BENTON LTD   *45 mins*

Bart Benton Ltd is a fairly new company at the leading edge of paint-spraying technology. Presently it has three customers - Gianni, Falke and Redaelli - whose bare metal products are finished by Bart Benton Ltd.

Gianni's products require 7 coats of paint, Falke's 6 coats and Redaelli's 5 coats. Because the products are different shapes and sizes different quantities of paint are needed.

	Litres
Gianni	7.6
Falke	8.6
Redaelli	6.3

Paint is delivered in batches of various sizes, depending upon the finish required.

Production details for each product are budgeted as follows for the coming month.

	Gianni	Falke	Redaelli
Units sprayed	5,400	4,360	3,600
Batches of paint required	27	20	40
Machine attendant time	30 mins	45 mins	75 mins
Cost of paint per unit	£15.20	£11.18	£18.90

Machine attendants are paid £5.30 per hour.

Overhead costs are absorbed on a labour hour basis. The following overheads are anticipated in the coming month.

	£
Paint stirring and quality control	24,081
Electricity	104,700
Filling of spraying machines	64,914

REQUIREMENTS:

(a)   Calculate the unit cost to Bart Benton Ltd of each sprayed product for the coming month showing each cost element separately.

(b)   Given the following additional information calculate the unit cost to Bart Benton Ltd on an activity based costing approach.

Activity	*Cost driver*
Paint stirring and quality control	Batches of paint
Electricity	Coats of paint
Filling of spraying machines	Litres of paint

(c)   Using the costs calculated for parts (a) and (b) as illustration describe the role in activity based costing of cost drivers.

15   COST REDUCTION   *45 mins*

It has been suggested that much of the training of management accountants is concerned with cost control whereas the major emphasis should be on cost reduction.

REQUIREMENTS:

(a)   Distinguish between cost control and cost reduction.   **7 Marks**

(b)   Give *three* examples *each* of the techniques and principles used for (i) cost control and (ii) cost reduction.   **8 Marks**

(c) Discuss the proposition contained in the statement.

10 Marks

Total Marks = 25

16 BB COMPANY   *45 mins*

For some time the BB company has sold its entire output of canned goods to supermarket chains which sell them as 'own label' products. One advantage of this arrangement is that BB incurs no marketing costs, but there is continued pressure from the chain on prices, and margins are tight.

As a consequence, BB is considering selling some of its output under the BB brand. Margins will be better but there will be substantial marketing costs.

The following information is available.

	Current year's results - 20X2 *(adjusted to 20X3 cost levels)*	*Forecast for 20X3* *(assuming all 'own label' sales)*
Sales (millions of cans)	18	19
	£ million	£ million
Sales	5.94	6.27
Manufacturing costs	4.30	4.45
Administration costs	1.20	1.20
Profit	0.44	0.62

For 20X3 the unit contribution on BB brand sales is expected to be $33\frac{1}{3}\%$ greater than 'own label' sales, but variable marketing costs of 2p per can and fixed marketing costs of £400,000 will be incurred.

REQUIREMENTS:

(a) Prepare a contribution breakeven chart for 20X3 assuming that all sales will be 'own label'.

9 Marks

(b) Prepare a contribution breakeven chart for 20X3 assuming that 50% of sales are 'own label' and 50% are of the BB brand.   **9 Marks**

Note. The breakeven points and margins of safety must be shown clearly on the charts.

(c) Comment on the positions shown by the charts and your calculations and discuss what other factors management should consider before making a decision.   **7 Marks**

Ignore inflation.   **Total Marks = 25**

17 ABC LTD (PILOT PAPER)   *45 mins*

ABC Ltd manufactures one product in each of its three factories in Anytown. Each factory makes the same complete product. One factory is located to the north of the town, another is in the central area, and a third is located in the south of the town. ABC Ltd owns a warehouse to the east of the town which it uses as a distribution centre and also to store finished goods. These locations are illustrated below.

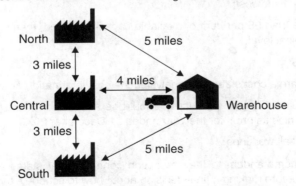

The company is now preparing its budgets for the year to 31 December 20X3 and has recognised that demand for its product will be 30 per cent less than its activity during the year ended 31 December 20X1. ABC Ltd is therefore considering the resources that it has available and seeks to identify the most profitable way of reducing its activity level. Factory closure is being considered, provided that at least one of the remaining factories is utilised at maximum capacity. All units to be sold in the year ending 31 December 20X3 will have to be made in that year because the company has no spare

BPP
PUBLISHING

capacity in the year ending 31 December 20X2. This is due to its acceptance of some subcontracting work. This contract will be completed on 31 December 20X2 and it is not expected to be renewed.

Cost statements for the three factories for the year ended 31 December 20X1 are set out below.

	North	Central	South
Number of units produced	100,000	200,000	150,000
	£'000	£'000	£'000
Direct materials	500	1,000	750
Direct wages	800	1,600	1,200
Indirect materials	375	800	530
Indirect wages	250	1,000	750
Indirect expenses	1,000	2,000	750
Administration	300	550	350
Transport	500	800	750
Total cost	3,725	7,750	5,080

Additional information

1   Direct costs are totally variable, and are dependent on the number of units produced.

2   Indirect production costs are semi-variable. The variable element varies in relation to the number of units produced. Analysis has revealed that the variable element in each factory is as follows:

	North	Central	South
	%	%	%
Indirect materials	80	75	85
Indirect wages	20	15	20
Indirect expenses	35	30	40

The fixed cost element of the indirect production costs is avoidable if the factory is closed.

3   The administration costs include £900,000 for head-office costs. These costs have been apportioned to the factories based on the number of units produced. The balance of administration costs are fixed costs specific to each factory.

4   Transport costs represent the costs of transporting finished goods from the factory to the warehouse. The transport costs are variable and were allocated using 'unit mile' as the cost unit.

5   The annual production capacity of the factories is as follows:

	Units
North	160,000
Central	250,000
South	180,000

It is estimated, based on trade/industry averages, that:

- if production levels exceed 85 per cent of capacity, then there is a 40 per cent increase in specific fixed cost;

- if more than 95 per cent of available capacity is used, then specific fixed cost doubles from its original level.

REQUIREMENTS:

(a) (i)   Prepare a cost statement analysing the cost information provided by behaviour.   **6 Marks**

     (ii)   Calculate how the production should be scheduled for the factories of ABC Ltd so as to maximise its profit for the year ended 31 December 20X3.

            Show all workings.   **14 Marks**

(b) Prepare a memorandum to the production controller that states other factors which should be considered before making a final decision about how to schedule the production.   **5 Marks**

Total Marks = 25

18   RAB CONSULTING LTD (PILOT PAPER)   *45 mins*

RAB Consulting Ltd specialises in two types of consultancy project.

- Each Type A project requires twenty hours of work from qualified researchers and eight hours of work from junior researchers.

- Each Type B project requires twelve hours of work from qualified researchers and fifteen hours of work from junior researchers.

Researchers are paid on an hourly basis at the following rates:

Qualified researchers £30/hour
Junior researchers £14/hour

Other data relating to the projects:

Project type	A	B
	£	£
Revenue per project	1,700	1,500
Direct project expenses	408	310
Administration*	280	270

* Administration costs are attributed to projects using a rate per project hour. Total administration costs are £28,000 per four-week period.

During the four-week period ending on 30 June 20X0, owing to holidays and other staffing difficulties the number of working hours available are:

Qualified researchers 1,344
Junior researchers 1,120

An agreement has already been made for twenty type A projects with XYZ group. RAB Consulting Ltd must start and complete these projects in the four-week period ending 30 June 20X0.

A maximum of 60 type B projects may be undertaken during the four-week period ending 30 June 20X0.

RAB Consulting Ltd is preparing its detailed budget for the four-week period ending 30 June 20X0 and needs to identify the most profitable use of the resources it has available.

REQUIREMENTS:

(a) (i) Calculate the contribution from each type of project. **4 Marks**

(ii) Formulate the linear programming model for the four-week period ending 30 June 20X0. **4 Marks**

(iii) Calculate, using a graph, the mix of projects that will maximise profit for RAB Consulting Ltd for the four-week period ending 30 June 20X0.

(Note: projects are not divisible.) **9 Marks**

(b) Calculate the profit that RAB Consulting Ltd would earn from the optimal plan. **3 Marks**

(c) Explain the importance of identifying scarce resources when preparing budgets and the use of linear programming to determine the optimum use of resources. **5 Marks**

Total Marks = 25

19 XYZ LTD *45 mins*

(a) The following details are taken from the forecasts for 20X1 of XYZ Ltd.

Sales demand	Thousands of units per annum, maximum
Super deluxe model (x_1)	500
Deluxe model (x_2)	750
Export model (x_3)	400

Two production facilities are required, machining and assembly, and these are common to each model.

Capacity in each facility is limited by the number of direct labour hours available.

	Direct labour, total hours available in millions	Direct labour hours per unit		
		x_1	x_2	x_3
Machining (x_4)	1.4	0.5	0.5	1.0
Assembly (x_5)	1.2	0.5	0.5	2.0

Contribution is estimated as follows.

Model	Contribution per thousand units £
x_1	1,500
x_2	1,300
x_3	2,500

REQUIREMENTS:

Prepare formulae for this problem using the Simplex method of linear programming.　　**10 Marks**

(b) Interpret the following tableau, given that it is the final solution to the above problem. The s variables (s_1, s_2, s_3, s_4, s_5) relate to the constraints in the same sequence as presented in (a) above.

x_1	x_2	x_3	s_1	s_2	s_3	s_4	s_5	
1	0	0	1	0	0	0	0	500
0	0	0	0.25	0.25	1	0	-0.5	112.5
0	0	1	-0.25	-0.25	0	0	0.5	287.5
0	0	0	-0.25	-0.25	0	1	-0.5	487.5
0	1	0	0	1	0	0	0	750
0	0	0	875	675	0	0	1,250	2,443,750

15 Marks

Total Marks = 25

Exam answer bank

1 STANDARD COSTS

(a) Standard cost

A standard cost is a predetermined cost calculated in relation to a prescribed set of working conditions, correlating technical specifications and scientific measurements of materials and labour to the prices and wage rates expected to apply during the period to which the standard cost is intended to relate (with an addition of an appropriate share of budgeted overhead if absorption costing is used).

The CIMA *Official Terminology* defines standard cost as 'The planned unit cost of the products, components or services produced in a period' whose main uses are 'in performance measurement, control, stock valuation and the establishment of selling prices'.

(b) The benefits of standard costing

(i) Carefully planned standards are an aid to more accurate budgeting.

(ii) Standard costs provide a yardstick against which actual costs can be measured.

(iii) The setting of standards involves determining the best materials and methods which may lead to economies.

(iv) A target of efficiency is set for employees to reach and cost-consciousness is stimulated.

(v) Variances can be calculated which enable the principle of 'management by exception' to be operated. Only the variances which exceed acceptable tolerance limits need to be investigated by management with a view to control action.

(vi) Standard costs and variance analysis can provide a way of motivation to managers to achieve better performance. However, care must be taken to distinguish between controllable and non-controllable costs in variance reporting.

(c) Problems of standard costing

(i) Deciding how to incorporate inflation into planned unit costs.

(ii) Agreeing a short-term labour efficiency standard (current, attainable or ideal).

(iii) Deciding on the quality of materials to be used (a better quality of material will cost more, but perhaps reduce material wastage).

(iv) Deciding on the appropriate mix of component materials, where some change in the mix is possible (for example in the manufacture of foods and drink).

(v) Estimating materials prices where seasonal price variations or bulk purchase discounts may be significant.

(vi) Finding sufficient time to construct accurate standards. Standard-setting can be a time-consuming process.

(vii) Incurring the cost of setting up and maintaining a system for establishing standards.

(viii) Dealing with possible behavioural problems. Managers responsible for the achievement of standards might resist the use of a standard costing control system for fear of being blamed for any adverse variances.

2 BACKE AND SMASH LTD

Materials price variance

	£	£
37,100 metres of wood should cost ($\times$ £0.30)	11,130	
but did cost	11,000	
Wood price variance		130 (F)
29,200 metres of gut should cost ($\times$ £1.50)	43,800	
but did cost	44,100	
Gut price variance		300 (A)
Wood and gut price variance		170 (A)

Material usage variance

3,700 units of Winsome should use	(× 7m)	25,900 m	(× 6 m)	22,200 m
1,890 units of Boastful should use	(× 5m)	9,450 m	(× 4 m)	7,560 m
		35,350 m		29,760 m
Together they did use		37,100 m		29,200 m
Material usage variance in metres		1,750 m(A)		560 m (F)
× standard cost per metre		× £0.30		× £1.50
Material usage variance				
Wood		£525 (A)		
Gut				£840 (F)

Other materials cost variance

	£
3,700 units of Winsome should cost (× £0.20)	740.00
1,890 units of Boastful should cost (× £0.15)	283.50
	1,023.50
Together they did cost	1,000.00
Other materials cost variance	23.50 (F)

Direct labour rate

	£
2,200 hours of labour should cost (× £3)	6,600
but did cost	6,850
Direct labour rate variance	250 (A)

Direct labour efficiency

3,700 units of Winsome should take (× 30 minutes)	1,850 hrs
1,890 units of Boastful should take (× 20 minutes)	630 hrs
	2,480 hrs
Together they did take	2,200 hrs
Efficiency variance in hrs	280 hrs (F)
× standard rate per hour	× £3
Direct labour efficiency variance	£840 (F)

Variable overhead costs

	Hours	Units
Budgeted hours: Winsome	2,000	4,000
Boastful	500	1,500
	2,500	

	£
Power cost per standard hour (£1,500 ÷ 2,500 hrs)	0.60
Maintenance cost per standard hour (£7,500 ÷ 2,500 hrs)	3.00
	3.60

Variable overhead efficiency variance	
= (as labour) 280 hours (F) × £3.60 =	£1,008 (F)

	£	£
Variable overhead cost of 2,200 hours should be (× £3.60)		7,920
but was: power	1,800	
maintenance	6,900	
		8,700
Variable overhead expenditure variance		780 (A)

Fixed overhead

Budgeted fixed costs	£21,000
Budgeted hours (see calculation for variable overheads)	2,500 hrs
Absorption rate per hour	£8.40

Fixed overhead expenditure variance

	Budgeted expenditure	Actual expenditure	Expenditure variance
	£	£	£
Supervision	8,000	7,940	60 (F)
Heating and lighting	1,200	1,320	120 (A)
Rent	4,800	4,800	-
Depreciation	7,000	7,000	-
Total	21,000	21,060	60 (A)

Fixed overhead volume variance

		£	£
Actual production at standard rates			
Winsome (3,700 × £8.40 × 1/2 hr)		15,540	
Boastful (1,890 × £8.40 × 1/3 hr)		5,292	
Budgeted production at standard rates			20,832
Winsome (4,000 × £8.40 × 1/2 hr)		16,800	
Boastful (1,500 × £8.40 × 1/3 hr)		4,200	21,000
			168 (A)

Fixed overhead efficiency variance

Efficiency variance in hours (as labour)	280 hrs (F)
x absorption rate per hour	£8.40
Fixed overhead efficiency variance	£2,352 (F)

Fixed overhead capacity variance

Budgeted hours of work	2,500 hrs
Actual hours of work	2,200 hrs
Capacity variance in hours	300 hrs (A)
× absorption rate per hour	× £8.40
Fixed overhead capacity variance	£2,520 (A)

Calculation of unit standard costs

		Winsome £ per unit	Boastful £ per unit
Direct materials:	wood	2.10	1.50
	gut	9.00	6.00
Other materials		0.20	0.15
Direct labour		1.50	1.00
Variable overhead at £3.60 per hour		1.80	1.20
Fixed overhead at £8.40 per hour		4.20	2.80
Total standard cost per unit		18.80	12.65

OPERATING STATEMENT FOR OCTOBER

		£
Standard cost of actual output:	Winsome 3,700 × £18.80	69,560.00
	Boastful 1,890 × £12.65	23,908.50
		93,468.50

	(F) £	(A) £	
Cost variances			
Wood price	130		
Gut price		300	
Wood usage		525	
Gut usage	840		
Other materials cost	23.50		
Direct labour rate		250	
Direct labour efficiency	840		
Variable overhead efficiency	1,008		
Variable overhead expenditure		780	
Fixed overhead expenditure		60	
Fixed overhead efficiency	2,352		
Fixed overhead capacity		2,520	
	5,193.50	4,435	758.50 (F)
Actual cost of output			92,710.00

BPP
PUBLISHING

3   **HOPSCOTCH LTD**

Workings

The area of one floor tile is $^1/2 \times {}^1/4$ = 0.125 sq m. In a standard batch of 100 sq m there will be 800 tiles. The standard cost per tile is therefore as follows.

Material	Quantity kg	Price £	Std cost £
A	0.0500	1.50	0.0750
B	0.0375	1.20	0.0450
C	0.0125	1.40	0.0175
D	0.0250	0.50	0.0125
	0.1250	1.20	0.1500

(a) **Cost variance**

	A £	B £	C £	D £	Total £
46,400 tiles should cost	3,480	2,088	812	580	6,960
but did cost	3,520	2,200	750	700	7,170
Cost variance	40(A)	112(A)	62(F)	120(A)	210(A)

(b) **Price variance**

Material	Quantity kg	Should cost £	Did cost £	Price variance Per kg £	Total £
A	2,200	1.50	1.60	0.10 (A)	220 (A)
B	2,000	1.20	1.10	0.10 (F)	200 (F)
C	500	1.40	1.50	0.10 (A)	50 (A)
D	1,400	0.50	0.50	-	-
Total price variance					70 (A)

(c) **Mix variance**

The standard weighted average price of the input materials is £120/100 kg = £1.20 per kg.

Actual input = (2,200 + 2,000 + 500 + 1,400) kgs = 6,100 kg

Standard mix of actual input

A	40/100 × 6,100 kgs =	2,440 kgs
B	30/100 × 6,100 kgs =	1,830 kgs
C	10/100 × 6,100 kgs =	610 kgs
D	20/100 × 6,100 kgs =	1,220 kgs
		6,100 kgs

Material	Actual input kg	Standard mix of actual input kg	Difference kg	x difference between w. av. price and std price		Mix variance £
A	2,200	2,440	(240)	(£1.20 – £1.50)	(0.30)	72 (F)
B	2,000	1,830	170	(£1.20 – £1.20)	–	–
C	500	610	(110)	(£1.20 – £1.40)	(0.20)	22 (F)
D	1,400	1,220	180	(£1.20 – £0.50)	0.70	126 (F)
	6,100	6,100	-			220 (F)

(d) **Yield variance**

Each unit of output (800 tiles) requires

40	kg of A, costing	£60
30	kg of B, costing	£36
10	kg of C, costing	£14
20	kg of D, costing	£10
100 kg		£120

6,100 kgs should have yielded (× 800 tiles/100 kgs)	48,800 tiles
but did yield	46,400 tiles
	2,400 tiles (A)
× standard cost per tile	× £0.15
	£360 (A)

4 WIMBRUSH LTD

(a) (i) **Traditional variance analysis**

2,000 Widgets should use (× 5 kg)	10,000 kg
but did use	10,800 kg
Material X usage variance in kgs	800 kg (A)
× standard cost per kg	× £3
Material X usage variance in £	£2,400 (A)

	£
10,800 kg of X should cost (× £3)	32,400
but did cost	51,840
Material X price variance	19,440 (A)

500 Splodgets should use (×1.5 tonnes)	750 tonnes
but did use	700 tonnes
Material Z usage variance in tonnes	50 tonnes (F)
× standard cost per tonne	× £30
Material Z usage variance in £	£1,500 (F)

	£
700 tonnes of Z should cost (× £30)	21,000
but did cost (× £25)	17,500
Material Z price variance	3,500 (F)

Summary	Material X variances £	Material Z variances £	Total £
Price variance	19,440 (A)	3,500 (F)	15,940 (A)
Usage variance	2,400 (A)	1,500 (F)	900 (A)
	21,840 (A)	5,000 (F)	16,840 (A)

(ii) **Planning and operational variances**

Widgets: the revised standard was 5 kg at £4.50 per kg

	£
10,800 kg of X should have cost (× £4.50)	48,600
but did cost	51,840
Material X price variance (operational variance)	3,240 (A)

Usage variance for X = 800 kg (A) × £4.50 = **(operational variance)**   3,600 (A)

The **planning variance** is calculated as follows.

	£
Original standard (using X) 2,000 units × 5 kg × £3 =	30,000
Revised standard (using X) 2,000 units × 5 kg × £4.50 =	45,000
Planning variance £1.50 (A) per kg, or	15,000 (A)

(*Note*. The variance is adverse because the original standard was too optimistic, overstating the profits by understating the realistic cost.)

Splodgets: the revised realistic standard is 1.5 tonnes of Z at £23 =   £34.50

	£
700 tonnes of Z should cost (× £23)	16,100
did cost (× £25)	17,500
Material Z price variance (operational variance)	1,400 (A)

Material Z usage variance = 50 tonnes (F) × £23 = **(operational variance)** — £1,150 (F)

Planning variance — £

Original standard 500 units × 1.5 tonnes × £30 per tonne = — 22,500

Revised standard 500 units × 1.5 tonnes × £23 per tonne = — 17,250

Total planning variance (£7 per tonne (F)) or — 5,250 (F)

Summary	Material X £	Material Z £	Total £
Price variance	3,240(A)	1,400(A)	4,640(A)
Usage variance	3,600(A)	1,150(F)	2,450(A)
Operational variances	6,840(A)	250(A)	7,090(A)
Planning variances	15,000(A)	5,250(F)	9,750(A)
Total variances	21,840(A)	5,000(F)	16,840(A)

(b) (i) The distinction between planning and operational variances is a development of the opportunity cost approach to variance analysis. *Demski* argued that **more helpful** and **meaningful information will be provided for management control decisions** if variances are reported using an ex-post (revised) standard, that is a **standard which in hindsight should have been used**, when the actual standard used (or the budget) is unrealistic for the conditions which actually prevailed. Thus, when it is realised in retrospect that the planned standard is inaccurate, a more realistic (ex-post) standard should be used to calculate operational variances. The **final reconciliation between budgeted and actual profit** would then be made as a **planning variance**, which measures the **extent to which the budget targets are at fault** because the original standard used was incorrect. (A planning variance is similar to a budget revision variance.)

(ii) The **opportunity cost approach** may be useful to companies by **indicating more clearly the actual loss sustained by faults which gave rise to the particular variances**. There is an attempt to equate variance with the amount of profit or loss sustained, which traditional variances often fail to do. **Examples** are as follows.

(1) Traditional absorption costing variances for sales volume and production volume do not show the true effect of the variations from budget on company profitability.

(2) When a standard is incorrect, traditional variances will mislead managers about the true costs incurred. In the case of Wimbrush Ltd the error in the original standard price of material X means that traditional variances would have reported a misleading variance to the purchasing department for price, and a mis-valuation of the usage variance would report the cost of the adverse usage of material X and the favourable usage of Z incorrectly.

Planning and operational variances attempt to **indicate** the following constructively.

(1) What the real cost of variances should be.

(2) Which of these variances might have been controllable by better management performance and which were unavoidable.

(3) The effect on financial targets of a failure to construct realistic standards.

The approach is only different from traditional variance analysis, however, when the revised and original standards are different.

(iii) The main **difficulty** with the approach is deciding in retrospect **what the realistic standard should have been**. Unless some objective, readily available yardstick is available, the selection of an ex-post standard might be subjective and designed to provide a cover-up of responsibility rather than to reveal constructive control information.

5   M LTD

> **Tutorial note.** Our answer mirrors the model answer produced by CIMA but you may have put a different interpretation on the question
>
> - You may have valued the sales volume variance at the revised profit per unit of £24.96 (although the question did say that the original standard should be used for stock valuation), giving a variance of £2,496(A).
>
> - You may have based the labour rate planning variance on 1,000 units × 3 hours × £0.18, giving a variance of £540(A).
>
> - You would then have had to make an adjustment for the planning variance left in stock of (1,050 – 900) units × £0.54 = £81.

(a)   *Workings*

(i)

Budgeted sales volume	1,000 units
Actual sales volume	900 units
Variance in units	100 units (A)
× standard profit per unit	£25.50
Sales volume variance	£2,550 (A)

(ii)

	£
900 units should have sold for (× £120)	108,000
but did sell for	118,000
Sales price variance	10,800 (F)

(iii)   Material A – provided in question - £567 (A)
Material B – provided in question - £3,661 (F)

(iv)   Standard weighted average cost   =   standard cost/standard quantity

   =   £(40 + 12.50)/(5 + 10) kgs

   =   £3.50 per kg

Actual input = (5,670 + 10,460) kgs = 16,130 kgs

Standard mix of actual input

A =   16,130 × 5/15 =   5,376.67 kgs
B =   16,130 × 10/15 =   10,753.33 kgs
   16,130.00

	Actual Input Kgs	Standard mix of actual input Kgs	Difference Kgs	× difference between w. av. price and std. price £	Variance £
A	5,670	5,376.67	293.33	(£3.50 – £2.50) 1.00	293.33 (F)
B	10,460	10,753.33	(293.33)	(£3.50 – £4.00) (0.50)	146.67 (F)
	16,130	16,130.00	-		440.00 (F)

(v)   Yield variance   =   (actual total quantity used – quantity that should have been used for actual output) × standard weighted average cost per unit input.

   =   ((5,670 + 10,460) – (1,050 × 15) × £3.50 = £1,330 (A)

(vi)   Revised labour rate £6 × 103% = £6.18

	£
Revised standard cost (1,050 units × 3hrs × £6.18)	19,467
Original standard cost (1,050 units × 3hrs × £6)	18,900
Planning variance	567 (A)

		£
With revised standard, 3,215 hours should have cost (× £6 × 103%)		19,869
but did cost		19,933
Labour rate operating variance		64 (A)

(vii)

		hrs
1,050 units should have taken (× 3hrs)		3,150 hrs
but did take		3,215 hrs
Variance in hrs		65 hrs (A)
× revised standard rate per hr (× £6 × 103%)		× £6.18
Labour efficiency variance		£402 (A)

(viii)

		£
3,215 hours of variable overhead should have cost (× £3)		9,645
but did cost		10,288
Variable production overhead expenditure variance		643 (A)

(ix)

1,050 units should have taken (× 3hrs)		3,150 hrs
but did take		3,215 hrs
Variance in hrs		65 hrs (A)
× standard rate per hr		× £3
Variable production overhead efficiency variance		£195 (A)

(x)

		£
Budgeted expenditure (£180,000/12)		15,000
Actual expenditure		15,432
Fixed production overhead expenditure variance		432 (A)

(xi)

Budgeted labour hours		3,000 hrs
Actual labour hours		3,215 hrs
Variance in hrs		215 hrs (F)
× standard absorption rate per hr		× £5
Fixed production overhead capacity variance		£1,075 (F)

(xii)

		£
Variable overhead efficiency variance in hrs		65hrs (A)
× standard absorption rate per hr		× £5
Fixed production overhead efficiency variance		£325 (A)

PROFIT RECONCILIATION STATEMENT (BUDGET TO ACTUAL) JANUARY 20X0

			£
Budgeted profit (1,000 units × £25.50)			25,500
Planning variances: labour rate			567 (A)
Revised budgeted profit			24,933
Sales volume variance			2,550 (A)
Revised standard profit from sales achieved			22,383

Operating variances		£	£
		(F)	(A)
Selling price		10,800	
Material price	- A		567
	- B	3,661	
Material mix	- A	420	
	- B	20	
Material yield			1,330
Labour rate			64
Labour efficiency			402
Variance production overhead expenditure			643
Variable production overhead efficiency			195
Fixed production overhead expenditure			432
Fixed production overhead capacity		1,075	
Fixed production overhead efficiency			325
		15,976	3,958

	12,018 (F)
Actual profit	34,401

We can do a check on the actual profit figure in the reconciliation statement by calculating actual profit based on the figures given in the exam. Closing stock is to be valued at standard cost.

> **Tutorial note**. Only do this if you have time in the exam – perhaps at the very end if you have five minutes to spare.

Check	£	£
Sales		118,800
Costs incurred	98,574	
Closing stock (150 × £94.50)	(14,175)	
		84,399
Actual profit		34,401

(b) The transfer pricing system being used by M Ltd is based on a **'cost-plus' approach. User departments** are simply **charged actual costs plus,** in this instance, **20%.** Such an approach is generally considered to be **unfair** and/or **inappropriate**.

(i) The **user departments** (the production department of M Ltd in this scenario) are **charged for any overspending and inefficiency in the service department.** On the other hand, user departments **benefit from cost savings and efficiency improvements made by the service departments.** There is therefore **no incentive for supplier departments to be cost efficient,** and **user departments are charged with costs they cannot control.**

(ii) If the **service departments are not working at full capacity, the charge per unit** of service is **higher** than if the department is busier. This might discourage the user departments from using the services, to avoid high charges.

(iii) The **functioning charges** which can result form the use of actual costs could make it **difficult for the user departments to plan and control costs**.

A more appropriate system would be to charge user departments with a standard, predetermined cost for services. Such a standard cost should be based on (standard total costs ÷ budgeted service activity). User departments are therefore not penalised for all the overspending and inefficiency or under-capacity in the service department. There are two problems with such an approach however.

(i) The standard cost must be reviewed regularly and frequently so that user departments do not get a false impression of the cost of services.

(ii) It may be difficult to determine what the budgeted service activity level should be.

The use of a **mark up** is a **matter of policy** for the organisation but it can cause **dysfunctional decision making.** If service departments are able to **provide their services to external customers** however, a **mark-up may be necessary** to ensure that they continue to supply internal user departments.

6   BENCHMARKING

By comparing various indicators drawn from the budget before the implementation of the IT initiative with both those drawn from the budget after its implementation and recent industry average statistics, the **effectiveness of the sales order department** can be assessed.

	Industry average		Cognet plc Current	Post – IT
Cost per customer per year	£300	(W1)	£370.00	£350.00
Cost per home order processed	£50	(W2)	£43.20	£52.91
Cost per export order processed	£60	(W3)	£110.00	£93.00
Cost per despatch	£8	(W4)	£11.13	£8.64
Sales literature cost per customer	£35	(W5)	£45.00	£27.69
Average no. of orders per customer pa	4.1	(W6)	3.10	2.88
Average no. of despatches per order	3.3	(W7)	1.85	2.50

BPP PUBLISHING

Activity measures

Number of customers	2,000	2,600
Number of negotiations	3,000	6,000
Number of home orders	5,000	5,500
Number of export orders	1,200	2,000
Number of despatches	11,500	18,750

Workings

1   Total cost ÷ number of customers
2   Cost of processing home orders ÷ number of orders
3   Cost of processing export orders ÷ number of orders
4   Cost of implementing despatches ÷ number of despatches
5   Sales literature cost ÷ number of customers
6   Number of orders (home + export) ÷ number of customers
7   Number of despatches ÷ number of orders (home and export)

The implementation of the IT initiative will cause **customer numbers** to increase by 30% to 2,600, **home orders** to increase by 10% to 5,500 and **export orders** to increase by 67% to 2,000. Industry average statistics are not available for these measures and so it is impossible to tell whether Cognet plc's level of business is below, in line with or above what one would expect.

The implementation of the IT initiative should cause the **cost per customer per year** to fall by 5.4% (£20) but this cost is still 16.7% (£50) above the industry average.

The IT initiative is likely to cause the **cost per home order processed** to increase by 22.5% (£9.71), causing it to move from below the industry average of £50 to above it. The **cost per export order processed** should fall as a result of the IT initiative (by 15.5% from £110 to £93), but it is still way above the industry average of £60.

After the implementation of the IT initiative the **export orders will be 27% of total orders**, compared with 19% before the implementation. An industry average statistic would enable us to ascertain whether this represents a common trend or an increasing market share for Cognet plc.

The **average number of orders per customer per annum** was below the industry average of 4.1 before the implementation of the IT initiative but has dropped even further from 3.1 to 2.88.

Despite the increase in customer numbers (which might have led to inefficiencies, additional fixed costs and so on), the IT initiative has led to a significant drop (38.47%) in the **sales literature cost per customer** from £45 to £27.69, bringing it under the industry average cost of £35.

Although the IT initiative has led to a 22.4 % fall in the **cost per despatch**, from £11.13 to £8.64, the industry average is still lower at £8. If the majority of the despatch costs are fixed in nature, the fall in the cost per despatch could well be due to the increase in despatches to 18,750.

The question indicated that the **despatching of part orders** to customers is to the benefit of both customers and the company as it helps to reduce Cognet plc's stock holding costs and helps customers in their work flow management. The implementation of the IT initiative has caused the **average number of despatches per order** to move to the advantage of customers and the company, increasing from 1.85 to 2.5, but it still falls short of the industry average of 3.3.

It would also be useful to have information which would allow us to ascertain **whether additional contribution will be earned** as a result of the IT initiative to cover its cost for the year.

7   **HYMAN OLD ERSKINE FLINT LTD**

(a)   A cash budget is used to estimate cash receipts and cash payments during the forthcoming period. The cash flows in this period of time (typically one year) will be analysed into smaller time periods (usually months) for control purposes.

The **importance** of cash budgeting lies in the fact that a company **may be operating profitably, but may still run short of cash**. A cash shortage would threaten the company with liquidation. Conversely, a cash surplus can be used more efficiently if management are forewarned of its timing and duration.

It is therefore essential in budgeting that there will either be a sufficiency of cash or a large enough overdraft facility, throughout the budget period. Should actual cash flows differ from the budget in any control period, management is in a position to estimate the consequences of this change on liquidity, and to attempt whatever remedial action might be necessary.

(b) **HYMAN OLD ERSKINE FLINT LTD**
CASH BUDGET

	October £	November £	December £	Total £
Receipts				
Discount sales (W1)	38,220	50,960	63,700	152,880
Non-discount sales (W1)	74,250	94,500	121,500	290,250
Mortgage		40,000		40,000
	112,470	185,460	185,200	483,130

	£	£	£	£
Payments				
Trade creditors	35,000	40,000	40,000	115,000
Wages (W2)	26,000	20,500	16,500	63,000
Production overhead (W3)	19,000	17,000	11,000	47,000
Sales commission (W4)	600	700	750	2,050
Other sales overhead (W4)	12,350	13,775	15,675	41,800
Administrative overhead (W5)	11,000	10,000	9,000	30,000
New machine		3,600		3,600
Mortgage			2,000	2,000
Dividend	30,000			30,000
	133,950	105,575	94,925	334,450

	£	£	£	£
Receipts less payments	(21,480)	79,885	90,275	148,680
Opening cash balance	5,000	(16,480)	63,405	5,000
Closing cash balance	(16,480)	63,405	153,680	153,680

Workings

1

	July £'000	Aug £'000	Sept £'000	Oct £'000	Nov £'000	Dec £'000
Sales	40.00	60.00	100.00	120.00	160.00	200.00
Cash sales (10%)	4.00	6.00	10.00	12.00	16.00	20.00
Credit sales	36.00	54.00	90.00	108.00	144.00	180.00
Credit sales with discount (25%)	9.00	13.50	22.50	27.00	36.00	45.00
Other credit sales	27.00	40.50	67.50	81.00	108.00	135.00
Total sales with discount (cash and credit)	13.00	19.50	32.50	39.00	52.00	65.00
Discount (2%)				0.78	1.04	1.30
Cash receipts				38.22	50.96	63.70
Other credit sales (see above)	27.00	40.50	67.50	81.00	108.00	135.00
Receipts	13.50					
		13.50				
		20.25				
			20.25			
			33.75			
				33.75		
				40.50		
					40.50	
					54.00	
						54.00
						67.50
				74.25	94.50	121.50

2   *Wages*

		Total £'000		Payable in	
		Total £'000	Oct £'000	Nov £'000	Dec £'000
Wages incurred in:					
	September	20	5		
	October	28	21	7.0	
	November	18		13.5	4.5
	December	16			12.0
			26	20.5	16.5

3   *Production overhead*

		Total £'000		Payable in	
		Total £'000	Oct £'000	Nov £'000	Dec £'000
Overhead excluding depreciation:					
	September	18	9		
	October	20	10	10	
	November	14		7	7
	December	8			4
			19	17	11

4   *Sales overhead*

	Sept £	Oct £	Nov £	Dec £	Total £
Overhead	12,000	14,000	15,000	18,000	
Commission (5%)	600	700	750	900	
Other costs	11,400	13,300	14,250	17,100	
Which are payable in					
October	5,700	6,650			12,350
November		6,650	7,125		13,775
December			7,125	8,550	15,675

5   *Administration overhead*

		Total £'000		Payable in	
		Total £'000	Oct £'000	Nov £'000	Dec £'000
Overhead incurred in					
	September	10	5		
	October	12	6	6	
	November	8		4	4
	December	10			5
			11	10	9

8   TERRY HENDSETTER

(a) **Graph of sales**

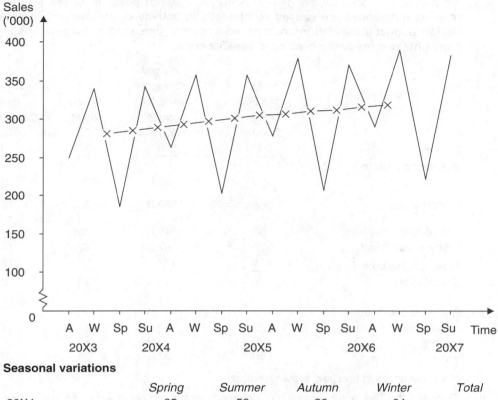

(b) **Seasonal variations**

	Spring	Summer	Autumn	Winter	Total
20X4	−95	+58	−26	+64	
20X5	−94	+56	−27	+73	
20X6	−104	+58	−27	+71	
	−293	+172	−80	+208	
Average variation	−97.7	+57.3	−26.7	+69.3	+2.2
Adjust to nil	− 0.5	− 0.5	−0.6	− 0.6	−2.2
	-98.2	+56.8	−27.3	+68.7	0.0
Round	−98	+57	−28*	+69	0

*Adjusted to keep the total of seasonal variations at zero.

(c) The **trend line shows increases in sales of about three thousand per quarter**, and so a forecast of sales will be based on this assumption.

			Trend line	Variation	Forecast
20X6	Winter	Trend line value	320		
20X7	Autumn	Estimate 320 + (3 × 3)	329	−28	301
	Winter	Estimate 320 + (4 × 3)	332	+69	401

The **forecasts** of sales, based on the calculations and assumptions here, are **301,000 units of product XN30 in autumn 20X7** and **401,000 units of products XN30 in winter 20X7**.

9   PRESENTATION

(a)   The **comparison of the actual results for 4,500 units with the budget data for 5,000** units is not particularly useful for the general manager. It is **not possible to tell whether cost and revenue differences are caused by changes in activity or by changes in expenditure**. A **flexible budget presentation** would be more relevant, presented in **marginal costing format** to **highlight the more easily controlled variable costs**.

	Original budget for 5,000 units £'000	Flexed budget for 4,500 units £'000	Actual result £'000	Variance against flexed budget £'000
Sales	600	540.0	550	10
less variable costs				
Direct materials	150	135.0	130	5.0
Direct labour	$200 \times \frac{4,500}{5,000}$	180.0	189	(9.0)
Production overhead	50	45.0	46	(1.0)
Selling overhead	75	67.5	72	(4.5)
Total variable cost	475	427.5	437	(9.5)
Contribution	125	112.5	113	0.5
less fixed overhead:				
Production	25	25.0	29	(4.0)
Selling	50	50.0	46	4.0
Profit	50	37.5	38	0.5

Note. Variances in brackets are adverse.

(b)   *Tutorial note.* The variances will be calculated using marginal costing principles. This means that there will be no variance for fixed production overhead volume capacity or volume efficiency - these two variances explain the reasons for under- or over-absorbed fixed production overhead, which cannot arise with marginal costing. The other main difference compared with absorption costing variances is that the sales volume variance is valued at the standard *contribution* per unit.

Workings

1   Standard contribution per unit:

	for 5,000 units	£ per unit
Sales price	£600,000	120
Direct materials	£150,000	30
Direct labour	£200,000	40
Variable production overhead	£50,000	10
Variable selling overhead	£75,000	15
Standard contrib'n per unit		25

2   Standard labour rate per hour = £200,000/50,000 = £4 per hour

3   Standard variable production overhead per hour = £50,000/50,000 = £1 per hour

Variances (*Note.* Variances in brackets are adverse)

			Variance against flexed budget
		£	£
(i)	**Selling price variance**		
	Margin on 4,500 units should have been	112,500	
	but was (£(550,000 – 427,500))	122,500	
			10,000
(ii)	**Direct material cost variance**		
	No further analysis than that in (a) possible		5,000
(iii)	**Direct labour rate variance**		
		£	
	47,500 hrs should cost (× £4)	190,000	
	but did cost	189,000	
			1,000
	Direct labour efficiency variance		
	4,500 units should have taken (× 10 hrs)	45,000 hrs	
	but did take	47,500 hrs	
	Variance in hours	2,500 hrs	
	× standard rate per hour	× £4	
			(10,000)
(iv)	**Variable production overhead efficiency variance**		
	2,500 hrs × standard rate per hour (× £1)		(2,500)
	Variable production overhead expenditure variance		
		£	
	47,500 hrs should cost (× £1)	47,500	
	but did cost	46,000	
			1,500
(v)	**Variable selling overhead expenditure variance**		
		£	
	4,500 units should cost (× £15)	67,500	
	but did cost	72,000	
			(4,500)
Total contribution variance			500
(vi)	**Fixed production overhead expenditure variance**		
	= budget expenditure – actual expenditure		
	= £(25,000 – 29,000)		(4,000)
(vii)	**Fixed selling overhead expenditure variance**		
	= budget expenditure – actual expenditure		
	= £(50,000 – 46,000)		4,000
(viii)	**Sales volume variance**		
	= [actual units – budget units] × std contribution/unit		
	= (4,500 – 5,000) × £25		(12,500)
Variance against original budget			(12,000)

REPORT

(c)   To: General manager
       From: Management accountant
       Date: 1 December 20X0
       Subject: The principles upon which the redrafted statement is based

As requested, I outline below the principles upon which the redrafted statement is based and the information it provides.

(i)   Marginal costing principles

The report has been prepared using marginal costing principles. Marginal costing highlights the variable costs, which may be more controllable than the fixed costs.

The report concentrates management attention on contribution, which is often the more easily controlled performance measure. The contribution is so called because it contributes towards fixed costs and profits.

(ii)   Flexible budget principles

The report has also used flexible budget principles. Flexible budgets use the available knowledge about cost behaviour patterns to 'flex' the budget. The resulting flexed budget contains more realistic targets for costs and revenues at the actual activity level for the period.

The report thus enables managers to compare like with like. There is little to be gained by comparing the actual costs and revenues for 4,500 units with the budget figures for 5,000 units. It would not be possible to tell which differences were caused by the volume change, and which were caused by over- and under-spending.

The most important piece of information in the re-drafted budget statement is the large variance caused by the volume shortfall. The net profit from sales was only £500 different from the flexed budget, but the large volume shortfall caused a major reduction of £12,500 in the profit result when compared with the original budget.

10   BUDGETS AND PEOPLE

There is one major **reason why managers may be reluctant to participate** fully in setting up budgets and that is a **lack of education** in the purposes of the budgeting process. The budget's major role is to communicate the various motivations that exist among management so that everybody sees, understands and co-ordinates the goals of the organisation.

Specific reasons for the reluctance of managers to participate

(a)   Managers view budgets as too rigid a constraint on their decision making. For example, a manager may be unable to sanction an item of expenditure if it has not been budgeted for. The natural reaction to this supposed restriction of their autonomy is resistance and self defence.

(b)   Managers feel that the top management goals expressed by the budget will interfere with their personal goals (for example their desire to 'build an empire' with substantial resources under their control, large personal income and so on). A successful budgetary system will harmonise the budget goals with the managers' personal goals, but it is by no means easy to achieve a successful system.

(c)   Managers imagine that the purpose of budgets is to provide senior management with a rod with which to chastise those who do not stay within budget. They will be unwilling to help in the construction of such a rod.

(d)   Managers view the budgeting process as one in which they must fight for a fair share of the organisation's resources in competition with colleagues with other responsibilities.

(e)   Managers misinterpret the control function of the budgeting system to be a method whereby blame can be attached. By not participating in the budget setting process, they are able to blame an 'unattainable' or 'unrealistic' budget for any poor results they may have.

As a reaction to these uneducated notions, the behaviour of managers involved in budget preparation can conflict with the desires of senior management. Such **behaviour** is often described as **dysfunctional**; it is counter-productive because it is not goal congruent.

The **unwanted side effects** which may **arise from the imposition of budgets** by senior management (for example under an authoritative rather than a participative budgetary system) are examples of **dysfunctional behaviour** and include the following.

(a)   There may be a reluctance to reduce costs for fear that future budget allowances may be reduced as a consequence of successful cost cutting.

(b)   Managers may spend up to their budget in order to justify levels of expenditure. This is particularly the case in local government circles where there is a tendency to spend any available cash at the end of a financial year.

(c)   There may be padding, whereby managers request inflated allowances. In turn senior management may cut budgets where they suspect padding exists. Padding is sometimes called slack and represents the difference between the budget allowance requested and the realistic costs necessary to accomplish the objective.

(d)   In extreme cases of authoritative budgeting the 'emotional' responses of managers can be highly detrimental to the goals of the organisation, for example non-cooperation.

11   MPL LTD

> **Tutorial note.** The key point to note in the scenario detail is that budgets are issued to the consultants, implying that an imposed system of budgeting is in place.

REPORT

(a)   To: Board of Directors of MPL Ltd
       From: Management accountant
       Date: 23 April 20X0
       Subject: Budgeting

This report considers our present approach to budgeting, including the appropriateness of the format of the opening statement currently prepared.

Present approach to budgeting

Given that the budgets are **'issued to' consultants**, they clearly have very **little or no input to the budget process**. Budgets are **set centrally by senior management** and are **imposed** on consultants without consultants participating in their preparation.

Although there are advantages to such an approach (for example, strategic plans are likely to be incorporated into planned activities, there is little input from inexperienced or uninformed employees and the period of time taken to draw up the budgets is shorter, **dissatisfaction, defensiveness and low morale** amongst employees who must work with the budgets is often apparent. The budget may be seen as a **punitive device** and **initiative may be stifled**. More importantly, however, it is **difficult for people to be motivated to achieve targets that have been set by somebody else.**

- **Targets** that are **too difficult** will have a **demotivating** effect because **adverse efficiency variances** will always be reported.

- **Easy targets** are also **demotivating** because there is **no sense of achievement** in attaining them.

- **Targets set at the same levels as have been achieved in the past** will be too low and might **encourage budgetary slack.**

Academics have argued that each individual has a **personal 'aspiration level'** which the individual undertakes for himself to reach, and so it may be more appropriate to adopt a **participative approach** to budgeting. Budgets would be developed by the consultants and would be based on their perceptions of what is achievable and the associated necessary resources.

Consultants are more likely to be **motivated** to achieve targets that they have set themselves and overall the budgets are likely to be more **realistic** (as senior management's overview of the business is mixed with operational level details and the expectations of both senior management and the consultants are considered).

Allowing participation in the budget-setting process is **time consuming**, however, and can produce **budget bias.** It is generally assumed that the bias will operate in one direction only, consultants building **slack** into their budgets so targets are easy to achieve. But **bias can work in**

two directions. Optimistic forecasts may be made with the intention of pleasing senior management, despite the risk of displeasing them when optimistic targets are not met.

Format of the operating statement

The current format of the operating statement **classifies costs as either fixed or variable** in relation to the number of chargeable consultancy hours and **compares expected costs for the budgeted number of chargeable consultancy hours with actual costs incurred.**

For **control purposes**, however, there is little point in comparing costs and revenues for the budgeted numbers of chargeable hours with actual costs and revenues if budgeted and actual hours differ. Rather, the **costs that should have been incurred given the actual number of chargeable consultancy hours should be compared with the actual costs incurred.** Although fixed costs should be the same regardless of the hours charged, such a comparison requires **variable costs to be flexed** to the actual activity level. More appropriate **variances** could then be calculated and denoted as either **adverse or favourable.**

The report should also **distinguish** between those **costs** which are **controllable** by consultants and those which are **uncontrollable.** Consultants' attention will then be focused on those variances for which they are responsible and which, if significant, require action.

I hope this information has proved useful. If you have any further questions, please do not hesitate to contact me.

(b) A spreadsheet model which requires only actual data to be input so that a flexed budget and variance calculations are produced would require three separate areas.

The **output area** would require four columns (original budget, flexed budget, actual costs and variances) and rows for chargeable consultancy hours, each cost classification (in total, not split into its fixed and variable components), total costs, fees charged and profit.

The **input area** would require cells containing the following details.

- Budget chargeable consultancy hours
- Actual consultancy hours
- Budget variable cost per consultancy hour for each cost classification
- Budget fixed cost for each cost classification

The **calculation area** would contain the formulae to do the following.

- **Produce the budget column.** For example, if the budget variable cost per chargeable consultancy hour for motor and travel costs was contained in cell B34, the budget fixed cost for motor and travel cost was contained in cell B35 and the budget chargeable hours in cell B27 (say), the formula would be B34*B27 + B35.

- **Produce the flexed budget.** If the value for actual chargeable hours was contained in cell B28, the formula for the motor and travel costs would be B34*B28 + B35 (given that the budget fixed cost should be the same regardless of the number of chargeable hours).

- **Produce the variances column.** The formulae would simply be the difference between the values in the flexed budget cells of the output area and those in the actual results cells. The formulae would need to be constructed in such a way that adverse and favourable variances were appropriately designated, brackets or minus signs perhaps signifying adverse variances.

- **Produce the budget, flexed budget, actual and variance total costs and profit figures.**

Actual costs could then be **inserted** directly into the output area and the operating statement would be automatically prepared.

12   TRANSFER PRICING

(a) **Main variants of market price based transfer prices**

- Full market price
- Market price discounted by any costs saved by making internal transfers.

Advantages of market price based transfer prices

(i)   The use of market price simulates the competitive characteristics of the free market and ensures that both transferor and transferee behave as if at arm's length. It is argued that this will lead to optimal decision making.

(ii)   The market price (as discounted if necessary) should be seen to be fair by both the transferor and the transferee.

(iii) The profit sharing achieved under such a system can be considered to be objective since it is based on external factors and is not distorted by subjective or internal considerations.

Disadvantages of market price based transfer prices

(i)   The market price may be a temporary one, induced by adverse economic conditions, or dumping.

(ii) A transfer price at market value might, under some circumstances, act as a disincentive to use up any spare capacity in the buying divisions. A price based on incremental cost, in contrast, might provide an incentive to use up the spare resources in order to provide a marginal contribution to profit.

(iii) Many products in a part-finished state do not have a market price.

(b) **Main variants of cost based transfer prices**

- Full cost plus
- Marginal cost plus

Furthermore, each variant could be operated on the following basis.

- Standard cost
- Actual cost

In the absence of a market price the optimum transfer price is likely to be one based on standard cost plus. Its advantages are as follows.

(i)   The transfer price can be fixed and agreed in advance without being subject to external fluctuations.

(ii) Such a transfer price should motivate divisional managers to increase output and reduce expenditure levels.

(iii) The transfer price can be set in such a way as to ensure a fair division of profit between divisions.

Disadvantages of a cost based transfer pricing system

(i)   Reaching agreement between the transferor and the transferee as to an appropriate mark-up can be difficult.

(ii) Such a system is dependent on cost behaviour and can only be used for ranges of production over which costs vary linearly with output.

(iii) The use of a cost based transfer price may encourage dysfunctional behaviour if one division feels that the price is wrong.

13   JUST-IN-TIME

> **Tutorial note.** In the exam you would probably only need to provide five (relevant) financial benefits in part (b) to gain the full five marks.

(a) JIT production systems will include the following features.

Multiskilled workers

In a JIT production environment, production processes must be shortened and simplified. **Each product family is made in a workcell based on flowline principles**. The variety and complexity of work carried out in these work cells is increased (compared with more traditional processes), necessitating a group of dissimilar machines working within each work cell. **Workers must therefore be more flexible and adaptable, the cellular approach enabling each operative to operate several machines.** Operatives are trained to operate all machines on the line and **undertake routine preventative maintenance**.

Close relationships with suppliers

JIT production systems often go hand in hand with JIT purchasing systems. **JIT purchasing** seeks to **match the usage of materials with the delivery of materials** from external suppliers. This means that **material stocks can be kept at near-zero levels**. For JIT purchasing to be successful this requires the organisation to have confidence that the supplier will deliver on time and that the supplier will deliver materials of 100% quality, that there will be no rejects, returns and hence no consequent production delays. The **reliability of suppliers is of utmost importance** and hence the company must **build up close relationships** with their suppliers. This can be achieved by doing **more business with fewer suppliers** and placing **long-term orders** so that the supplier is assured of sales and can produce to meet the required demand.

Machine cells

With JIT production, factory layouts must change to reduce movement of workers and products. Traditionally machines were grouped by function (drilling, grinding and so on). A part therefore had to travel long distances, moving from one part of the factory to the other, often stopping along the way in a storage area. All these are non-value-added activities that have to be reduced or eliminated. **Material movements between operations are therefore minimised by eliminating space between work stations and grouping machines or workers by product or component** instead of by type of work performed. Products can flow from machine to machine without having to wait for the next stage of processing or returning to stores. **Lead times and work in progress are thus reduced.**

Quality

Production management within a JIT environment seeks to both **eliminate scrap and defective units during production and avoid the need for reworking of units**. Defects stop the production line, thus creating rework and possibly resulting in a failure to meet delivery dates. Quality, on the other hand, reduces costs. Quality is assured by **designing products and processes with quality in mind, introducing quality awareness programmes** and **statistical checks on output quality**, providing **continual worker training** and implementing **vendor quality assurance programmes** to ensure that the correct product is made to the appropriate quality level on the first pass through production.

Set-up time reduction

If an organisation is able to **reduce manufacturing lead time** it is in a better position to **respond quickly to changes in customer demand**. Reducing set-up time is one way in which this can be done. Machinery set-ups are non-value-added activities which should be reduced or even eliminated. **Reducing set-up time** (and hence set-up costs) also makes the manufacture of **smaller batches more economical and worthwhile**; managers do not feel the need to spread the set-up costs over as many units as possible (which then leads to high levels of stock). Set-up time can be reduced by the **use of one product or one product family machine cells**, by **training workers** or by the use **of computer integrated manufacturing (CIM)**.

(b)   JIT systems have a number of financial **benefits**.

- Increase in labour productivity due to labour being multiskilled and carrying out preventative maintenance

- Reduction of investment in plant space

- Reduction in costs of storing stock

- Reduction in risk of stock obsolescence

- Lower investment in stock

- Reduction in costs of handling stock

- Reduction in costs associated with scrap, defective units and reworking

- Higher revenue as a result of reduction in lost sales following failure to meet delivery dates (because of improved quality)

- Reduction in the costs of setting up production runs

- Higher revenues as a result of faster response to customer demands

14   BART BENTON LTD

(a)   **Unit cost using absorption costing**

	Gianni	Falke	Redaelli
	£	£	£
Paint	15.20	11.18	18.90
Labour (W1)	2.65	3.98	6.63
Stirring and quality control (W2)	1.15	1.73	2.88
Electricity (W2)	5.00	7.50	12.50
Filling of machines (W2)	3.10	4.65	7.75
	27.10	29.04	48.66

(b)   **Unit cost using activity based costing**

	Gianni	Falke	Redaelli
	£	£	£
Paint	15.20	11.18	18.90
Labour	2.65	3.98	6.63
Stirring and quality control (W3)	1.38	1.27	3.08
Electricity (W3)	8.94	7.66	6.39
Filling of machines (W3)	4.87	5.52	4.04
	33.04	29.61	39.04

(c)   **Cost drivers** are activities or transactions that are significant determinants of cost, in other words the activities that cause costs to occur. Activity based costing acknowledges that some costs vary not with volume of output but with some other activity.

The logic of this approach is clearly illustrated by the facts given in the question. If paint delivered is stirred and inspected in batches, then it is the number of batches rather than units or labour hours that determine how much stirring and inspection is to be done.

The use of electricity best illustrates the **difference between the two methods** in this example. Under absorption costing Redaelli's products absorb the largest part of the electricity overhead because Redaelli's involve more labour time than the other products. Under activity based costing Redaelli's have the smallest share of the electricity overhead, recognising that use of labour time and consumption of electricity are not necessarily related. (Note that Redaelli's use more different batches of paint than the other products: the labour time is probably spent adjusting the machinery while it is idle rather than operating it and using electricity.)

The **consequences of adopting activity based costing** are a significant change in the unit cost of Redaelli's mainly at the expense of Gianni's. This will have implications for valuing work in progress and also for pricing the service and assessing its overall validity.

Workings

1   *Labour cost per unit*

	Gianni	Falke	Redaelli
Labour hours per unit	0.50	0.75	1.25
Rate per hour	£5.30	£5.30	£5.30
Cost per unit	£2.65	£3.98	£6.63

2   *Overheads - absorption costing*

	Gianni	Falke	Redaelli	Total
Units	5,400	4,360	3,600	13,360
Labour hours/unit	0.5	0.75	1.25	
Total labour hours	2,700	3,270	4,500	10,470

	Total overhead	Total hours	Rates per hour
	£	Hrs	£
Paint stirring and quality control	24,081	10,470	2.30
Electricity	104,700	10,470	10.00
Filling of spraying machines	64,914	10,470	6.20

	Gianni £	Falke £	Redaelli £
Stirring @ £2.30 per hour (× 0.5/0.75/1.25)	1.15	1.73	2.88
Electricity @ £10 per hour	5.00	7.50	12.50
Filling @ £6.20 per hour	3.10	4.65	7.75

3   *Overheads - activity based costing*

    (a)   Paint stirring and quality control

	Gianni	Falke	Redaelli	Total
Units	5,400	4,360	3,600	
Batches	27	20	40	87
Share of overhead (27:20:40)	£7,473	£5,536	£11,072	£24,081
Per unit	£1.38	£1.27	£3.08	

    (b)   Electricity

	Gianni	Falke	Redaelli	Total
Coats per unit	7	6	5	
Total coats	37,800	26,160	18,000	81,960
Share of overhead	£48,288	£33,418	£22,994	£104,700
Per unit	£8.94	£7.66	£6.39	

Tutorial note. An easy mistake to make here would be to divide the overhead in the ratio of number of coats but this would not be correct: Gianni's products have substantially more costs overall because more Gianni units are sprayed overall.

    (c)   Filling

	Gianni	Falke	Redaelli	Total
Litres per unit	7.6	8.6	6.3	
Total litres	41,040	37,496	22,680	101,216
Share of overhead	£26,321	£24,048	£14,545	£64,914
Per unit	£4.87	£5.52	£4.04	

15   COST REDUCTION

(a)   **Cost control** is the regulation of the costs of operating a business and is concerned with keeping costs within acceptable limits.

In contrast, **cost reduction** is a planned and positive approach to reducing expenditure. It starts with an assumption that current or planned cost levels are too high and looks for ways of reducing them without reducing effectiveness.

Cost control action ought to lead to a reduction in excessive spending (for example when material wastage is higher than budget levels or productivity levels are below agreed standards). However, a cost reduction programme is directed towards reducing expected cost levels below current budgeted or standard levels.

Cost control tends to be carried out on a routine basis whereas cost reduction programmes are often ad hoc exercises.

(b)   **Three examples of cost control techniques**

    (i)   **Budgetary control**. Cost control is achieved by setting predetermined absolute levels for expenditure. If flexible budgeting is used then the budget cost allowance can be flexed in line with changes in activity. Control action is taken if actual expenditure differs from planned expenditure by an excessive amount.

    (ii)   **Standard costing**. Designed to control unit costs rather than absolute levels of expenditure, the use of standard costing depends on the existence of a measurable output which is produced in standard operations. Control action is taken if the actual unit costs differ from standard unit costs by an excessive amount.

    (iii)   **Limits on authority to incur expenditure**. Many organisations restrict the authority for their managers to incur expenditure. For example a budget manager may have an overall budget for overheads in a period, but even within this budget the manager may be required to seek separate authorisation for individual items of expenditure which are above a certain amount.

Three examples of cost reduction techniques

(i) **Value analysis**. The CIMA defines value analysis as 'a systematic inter-disciplinary examination of factors affecting the cost of a product or service, in order to devise means of achieving the specified purpose most economically at the required standard of quality and reliability.' The aim in a value analysis exercise is to eliminate unnecessary costs without reducing the use value, the esteem value or the exchange value of the item under consideration.

(ii) **Work study**. This is a means of raising the production efficiency of an operating unit by the reorganisation of work. The two main parts to work study are method study and work measurement. Method study is the most significant in the context of cost reduction. It looks at the way in which work is done and attempts to develop easier and more effective methods in order to reduce costs.

(iii) **Variety reduction**. This involves standardisation of parts and components which can offer enormous cost reduction potential for some manufacturing industries. Variety reduction can also be used to describe the standardisation or simplification of an organisation's product range.

(c) The **statement suggests** that the training of management accountants should place the major **emphasis on cost reduction**.

This is true to some extent because of the changes in the competitive environment and the globalisation of markets. In order to remain competitive an organisation must provide goods and services of the right quality at prices which are attractive to the customer.

The **Japanese** in particular view costs as a **target** which must be reached rather than as a limit on expenditure. They employ cost reduction techniques to bring costs down below a target price with the result that prices dictate costs and not vice versa.

If companies are to compete effectively then they must adopt a similar philosophy. The management accountant needs to be trained to provide information which is useful for cost planning and cost reduction. An emphasis on cost control might create a tendency to concentrate effort and resources on the mechanics of recording and reporting historic costs, rather than on the planning and reducing of future costs.

On the other hand it is **still necessary to control costs** and to record and report actual costs so that management can take control action if necessary. An efficient plan will ensure that the organisation is starting out with the most effective cost targets, but only by recording the actual costs and comparing them with the targets will management know whether those targets have been achieved.

Despite the implied criticism of management accounting training, an increasing awareness of the need for a **more strategic approach to management accounting** does exist, both among trainee and qualified management accountants. Active discussion is also taking place on the need to adapt information systems to be more useful in an advanced manufacturing technology environment.

In **conclusion** while there may be a case for a **slight change in emphasis** in the training of management accountants, this should not lead to the total abandonment of cost control principles and techniques.

16   BB COMPANY

Assumption. Manufacturing costs for the BB brand will be the same as for own label brands.

Initial workings

Manufacturing costs

We need to analyse the cost behaviour patterns by separating the manufacturing costs into their fixed and variable elements, using the high-low method.

BPP PUBLISHING

	Sales Millions	Costs £ million
20X3	19	4.45
20X2	18	4.30
	1	0.15

Variable manufacturing cost per can = £0.15

Fixed manufacturing cost	= £4.45 million – (19 million × £0.15)
	= £1.6 million

Selling prices

Selling price per can in 20X3		= 6.27/19	= £0.33
∴	Unit contribution per can	= £0.33 – £0.15	= £0.18
∴	Contribution per can of BB brand	= £0.18 × 133 1/3%	= £0.24
	Variable cost per can of BB brand	= £0.15 + £0.02	= £0.17
∴	Selling price per can of BB brand	= £0.17 + £0.24	= £0.41

(a) **Data for chart**

		£ million	£ million
Variable costs	(19 million × £0.15)		2.85
Fixed costs:	manufacturing	1.60	
	administration	1.20	
			2.80
Total costs			5.65

$$\text{Breakeven point} = \frac{\text{fixed costs}}{\text{contribution}} = \frac{£2.8m}{£0.18}$$

= 15.55 million cans
= £5.13 million sales

Margin of safety = 19m – 15.55m = 3.45 million cans = £1.14 million sales

Breakeven chart for 20X3 - all 'own label' sales

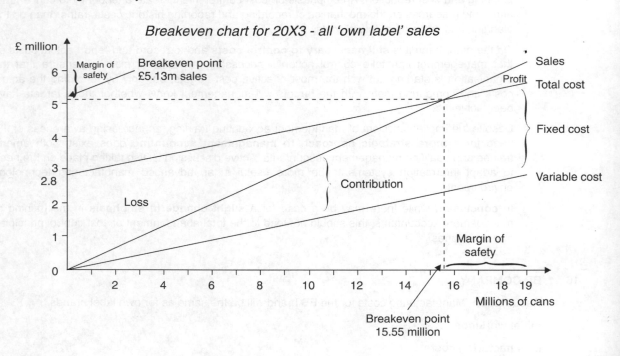

(b) **Data for chart**

		£ million	£ million
Variable costs	own label (9.5m × £0.15)		1.425
	BB brand (9.5m × £0.17)		1.615
			3.040
Fixed costs:	manufacturing	1.600	
	administration	1.200	
	marketing	0.400	
			3.200
Total costs			6.240
Sales value:	own label (9.5m × £0.33)		3.135
	BB brand (9.5m × £0.41)		3.895
			7.030

Our standard mix is 1 own label, 1 BB brand.

$$\text{Breakeven point} = \frac{\text{fixed costs}}{\text{contribution per mix}} = \frac{£3.2\text{m}}{£(0.18 + 0.24)} = \frac{£3.2\text{m}}{£0.42}$$

$$= 7.62 \text{ million mixes} = 15.24 \text{ million cans}$$
$$= 7.62 \times (£(0.33 + 0.41)) \text{ million sales} = £5.64 \text{ million sales}$$

Margin of safety $= 19\text{m} - 15.24 \text{ million} = 3.76 \text{ million cans} = 1.88 \text{ million mixes}$
$= 1.88 \times (£(0.33 + 0.41)) \text{ million sales}$
$= £1.39 \text{ million sales}$

Profit $= £7.03 \text{ million} - £6.24 \text{ million} = £790,000$

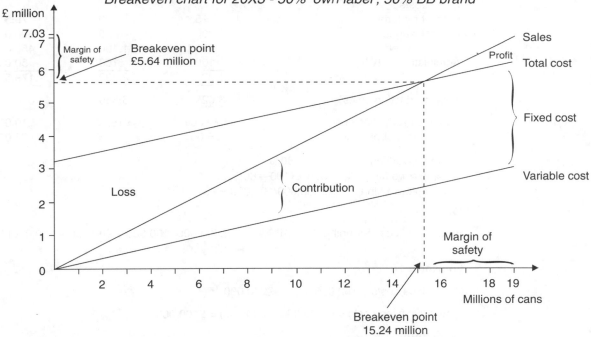

Breakeven chart for 20X3 - 50% 'own label', 50% BB brand

(c) The **first chart** shows a breakeven point of £15.55 million cans (£5.13m sales value) and a margin of safety of 3.45 million cans (£1.14m sales value). Forecast profit for sales of 19 million cans is £620,000.

The **second chart** shows a breakeven point of 15.24 million cans (£5.64m sales value) and a margin of safety of 3.76 million cans (£1.39m sales value). Forecast profit for sales of 19 million cans is £790,000.

Option 2 therefore results in a higher profit figure, as well as a lower breakeven point and increased margin of safety. On this basis it is the better of the two options.

Other factors which management should consider before making a decision

(i)   The supermarket chains may put the same pressure on margins and prices of the BB brand as they do on the own label brands.

(ii)   Customers may realise that the BB brand is the same product as the own label brand and may not be willing to pay the premium price.

(iii)   If the mix of sales can be changed in favour of the BB brand then profits will improve still further.

---

17   ABC LTD

> **Tutorial note**. An analysis by behaviour (part (i)) means analysing the costs into those that are fixed and those that are variable.
>
> For each of the six options in part (ii) one factory is closed, one factory operates to 100% capacity and so the third factory produces the balance of the units.

(a)   (i)

	North	*Central*	*South*
	£'000	*£'000*	*£'000*
Variable costs			
Direct materials	500	1,000	750.0
Direct wages	800	1,600	1,200.0
Indirect materials	300*	600	450.5
Indirect wages	50	150	150.0
Indirect expenses	350	600	300.0
	2,000	3,950	2,850.5
Fixed costs			
Indirect materials	75**	200	79.5
Indirect wages	200	850	600.0
Indirect expenses	650	1,400	450.0
Administration (W)	100	150	50.0
	1,025	2,600	1,179.5
Total production costs	3,025	6,550	4,030
Variable production cost per unit	£20.00	£19.75	£19.00
Transport cost per unit ***	£5.00	£4.00	£5.00

* Sample working: $375 \times 80\%$

** Sample working: $375 \times (100 - 80)\%$

*** Sample working: £500,000/100,000 = £5

Workings

Head-office cost per unit produced   = £900,000/(100,000 + 200,000 + 150,000)

                                          = £2

For North:

Head office costs = 100,000 × £2 = £200,000

∴ Specific fixed costs = £(300,000 − 200,000) = £100,000

For Central:

Head office costs = 200,000 × £2 = £400,000

∴ Specific fixed costs = £(550,000 − 400,000) = £150,000

For South:

Head office costs = 150,000 × £2 = £300,000

∴ Specific fixed costs = £(350,000 − 300,000) = £50,000

(ii)   There are **six possible options**. Each option requires the closure of one factory and the relocation of that factory's production so that production is at maximum capacity in one of the remaining factories. Demand in 20X3 = 70% × 20X1 demand = 70% × 450,000 = 315,000 units.

Option	North '000 units	North % of annual capacity	Central '000 units	Central % of annual capacity	South '000 units	South % of annual capacity
1	Close	0	250	100	65	36
2	Close	0	135	54	180	100
3	160	100	Close	0	155	86
4	135*	84	Close	0	180	100
5	160	100	155	62	Close	0
6	65	41	250	100	Close	0

* Sample working: (135,000/160,000) x 100%

Costs of each option

Variable cost = production cost + transport cost per unit

Option		North £'000	Central £'000	South £'000	Total £'000
1	Variable	-	5,937.50	1,560.0	
	Fixed	-	5,200.00	1,179.5	
		-	11,137.5 (W1)	2,739.5 (W2)	13,877
2	Variable	-	3,206.25	4,320.0	
	Fixed	-	2,600.00	2,359.0	
		-	5,806.25 (W3)	6,679.0 (W4)	12,485.25
3	Variable	4,000	-	3,720.0	
	Fixed	2,050	-	1,651.3	
		6,050 (W5)	-	5,371.3 (W6)	11,421.3
4	Variable	3,375	-	4,320.0	
	Fixed	1,025	-	2,359.0	
		4,400 (W7)	-	6,679.0 (W4)	11,079
5	Variable	4,000	3,681.25	-	
	Fixed	2,050	2,600.00	-	
		6,050 (W5)	6,281.25 (W8)	-	12,331.25
6	Variable	1,625	5,937.50	-	
	Fixed	1,025	5,200.00	-	
		2,650 (W9)	11,137.50 (W1)	-	13,787.5

Workings

1 **100% capacity**

Variable costs = 250,000 × £(19.75 + 4.00)
Fixed costs = £2,600,000 × 2

2 **36% capacity**

Variable costs = 65,000 × £(19 + 5)
Fixed costs = £1,179,500

3 **54% capacity**

Variable costs = 135,000 × £(19.75 + 4)
Fixed costs = £2,600,000

4 **100% capacity**

Variable costs = 180,000 × £(19 + 5)
Fixed costs = £1,179,500 × 2

5 **100% capacity**

Variable costs = 160,000 × £(20 + 5)
Fixed costs = £1,025,000 × 2

6   **86% capacity**

Variable costs = 155,000 × £(19 + 5)
Fixed costs = £1,179,500 × 140%

7   **84% capacity**

Variable costs = 135,000 × £(20 + 5)
Fixed costs = £1,025,000

8   **62% capacity**

Variable costs = 155,000 × £(19.75 + 4)
Fixed costs = £2,600,000

9   **41% capacity**

Variable costs = 65,000 × £(20 + 5)
Fixed costs = £1,025,000

The lowest cost option is Option 4. To maximise profits the Central factory should be closed, South factory should produce to full capacity and North factory should produce 135,000 units.

(b)   MEMO

To: Production controller
From: Management accountant
Date: 17 March 20X2
Subject: **Production scheduling**

Further to our meeting on Tuesday, I can confirm that, **on the basis of the cost and output information available**, the **Central factory should be closed, South factory should produce to full capacity** and **North should produce 135,000 units** if we wish to maximise profits. The following **factors** should also be taken into account, however, before a final decision is made.

(i)   Employees at the Central factory would either need to be transferred to the other two factories or made redundant. Transfers are known to cause dissatisfaction to employees. Redundancy costs could be high.

(ii)   There may be other costs associated with the closure of the Central factory such as machinery decommissioning costs.

(iii)   If employees from the Central factory are not willing to transfer, additional staff will need to be recruited for the North and South factory.

(iv)   The South factory would be required to operate at maximum capacity. This may cause administrative burdens for management and pressures of work might reduce efficiency and effectiveness.

(v)   If demand were to increase in the future we may be unable to satisfy it with the capacity available from the North and South factories alone.

(vi)   Employee morale in the organisation as a whole may suffer if we appear to be motivated by profit alone.

(vii)   The closure of the factory and the possible redundancies may tarnish the organisation's public image and this might have repercussions on sales demand.

(viii)   Demand forecasts may be inaccurate.

Give me a call if you have any further questions.

18   RAB CONSULTING LTD

> **Tutorial note.** This is a straightforward linear programming question. The examiner has stated that he will keep new topics such as linear programming in the optional sections of the paper for the first couple of sittings.

(a)   (i)

		Type A £ per project		Type B £ per project
Revenue		1,700		1,500
Variable costs				
Labour				
- qualified researchers	(20 hrs × £30)	600	(12 hrs × £30)	360
- junior researchers	(8 hrs × £14)	112	(15 hrs × £14)	210
Direct project expenses		408		310
		1,120		880
Contribution		580		620

(ii)   **Define variables**

Let a = number of type A projects
Let b = number of type B projects

Establish objective function

Maximise contribution (C) = 580a + 620b, subject to the constraints below.

Establish constraints

Qualified researchers time:	$20a + 12b \leq 1,344$
Junior researchers time:	$8a + 15b \leq 1,120$
Agreement for type A:	$a \geq 20$
Maximum for type B:	$b \leq 60$
Non-negativity:	$a \geq 0, b \geq 0$

(iii)   **Graphing the constraints**

Qualified researcher time:	if a = 0, b = 112 if b = 0, a = 67.2
Junior researcher time:	if a = 0, b = 74.67 if b = 0, a = 140
Agreement for type A:	graph the line a = 20
Maximum for type B:	graph the line b = 60

Iso-contribution line

580a + 620b = 35,960 (where 35,960 = 58 × 62 × 10) goes through the points (62, 0) and (0, 58)

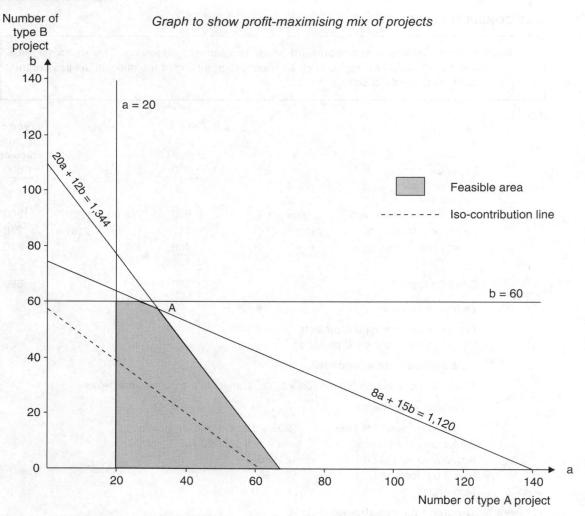

Graph to show profit-maximising mix of projects

Moving the iso-contribution line away from the origin, we see that it leaves the feasible area at the intersection of the two time constraints (point A).

Find the coordinates of A

$20a + 12b$	$= 1,344$	(1)	
$8a + 15b$	$= 1,120$	(2)	
$20a + 37.5b$	$= 2,800$	(3)	(2) × 2.5
$25.5b$	$= 1,456$		(3) − (1)
b	$= 57.09$		
$20a + 685.08$	$= 1,344$		substitute into (1)
a	$= 32.946$		

The profit-maximising mix of projects is 33 of type A and 57 of type B.

(b) **Profit for profit-maximising mix**

		£
Contribution from type A:	33 × £580	19,140
Contribution from type B	57 × £620	35,340
Total contribution		54,480
Less: fixed costs		(28,000)
		26,480

(c) **The importance of identifying scarce resources when preparing budgets**

Scarce resources restrict the activity level at which an organisation can operate. For example, a sales department might estimate that it could sell 1,000 units of product X, which would require 5,000 hours of grade A labour. If there are no units of product X in stock, and only 4,000 hours of grade A labour available in the period, the company would be unable to make and sell 1,000 units of X because of the shortage of labour hours. Management must choose one of the following options.

- Reduce budgeted sales by 20%.
- Increase the availability of grade A labour by recruitment or overtime working.
- Sub-contract some production to another manufacturer.

If the fact that grade A labour is a **scarce resource** is **ignored** when the **budget** is prepared, it will be **unattainable** and of **little relevance for planning and control.**

Most organisations are **restricted** from making and selling more of their products because there would be **no sales demand for the increased output** at an acceptable price. The organisation should therefore budget to produce and sell the volume of its product(s) demanded.

The **scarce resource** might be machine capacity, distribution and selling resources, raw materials or cash.

(i) If an organisation **produces just one product**, the **budget for the scarce resources is usually the starting point in the budget preparation process.**

(ii) If an organisation **produces two or more products** and there is only **one scarce resource, limiting factor analysis** must be used to determine the most profitable use of the scarce resource.

(iii) When there is **more than one scarce resource, linear programming** must be used to identify the most profitable use of resources.

The use of linear programming to determine the optimum use of resources

Linear programming is a technique which **determines the most profitable production mix, taking into account resource constraints and limitations** faced by an organisation. **All costs are assumed to be either fixed or variable in relation to a single measure of activity (usually units of output).**

The **problem** is **formulated** in terms of an **objective function** and **constraints** are then **graphed**. This process **highlights all possible output combinations** given the resource constraints and limitations and allows for the **identification of the output combination which would maximise contribution (the optimal solution).**

If there are **more than two types of output,** the graphical approach is not possible and the **Simplex method** must be used instead.

19 XYZ LTD

(a) **Define variables**

Let x_1 be the number of Super deluxe produced
Let x_2 be the number of Deluxe produced
Let x_3 be the number of Export produced

Establish objective function

Maximise contribution (C) = $1,500x_1 + 1,300x_2 + 2,500x_3$ (subject to the constraints below).

Establish constraints

$$
\begin{aligned}
x_1 &\leq 500 &&\text{(super deluxe demand)} \\
x_2 &\leq 750 &&\text{(deluxe demand)} \\
x_3 &\leq 400 &&\text{(export model demand)} \\
0.5x_1 + 0.5x_2 + x_3 &\leq 1,400 &&\text{(machining capacity)} \\
0.5x_1 + 0.5x_2 + 2x_3 &\leq 1,200 &&\text{(assembly capacity)} \\
x_1, x_2, x_3 &\geq 0
\end{aligned}
$$

Introduce slack variables

Slack variables are introduced as follows.

s_1 is the amount by which demand for x_1 falls short of 500

s_2 is the amount by which demand for x_2 falls short of 750
s_3 is the amount by which demand for x_3 falls short of 400
s_4 is the unused machine capacity in hours
s_5 is the unused assembly capacity in hours

Then $x_1 + s_1 = 500$
                $x_2 + s_2 = 750$
                $x_3 + s_3 = 400$
                $0.5x_1 + 0.5x_2 + x_3 + s_4 = 1,400$
                $0.5x_1 + 0.5x_2 + 2x_3 + s_5 = 1,200$
and $C - 1,500x_1 - 1,300x_2 - 2,500x_3 + 0s_1 + 0s_2 + 0s_3 + 0s_4 + 0s_5 = 0$

(b) The **optimal solution** must be determined by looking for **variables which have a zero in every row of their column, except for one row which has a figure 1**. This is the solution for that variable.

(i)   Produce   500,000 units of the super deluxe model   ($x_1 = 500$)
                             750,000 units of the deluxe model   ($x_2 = 750$)
                and   287,500 units of the export model   ($x_3 = 287.5$)

(ii)   This means that demand for the export model will be 112,500 units short of the maximum demand ($s_3 = 112.5$)

(iii)   There will be 487,500 unused direct labour hours in machining ($s_4 = 487.5$)

(iv)   The total contribution will be £2,443,750.

(v)   The shadow price of s_1 is £875 and that of s_2 is £675.

      (1)   Contribution would therefore increase (or decrease) by £875 for each one thousand units by which the demand constraint for the super deluxe model increased (or decreased). For example if the maximum demand for the super deluxe fell to 490,000 ($x_1 \le 490$), maximum contribution would fall by $10 \times £875 = £8,750$ to £2,435,000.

      (2)   Similarly, contribution would increase (or decrease) by £675 for each one thousand units by which the demand constraint for the deluxe model increased (or decreased).

(vi)   The shadow price of assembly time is £1,250 per thousand hours. This means that for every thousand hours extra (or less) of assembly time available, provided that the cost of this time remains at its normal variable cost per hour, maximum contribution would be £1,250 higher (or lower). This is readily apparent in this particular problem, because the extra time would have to be used to make the export model (since the other two models are already being produced up to maximum demand). One thousand extra hours of assembly time would be sufficient to produce 500 units of the export model, to earn a contribution of 50% of £2,500 = £1,250. This shadow price is only valid up to the point where demand for the export model is satisfied (an extra 112,500 units, or 225,000 hours), given that sufficient machining capacity does exist to produce all of these extra units.

Multiple choice
questions

1

Y Ltd has been making a new product and the time taken to produce successive units has been recorded.

Cumulative output	Total time taken
Units	Hours
2	500
3	635
4	750
6	951
8	1,125

Which one of the following learning rates is the company experiencing?

A   50%   B   60%   C   70%   D   75%

2

The learning curve formula $Y_x = aX^{-0.322}$ applies to the production of product J, the first unit of which took 25 hours to make in period 1 of year 1. By the end of period 5 in year 1, 75 units of product J had been produced. The production budget for period 6 in year 1 is 20 units.

What is the budgeted total labour time for the production of product J in period 6 of year 1?

A   115.380 hours   B   81.180 hours   C   124.500 hours   D   548.055 hours

3

Which of the following statements about standards is/are true?

I   Can be prepared for all functions, even where output cannot be measured
II   Must be expressed in money terms
III   Aids control by setting financial targets or limits for a forthcoming period
IV   Should be revised every time prices or levels of efficiency change

A   None of the above   B   All of the above   C   III and IV   D   I, II and IV

The following information relates to questions 4 and 5.

The standard cost and selling price structure for the single product that is made by CD Ltd is as follows.

	£ per unit
Selling price	82
Variable cost	(47)
Fixed production overhead	(29)
	6

The budgeted level of production and sales is 3,200 units per month.

Extract from the actual results for March

Fixed production overhead volume variance   £8,700 favourable
Fixed production overhead expenditure variance   £2,200 adverse
Stock levels reduced by 200 units during the period.

4

What was the actual expenditure on fixed production overhead during March?

A   £86,300   B   £90,600   C   £92,800   D   £95,000

5

What was the actual sales volume during March?

A 2,900 units   B 3,300 units   C 3,500 units   D 3,700 units

6

The sales budget of product R for control period 4 was 1,000 units. The budgeted selling price was £15 per unit and the budgeted unit variable cost £7.

The actual sales volume achieved was 1,000 units but, upon reviewing the period's performance, management realised that a standard selling price of £18 might have been more appropriate given that the actual price achieved on the 1,000 units was £20. The actual total variable cost was £7,000.

What are the planning and operational selling price variances?

	Planning	Operational
A	£5,000 (F)	-
B	-	£5,000 (F)
C	£3,000 (F)	£2,000 (F)
D	£3,000 (A)	£2,000 (A)

7

Standard material usage for product L is 5 kgs. The expected standard deviation around this average is 0.08 kgs. A variance of 0.2 kgs is reported. Which of the following statements is/are true?

I   A 95% significance level rule would state that the variance should be investigated.
II   A 0.05 significance level rule would state that the variance should not be investigated.
III   A 99% significance level rule would state that the variance should be investigated.
IV   A 0.01 significance level rule would state that the variance should not be investigated.

A I only   B I and IV   C II and III   D I, III and IV

8

Which of the following might be appropriate action for management to take in response to an adverse material usage variance?

I   Change supplier.
II   Ensure stores are secure.
III   Assess whether workers require more supervision.
IV   Continue to use higher quality material if there are no cost implications.

A All of the above   B III only   C III and IV   D I, II and III

9

Which of the following are features of information for strategic planning?

I   Relevant to the long term
II   Prepared routinely and regularly
III   Task specific
IV   Incapable of providing complete certainty

A None of the above   B All of the above   C I, II and III   D I and IV

10

K Ltd manufactures product E. Budgeted sales for control periods 1 to 5 are as follows.

Control period	Units
1	750
2	690
3	540
4	820
5	910

Opening stock of product E at the beginning of a control period should be sufficient to cover 30% of the anticipated sales in the control period.

8% of input during the production process is wasted. How many units must be input to the production process during control period 3?

A   679 units   B   624 units   C   587 units   D   674 units

11

Sales of product D during 20X0 (control periods 1 to 13) were noted and the following totals calculated.

$\Sigma X = 91$ $\Sigma Y = 1,120$ $\Sigma XY = 9,247$ $\Sigma X^2 = 819$

There is a high correlation between time and volume of sales. Using a suitable regression line, what is the predicted sales level of product D in control period 4 of 20X1, when a seasonal variation of −13 is relevant?

A   552   B   158   C   150   D   176

12

Actual sales volumes during years 3 and 4 were as follows.

Year	Quarter	Actual sales volume '000 units
3	1	47
	2	59
	3	92
	4	140
4	1	35
	2	49
	3	89
	4	120

What trend figures can be calculated from the information above?

Year	Quarter	A	B	C	D
3	2	338	-	-	84.50
	3	326	83.000	84.50	81.50
	4	316	80.250	81.50	79.00
4	1	313	78.625	79.00	78.25
	2	293	75.750	78.25	73.25
	3	-	-	73.25	-

13

A company manufactures a single product and has produced the following flexed budget for the year.

	Level of activity		
	70%	80%	90%
	£	£	£
Direct materials	17,780	20,320	22,860
Direct labour	44,800	51,200	57,600
Production overhead	30,500	32,000	33,500
Administration overhead	17,000	17,000	17,000
Total cost	110,080	120,520	130,960

Which of the following is the budget flexed at 45% activity?

	A	B	C	D
	£	£	£	£
Direct materials	11,430	11,430	17,780	11,430
Direct labour	28,800	28,800	44,800	28,800
Production overhead	16,750	16,750	30,500	26,750
Administration overhead	8,500	17,000	17,000	17,000
Total cost	65,480	73,980	110,080	83,980

14

What is budgetary slack?

A   The difference between the costs built into the budget and the costs actually incurred
B   The difference between the minimum necessary costs and the costs actually incurred
C   The sum of the minimum necessary costs and the costs built into the budget
D   The difference between the flexible budget and the costs actually incurred

15

Labour cost per unit manufactured is an appropriate measure for which perspective of the balanced scorecard?

A   Customer
B   Internal
C   Innovation and learning
D   Financial

16

Which of the following is/are not a disadvantage of using market value as a transfer price?

I   The market price might be a temporary one.
II   It might act as a disincentive to use up spare capacity.
III   A market price might not exist.
IV   The external market might be perfect.

A   I, II and III   B   III only   C   IV only   D   All of the above

17

Which of the following is/are part of an FMS?

I   JIT
II   CIM
III   MHS
IV   ASRS

A   All of the above   B   None of the above   C   II and IV   D   III only

18

A kanban is associated with what type of system?

A   An MRP II system
B   A JIT system
C   An ABC system
D   An ERP system

The following information relates to questions 19 and 20

A firm of financial consultants offers short revision courses on taxation and auditing for professional exams. The firm has budgeted annual overheads totalling £152,625. Until recently the firm had applied overheads on a volume basis, based on the number of course days offered. The firm has no variable costs and the only direct costs are the consultants' own time which they divide equally between the two courses. The firm is considering the possibility of adopting an ABC system and has identified the overhead costs as shown below.

	£
Centre hire	62,500
Enquiries administration	27,125
Brochures	63,000

The following information relates to the past year and is expected to remain the same for the coming year.

Course	No of courses sold	Duration of course	No of enquiries per course	No of brochures printed per course
Auditing	50	2 days	175	300
Taxation	30	3 days	70	200

All courses run with a maximum number of students (30), as it is deemed that beyond this number the learning experience is severely diminished, and the same centre is used for all courses at a standard daily rate. The firm has the human resources to run only one course at any one time.

19

What is the overhead cost per course for both auditing and taxation using traditional volume based absorption costing?

	Auditing £	Taxation £
A	1,606.58	2,409.87
B	2,409.87	1,606.58
C	3,815.63	5,723.44
D	5,723.44	3,815.63

20

What are the overhead costs for both auditing and taxation using ABC?

	Auditing £	Taxation £
A	1,995.40	1,761.85
B	1,337.50	775.00
C	1,606.58	2,409.87
D	1,095.40	1,161.85

21

A retail organisation has recently introduced a 'petite' range in its women's clothing range. Which aspect of the value of the women's clothing range should have increased?

A   Cost   B   Exchange   C   Use   D   Esteem

22

ABC Ltd manufactures and sells two products, Y and Z.

	Y	Z
	£ per unit	£ per unit
Selling price	57	41
Variable cost	35	20
Contribution	22	21

For every six units of Y sold, seven units of Z are sold. Annual fixed costs are £558,000.

Budgeted annual sales revenue in the standard mix is £1,446,700. What is the margin of safety?

A   15%   B   13.04%   C   0.1304%   D   Cannot be calculated from the information provided

23

Which of the following is not true?

A   The shadow price of a resource is its internal opportunity cost.

B   The marginal revenue-earning potential of a limiting factor at the profit-maximising output level is its shadow price.

C   A shadow price is an increase in value which would be created by having available one additional unit of a limiting resource at the original cost.

D   The shadow price of a limiting factor is its dual price.

24

An organisation manufactures two products. Product X requires six minutes of labour grade A time, Product Y ten minutes. If x represents the number of product X manufactured and y represents the number of Y manufactured and in the next control period 720 hours of labour grade A time are available, how can the labour grade A constraint on production of X and Y be written as an inequality?

A $0.1x + 0.167y \geq 43,200$
B $10x + 6y \leq 720$
C $x + 1.67y \leq 720$
D $0.1x + 0.167y \leq 720$

25

Where can the value of the objective function be found in a final simplex tableau?

A   The bottom right hand corner
B   The top of the right hand column of figures
C   The bottom of the left hand column of figures
D   It cannot be found on the final tableau

1 **The correct answer is D**.

The key to this question is to calculate what happens to the average unit time when output doubles.

Cumulative output		Average time per unit
Units		Hours
2	(500 ÷ 2)	250.000
4	(750 ÷ 4)	187.500
8	(1,125 ÷ 8)	140.625

187.5/250 = 0.75 and 140.625/187.5 = 0.75

Alternatively, you could try applying each of the learning rates supplied in the four options and you will find that the only option which fits the data supplied is option D. For example, option A does not apply because the total time taken for the first four units would be $500 \times 2 \times 50\% = 500$ hours.

Option B does not apply because the time taken for the first four units would be $500 \times 2 \times 60\% = 600$ hours. For option C the first four units would take $500 \times 2 \times 70\% = 700$ hours.

2 **The correct answer is B**.

Cumulative average time per unit when 75 units are produced

If $Y_x = aX^{-0.322}$, then if X = 75 and a = 25, $Y = 25 \times 75^{-0.322} = 6.225$

Cumulative average time per unit when 95 units are produced

Now if X = 75 + 20 = 95, $Y = 25 \times 95^{-0.322} = 5.769$

Extra time needed to produce the 20 units in period 6

$= (95 \times 5.769) - (75 \times 6.225) = 81.18$ hours

If you choose option A, you calculated 20×5.769.

If you choose option C, you calculated 20×6.225.

If you choose option D, you found the total time to produce 95 units.

3 **The correct answer is A**.

I   The use of standards is limited to situations where repetitive actions are performed and output can be measured.

II   Standards need not be expressed in monetary terms.

III   Standards achieve control by comparison of actual results against a predetermined target.

IV   The most suitable approach is probably to revise standards whenever changes of a permanent and reasonably long-term nature occur.

4 **The correct answer is D**.

	£
Budgeted fixed overhead expenditure (3,200 units × £29)	92,800
Fixed production overhead expenditure variance	2,200 (A)
Actual fixed production overhead expenditure	95,000

If you selected option A, you adjusted the budgeted overhead unnecessarily for the fixed overhead volume variance.

If you selected option B, you had the right idea about adjusting the budgeted overhead for the expenditure variance, but you should have added the variance rather than subtracting it.

If you selected option C, you chose the budgeted fixed overhead expenditure for the month.

5   **The correct answer is D**.

	Units
Budgeted production	3,200
Volume variance in units (£8,700 ÷ £29)	300 (F)
Actual production for March	3,500
Reduction in stock volume	200
Actual sales for March	3,700

If you selected option A, you subtracted the volume variance in units from the budgeted production. However the volume variance is favourable and so the actual production must be higher than budgeted.

If you selected option B, you subtracted the stock reduction from the actual production volume. However if stocks reduce, sales volume must be higher than production volume.

Option C is the actual production for March. Since the stock volume altered, sales must be different to the production volume.

6   **The correct answer is C**.

Planning variance

	£
Original budget was (1,000 × £15)	15,000
but should have been (1,000 × £18)	18,000
	3,000 (F)

Operational variance

	£
Revenue should have been (1,000 × £18)	18,000
but was (1,000 × £20)	20,000
	2,000 (F)

If you chose options A or B, you compared the original standard and the actual result.

If you chose option D, you muddled up favourable and adverse: the original budget was too low so the planning variance is favourable, and the actual revenue was greater than the revised standard revenue and so the operational variance is favourable.

7   **The correct answer is B**.

The actual result is 0.2/0.08 = 2.5 standard deviations from the standard.

A 95% or 0.05 significance level rule would state that the variance should be investigated because it is greater than 1.96 standard deviations.

A 99% or 0.01 significance level rule would state that the variance should not be investigated because it is less than 2.58 standard deviations.

8   **The correct answer is D**.

A high quality material would be more likely to produce a favourable usage variance.

9   **The correct answer is D**.

II is a feature of information for budgetary/tactical planning.

III is a feature of information for operation planning.

10   **The correct answer is A**.

Opening stock + production – closing stock = sales

Opening stock = 30% × 540 = 162

Closing stock = 30% × 820 = 246

∴ Good production = 540 + 246 – 162 = 624

∴ Total production = 624/0.92 = 679 units

If you chose option B, you forgot to take account of the wastage rate.

If you chose option C, you forgot to take account of opening and closing stock and based your wastage calculation on the sales figure.

If you chose option D, you multiplied good production by 1.08, instead of dividing it by 0.92.

11   The correct answer is C.

During 20X0, there are 13 control periods and so n = 13. The regression line is Y = a + bX.

$$b = \frac{n\Sigma XY - \Sigma X\Sigma Y}{n\Sigma X^2 - (\Sigma X)^2}$$

$$= \frac{(13 \times 9,247) - (91 \times 1,120)}{(13 \times 819) - (91)^2}$$

$$= 7.731$$

$$a = \frac{\Sigma Y}{n} - \frac{b\Sigma X}{n}$$

$$= \frac{1,120}{13} - \frac{(7.731 \times 91)}{13}$$

$$= 32.037$$

Regression line is Y = 32.037 + 7.731X

Control period 4 of 20X1, X = 17

$\therefore$ Y = 32.037 + (7.731 $\times$ 17) = 163 units

Adjusting by the seasonal variation of –13, predicted sales = 163 – 13 = 150 units

If you chose option A, you mixed up your 'a' and 'b' values and forgot the seasonal adjustment.

If you chose option B, you used X = 18.

If you chose option D, you added the seasonal variation instead of deducting it.

12   The correct answer is B.

Year	Quarter	Actual sales '000 units	Moving total of 4 quarters' sales '000 units	Moving average '000 units	Mid-point Trend '000 units
3	1	47			
	2	59			
			338	84.5	
	3	92			83.000
			326	81.5	
	4	140			80.250
			316	79.0	
4	1	35			78.625
			313	78.25	
	2	49			75.750
			293	73.25	
	3	89			
	4	120			

BPP PUBLISHING

13 **The correct answer is D.**

Variable costs

	£ per 1%	£
Direct materials	254	11,430
Direct labour	640	28,800
Production overhead	150 (W)	6,750
		46,980

Fixed costs

	£
Production overhead	20,000 (W)
Administration overhead	17,000
	37,000
	83,980

Working

Production overhead is a semi-variable cost.

Range of activity = 90% − 70% = 20%

Range of cost = £(33,500 − 30,500) = £3,000

Variable cost per 1% change in activity = £3,000/20 = £150

Fixed cost = £33,500 − (90 × £150) = £20,000

If you chose option A, you simply took half of the 90% budget. This approach can be used for variable costs but not for mixed and fixed costs.

If you chose option B, you failed to recognise that production overhead was a mixed cost. You treated it as a variable cost (based on 90% data).

If you chose option C, you may have thought that the costs could not be reduced below the 70% budget level.

14 **The correct answer is B.**

15 **The correct answer is B.**

It can be used to show how internal processes are improving.

16 **The correct answer is C.**

An imperfect external market is a disadvantage.

17 **The correct answer is A.**

FMS: Flexible manufacturing system
JIT: Just-in-time
CIM: Computer-integrated manufacturing
MHS: Materials handling system
ASRS: Automated storage and retrieval system

18 **The correct answer is B.**

A kanban, or signal, ensures that products/components are only produced when needed by the next process. In a JIT system, nothing is produced in anticipation of need, to then remain in stock, consuming resources.

19 **The correct answer is A.**

	Auditing	Taxation	Total
Number of courses sold	50	30	
Duration of course (days)	2	3	
Number of course days	100	90	190

$$\text{Overhead cost per course day} = \frac{£152,625}{190} = £803.29$$

Overhead cost per course

Auditing   £803.29 × 2 days = £1,606.58
Taxation   £803.29 × 3 days = £2,409.87

If you chose option B, you got the course durations muddled up.

If you chose option C, you used number of courses sold as the activity level in the calculation of the overhead cost per course day, rather than the number of course days.

If you chose option D, you made the same mistake as in option C and you got the number of courses sold muddled up.

20   The correct answer is A.

Centre hire cost per course day = $\dfrac{£62,500}{190 \,^*}$ = £328.95

* See working in question 19.

Enquiries administration cost per enquiry = $\dfrac{£27,125}{(50 \times 175) + (30 \times 70)}$ = £2.50

Brochure cost per brochure printed = $\dfrac{£63,000}{(50 \times 300) + (30 \times 200)}$ = £3

Overhead costs per course using ABC

		Auditing £ per course		Taxation £ per course
Centre hire at £328.95 per day	(× 2)	657.90	(× 3)	986.85
Enquiries admin at £2.50 per enquiry	(× 175)	437.50	(× 70)	175.00
Brochures at £3 per brochure printed	(× 300)	900.00	(× 200)	600.00
		1,995.40		1,761.85

If you chose option B, you forgot to include the centre hire.

If you chose option C, you used absorption costing instead of ABC.

If you chose option D, you forgot to include the cost of brochures.

21   The correct answer is D.

22   The correct answer is B.

Contribution per mix = (£22 × 6) + (£21 × 7) = £279

Breakeven point	=	fixed costs/contribution per mix
	=	£558,000/£279 = 2,000 mixes
	=	(2,000 × 6) 12,000 units of Y and (2,000 × 7) 14,000 units of Z
	=	(12,000 × £57) £684,000 revenue from Y and (14,000 × £41) £574,000 revenue from Z
	=	£1,258,000 in total
Margin of safety	=	budgeted sales – breakeven sales
	=	£(1,446,700 – 1,258,000)
	=	£188,700
Margin of safety (%)	=	(£188,700/£1,446,700) × 100%
	=	13.04%

If you chose option A, you used breakeven sales as the denominator in the final calculation.

If you chose option C, you forgot to multiply by 100%.

23   The correct answer is B.

It should be the marginal contribution-earning potential, not revenue-earning potential.

24   The correct answer is D.

X requires 0.100 hours of labour grade A time.

Y requires 0.167 hours of labour grade A time.

720 hours are available.

$\therefore 0.1x + 0.167y \leq 720$

If you chose option A, you had the inequality the wrong way round. The labour time used must be less than or equal to the time available. You also converted the labour availability into minutes but showed the product requirements in hours.

If you chose option B, you forgot to convert the times for X and Y into hours.

If you chose option C, you converted the product requirements from minutes into hours incorrectly.

25   **The correct answer is A.**

Index

Note: **Key Terms** and their references are given in **bold**.

ABB, 120, 161, 266
ABC, 218
Absorption costing, 221
Activity based budgeting (ABB), 120, 161, 226
Activity based costing (ABC), 218, 219
Additive model, 140, 143
Advanced manufacturing technology (AMT), 197
Alternative approaches to budgeting, 113
AMT, 197
Appraisal costs, 211
Aspiration level, 170
Aspirations budget, 171
Attainable standards, 8
Automated guided vehicles (AGV), 198
Automated storage and retrieval systems (ASRS), 198

Balanced scorecard, 173
Balanced scorecard approach, 173
Balancing transactions, 220
Basic standard, 8
Batch processing, 195
Behavioural implications of budgeting, 163
Benchmarking, 82, 83
Bottom-up budgeting, 166
Breakeven analysis, 246
Breakeven chart, 246, 255
Breakeven point, 246
BS EN ISO 9000, 207
Budget, 90
Budget centre, 161
Budget committee, 93
Budget cost allowance, 155
Budget manual, 92
Budget period, 92
Budget preparation, 93
Budgetary control, 157
Budgetary control reports, 161
Budgetary slack, 170
Budgeted balance sheet, 112
Budgeted capacity, 10
Budgeted profit and loss account, 112
Budgeting, 89
   behavioural implications of, 163
   imposed style of, 166
   negotiated style of, 167
   participative style of, 166

Budgets for worst possible, best possible and most likely outcomes, 120
Business models, 146

C/S ratio, 246
Capacity levels, 9
   budgeted, 10
   full, 10
   idle, 10
   practical, 10
Capacity ratios, 10
Cash budgets, 104
Cellular manufacturing, 196
Centralisation, 181
Change transactions, 221
Coefficient of correlation (r), 134
Coefficient of determination (r^2), 135
Competitive benchmarking, 83
Composite variances, 76
Computer numerically controlled (CNC) machines, 198
Computer-aided design (CAD), 197
Computer-aided manufacturing (CAM), 198
Computer-integrated manufacturing (CIM), 198
Computerised materials handling systems (MHS), 198
Computers, 161
   and flexible budgets, 161
Constraints, 281, 306
Continuous improvement, 207
Contribution (contribution breakeven) chart, 246
Contribution/sales (C/S) ratio, 246
Control chart, 75
Controllable cost, 168, 180
Corporate planning, 91
Corporate profit maximisation, 183
Correlation, 131, 132
   and causation, 135
   curvilinear, 133
   negative, 134
   non-linear, 133
   partial, 133
   perfect, 132
   positive, 134
Cost centre, 179
Cost control, 229
Cost driver, 161, 220, 223
Cost experience curve, 17, 18

BPP PUBLISHING

Cost of appraisal, 211
Cost of conformance, 211
Cost of external failure, 211
Cost of internal failure, 211
Cost of non-conformance, 211
Cost of prevention, 211
Cost of quality, 210, 211
Cost of quality reports, 210
Cost pools, 220
Cost reduction, 229, 230
   methods of, 233
Cost value, 237
Cost-volume-profit analysis, 245
Cumulative average time model, 16
Current standards, 8
Cusum chart, 76
CVP analysis, 245
Cyclical variations, 140

Decentralisation, 181
Decision packages, 114
Decision units, 114
Decision variables, 305
Decision variables, 289
Dedicated cell layout, 196
Departmental budget, 93
Dependent variable, 127
Direct model, 16
Discretionary cost, 117, 118
Divisional autonomy, 182
Divisional performance measurement, 183
Double loop feedback, 162
Dual price, 274

Economic order quantity (EOQ), 101
Efficiency ratio, 11
Electronic data interchange (EDI), 198
Employee empowerment, 195
Enterprise resource planning (ERP)
   systems, 200
EOQ, 101, 102
Esteem value, 237
Ex ante, 58
Ex post, 58
Exchange value, 237
Expectations budget, 171
External failure costs, 211
Extrapolation, 130

Feasible area, 284
Feasible polygon, 284
Feasible region, 284

Feedback, 162
   negative, 162
   positive, 162
Feedforward control, 112, 162
Final tableau, 309
Fixed budget, 154
Fixed overhead capacity variance, 35
Fixed overhead expenditure variance, 35
Fixed overhead total variance, 35
Fixed overhead (volume) capacity
   variance, 35
Fixed overhead (volume) efficiency
   variance, 35
Fixed overhead volume variance, 35
Flexed budgets using ABC, 226, 227
Flexible budget, 154
   and computers, 161
Flexible manufacturing system (FMS), 198
Forecast, 96
Forecasting, 126, 136
   regression and, 136
   time series analysis and, 145
   using historical data, 127
Full capacity, 10
Functional analysis, 240, 241
Functional benchmarking, 83
Functional budget, 93

Get it right, first time, 207
Goal congruence, 163, 169, 183
Graphing equations, 283

Hierarchy of cost, 224
Higher level feedback, 162
High-low method, 155
Historigram, 137
Hopwood, 169

Ideal standard, 8
Idle capacity, 10
Idle capacity ratio, 10
Imposed budget, 166
Incremental model, 16
Incremental budgeting, 113
Incremental packages, 114
Independent variable, 127
Inequalities, 281
Inflation, 156
Initial tableau, 307
Innovation, 195
Inspection, 209
Internal benchmarking, 83

Internal failure costs, 211
Internal opportunity cost, 274
Interpolation, 130
Interpreting variances, 77
Islands of automation (IAs), 198
Iso-contribution lines, 287

Jobbing industries, 195
Just-in-time (JIT), 201
Just-in-time production, 201
Just-in-time purchasing, 201
Just-in-time systems, 201

Kanban, 202
Key budget factor, 94
Key factor, 263

Labour mix variance, 56
Labour output variance, 56
Labour variances, 28
Labour yield variance, 56
Learning coefficient, 15
Learning curve, 8, 12
  formula for, 15
Learning curve effect, 8, 11
Learning curve theory, 12
Learning effect, 12
Learning index, 15
Least squares technique, 128
Limited freedom of action, 269
Limiting budget factor, 94
Limiting factor, 263
  and opportunity costs, 273
Limiting factor analysis, 263
Limiting factor sensitivity analysis, 296
Line of best fit, 128, 131
Linear equation, 283
Linear programming, 280
  assumptions of, 318
  practical difficulties with using, 319
  uses of, 319
Linear regression analysis, 127
Linear relationships, 127
Logistical transactions, 220
Long-range planning, 91

Machine cells, 202
Make or buy decisions, 271
Managerial performance, 169
Manufacturing resource planning (MRPII), 199

Marginal model, 16
Margin of safety, 246
Margin of safety for multiple products, 254
Mass production, 196
Master budget, 112
Material variances, 26
Materials mix variance, 50
Materials requirement planning (MRPI), 199
Materials yield variance, 50
Maximum level, 101
Method study, 233
Minimisation problems, 294
Minimum level, 101
Modern business environment, 194
Motivation, 163
  and pay, 165
  management accountant and, 171
Moving averages, 140
Multiple product CVP analysis, 245
Multiplicative model, 144

Negative correlation, 134
Negotiated budget, 167
Non value-added costs/activities, 203
Non-negativity constraints, 282

Objective function, 281, 306
Operating statement, 39
Operating variance, 58
Operation planning, 91
Operational variance, 58
Opportunity cost, 273
Optimised production technology (OPT), 200
Organisation and methods (O&M), 234

P/V charts, 246, 56
Participation, 165
Participative budgeting, 166
Pearsonian coefficient of correlation, 134
Performance evaluation, 168
Performance standard, 7
Periodic budget, 119
Planning, 91
Planning variance, 58
PPBS, 117
Positive correlation, 134
Practical capacity, 10
Prevention costs, 211
Principal budget factor, 94
Product life cycle, 194
Product moment correlation coefficient, 134

Production capacity, 9
Production management strategies, 199
   manufacturing resource planning
     (MRPII), 199
   materials requirement planning (MRPI),
     199
   optimised production technology (OPT),
     200
Production volume ratio, 11
Profit centre, 179, 182
Profit targets, 253
Profit/volume (P/V) chart, 246, 256
Programme planning and budgeting system
   (PPBS), 117
Proportional model, 144

Quality, 206
Quality assurance procedures, 207
Quality assurance scheme, 207
Quality control, 209
Quality transactions, 220
Quality-related costs, 210

Rationalisation, 235
Regression, 136
Reorder level, 101
Resource planning systems, 199
Responsibility accounting, 91, 178, **179**
Responsibility centre, 179
Restricted freedom of action, 269
Reverse engineering, 83
Revision variance, 58
Robots, 198
Rolling budget, 106, **119**
Rule-of-thumb models, 73

Sales budget, 96
Sales forecasting, 136
Sales price sensitivity analysis, 298
Sales variances, 38
Sales/product mix decisions, 251
Scarce resources, 271
Scatter diagrams, 131
Scattergraph method, 155
Seasonal variations, 139
Sensitivity analysis, 148, **296,** 313
Shadow price, 274, 296, 314
Short-term tactical planning, 91
Simplex method, 304
   using computer packages, 317
Simplex tableaux, 307

Simultaneous equations, 291
Single loop feedback, 162
Slack, 294
Slack variable, 305, **306**
Spreadsheet, 146
Spreadsheet packages, 146
Standard absorption costing, 42
Standard cost, 5
Standard costing, 5
   behavioural implications of, 18
   criticisms of, 21
   uses of, 5
Standard hour, 97
Standard marginal costing, 42
Standards, 3
   attainable, 8
   basic, 8
   current, 8
   ideal, 8
   review of, 20
   revision of, 20
   setting, 6
   types of, 7
   updating, 19
Statistical control charts, 75
Statistical significance model, 74
Stock control formulae, 101
Strategic benchmarking, 83
Strategic planning, 91
Surplus, 294
Surplus variables, 305
Synchronous manufacturing, 205

Target profits for multiple products, 253
Team composition variance, 56
Team productivity variance, 56
Three tier approach to budgeting, 122
Time series, 137
Time series analysis, 137
Top-down budget, 166
Total Quality Management (TQM) , 206,
   207, 213
   standard costing and, 212
Transactions analysis, 220
Transfer price, 182
   adjusted market price as, 184
   at actual cost plus, 188
   based on a two part charging system, 188
   based on standard variable cost, 187
   market price as, 183
   use of market price as a basis for, 183
Transfer pricing, 188

cost-based approaches to, 185
fixed costs and, 188
Trend, 138
Two-plus constraint/limitation problem, 279
Two-plus constraint/limitation problem for
two-plus products, 304

Uncontrollable costs, 180
Uniform loading, 202
Use value, 237

Value, 237
cost, 237
esteem, 237
exchange, 237
use, 237
Value added, 203
Value analysis, 236, 237, 238, 243
defining, 236
stages in, 239
Value chain, 214
Value engineering, 237
Variable production overhead variances, 32
Variables, 281
Variance, 26, 158
composite, 76
direct labour efficiency, 29
direct labour rate, 29
direct material price , 26
direct material usage, 26
fixed production overhead, 33
idle time, 30

interpreting, 77
interrelationship of, 70
labour cost, 28
labour mix, 56
labour yield, 57
materials mix, 49
materials yield, 49
operational, 58, 60
planning, 59
sales volume profit, 38
selling price, 38
significance of, 73
variable production overhead, 32
variable production overhead efficiency,
33
variable production overhead expenditure,
33
Variance analysis, 25, 26
Variance investigation models, 73
Variance trend, 70
Vendor rating, 207
Volume capacity, 9

What if? analysis, 147, 154
Work measurement, 233
Work study, 233
World Class Manufacturing (WCM), 214

ZBB, 113, 226
Zero base budgeting (ZBB), 113, 226

BPP PUBLISHING

REVIEW FORM & FREE PRIZE DRAW

All original review forms from the entire BPP range, completed with genuine comments, will be entered into one of two draws on 31 January 2002 and 31 July 2002. The names on the first four forms picked out on each occasion will be sent a cheque for £50.

Name: _____ Address: _____

_____

How have you used this Text?
(Tick one box only)

☐ Self study (book only)

☐ On a course: college (please state)_____

_____

☐ With 'correspondence' package

☐ Other _____

Why did you decide to purchase this Text?
(Tick one box only)

☐ Have used BPP Texts in the past

☐ Recommendation by friend/colleague

☐ Recommendation by a lecturer at college

☐ Saw advertising

☐ Other _____

During the past six months do you recall seeing/receiving any of the following?
(Tick as many boxes as are relevant)

☐ Our advertisement in CIMA *Insider*

☐ Our advertisement in *Financial Management*

☐ Our advertisement in *Pass*

☐ Our brochure with a letter through the post

☐ Our website www.bpp.com

Which (if any) aspects of our advertising do you find useful?
(Tick as many boxes as are relevant)

☐ Prices and publication dates of new editions

☐ Information on product content

☐ Facility to order books off-the-page

☐ None of the above

Which BPP products have you used?

Text ☐   Kit ☐   Passcard ☐   MCQ cards ☐   Tape ☐   Video ☐

[For foundation only] How did you/will you take the exam for this paper (Tick one box only)

Written exam ☐   Computer based assessment ☐

Your ratings, comments and suggestions would be appreciated on the following areas

	Very useful	Useful	Not useful
Introductory section (Key study steps, personal study)	☐	☐	☐
Chapter introductions	☐	☐	☐
Key terms	☐	☐	☐
Quality of explanations	☐	☐	☐
Case examples and other examples	☐	☐	☐
Questions and answers in each chapter	☐	☐	☐
Chapter roundups	☐	☐	☐
Quick quizzes	☐	☐	☐
Exam focus points	☐	☐	☐
Question bank	☐	☐	☐
MCQ bank	☐	☐	☐
Answer bank	☐	☐	☐
Index	☐	☐	☐
Icons	☐	☐	☐
Mind maps	☐	☐	☐

	Excellent	Good	Adequate	Poor
Overall opinion of this Study Text	☐	☐	☐	☐

Do you intend to continue using BPP products?   ☐ Yes   ☐ No

Please note any further comments and suggestions/errors on the reverse of this page. The BPP author of this edition can be e-mailed at: alisonmchugh@bpp.com

Please return this form to: Alison McHugh, CIMA Range Manager, BPP Publishing Ltd, FREEPOST, London, W12 8BR

REVIEW FORM & FREE PRIZE DRAW (continued)

Please note any further comments and suggestions/errors below.

FREE PRIZE DRAW RULES

1   Closing date for 31 January 2002 draw is 31 December 2001. Closing date for 31 July 2002 draw is 30 June 2002.

2   Restricted to entries with UK and Eire addresses only. BPP employees, their families and business associates are excluded.

3   No purchase necessary. Entry forms are available upon request from BPP Publishing. No more than one entry per title, per person. Draw restricted to persons aged 16 and over.

4   Winners will be notified by post and receive their cheques not later than 6 weeks after the relevant draw date.

5   The decision of the promoter in all matters is final and binding. No correspondence will be entered into.

See overleaf for information on other
BPP products and how to order

CIMA Order

To BPP Publishing Ltd, Aldine Place, London W12 8AW
Tel: 020 8740 2211. Fax: 020 8740 1184
www.bpp.com Email publishing@bpp.com
Order online www.bpp.com

Mr/Mrs/Ms (Full name)

Daytime delivery address

Postcode

Email

Date of exam (month/year)

Daytime Tel

POSTAGE & PACKING

Study Texts	First	Each extra
UK	£3.00	£2.00
Europe***	£5.00	£4.00
Rest of world	£20.00	£10.00

Kits/Passcards/Success Tapes	First	Each extra
UK	£2.00	£1.00
Europe***	£2.50	£1.00
Rest of world	£15.00	£8.00

Breakthrough Videos	First	Each extra
UK	£2.00	£2.00
Europe***	£2.00	£2.00
Rest of world	£20.00	£10.00
MCQ cards	£1.00	£1.00

£ ☐ £ ☐ £ ☐
£ ☐ £ ☐ £ ☐
£ ☐ £ ☐ £ ☐ £ ☐

Grand Total (Cheques to *BPP Publishing*) I enclose a
cheque for (incl. Postage) £ ☐
Or charge to Access/Visa/Switch

Card Number

Expiry date   Start Date

Issue Number (Switch Only)

Signature

Order Table

	7/01 Texts £20.95	1/01 Kits £10.95	1/01 Passcards £5.95	9/00 Tapes £12.95	7/00 Videos £25.95	8/01 i-Pass £24.95 / 1/02 i-Pass £29.95	1/02 i-Learn £19.95	7/01 MCQ cards £5.95
FOUNDATION								
1 Financial Accounting Fundamentals	£20.95	£10.95	£5.95	£12.95	£25.95	£24.95	£19.95	£5.95
2 Management Accounting Fundamentals	£20.95	£10.95	£5.95	£12.95	£25.95	£24.95	£19.95	£5.95
3A Economics for Business	£20.95	£10.95	£5.95	£12.95	£25.95	£24.95	£19.95	£5.95
3B Business Law	£20.95	£10.95	£5.95	£12.95	£25.95	£24.95	£19.95	£5.95
3C Business Mathematics	£20.95	£10.95	£5.95	£12.95	£25.95	£24.95	£19.95	£5.95
INTERMEDIATE								
4 Finance	£20.95	£10.95	£5.95	£12.95	£25.95	£29.95	£19.95	£5.95
5 Business Tax (FA 2001)	£20.95 (9/01)	£10.95	£5.95	£12.95	£25.95	£29.95	£19.95	£5.95
6 Financial Accounting	£20.95	£10.95	£5.95	£12.95	£25.95	£29.95	£19.95	£5.95
6I Financial Accounting International	£20.95	£10.95		£12.95	£25.95	£29.95	£19.95	£5.95
7 Financial Reporting	£20.95	£10.95	£5.95	£12.95	£25.95	£29.95	£19.95	£5.95
7I Financial Reporting International	£20.95	£10.95		£12.95	£25.95	£29.95	£19.95	£5.95
8 Management Accounting – Performance Management	£20.95	£10.95	£5.95	£12.95	£25.95	£29.95	£19.95	£5.95
9 Management Accounting – Decision Making	£20.95	£10.95	£5.95	£12.95	£25.95	£29.95	£19.95	£5.95
10 Systems and Project Management	£20.95	£10.95	£5.95	£12.95	£25.95	£29.95	£19.95	£5.95
11 Organisational Management	£20.95	£10.95	£5.95	£12.95	£25.95	£29.95	£19.95	£5.95
FINAL								
12 Management Accounting – Business Strategy	£20.95	£10.95	£5.95	£12.95	£25.95	£29.95	£19.95	£5.95
13 Management Accounting – Financial Strategy	£20.95	£10.95	£5.95	£12.95	£25.95	£29.95	£19.95	£5.95
14 Management Accounting – Information Strategy	£20.95	£10.95	£5.95	£12.95	£25.95	£29.95	£19.95	£5.95
15 Case Study								
(1) Workbook	£20.95			£12.95	£25.95			
(2) Toolkit for 11/01 exam: available 9/01		£19.95						
(3) Toolkit for 5/02 exam: available 3/02		£19.95						

Total ☐

We aim to deliver to all UK addresses inside 5 working days. A signature will be required. Orders to all EU addresses should be delivered within 6 working days. All other orders to overseas addresses should be delivered within 8 working days.